Return to Putin's Russia

Return to Putin's Russia

Past Imperfect, Future Uncertain

Fifth Edition

Edited by
Stephen K. Wegren

ROWMAN & LITTLEFIELD PUBLISHERS, INC.
Lanham • Boulder • New York • Toronto • Plymouth, UK

Published by Rowman & Littlefield Publishers, Inc.
A wholly owned subsidiary of The Rowman & Littlefield Publishing Group, Inc.
4501 Forbes Boulevard, Suite 200, Lanham, Maryland 20706
www.rowman.com

10 Thornbury Road, Plymouth PL6 7PP, United Kingdom

British Library Cataloguing in Publication Information Available

Library of Congress Cataloging-in-Publication Data

Return to Putin's Russia : past imperfect, future uncertain / edited by Stephen K. Wegren.—Fifth edition.
  pages ; cm
 Previously published under title: After Putin's Russia.
 Includes bibliographical references and index.
 ISBN 978-1-4422-1345-6 (cloth : alkaline paper)
 ISBN 978-1-4422-1346-3 (paperback : alkaline paper)
 ISBN 978-1-4422-1347-0 (electronic) (print)
  1. Russia (Federation)—Politics and government—21st century.   2. Putin, Vladimir Vladimirovich, 1952–   I. Wegren, Stephen K., 1956–, editor.
DK510.763.R477   2013
947.086'3—dc23

                                                                    2012034710

Printed in the United States of America

Contents

Preface to the Fifth Edition

Since the publication of the fourth edition of this book, Dmitry Medvedev completed his term as president, giving way to Vladimir Putin, who was elected to a third (nonconsecutive) term in March 2012. Putin was inaugurated in May 2012 and will serve as president for six years, the first time a president has a six-year term in Russia's history. Russia is at a crossroads, and critical questions are more important than ever. Where does Russia go from here? Will Putinism evolve? Will Putin be able to understand and adapt to a new political climate, or will he constantly be behind the curve as was Gorbachev, who in trying to reform the Communist Party did not understand the forces he unleashed? More broadly, what kind of society is Russia evolving into? In the economy, will oil revenues be sufficient to fund economic development and modernization or will they hinder democratization, the so-called resource curse? Will Russia's population stabilize or will demographic decline continue, with economic and military ramifications? Will Putin resort to the adversarial relations with the West that characterized his first two terms in office?

Analyzing change across wide-ranging policy issues requires the combined efforts of an excellent group of scholars. Because Russian trends are difficult for nonspecialists to discern, I have endeavored to recruit some of "the best and brightest." This edition contains many of the top scholars—a who's who—in Russian studies. Most of the authors who wrote chapters for the fourth edition are included in the fifth edition. Building on the success of previous editions, a decision was made to widen the scope of coverage, and the fifth edition adds three new authors: Alfred Evans, who writes on civil society; Pekka Sutela, who writes on economic policy; and Jeffrey Mankoff, who writes on Russian-EU relations. I am deeply grateful to all of the authors who contributed to this fifth edition.

In addition, I would like to thank several people at Rowman & Littlefield: Susan McEachern for her support of this project; Carrie Broadwell-Tkach for discovering the book cover and for general production support; and Jehanne Schweitzer, for her excellent editorial skills in producing this book. I also thank Christine Carberry, who expertly prepared the index. Finally, this book is dedicated to our collective students so that they may better understand the riddle, wrapped in a mystery, inside an enigma that we call Russia.

Introduction

Stephen K. Wegren

As this book progresses from its fourth to its fifth edition, some questions about Russia have been answered and new ones have appeared. This edition, titled *Return to Putin's Russia*, marks the departure of Dmitry Medvedev from the presidency and the reelection of Vladimir Putin to his third (non-consecutive) term, Putin 3.0. Arguably, this edition is the most important yet. As Putin retakes power, the country stands at a crossroads and faces critical questions about its future.

For many months speculation was rife over the 2012 presidential election—would Medvedev run for reelection or would Putin return to power? Medvedev repeatedly stated that he wanted to run for reelection and had grown to like the job, but he nuanced his statements by saying that he and Putin would sit down and decide together what was best. On September 24, 2011, the answer came before a Congress of United Russia: Dmitry Medvedev conceded to Vladimir Putin, who announced he would return to the presidency; Putin in turn indicated that he would nominate Medvedev for prime minister. Putin was elected in March 2012 with 63.6 percent of the vote according to official statistics. Putin was inaugurated on May 7, 2012; one day later, the Duma approved Medvedev as prime minister. The game of musical chairs continues, with two players and two chairs.

The run-up to Putin's return to power was not met with the same societal support as the first two times he was elected. The December 2011 election for the State Duma ignited widespread protest over alleged fraud, which gave more support to the party of power, United Russia. Officially, the party backed by the Kremlin, United Russia, received just under 50 percent of the vote, enough to obtain a majority of seats in the Duma. This result, however, represented a drop from the 64 percent of the vote and two-thirds of the deputies that it received in the December 2007 Duma election. Allegations of widespread fraud and falsification in the December 2011 election fueled large-scale demonstrations in Moscow. According to the Levada Center, a leading polling organization in Russia, one-third of the population thought the election had been "largely" or "entirely" honest, but almost one-half did not think that the election was honest.[1] Another authoritative source, GOLOS, estimated that United Russia was given up to 15 million extra votes, so that it really obtained just 34 percent of the vote.[2] Protesters demanded that election results be canceled and a new election held. That position was rejected, but afterward Medvedev indicated that some concessions would be considered, such as reviving single-mandate districts, restoring the right to vote "against all," and allowing regional governors to be directly elected again.

For the March 2012 presidential election, therefore, unprecedented efforts were taken to make the election appear fair and honest. Acting upon the suggestion of Putin himself, Web cameras were installed in all 93,000 polling places that recorded the proceedings from 8 a.m. to 8 p.m. Some cases of fraud were caught and the results invalidated.[3] Even so, in the aftermath of the March 2012 election there were demonstrations against Putin and a return to Putinism. To be sure, protesters were not united in their message. Some protested over the blatant manipulation of the political system. Others were sick and tired of the corruption that defined the political system. My own conversations with ordinary Russians in Moscow a few days before Putin's May 7 inaugural indicated a variety of feelings as to why Putin was less popular the third time around: three terms is too many for one individual; Medvedev represented an alternative to Putinism and his leadership should have been given a chance to develop; and Putin is a Soviet-era KGB relic who has simply outlived his usefulness. In short, Russia and Russians had changed since 2000, and there seemed to be a sense that whereas Russia needed Putin in 2000, that was much less true in 2012. To be fair, however, outside of Moscow, sentiments are often different, as people are more prone to support Putin. On May 7 when Putin was inaugurated, protests in Moscow again occurred with an estimated 400 people arrested in Moscow. Does this portend the start of a rocky next six years for Putin?

Analysts have been quick to point out that Russian protests and protesters have little in common with those that occurred during the Arab Spring—Russian protesters tend to be young, educated, and prosperous, and they avoid violence.[4] Although no one questioned whether Putin actually won the presidential election, a large percentage of voters did not believe that the results were honest. For the first time, the Russian people protested against Putin as leader. Coming on the heels of demonstrations in Moscow and elsewhere over massive fraud in the Duma election of December 2011, it appeared that a genuine civil society was developing in Russia (see chapter 5 by Evans). A passive population that had tolerated political games, manipulation, and dishonesty for twenty years suddenly awoke. As one Russian academic argued, "The decade of economic growth and socio-political stability led to the appearance of a layer within society that wants to have the right to its own voice and is ready to put pressure on the authorities."[5]

MEDVEDEV'S LEGACY

Looking back on the years that Russia was governed by Dmitry Medvedev, 2008–2012, the results are contradictory. There is a lingering feeling that more was promised than was delivered and that four years were spent essentially marking time. Critics satirized Medvedev by saying his only accomplishment was putting Russia on permanent daylight saving time. This judgment may be harsh, but the reality is that Medvedev's record was spotty at best, results did not match rhetoric, and the Russian population did not perceive him as the real leader of the country. Thus, his record as a reformer was weak. The early verdict on Medvedev is that he merely continued Putinism. On the other hand, Richard Sakwa in his chapter argues that Medvedev's major achievement was to outline something different from what had preceded his presidency; in other words, to create expectations about what liberal democracy might look like in Russia.

During Medvedev's presidency there was a consensus by both Western and Russian political observers that Putin remained the real power in government. Both men were respectful of each other, but often Putin overshadowed Medvedev.[6] The traditional "reserved domain" of presidents was blurred, and Putin showed a willingness to exert his presence or comment on any aspect of economic policy, any political issue, or any foreign policy problem that he pleased, and Medvedev allowed him to do so (see the chapter by Thomas Remington in this volume). The historical legacy of Medvedev has yet to be written—it is too early to accurately assess his impact on Russia and its future—but we can begin to outline the contours of his legacy.

Medvedev's Record on Reform

Because of the failure to seize opportunities for meaningful change, it is unlikely that Medvedev will be remembered as a significant reformer. Perhaps if Medvedev had assembled a record of reform that resonated with the population, the momentum for Putin's return to power would have been considerably less. After all, the official explanation for Putin's return was that he was more popular and offered the best chance to galvanize support for policies going forward.

Medvedev entered office talking about wide-ranging political reform and deepening democratization, thereby raising hopes abroad and among liberals in Russia that his rule would usher in a softer, more democratic governance than under Putin.[7] A liberal and enlightened public persona was cultivated by the Kremlin, which released information about Medvedev's tastes in rock music and the fact that he was an active blogger. The reality of Medvedev's rule was quite different from the public image. From May 2008 to April 2012 the singular significant political reform was to lengthen the presidential term from four to six years. In contrast, Medvedev was not squeamish about authorizing force to disband and disrupt political demonstrations. Various uses of coercion and intimidation continued just as they had under Putin 2.0, as did various dirty tricks such as sending the tax inspectorate to investigate NGOs, human rights organizations, and political opponents; the removal or barring of political candidates from ballots; the continued suppression of the media; and the overt use of force against demonstrators.

It is well to recall Medvedev's political agenda when he entered office. In his first State of the Union speech in November 2008, Medvedev repeated a theme from Putin's early days as president that corruption needs to be eliminated from Russian society. Medvedev stated that "corruption is the number one enemy for a free, democratic and just society."[8] He indicated that a package of reforms was under consideration for the bureaucracy at the federal and regional levels, in the courts, and in municipal governments. These reforms included a declaration of income and its sources by state and municipal employees, including their families. The accuracy of the information supplied by bureaucrats was to be "thoroughly" checked through the use of "intelligence and investigation capabilities."[9] The reality was that tens of thousands of state and municipal employees provided inaccurate income information, leading Medvedev to say that a second chance would be given but after that discipline would be imposed.[10] In February 2012 Russia's prosecutor general announced that "the fight against corruption in most of Russia's regions failed."[11] According to international indices Russia remained one of the most corrupt nations in the world. In March 2012, a poll by the Public Opinion Fund showed that 81 percent of Russian citizens believed the level of corruption in the country is high, up from 75 percent in 2010.[12] In early 2011, Medvedev noted that his campaign had seen "almost no success," confessing that the skeptics who had predicted he would fail were "absolutely right." Then in a live TV interview in April 2012 Medvedev stated, "It would be a massive exaggeration to say that nothing is being done. But if we are talking of results, then they are, of course, modest."[13]

Another important item on his agenda was judicial reform. In a March 2008 interview, the first after his election, Medvedev offered his thoughts on a society based on the rule of law and the elimination of what he called legal nihilism, noting that "Russia is a country where people don't like to observe the law. It is, as they say, a country of legal nihilism." Medvedev offered a three-point plan. First, assert the law's supremacy over executive power and individual actions. Second, create "a new attitude toward the law." He argued that "we need to make sure that every citizen understands . . . the necessity and desirability of observing the law." Third, he argued for the need to "create an effective courts system, above all by assuring independence of the judiciary."[14] The reality is that it is difficult to build a state governed by the rule of law when the state itself applies laws arbitrarily and inconsistently. Further, by the end of his term the court system continued to lack independence and remained a tool of the Kremlin.

Finally, Medvedev spoke about the development of democracy and a system with more political accountability. In his December 2008 interview he stated that "I am a supporter of the values of democracy in the form that humanity has developed them over the last few centuries. My definition of democracy as the power of the people is in no way different from classical definitions that exist in all countries."[15] He also expressed confidence that Russia could develop along the lines of other countries that have chosen "the democratic path." In reality, the Medvedev years are hardly an example of political enlightenment; his actions reflect his real conception of democracy.

It is telling, for instance, that Medvedev participated in and did not speak out against the sham presidential election in March 2008 that was in essence a transfer of power by appointment. This election, which brought him to power, was a clear expression of managed democracy; opposition candidates had no realistic chance to win and in certain instances were overtly repressed (e.g., Gary Kasparov). The Kremlin stage-managed the electoral process and mobilized the population to validate the outcome, not unlike Soviet elections. As one Moscow journalist, Sergei Strokan, remarked, "Putin could have nominated his dog, and it would be duly elected and inaugurated as president."[16] In other words, Medvedev directly benefited from the faux democracy that characterizes Russia's electoral politics.

As president Medvedev did little to rein in the powers of the secret police, powers that had increased significantly under Putin. Files on foreigners are actively maintained, acquaintances and friends are pressured to become informants, and threats are made against Russians and their families who refuse to cooperate. According to this mindset, any information that is derogatory—or merely revealing—about Russia is considered harmful to national interests. An example of this mindset was evident at the end of December 2008. A man named Aleksandr Bragin was arrested by the Interior Ministry for publishing information that tarnished the region's image. His crime: posting on a website facts about the socioeconomic situation in Ulyanovsk, a city some 900 kilometers east of Moscow on the Volga. His article contained open source information about unemployment, wage arrears, and inflation.[17]

Furthermore, Medvedev talked about political accountability of the executive to the legislature, but this was empty rhetoric when the legislature was dominated and controlled by a pro-Kremlin party. During the second half of his administration Medvedev occasionally criticized United Russia for its actions but did little to stop the dirty tricks and electoral manipulation that allowed United Russia to retain power in regional legislatures. In the final regional election during Medvedev's term (March 2012), he did nothing to stop electoral fraud in regional elections that returned United Russia candidates to power and that in turn sparked protests. In Astrakhan, for instance, activist Oleg Shein went on a long hunger strike; in the town of Lermontov in Stavropol Krai the election was canceled because activists staged a hunger strike to protest the exclusion of two opposition candidates.[18] Shortly after becoming prime minister in May 2012, Medvedev not only assumed leadership of United Russia but also joined the party, something Putin had never done. Thus, if we look at what Medvedev offered as an agenda for reform and what he achieved, his record is far from impressive.

That said, in his last weeks in office Medvedev returned to political reform, although the net effect may be less than originally expected. In April 2012 he signed a new law on parties that made it easier for parties to form and get on the ballot by lowering the number of signatures from 40,000 to 500. The law also reduced the power of the electoral commission to remove candidates from a ballot. A cynic may be tempted to suggest that a proliferation of parties only serves to fracture and divide political opposition. In particular, liberal parties are likely to proliferate, which will only serve to splinter the electorate. Further, ultimate power rests with those who count the vote, irrespective of the candidates on the ballot. Nikolai Petrov, who with Darrell Slider contributes a chapter in this book, concludes that the new law seems to be "a concession to the opposition . . . but in reality, this would actually be a serious obstacle to the development of a full-fledged multiparty system and the strengthening of representative government."[19]

Following the December 2011 demonstrations, Medvedev also suggested a return to elected regional governors, which had been banned since 2004. The new law was signed in May 2012, but in the run-up to the law taking effect, the Kremlin was busy taking steps to ensure that its impact would be minimal, at least in the short term. From January 1, 2012, through May 22, 2012, twenty regional governors—almost one in four—were replaced. Some were replaced because they were weak and not able to deliver the vote that the Kremlin desired in recent elections. In other cases the Kremlin wanted to ensure that it had "its man" in place for the next five years before the next election. Furthermore, of the eleven regional elections to take place in 2012, only four will be held, and none is a region that appears poised to leave the Kremlin's orbit.[20] In any event, the new method for selecting governors diluted the original intent—free election of governors. The introduction of various "filters" will protect the interests of the Kremlin (see chapter 3). Critics argue that these two reforms do not change the essence of the political system, which is controlled by the Kremlin and which gives the Kremlin multiple levers to manipulate political outcomes.

Nonetheless, Medvedev *may* be remembered for navigating Russia through a succession of crises during his term. During his four years in power Medvedev faced no fewer than four serious economic crises: (1) the collapse in the price of oil after mid-2008, which affected revenue flows into Russia's budget; (2) the August 2008 war with Georgia, which, although short-lived, brought global condemnation upon Russia and delayed its entry into the WTO by several years; (3) the 2009 global financial crisis, which hit Russia harder than any G20 power and led to a significant drop in its GDP; as a consequence, analysts and commentators predicted political instability inside Russia;[21] and (4) the 2010 drought and heat wave that led to one-third of the harvest being destroyed, thereby driving food prices up and depriving the government of export earnings. By 2011 the government announced that the decline in agricultural production was over, and in 2012 Putin said that macroeconomic indicators showed that growth had returned to the Russian economy.

Medvedev also enjoyed some policy successes. Relations with America became less tense, and the March 2009 reset led to a historic arms reduction agreement in early 2010 between the two nations. One of the disappointments had to be that the bilateral relationship did not develop further. The admission of Russia into the WTO was a significant achievement, bringing an end to eighteen years of disappointment and hard feelings. WTO membership gives Russia status that it did not have before, essentially allowing it equal status with other major nations and providing a psychological lift. Accession is expected to increase economic growth in the medium and long term, lower import prices, increase competition, and spur foreign investment. Further, accession helps to enforce the rule of law and provide investors access to the WTO's dispute resolution process. Medvedev also put Russia on the road to being globally influential again, both with his personality and style, and because of policies that he initiated. In terms of domestic policies, Medvedev oversaw a large increase in military spending that will allow Russia to modernize its armed forces. A major push for innovation and modernization in the economy was undertaken with the goal to make Russia a technological superpower, akin to Silicon Valley in the United States.

Medvedev's Historical Role

Just as history may remember Medvedev for the lack of significant political reform, it will also judge his historical importance. What was his role? On the one hand, the handing of power to Medvedev was "nothing more than a chess move to keep Putin in power without violating the letter of the constitution."[22] In this interpretation, Medvedev's role was to be loyal to Putin, to keep the presidential seat warm for four years and then turn the presidency back to Putin. In this role Medvedev played his part well. This scenario makes sense, because Putin would not have promoted him up the political ladder if he believed that Medvedev were not responsible, capable, and most of all, loyal. Putin could count on Medvedev to step aside when Putin decided to return to power, exactly what happened. Moreover, Putinism would survive because the two men have a good working relationship that has developed over many years, and this relationship is due in no small part to the fact that they shared similar views and values. Despite the fact than enormous time and effort was spent by Western journalists and others to find (or create) anything that smacked of division between the two when Medvedev was president, Medvedev never gave any reason to doubt his loyalty to his mentor. In the relationship there were, of course, at times differences over language or emphasis, as would be expected in any political relationship, but these differences were often minor.

Toward the end of Medvedev's term there were rumors that the tandem had ruptured, that Medvedev's "political partnership with Putin appears to have outlived its sell-by date," and that Putin may backtrack on his promise to make Medvedev prime minister.[23] This did not happen, as Medvedev was confirmed as prime minister, and a fracturing of the political elite into the Putin camp and Medvedev camp never occurred. Medvedev as loyal client continued when the new cabinet was revealed the third week of May 2012, showing a cadre that was stacked with Putin loyalists and former colleagues. It is well to remember that according to the constitution the prime minister is to formulate the cabinet, but in reality it is clear that Putin had significant input and Medvedev conceded. On the whole, therefore, Putin trusted, and continues to trust, and Medvedev plays the loyal protégé, aided by the fact that for all intents and purposes the two men share common values and perceptions.

On the other hand, a second historical role views the transfer of power to Medvedev as "a clever way to transition out of the authoritarian system

Putin built into a more pluralistic model."[24] In this role, Medvedev spoke out against corruption and for democratization, thereby raising hopes and expectations in the young, educated, and urban population, and, according to some analysts, among a technocratic elite that has grown weary of Putinism. The problem with this interpretation is twofold. First, Medvedev talked a better game than he played; as noted above, his record in political reform was less than impressive, although he certainly said the right things in his speeches. The problem was he did not deliver on his promises or his vision. To argue that Medvedev's attempt to democratize was blocked by Putin or the *siloviki*, we would need insider information to that effect. More likely, in my opinion, is simply that Medvedev held essentially the same values as Putin. Furthermore, if Medvedev was ineffective in transforming the political system as president, it is hard to see how he will do so as prime minister, a position that by constitutional norms is subordinate to the president, as well as the fact that Putin is clearly the superior personality.

The second problem with this view is that Medvedev appeared to be no less a law-and-order man than was Putin. During Medvedev's term police were used many times to break up demonstrations. Protesters were arrested and sent to jail. The press was no less censored. The use of intimidation against the press was no less severe. Furthermore, Medvedev missed a major opportunity and failed the democracy litmus test by not only refusing to pardon Mikhail Khodorkovsky, but also allowing his retrial in December 2010 and the extension of his sentence to 2017 in what would be considered double jeopardy in the West. Rumors swirled that the judge in the December 2010 trial was pressured and the sentence was prepared elsewhere and delivered to him. In the run-up to the retrial, Khodorkovsky published editorials critical of Medvedev and the political regime in *Vedomosti, New York Times, International Herald Tribune,* and *Nezavisimaia Gazeta.* The article in *Vedomosti* came in response to Medvedev's article on "Forward Russia," in which Khodorkovsky argued that "authoritarianism in its current Russian form does not meet many key humanitarian requirements customary for any country that wishes to consider itself modern and European."[25]

These two views of Medvedev's historical role are important because they are directly relevant to Medvedev's political future. If the first view is accurate, Medvedev is expendable and he has fulfilled his usefulness, and it is possible that he will disappear from the political scene as did many before him—Chernomyrdin and Kasianov. The question then becomes how long he will last as prime minister. Even before taking office some speculation suggested that Medvedev is ill-suited to be prime minister because of deficiencies in organizational skills; others say the cabinet will not be his and he lacks political support. If rumors of a rupture in the tandem are true, then it would be expected that Medvedev would not last long—Putin may replace him at any time. A month before Medvedev assumed the position there were rumors that Aleksei Kudrin, a close friend of Putin, may be akin to a shadow prime minister, or even a co-premier.[26] Other speculation suggests that a future budget deficit—fueled in part by Putin's promise of $160 billion in extra spending for wage and salary increases over six years as part of his electoral campaign—will tie Medvedev's hands and may cripple his effectiveness.[27] If nothing else, these rumors testify to political infighting among political elites as they jockey for power and position in the new administration.

If the second view of Medvedev's historical role is more accurate, it suggests that Medvedev still has a useful role to play, and we may not have seen the last of him in a political role. Putin bided his time as prime minister; can Medvedev do the same? In 2018 Putin will be sixty-six, which is not especially old, but health problems are always an unknown. Further, if opposition to Putin continues to spread during the next six years, maybe Putin would be unable to win a fourth term without massive fraud, a prospect I doubt he wants to face because of its destabilizing potential for Russia. Medvedev himself has not conceded that his political career is over. At the end of January 2012 he stated that "I have never said that I would not run for office again. I will remind you that I am only forty-six, and this is not an old enough age to give up any future political battles."[28] Unfortunately, the answer about Medvedev's political future does not necessarily rest with him.

WHITHER PUTINISM? PUTIN 3.0 AND RUSSIA'S FUTURE

Russia's future is more uncertain than perhaps at any time in its post-Soviet history. New questions have arisen, and the nation seems to be at a critical juncture in its history. Is Putin's reelection the beginning of the end for managed democracy? Will nascent civil society and political opposition be crushed or allowed to evolve? Is Russia heading toward its own version of an Orange Revolution?

The fourth edition identified several characteristics that defined Putinism. Putin created a more centralized and authoritarian state than his predecessor Boris Yeltsin. A central feature of Putinism is an unfree media, and it became increasingly less so as time went on. Political opposition was silenced one way or another. Politicians who opposed the Kremlin were suppressed, such as Gary Kasparov, Mikhail Kasianov, and Boris Nemtsov; others such as Grigori Yavlinsky were essentially marginalized. Oligarchs and businessmen such as Vladimir Gusinsky and Boris Berezovsky were driven from the country, or in the case of Mikhail Khodorkovsky, jailed.

Journalists and writers who criticized the Kremlin were silenced by force, witnessed by the murder of Anna Politkovskaia and Paul Klebnikov. There were attempts to silence political voice at the mass level as popular demonstrations often did not receive permission to gather and were forcibly broken up if they did.

Center-periphery relations were redefined, with a shift of power to the center at the cost of regional autonomy. Political parties were brought under control, as a "party of power" (United Russia) was constructed that dominated elected institutions at federal and regional levels. As a result, elections, at every level, became less competitive and offered voters limited choice.[29] The court system, judges, and courts became less independent and served to back the position of the Kremlin. Physical force, violence, and arbitrary applications of the law defined the relationship between the governed and those who governed. This particularly pertained to individuals who spoke out against the regime or Putin himself. While the term "thug state," which appeared in some Western papers, may be too strong of a description for Putinism, certain behaviors suggested movement in that direction, such as the beating of journalists, the use of force to break up demonstrations, and suspected political assassinations. Putinism, therefore, led to a Russia that was much less free at the end of Putin's second term than when he took power in 2000, although it was freer and more pluralistic than during the communist period.

To be sure, the country that Putin inherited in 2000 was chaotic and collapsing. In that respect some form of Putinism was probably necessary to reverse the course of decline. But twelve years later one may question whether Putinism still has relevance for Russia. Going forward, the crucial questions for Russia's future are twofold: (1) Is Putinism adaptable? (2) Has Russia changed so that Putinism has become an ossified paradigm, a relic of the past that has little use?

During his first eight years in office Putin showed himself not to be a risk taker or a president prone to reckless action. He moved cautiously and did not stray from his sources of support and power. At present, the central features of Putinism appear not to have changed much at all, namely the desire for a strong state and the centrality of the state in all realms of political and economic life. Thus, the words that Putin articulated in his millennium speech in January 2000 continue to reflect his value system in 2012, namely, "For Russians a strong state is not an anomaly that should be gotten rid of. Quite the contrary, they see it as a source and guarantor of order and the initiator and main driving force of any change."[30]

Furthermore, Russian nationalism and a healthy dose of xenophobia continue as major elements of Putinism. In the aftermath of his electoral victory in March 2012, Putin dismissed the protesters' demands, casting them as a coddled minority of urban elites working at Western behest to weaken Russia. His claims that the United States was behind the opposition protests appealed to people who are suspicious of Western intentions after years of state propaganda. Putin argued that the vote showed the majority of Russians has rejected "political provocations" by his opponents aimed at "destroying Russia's statehood and usurping power."[31]

In short, Putin 3.0 is unlikely to be significantly different—or any more democratic—from Putin 1.0 and Putin 2.0. What is likely is that Putin will remain dependent upon the business, political, and security elites that brought him to power in the first place and that remain influential, which means that the *siloviki* will remain a potent force in Russian politics. We should not expect that Putin can or will break out of the mold that defined his first two terms; in the vernacular of today, Putin is who we thought he was. The next six years will indicate whether Putinism is adaptable or whether Putin runs the risk of repeating Gorbachev's mistake of not understanding the forces that had been unleashed and, as a consequence, always lagging behind the curve of reform. In the end, societal change left Gorbachev and the Soviet system behind. The same is possible for Putin and authoritarian Putinism.

There are abundant signs that Russia has changed, that the Russia of 2012 is significantly different from the Russia of 2000 when Putin first took power. The willingness to be politically active, to protest and demonstrate against a fraudulent Duma election and then the presidential election is remarkable for a population known for its passivity. The fact that 50 percent of the population does not trust the electoral outcomes can only be interpreted as a loss of legitimacy, or at least the start of a process of delegitimation of the political system.[32] It is telling that in the December 2011 Duma election United Russia received less support in large cities and more support in rural areas.[33] This is a reversal of the pattern during the early era of democratization under Gorbachev when democratic parties won the urban vote and communists gained support from rural areas.[34] The contemporary voting pattern suggests the rise of an educated, prosperous middle class that has withdrawn its support for the Kremlin-backed United Russia and is extending its demands to include political freedom and a genuinely competitive political system.[35] In the March 2012 presidential election, the city of Moscow was relatively clean, whereas electoral fraud was highest in ethnic minority republics.[36] As future budgetary cuts in social spending and higher utility bills hit average Russians, the potential for more and larger protests increases. In short, it may be that the protests that occurred in December 2011 are the start of a process rather than an end.

A second sign of a changed Russia concerns new openness that is bound to have political effects. More and more Russian citizens get their information and news from the Internet, which is not as strictly controlled as the print media and TV (see the chapter by Lipman). Russians may subscribe to satellite dish TV to receive BBC news or CNN International. Cell phones are ubiquitous, making international communication easy and convenient. Russian tourism to foreign destinations has increased significantly during the past ten years, allowing everyday citizens to experience the political freedoms found in other nations. The opening of Russian society creates dissonance with the mindset espoused by Putinism that foreigners want to undermine Russia or deny it status as a global power. In the same way that Soviet citizens learned to tune out the political propaganda from the Soviet regime, so too may educated, urban voters become indifferent to Putin's message, thereby delegitimating not only Putin's rule but also the way in which political institutions are used.

It would be a mistake to think that Putin and Putinism will simply recede. The new Putin regime in the first month in office displayed an ability to adapt and use a combination of old techniques—police raids, intimidation, and arrests—along with the new legal maneuvers to quell protests. In the run-up to a planned massive demonstration in Moscow on June 12, police raided the apartments of protest leaders and summoned protest leaders to police stations to answer questions, methods of intimidation used in the past. Then in early June 2012 President Putin signed a new law that increases fines for "violations" during demonstrations and protests, to nearly a year's salary (based on the average national salary) as a way to discourage participation.[37] This law was dismissed as unenforceable by commentators in Moscow and may serve to enflame the protest movement. In the end, neither coercion nor law stopped the June 12 demonstration, as an estimated 120,000 Muscovites took to the streets, whereas official estimates were closer to 20,000. Unlike previous demonstrations, the June 12 protest was peaceful. Nonetheless, once in office Putin 3.0 has displayed a proclivity to crack down and less willingness to negotiate or meet the demands of protesters.

That said, it may also be a mistake to overdramatize the prospects for political instability under Putin 3.0. Putin as president retains enormously powerful levers—both legal and extralegal—to maintain control. Further, we should not forget that he remains a popular leader, particularly in the regions. He won 64 percent of the vote, almost 50 percentage points ahead of the runner-up. Even if fraud was committed during the presidential election, the net impact was probably only a small percentage. It's not as if he reversed the will of the people and stole the election as happened with Yanukovych and Yushchenko in Ukraine in November 2004. The few thousand protesters who took to the streets in Moscow in February, March, and May 2012, however brave they are, represent less than one-tenth of 1 percent of the population of Moscow. In short, the powers of the presidency have not been weakened, and Putin does not appear to have lost the will to use coercion, something that doomed Gorbachev. Opposition to Putin does not appear to be widespread, it is poorly organized, and protesters lack a coherent, unified message that can galvanize national support.

What, then, does the future hold for Russia? Predicting the future for Russia is always a hazardous business. Still, it is abundantly clear that Russia's recent past has been imperfect, and its future is uncertain. The chapters in this book present a road map for understanding the course ahead.

THE STRUCTURE OF THE BOOK

As with the fourth edition, the book is divided into three sections. Part I examines different aspects of domestic politics. Richard Sakwa begins by exploring the relationship between the nature of political leadership in Russia and the requisites for democratic development and societal modernity. He argues that a contradiction exists in Russia, indicated by the clear tension between liberal democratic aspirations and the state's inability to act as a coherent vessel in which these aspirations can be fulfilled. In particular, Sakwa shows that while Putin's administration certainly remained within the letter of the constitution, in fact it undermined the motivating spirit of democracy, political pluralism, and judicial impartiality. Moreover, a characteristic feature of modernity is the emergence of autonomous civic actors. As Putin attempted to manage various transformative actors, the larger contradictions within Russia's modernity were exposed. Medvedev did little to change this dynamic, although Sakwa argues that Medvedev as president was more significant than he is often given credit for.

Thomas Remington tackles the question of political development from a different angle, focusing on the Duma (the lower house of Russia's parliament) and the party system. Remington concentrates on two closely related developments: the subjugation of parliament and the creation of a party system in which United Russia dominates regional and federal elections and opposition parties are sidelined. Between the Yeltsin and Putin eras Russia's political system evolved from one in which "super-presidentialism" tended to undermine incentives for politicians to form competing programmatic parties to one in which politicians have a strong incentive to join the dominant pro-Kremlin party, United Russia. Efforts by Medvedev to introduce democratizing reforms into the political system largely failed to make any lasting impression. The success of the "castling move" by which Putin and Medvedev exchanged jobs in spring 2012 only underlined Putin's firm control over the regime. Yet there are serious reasons to question whether the Putin system is durable, and he argues that the Putin system, which was durable through the first decade of the 2000s, may need to give way to a more open and competitive system in the second decade.

Another critical area where recentralization occurred has been in center-periphery relations. Nikolai Petrov and Darrell Slider argue that rebalancing the relationship between the center and the periphery in favor of the center was one of Putin's goals. Putin aggressively pursued an antifederal policy designed to take away or circumscribe many powers exercised by regional leaders. His goal was to establish a unitary, centralized state under the guise of "restoring effective vertical power in the country," to use Putin's own description of his intentions. As a result, federalism eroded under Putin. During the period of joint rule by Medvedev and Putin from 2008–2012, the centralized model was further entrenched. By mid-2011 the Kremlin appeared to be shifting toward a path that would restore elements of a federal system, though reluctantly and with as many braking mechanisms as the political situation permitted.

A central aspect of a healthy democracy is a state governed by the rule of law and a court system that is both objective and honest (not corrupted). Kathryn Hendley provides a broad overview of Russian law and how it has developed since the end of the USSR. She argues that under both Putin and Medvedev, the Kremlin's legislative agenda was pushed through with a heavy hand and often with the result of curtailing human rights. In particular, Putin's willingness to use the courts as a weapon for punishing his political opponents quite rightly calls their independence into question. Moreover, the courts represent a central aspect of corruption and distribute resources (broadly defined) to individuals and their companies that are loyal and favored by the Kremlin. Such policies would be troubling in any context, but are particularly disquieting in post-Soviet Russia. They are disturbingly reminiscent of problem-solving tactics employed by Soviet leaders that would seem to have been renounced as part of the transition to a rule-of-law-based state (*pravovoe gosudarstvo*).

In a new contribution to this edition, Alfred Evans analyzes the development of civil society in Russia, with particular attention to protests. Evans begins with a discussion of civil society in Soviet society, tracing its development through the Gorbachev years and *perestroika*. In the 1990s, civil society in Russia was weak, and the two main reasons for the marginal condition of the vast majority of organizations in civil society were found in a culture of distrust of the public sphere and unfavorable economic circumstances for social organizations. Within a few years of becoming president, Putin turned his attention to bringing civil society into an integrated system of support for the centralized state. Putin also enhanced positive incentives for organizations in civil society to provide the kinds of services that the state considered most valuable. An upsurge in civil society, in particular the willingness to protest, began to emerge in 2005 with the attempt to monetize social benefits for large portions of the population. Thereafter, other protests occurred during 2005–2011. The chapter concludes with a discussion of the protests surrounding the December 2011 Duma election and the March 2012 presidential election.

The final chapter in part I concerns the Russian media and freedom of the press. Maria Lipman traces the rise of nongovernmental media through the 1990s and Putin's first two terms, 2000–2008. The theme of this coverage focuses on increased government control and regulation, progressively making the media less and less free. She then outlines a "political thaw" that occurred during the tandem rule of Dmitry Medvedev and Putin, arguing that a new permissiveness unleashed more criticism by the media. Although TV remained under state control, the newly energized media realm is filled with reportage and critical policy analysis. During the tandem period most major print and radio outlets rapidly developed Internet platforms. In addition, Internet, print, audio, and video are merging, which provides outlets for independent thought and criticism of the government. The fraudulent Duma election of December 2011 marked the end of political quiescence. She concludes that the repoliticization of the society is still in its very early stages, but in the coming years the new media are bound to play an important role in the revitalization of Russia's civil society.

Part II examines the economy and society. Timothy Heleniak opens the section by presenting a broad and comprehensive overview of demographics in Russia. The importance of demographics is reflected in Putin's 2006 State of the Union address, when he identified demographic decline as the country's largest problem. Heleniak's chapter examines population change, fertility, mortality, international migration, composition (gender, age, education, and nationality), and the spatial distribution of the population. The chapter also analyzes population projections. Russia will continue to have a negative natural increase where deaths exceed births and will continue to be a net immigration country. Although in recent years there has been a slight uptick in birth rates, there is only so much a government can do to affect fertility, mortality, and migration trends. Therefore, it is likely that the Russian population will decline from sixth largest in the world in 1991 to twelfth in 2025 and to fifteenth by 2050.

Pekka Sutela contributes a new chapter on economic policy. He begins with an overview of the tasks that Putin faced in trying to fix the economy in the early 2000s—balance the budget, fix the tax system, and monetize the economy. The chapter presents sections on monetary and fiscal policy. He then examines the impact of the 2008–2009 crisis and the steps that Russia took to combat it. The chapter concludes with a look at the Russian economy in 2020, based upon the program adopted in 2011–2012. He concludes that it is possible that Russia will engage in a new wave of reform, but many of the relatively easy tasks have already been tackled. Current and future challenges are complex and difficult, and Russia is unlikely to match its growth performance of the 2000s.

Louise Shelley analyzes crime and corruption. Whereas the Soviet regime hid these unpleasant realities, postcommunist Russia experienced a huge upsurge. The Putin years brought greater stability, but Russia has not been able to eliminate the high rates of violent crime, endemic corruption, or pervasive organized crime. High levels of money laundering and export of capital have continued to deprive Russia of the capital it needs for investment, although the record profits obtained during the boom years of oil revenues masked the impact. The crime problems have evolved in the years since the collapse of the Soviet Union, but they have remained an important element of the structure of the Russian economy, society, and political system. Russian society continues to experience high rates of homicide; high rates of youth crime and child exploitation; high rates of drug abuse and a rapidly escalating problem of international drug trade; and large-scale human smuggling and trafficking from, into, and through Russia. A more recent element has been corporate raiding, which results in insecure property rights and undermines entrepreneurship. The chapter also surveys the geographical distribution of crime and corruption and their characteristics.

Stephen Wegren examines agricultural policy. The chapter begins with a review of Russia's agricultural situation and achievements under former president Dmitry Medvedev. The chapter then considers priorities that Putin has in his third term as president (Putin 3.0). Medvedev's agrarian policy did not depart significantly from Putin's, and it is unlikely that Putin 3.0 will depart from policy directions defined during the Medvedev presidency. By 2018, when Putin's third term expires, Russia is likely to have had eighteen years of consistency in agrarian policy. Russia's agriculture has a twofold global importance. First, its production rebound influences world supply and affects global commodity prices. A Russia that is a supplier in a hungry world is better than a Russia that subtracts from global surplus. Second, a competitive agricultural sector is an integral part of the profile of a global power. Inasmuch as Putin hopes to return Russia to international influence, a strong agricultural sector furthers his goals. The chapter concludes with a survey of the challenges faced by Putin in making Russia a global food power.

Part III of the book analyzes foreign policy and military reform. Andrei Tsygankov begins this section by providing a broad survey of Russia's foreign policy. In particular, he presents an argument that Russian foreign policy has since fall 2009 become less assertive, thereby moderating policy that it followed since 2005. The new approach to foreign policy did not mean that Russia was returning to its pro-Western course of the early 1990s or attempting to build special ties with the United States in the manner that followed 9/11. The chapter first reviews the changing international conditions that have influenced Russia's worldview. The chapter then surveys policy and relations with different parts of the world, including relations with the West, Europe, China, the Middle East, and nations in the former Soviet region. Russia's new course, which combines elements of cooperation and assertiveness, is yet to be fully consolidated, and it remains to be seen whether the course will gather sufficient political support among top decision makers. Russia's new course depends on favorable developments in the global political and economic system.

Gregory Gleason analyzes relations between Russia and Central Asian nations. Central Asia is important for Russia because Russia wants to maintain control of its southern border, its traditional sphere of influence. Similarly, Russia is important for the Central Asian states. Even after independence Russia remains a major commercial partner for all the Central Asian states. What might be called Russia's political-gravitational field is palpable throughout the Central Asian states, where many of the media, financial, and technological influences originate primarily from Russia. Much of the competition pits Russian-based firms against the commercial prowess of firms from other countries of the world, including China, India, Europe, Turkey, the United States, and others. There is clearly competition over Central Asia's resources, markets, and future prospects. But despite the competition, the Central Asian states are not merely balancing "East against West," as was often perceived as the key foreign policy choices in the past two decades since independence. Today there are many competing sectors of influence: the energy sector, chiefly gas and oil but also electric power; the minerals sector; the agricultural sector; and, at least in Kazakhstan, the emerging banking sector. Today there are many vectors of influence—the Slavic relationship to the north is paralleled by a strong Turkic-language and cultural relationship to the west and a Persian cultural relationship to the south. China represents a new and rapidly accelerating commercial influence on Central Asia. Moreover, Central Asian states have conflictual relations with one another in ways that magnify the influences of foreign countries. In this context, Russia's role is more complex than dominance or competition.

A new contribution to this edition is from Jeffrey Mankoff, who analyzes relations with the European Union. Russia's relationship with the EU is deeply paradoxical. The EU is simultaneously Russia's most important economic partner and a multilateral, value-based organization that fits uncomfortably with Moscow's state-centric view of international relations. Though Russia is deeply tied by history and culture to Europe, the organizing principles of Russian politics and foreign policy are far removed from those at the heart of the EU. The chapter reviews Russia's place in Europe and its economic relations with the EU, which serve as the cornerstone of the partnership. The chapter also surveys the nature, tone, and content of cooperative relationships with European powers—Germany and France—as well as relationships fraught with more difficulty, such as with Poland and the Baltic states. Despite continued and often quite heated disagreements, Russia and the EU continue to need each other.

The final chapter is by Dale Herspring, who analyzes the question of whether military reform has ended, as postulated by Russia's political leadership. In the post-Soviet period it soon became clear that Russia's military needed structural reform. For a variety of reasons, however, little was accomplished under President Boris Yeltsin. When Putin took over it soon became clear to him that chaos existed in the military. Late in his second term President Vladimir Putin came to the conclusion that the Russian military had to be shaken up—that it was so corrupt that only an outsider could do the job. As a result, heads began to roll and major changes were introduced. Herspring traces the rise of Anatoly Serdiukov and the policies he has introduced to make the Russian military more efficient and cost-effective, as well as smaller. At the heart of the "New Look" policy was the decision to cut the Russian military from around 2 million to 1 million men. The chapter concludes with a survey of changes that remain and that need to be addressed. Modernizing the Russian military is and will continue to be both a lengthy and frustrating process.

NOTES

1. Stephen White, "From Soviet to 'Soviet' Elections?" *Russian Analytical Digest,* no. 109 (March 8, 2012): 4.

2. Arkady Lyubarev, "An Evaluation of the Results of the Duma Elections," *Russian Analytical Digest,* no. 108 (February 6, 2012): 2–5. See also Alexander Kynev, "Election Falsification and Its Limits: A Regional Comparison on the Eve of the Presidential Elections," *Russian Analytical Digest,* no. 110 (March 16, 2012): 17–19, who estimates that United Russia received only 32 percent of the vote, with a range of extra votes between 7 and 15 million.

3. Stephen White, "The Russian Presidential Election: What Next?" *Russian Analytical Digest,* no. 110 (March 16, 2012): 2.

4. Andrei Yakovlev, "Russia's Protest Movement and the Lessons of History," *Russian Analytical Digest,* no. 108 (February 6, 2012): 6.

5. Yakovlev, "Russia's Protest Movement," 9.

6. This was reflected early on by the fact that Putin took charge and was the national spokesman during the Georgian crisis. This was also seen by the fact that in early December 2008 Putin conducted a live, call-in radio program in which citizens asked questions and expressed concerns on a wide range of topics. Putin traditionally did this once a year when he was president. The fact that Putin continued to hold such a forum as prime minister was a symbol that Putin was still in charge.

7. See the discussion of Medvedev's early political rhetoric in Stephen K. Wegren and Dale R. Herspring, "Conclusion," in Stephen K. Wegren and Dale R.

Herspring, eds., *After Putin's Russia: Past Imperfect, Future Uncertain* (Lanham, MD: Rowman and Littlefield, 2010).

8. "Russian President Medvedev's First Annual Address to Parliament," *Johnson's Russia List*, no. 202 (November 6, 2008).

9. "Medvedev's First Annual Address," *Johnson's Russia List.*

10. Lyudmila Alexandrova, "Medvedev Says Anti-corruption Struggle Yields Results, Experts Disagree," ITAR-TASS, March 23, 2012, *Johnson's Russia List*, no. 55 (March 23, 2012).

11. "Russia's Corruption Is Invincible," *Russian Press Review*, February 22, 2012, *Johnson's Russia List*, no. 32 (February 22, 2012).

12. Alexandrova, "Medvedev Says Anti-corruption Struggle Yields Results."

13. "Medvedev Admits Failure in Fight against Corruption," *RIA Novosti*, April 26, 2012, *Johnson's Russia List*, no. 77 (April 26, 2012).

14. "Laying Down the Law: Medvedev Vows War on Russia's 'Legal Nihilism,'" *Johnson's Russia List*, no. 233 (December 26, 2008).

15. "Laying Down the Law," *Johnson's Russia List.*

16. "In These Times," *Johnson's Russia List*, no. 82 (April 28, 2008).

17. "Russian Opposition Figure Detained over Crisis Article," *RFE/RL*, December 30, 2008, at www.rferl.org.

18. Tom Balmforth, "Astrakhan Is Latest Battleground Between Kremlin, Opposition," April 10, 2012, www.rferl.org/content/astrakhan_battleground_kremlin_versus_opposition/24543764 (accessed April 10, 2012).

19. Nikolai Petrov, "The Devil in the Election Bill Details," *Moscow Times*, February 21, 2012, www.moscowtimes.com (accessed April 11, 2012).

20. See Nikolai Petrov, "Why I Am Optimistic About Putin's 4th Term," *The Moscow Times*, May 22, 2012, www.themoscowtimes.com (accessed May 22, 2012).

21. Masha Lipman, "For Russia, a Dark Horizon," *Washington Post*, January 3, 2009, *Johnson's Russia List*, no. 2 (January 5, 2009).

22. Brian Whitmore, "The Unraveling: The Tandem's Slow Death," April 2, 2012, www.rferl.org/content/the_tandem_disintegrated/24535389.html (accessed April 7, 2012).

23. Brian Whitmore, "The Tandem in Winter," February 2, 2012, www.rferl.org/content/the_tandem_in_winter/24471760.html (accessed April 7, 2012).

24. Whitmore, "The Unraveling."

25. *Vedomosti*, October 26, 2009.

26. Brian Whitmore, "Kudrin's Game: The Man in the Middle," April 3, 2012, www.rferl.org/content/kudrins_game_the_man_in_the_middle/245365581.html (accessed April 10, 2012).

27. Henry Meyer and Jason Corcoran, "Putin's Spending May Cripple Medvedev as Kudrin Eyes His Job," *Bloomberg*, March 23, 2012, *Johnson's Russia List*, no. 55 (March 23, 2012).

28. Cited in Brian Whitmore, "The Medvedev Legacy," January 25, 2012, www.rferl.org/content/the_medvedev_legacy/24463231 (accessed February 10, 2012).

29. Ian McAllister and Stephen White, "'It's the Economy, Comrade!' Parties and Voters in the 2007 Russian Duma Election," *Europe Asia Studies* 60, no. 6 (August 2008): 931–57.

30. Vladimir Putin, "Russia at the Turn of the Millennium," at government.gov .ru/english/statVP—engl—1.html.

31. Cited in Vladimir Isachenkov, "Putin Claims Victory in Russia's Presidential Vote," March 4, 2012, *Johnson's Russia List*, no. 40 (March 4, 2012).

32. Maxim Ivanov, "VCIOM: Less than 50% Respondents Trust the Outcome of Elections," *Kommersant*, March 15, 2012, *Johnson's Russia List*, no. 49 (March 15, 2012).

33. Lyubarev, "An Evaluation of the Results of the Duma Elections," 2–3.

34. Jerry F. Hough, *Democratization and Revolution in the USSR, 1985–1991* (Washington, DC: The Brookings Institution, 1997), 140–74.

35. Stepan Kravchenko and Henry Meyer, "Putin Grapples with Urban Russia's Ire as Challenge for Third Kremlin Term," *Bloomberg*, March 6, 2012, *Johnson's Russia List*, no. 42 (March 6, 2012).

36. See Anatoly Karlin, "The Provincialization of Russian Electoral Fraud," www .sublimeoblivion.com, March 6, 2012, Johnson's Russia List, no. 42 (March 6, 2012).

37. Kathy Lally, "Russian Police Raid Apartments of Protest Leaders," *Washington Post*, June 11, 2012, *Johnson's Russia List*, no. 105 (June 11, 2012); and BBC Monitoring, "Putin Signs New Law to Counter 12 June Protests—Analysts, Politicians," *Ekho Moskvy* Radio, June 8, 2012, *Johnson's Russia List*, no. 105 (June 11, 2012).

I

DOMESTIC POLITICS

1

Political Leadership

Richard Sakwa

> [I]t is clearly too early to assert that, this time, Russia will complete her
> real convergence with the West. But it is not too early to assert that, in
> the normal course, she hardly has anywhere else to go. . . . As has ever
> been the case since Peter, if Russia wants to be strong, she will have
> to Westernize. With her Communist identity gone, and with no other
> ideological identity possible, she has little choice but to become, as
> before 1917, just another "normal" European power, with an equally
> normal internal order.
>
> —Martin Malia[1]

The Putin phenomenon remains an enigma. A man with a legal training
who spent a large part of his formative adult years in the security apparatus,
following the fall of the communist system in 1991 he threw in his lot with
the democratic leader of St. Petersburg, Anatoly Sobchak. Elected president
for the first time in March 2000, he presided over the development of a
market economy and constantly reiterated his commitment to democracy,
yet following reelection for his second term in 2004 the system veered
toward some form of state capitalism. *Dirigisme* in the economy was accompanied by suffocating restrictions on the free play of political pluralism and
democratic competition. Putin came to power committed to the "normalization" of Russia, in the sense of aligning its internal order with the norms
practiced elsewhere and establishing Russia's foreign policy presence as just
another "normal great power," yet there remained something "extraordinary" about the country. Putin left the presidency as prescribed by the constitution in May 2008, but power was transferred to his nominee, Dmitry

Medvedev, while Putin himself became prime minister and was thus able to ensure that "Putinism after Putin" would continue.

The "tandem" form of rule during 2008–2012 ensured that neither the liberalizing aspirations of Medvedev nor Putin's more conservative inclinations could be given free rein. This was a prescription for stalemate and stagnation, as well as frustration for those who hoped that Medvedev's liberalizing rhetoric would be translated into more concrete action. His presidency was unable to reconcile the contradiction between the regime's avowed commitment to the development of a modern capitalist democracy, accompanied by declarations in favor of "modernization," with the consolidation of a power-hungry power system that absorbed all independent political life and suffocated the autonomy of civil society. The contradictions continued into Putin's renewed presidency. On September 24, 2011, Putin effectively announced that he planned to return to the presidency, while Medvedev was to become prime minister. The parliamentary election of December 2011 and the presidential election of March 2012 only formalized this decision, provoking massive protests against both the substance of the plan and the fraudulent elections through which it was achieved.

In May 2012 Putin returned to the Kremlin, while Medvedev swapped positions with him to become prime minister. The move was formally legitimized by elections, yet it was clear that Putin's decision was decisive. The regime had become increasingly personalistic, focused on Putin himself, although his prestige had suffered as a result of the bruising succession process. Medvedev's continued membership of a reconfigured "tandem" suggested that modernization and reform remained on the agenda. This was reflected in the relatively liberal composition of Medvedev's cabinet, with a strong bloc of reformers leading the economic ministries. The task of this chapter is to indicate some of the dimensions of Russia's continuing engagement with the problem of "becoming modern" and to present an analysis of the leadership dynamics accompanying this challenge.

THE DUAL STATE AND POLITICS

Under the leadership of Boris Yeltsin in the 1990s Russia emerged as a dual state. The divergence between, on the one hand, the formal constitutional order, the rule of law and autonomous expression of political and media freedoms and, on the other hand, the instrumental use of law and attempts to manage political processes was already evident, notably in the 1996 presidential election, which was effectively stolen by Yeltsin. Under Putin the gulf widened and became definitive of his system of rule. Putin's administration was careful not to overstep the bounds of the letter of the constitution, but the system of "managed democracy" conducted itself with relative impunity and lack of effective accountability. It was firmly located in the gray area of para-constitutionalism, a style of governance that remains true to the formal institutional rules but devises various strategies based on technocratic (rather than democratic) rationality to achieve desired political goals. Putin's para-constitutionalism did not repudiate the legitimacy of the constitution but in practice undermined the spirit of constitutionalism. The interaction of real constitutionalism and nominal para-constitutionalism in Russia can be compared to the development of the dual state in Germany in the 1930s. Ernst Fraenkel described how the prerogative state acted as a separate law system of its own, although the formal constitutional state was not dismantled. Two parallel systems of law operated, where the "normative state" operated according to sanctioned principles of rationality and impartial legal norms while the "prerogative state" exercised power arbitrarily and without constraints, unrestrained by law.[2]

The contrast between the *constitutional state* and the *administrative regime* defines contemporary Russia. To reflect the distinctive features of Russian development I use these terms in place of Fraenkel's "normative" and "prerogative" states. The fundamental legitimacy of the regime is derived from its location in a constitutional order that it is sworn to defend, yet on numerous occasions it applied the law for illegal purposes. The most egregious case of such abuse was the attack on Mikhail Khodorkovsky, the head of the Yukos oil company. In October 2003 he was arrested, and in the following year Yukos was dismembered. Although the rule of law in Russia remains fragile and, as the Yukos affair amply demonstrated, was susceptible to manipulation by the political authorities, no fully fledged prerogative state emerged. Instead, the administrative regime granted itself considerable latitude but formally remained within the letter of the constitution. Russia remains trapped in the gray area between a prerogative and a genuine constitutional state. The regime is able to rule *by* law when it suits its purposes, but the struggle for the rule *of* law, even by prominent members of the administration, is far from over.

Two political systems operate in parallel. On the one hand, there is the system of open public politics, with all of the relevant institutions described in the constitution and conducted with detailed regulation. At this level parties are formed, elections fought, and parliamentary politics conducted. However, at another level a second para-political world exists based on informal groups, factions, and operating within the framework of the inner court of the presidency. This Byzantine level never openly challenges the leader, but seeks to influence the decisions of the supreme ruler. This second level is more than simply "virtual" politics, the attempt to manipulate public opinion and shape electoral outcomes through the exercise of manipulative techniques.[3] However, by seeking to reduce the inevitable contradictions that accompany public politics into a matter of technocratic management, the contradictions between the groups within the regime itself were exacerbated. Putin placed a high value on civil peace and thus opposed a return to the antagonistic politics typical of the 1990s, but this reinforced the pseudo politics typical of court systems. The suffocation of public politics intensified factional processes within the regime.

The divisions of the dual state were exacerbated by the modernization program pursued by Putin in his first two terms as president. His rule was committed to the development of Russia as a modern state and society comfortable with itself and the world. However, at the same time it sought to overcome the failings of what it considered to be the excesses of the 1990s under Yeltsin, notably the pell-mell privatization, the liberalism that gave rise to inequality epitomized by the enormous wealth of a handful of "oligarchs," and the "anarcho-democracy" characterized by the hijacking of the electoral process by business-dominated media concerns and regional elites. However, instead of strengthening the state, it was the administrative system that was allowed to flourish, allowing officialdom to rule with arrogant high-handedness and the security apparatus to insinuate itself back into the control of daily life. While personal freedoms for the mass of the population flourished, including the free right to travel abroad, for intellectual, political, and business elites the suffocating hand of the administrative regime stifled initiative and restored elements of the atmosphere of the late Soviet years. The business environment deteriorated, encouraging capital flight while inhibiting inward investment, accompanied by an epidemic of "raiding" against companies. It also degraded the quality of governance, with the so-called vertical of power, a term Putin used when he first came to power but thereafter dropped, proving ineffective. Even the president's word was far from law. Some 1,800 policy-relevant decrees issued by Putin during his first eight years as president were not implemented. This was the price to pay for the attempt manually to manage everything.

Medvedev came to power committed to advancing the constitutional state, above all by strengthening the rule of law and tackling corruption, but he was afraid to openly challenge the prerogatives of the administrative regime. At the heart of Medvedev's rhetoric was a different concept of reform. It became clear that he came to view Putin's stability as a recipe for stagnation. At the same time, Medvedev was the alter ego of a different Putin from the one who had driven the country into an impasse and needed Medvedev to offer the prospect of an evolutionary passage out of the dead end. Medvedev was well aware of these dilemmas, and while committed to continue the broad outlines of "Putin's plan" (the term used in the 2007–2008 electoral cycle to describe Putin's policy agenda, later called Plan 2020)[4]—economic modernization and the creation of a more competitive diversified economy, international integration, social modernization, and efficacious political institutions—Medvedev changed the emphasis from "manual" management toward greater trust in the self-managing potential of the system. In his Civic Forum speech on January 22, 2008, he called for the struggle against corruption to become a "national program," noting that "legal nihilism" took the form of "corruption in the power bodies." Medvedev returned to this idea in his speech of January 29, 2008, to the Association of Russian Lawyers when he called on his fellow lawyers to take a higher profile in society and to battle "legal nihilism."[5] He clearly had two evils in mind: corruption in the traditional venal sense, characterized by the abuse of public office for private gain; and meta-corruption, where the judicial process is undermined by political interference, known in Russia as "telephone law," and which had been most prominently in evidence during the Yukos case, which itself had given rise to the term "Basmanny justice."

In a keynote speech to the Fifth Krasnoyarsk Economic Forum on February 15, 2008, Medvedev outlined not only his economic program but also his broad view of the challenges facing Russia. He focused on an unwieldy bureaucracy, corruption, and lack of respect for the law as the main challenges facing the country. He insisted that "freedom is better than lack of freedom—this principle should be at the core of our politics. I mean freedom in all of its manifestations—personal freedom, economic freedom, and, finally, freedom of expression." He repeated earlier promises to ensure personal freedoms and an independent and free press. He repeatedly returned to the theme of "the need to ensure the independence of the legal system from the executive and legislative branches of power" and once again condemned the country's "legal nihilism" and stressed the need to "humanize" the country's judicial system.[6] Renewed confrontation with the United States (but not, it should be stressed, to the same extent as with the European Union), especially evident during the Five-Day War of August 2008 with Georgia, however, threatened to derail Medvedev's aspirations as the country once again, as in Soviet times, appeared faced with a choice between modernization and militarization.

This was reflected in Medvedev's programmatic article "Forward, Russia!" which was published in September 2009.[7] The article reflected Medvedev's growing conviction that continued political drift was no longer an option, but it also suggested uncertainly over what was to be done. The article was presented as a discussion document for the president's annual state of the nation address to the Federal Assembly, but the harshly critical tone went beyond what would be acceptable on such a formal occasion. He characterized Russian social life as a semi-Soviet social system, "one that unfortunately combines all the shortcomings of the Soviet system and all the difficulties of contemporary life." The underlying thinking was that the rent-extraction model of Russian political economy was unsustainable in the long run. This model had been sustained by windfall profits from a booming natural resource sector, but this only rendered the economy extremely vulnerable to a fall in prices. The fundamental question was whether Russia, with its "primitive economy" and "chronic corruption," has a future. Medvedev attacked not Putin but the system that Putin represented, a balancing act that blunted his message.

The article listed a devastating series of problems, although it was weaker in suggesting ways in which the situation could be remedied. First, Medvedev argued that the country was economically backward and distorted by dependence on extractive industries. Who would act as the modernizing force, however, was not clear: the state or private enterprise? Second, corruption had long been one of Medvedev's bugbears, and here he once again condemned the phenomenon. It would require a wholly impartial and independent judiciary to achieve a breakthrough, yet as the endless cases of judges working closely with business "raiders" demonstrated, little progress was made in the Medvedev years. Third, Medvedev condemned the "paternalist mindset" prevalent in Russian society, with people looking to the state to solve their social problems.

At the Fifteenth St. Petersburg Economic Forum on June 17, 2011, Medvedev once again set out his goals. He insisted that

> modernization is the only way to address the many issues before us, and this is why we have set the course of modernizing our national economy, outlined our technology development priorities for the coming years, and set the goal of turning Moscow into one of the world's major financial centers.

The fruits of this, he admitted, were small, "but they are there." He went on to condemn overcentralization:

> It is not possible in the modern world to run a country from one single place, all the more so when we are talking about a country like Russia. In fact, we have already gone through the kind of system when everything operates only on the Kremlin's signal, and I know from my own experience that this kind of system is not viable and is always adjusted to suit the particular individual. We therefore need to change it.

He also stressed that reform of the judicial system would continue and the struggle against corruption would be intensified.[8]

Putin limited Medvedev's freedom of action, but when Medvedev ordered senior state officials to relinquish their directorial posts on the boards of state companies by July 1, 2011, which meant that Putin's allies would have to leave their posts, Putin reacted calmly. Even where there were instances of divisions, as over the Khodorkovsky trials, the Domodedovo airport bombing in January 2011, and the UN resolution on Libya, these were not enough to tear the tandem apart. However, they did expose real differences in style and political personalities. These were all trumped by Putin's *démarche* on September 24, 2011. Putin was back, and there would no longer be any ambiguity over who was really running the country. Nevertheless, it was a chastened Putin who returned to the Kremlin. The whole system had been rocked by the mass demonstrations against electoral fraud, and Medvedev's reformism was now backed by a popular movement.

The usual charge against Medvedev is that he was loud in rhetoric but achieved very little. There is some substance to the charge, since undoubtedly there is a mismatch between what he promised, or at least implied, and what he was actually able to do. However, the major achievement was to have outlined something different from what had preceded his presidency; but since this modified program was rooted in the system shaped by his predecessor, it was caught in a logical trap that prevented a radical breakthrough. Although the list of reforms begun by Medvedev is impressive, none were carried through to any sort of logical completion. In part this was because of his inherently cautious approach, with the experience of the chaos and disintegration of the *perestroika* years and the 1990s acting as a salutary warning of what could happen if liberalization was too radical and speedy. Hence there would be no *"perestroika* 2.0," no repeat of Mikhail Gorbachev's runaway reform process from 1985, which ended up with the dissolution of the communist system and the disintegration of the country in 1991. A new ideology of reform was developed that abandoned the postulates of "sovereign democracy" and instead advanced a range of ideas based on "humanism," restraints on the use of the coercive power of the state, attempts to strengthen the rule of law, and a softening of the harsh regulations constraining the opposition and civil society associations. Medvedev, for example, sought to mitigate the harsh environment for entrepreneurs, but he was unable seriously to restrain the prerogatives of the army of officialdom that continued to "nightmare" business (as he put it).[9] The tandem format was mutually constraining, allowing neither Putin nor Medvedev to show their true colors. Medvedev did not launch a revolution against Putin, something that his critics would have liked to see but that was never in the cards.

Four main themes emerge from this. The first is the remedial element. Putin's policy agenda emerged out of not only the legacy of seventy-four years of communism and the way that it was overcome, notably the disintegration of the Soviet Union in 1991, but also the need to overcome the perceived excesses of the 1990s, above all the development of inequality, mass poverty, oligarch domination of the media, and the excessive ambitions of the new business elite. The second feature is the type of developmental program that Putin ultimately favored, with a strong role for the state to ensure that the business of business remained business, and not politics, and to remain firmly in control of economic policy making, accompanied by support for national champions in the energy, military defense, and manufacturing sectors. The third feature is the political managerialism designed to counter what was perceived to be the irresponsibility engendered by an untutored democratic process, a theme that provoked an obsession with security by the *siloviki* (representatives of the security and military) in Putin's team. These three elements combined to create a profoundly tutelary regime that was in some ways reminiscent of the "trustee" democracy practiced in Singapore.[10] However, the fourth theme should not be forgotten: the ability of the regime itself to generate plans for reform. The duality of the system was starkly revealed by Medvedev's plans for reform, and this impulse was carried over into Putin's third presidency.

There is a profound historical reality behind the emergence of the guardianship system. As in so many other "third wave" countries that have embarked on the path toward greater political openness since 1974,[11] democracy in Russia was forced to create the conditions for its own existence. This is a type of giant boot-strapping operation described by Ernest Gellner in his work on the development of civil society in Russia and other postcommunist countries.[12] The social subjects of capitalist democracy were being created in the process of establishing capitalist democracy, a circular process that engendered numerous contradictions. The relationship between the various subsystems of a dynamic democracy, notably a functioning multiparty system, still has to be devised. Instead, the tutelary role of the administrative regime tended to become an end in itself, and its developmental functions came to substitute for and impede the development of autonomous structures in society. Thus there was a profound ambivalence about Putin's leadership and the nature of his developmental agenda, an ambivalence that is characteristic of Russia's long-term modernization in which adaptation to the technological and economic standards of the West has been accompanied by resistance to political Westernization.

PROBLEMS OF POWER CONCENTRATION

Democracy in Russia is faced with the task of creating the conditions for its own existence; to this postulate Putin has implicitly added that this cannot be done by following the logic of democracy itself. Therein lay a further level of duality—between the stated goals of the regime and its practices, which permanently subvert the principles that it proclaims. Putin's team dismantled the network of business and regional relationships that had developed under Yeltsin, and although in policy terms there was significant continuity between the two periods, where power relations are concerned, a sharp gulf separates the two leaderships. Putin recruited former associates from St. Petersburg and the security forces, and on this he built a team focused on the presidential administration in the Kremlin that drove through the new agenda.[13] The power of the most egregiously political oligarchs was reduced, and from their exile in London and Tel Aviv they plotted their revenge, further stoking the paranoia of the *siloviki*. With the fear of the oligarchic Jacobites abroad, instability spreading across the North Caucasus, and the specter of color revolutions, it is not surprising that the regime exhibited all the symptoms of a siege mentality, and its legitimism took an ever more conservative hue.

The Putin administration initially drew on staff from the Yeltsin team, notably Alexander Voloshin at the head of the presidential administration and Mikhail Kasianov as prime minister. At the same time, a parallel administration was built up in the Kremlin, and gradually it dispensed with the services of Yeltsin's old guard. This was accompanied by a shift in policy priorities in the middle period of Putin's leadership. The "over-mighty subjects" had been tamed, and now the Kremlin went on the offensive, not only to ensure its own prerogatives in economic policy and political life but also to forge a new model of political economy where the state's preferences predominated. The Yukos affair represented a major disciplinary act, not only ensuring that the business leaders stayed out of politics, but also bringing the state back into the heart of business life.[14] This was achieved not so much by renationalization as by "de-privatization." Economic policy was no longer a matter for autonomous economic agents but had to be coordinated with the state, while the state itself became a major player in the economic arena (in particular in the energy sector) through its "national champions," above all Gazprom and Rosneft.

The equivalent of de-privatization in the political sphere was "de-autonomization." The ability of political actors to act as independent agents was reduced through a not-so-subtle and at times brutal system of rewards and punishments, while the economic bases of independent political activity were systematically dismantled. The "imposed consensus" of Russia's elite, as Gel'man notes, was achieved through the Kremlin's use of "selective punishment of some elite sections and selective co-optation of others."[15] As long as the Kremlin had adequate resources, in material, political capital, and authority terms, to rein in potentially fractious elites, the system could continue, but there was an ever-present threat of defection. An unprecedented decade-long economic boom, accompanied by windfall energy rents, reinforced the position of the power elite. This allowed a new type of "neo-Stalinist compromise" to be imposed: a type of "social contract" whereby the government promised rising standards of living in exchange for restrictions on independent popular political participation, a pact that could only be sustained, as Gorbachev discovered to his cost in the late 1980s, as long as the economy could deliver the goods.

This was accompanied by the strengthening of the "party of power," United Russia (UR), which increasingly dominated the party system, but it was not allowed to challenge the prerogatives of the executive. The establishment of UR in 2001 represented a significant development, since it did not simply represent the existing power system but sought to set up an alternative structure in whose name a government could be formed.[16] Fear of the autonomous development of an independent political force in the past ensured that no party of power managed to make a credible showing in a second election, but UR's triumph in the December 2003 elections indicated that a new pattern of politics was emerging. This was confirmed by its even more convincing victory in the December 2007 Duma elections, and although its position fell back in 2011, it remains by far the single largest party. Amendments to the law on parties in the wake of that election made registration of new parties extremely easy, but the emergence of numerous small parties was unlikely to threaten the party's dominance. Putin headed the party from April 2008, but he had demonstratively not joined it. But in May 2012 Medvedev not only became UR's leader, he also became a party member.

The system survived the economic shock of 2008, but in the long term a decline in primary commodity prices threatened the support basis of the regime. Even before this, it was clear that the old Putinite social contract— stability, security, and regular wages in exchange for political exclusion and passivity—was no longer tenable. Medvedev as president was well aware of the problem but failed to negotiate a new social contract, and this remained on the agenda when he became prime minister. The fundamental problem of a concentrated power system is to ensure adequate renewal to avoid rendering itself so inward-looking as to become dysfunctional. The reliance on a small coterie of trusted followers and the resulting weakness of competent personnel leads to reduced governmental capacity and poor policy performance. The Putin years were marked by a remarkable "stability of cadres," with some cabinet ministers serving for nearly the whole period. Medvedev promised "substantial renewal" as he took up office as prime minister in May 2012, and over two-thirds of the cabinet was changed.

THE CHARACTER OF LEADERSHIP

Two decades after the fall of the Soviet regime there is no consensus about the nature of the Russian political system. A whole arsenal of terms has been devised in an attempt to capture the hybrid nature of Russian reality, including "managed democracy," "managed pluralism," "electoral authoritarianism," and "competitive authoritarianism."[17] Following the Orange Revolution in Ukraine in late 2004, Russia's presidential administration launched the term "sovereign democracy" to indicate that Russia would find its own path to democracy and that democracy in the country would have Russian characteristics. This was a theme Putin stressed in his state of the federation speech on April 25, 2005. He took issue with those who suggested that Russia was somehow not suited to democratic government, the rule of law, and the basic values of civil society: "I would like to bring those who think like that back to political reality. . . . Without liberty and democracy there can be no order, no stability and no sustainable economic policies." Responding to Western criticism, however, Putin stressed that the "special feature" of Russia's democracy was that it would be pursued in its own way and not at the price of law and order or social stability: "Russia . . . will decide for itself the pace, terms and conditions of moving towards democracy."[18] In other words, while the content of policy would be democracy, its forms and the tempo of development would be a directed and managed process, a division that helped sustain the dual state in Russia.

Under Medvedev the notion of sovereign democracy was dropped from public discourse, although it remained in the background as the general sentiment that Russia would have to do things in its own ways and would not take kindly to foreign interference in its domestic politics. With Putin's return, the theme of Russia's autonomy in domestic and foreign policy was reinforced, but this did not mean that Russia would turn its back on foreign engagement. However, his return, and the manner in which it was achieved, did strengthen the voice of critics, who now argued with greater confidence that Putin was a dictator and Russia an authoritarian country.[19] There was also a return to discussion over whether the constitution should be changed. If Russia had taken an unequivocal turn toward authoritarianism, then did the cause lie in the political culture of the people, the "natural resource curse" whereby energy rents allowed the political system to insulate itself from popular control, or did the problem lie in a flawed institutional design, namely, the excessive powers granted the presidency by the 1993 constitution? This chapter argues that it is still too early to write off Russia's development as a democracy, although the struggle continues.

The continuing debate about the character and direction of Russia's leadership reflects a broader debate about the nature of the new system. Is the country still in "transition" to an arguably more democratic system, despite numerous detours and reverses, a perspective that can be dubbed the "democratic evolutionist" view? Or is what has emerged under Putin more or less "it," stuck in some postcommunist syndrome where democratic accoutrements adorn a society and polity that mimic the authority patterns of the earlier order, although aware that there can be no return to the previous system, the "failed democratization" approach?[20] In the latter camp Steven Fish is unequivocal: "By the time of Vladimir Putin's re-election as president of Russia in 2004, Russia's experiment with open politics was over."[21]

One of the main reasons in his view for the re-creation of a monocratic system was the failure to free the economy from the grip of the bureaucracy. This inhibited the development of a vibrant economy, notably in the small and medium business sector. Contrary to what critics of the privatization of the 1990s argue,[22] Fish insists that more liberalization was required. The stunted development of an independent business sector deprived political life and the media of the sources of independent support, accompanied by widespread corruption and a corrosive venality in public life. The Yukos affair was a clear manifestation of the attempt to achieve economic goals by administrative means, using the law to achieve political purposes. While Putin's administration was clearly in favor of the creation of a capitalist market integrated into the world economy, it feared the free operation of market *forces*. In his 1997 doctoral dissertation Putin had argued for the creation of national champions, and this long-standing policy goal was reinforced by the concerns of the *siloviki* in Putin's team.[23]

The institutional choices embedded in the 1993 constitution, above all the establishment of a "super-presidential" system, are considered by many to have driven Russia toward monocracy. On the basis of his Parliamentary Powers Index, Fish finds that Russia is considered semi-presidential on rather weak grounds, and that in fact it is super-presidential. Only the right of the lower house to approve the president's nominee as prime minister gives it a tenuous claim to be semi-presidential, but the costs of rejecting the nomination three times are so high, namely dissolution and all the risks associated with a new election, that parliament would have to be suicidal to exercise its formal powers. However, defenders of the constitution, such as one of its authors, Viktor Sheinis, counter by arguing that the letter of the constitution has little to do with the issue; the key problem is that the spirit of constitutionalism is lacking. Democratic evolutionists see plenty of potential for the development of a more robust adherence to the spirit of legality, despite present setbacks.

The tutelary role of the regime may well have helped stabilize the state, but the quality of democracy suffered. The system in formal institutional terms is a liberal democracy, and this is what endows the present system with its legitimacy, but practice clearly often falls short of declared principles. The constitution of 1993 is a liberal document enshrining fundamental human rights, the rule of law, separation of powers, federalism, and accountable governance, but the powers of the executive are enormous and allow the emergence of a relatively autonomous power center unconstrained either vertically or horizontally. The dual state model calls this power center the administrative regime, to a degree unlimited by the constitutional constraints of the formal state order from above and relatively unaccountable to the representative system from below.[24] Nevertheless, the administrative regime can only survive in its present form by drawing on the normative and practical resources of the constitutional order; without at least formal obedience to the liberal constitutional norms, the regime would be exposed as little more than a dictatorship. The Constitutional Court remains a serious and authoritative body, and there have been sustained attempts to give muscle to the independence of the judicial system, including the widespread introduction of jury trials. However, in practice the various Putin administrations, while certainly remaining within the letter of the constitution, undermined the motivating spirit of democracy, political pluralism, and judicial impartiality. There is thus rich ground for disagreement, since partisans of both the democratic evolutionist and failed democratization camps can always find evidence to support their case.

A number of countries can be described as "para-democracies," where real power lies not with the constitutionally vested authorities but with groups outside the formal power system. This was the case, for example, in Greece following the end of the civil war in 1949 up to the military coup of 1967, with the formal democratic procedures vulnerable to interference from forces not subservient to the democratic process. Local bosses were able to carve out fiefdoms, and central government was prey to endless crises, with more than thirty governments between the end of the German occupation and 1967, and at all levels patronage relations prevailed. As in Russia, this system of controlled democracy was characterized by weak political parties, which were based on personalities rather than coherent programs. However, a fundamental difference with Russia is that in the latter there is no equivalent to repeated interventions by the military and the monarchy. Instead, in Russia the interventions come from within the dual system itself, and this endows both the formal institutions of the state and the administrative regime with a softness that inhibits either hardening into more or less autonomous structures. Instead, the two pillars of the dual state are in a condition of permanent tension. This degrades the coherent operation of both and undermines effective long-term strategic governance. The inner logic of the operation of the constitutional state cannot be given free rein, but at the same time, the authoritarian and corrupt inclinations of the administrative system are kept in some sort of check.

The logic of duality is reinforced by the international context in which Russia finds itself. The geopolitical dilemmas facing Putin and Medvedev have a strong historical resonance. Frustrated by the failure to achieve a viable framework for political relations between the post-Soviet states in Eurasia, the resolute geopolitical struggle with external great powers (America, the EU, China) in the region, and his exasperation with domestic liberal and democratic forces, Putin became ever more a legitimist of the type that Alexander I turned into in his final years before his death in 1825.[25] Putin's innate antirevolutionism was alarmed by the emergence of social movement "network" revolutions, which adopted a number of colors (rose, orange, and tulip) but which in all cases threatened his sense of the proper order of things. It is for this reason that he failed to recognize the underlying credibility of the demands of the "white" movement in the winter of 2011–2012 (the white ribbon became the symbol of the protest movement) and suggested that the demonstrators were in the pay of foreign governments. As befitting a person from the security apparatus who had witnessed the chaotic fall of communism in the German Democratic Republic in 1989, he had a deeply conservative view of how political change should take place. At the same time, Putin was unable to understand why Russia was not treated as just another of the great powers; since in his view there was no longer anything to fear from Russia, he assumed that the West would have "the serenity of spirit to understand her more."[26] Putin believed, with justice, that Russia was developing according to the same universal laws as the West, but later and more slowly. The decline in ideological hostility of the communist sort made possible a qualitatively better relationship with the West, but the Cold War spirit on both sides intruded.

Part of the reason for the remaining "extraordinary" elements in Russian politics is the nature of adaptation to contemporary modernity. We can briefly characterize this as a process of partial and dual adaptation.[27] Political adaptation is necessarily a partial process, since only in postcolonial and postwar contexts can one country try to copy wholesale the institutions of another. It is the nature and parameters of this *difference* that needs to be explored. Traditionalists insist that the gulf separating Russia from the West is enormous and therefore favor yet another *Sonderweg* (own path) that would affirm Russia's distinctive native traditions (*samobytnost'*). The security-focused part of the elite points to the danger to national security and national interests from full adaptation to external models. For economic liberals the elements of difference are precisely dysfunctional, and hence in their view Russia should adapt fully and unreservedly to the global economic order. These two worldviews are in rough balance, allowing a centrist authority to consolidate itself in the middle. The essence of Putin's leadership was the attempt to negotiate a new balance between adaptation and affirmation. A system of "partial adaptation" emerged, appealing to Russian political culture and shaped by security concerns while at the same time integrating into the international economy (notably, by joining the World Trade Organization in 2012). The partial nature of Putin's adaptation strategy was derived in part from the belief that excessive adaptation could be as dangerous as too little. While committed to a certain type of democratization, the Putin leadership insisted that democracy needs to be rooted in, and congruent with, national conditions.

The strategy of partial adaptation is therefore a balancing act torn by its inherent dualism. On the one hand it looks to the norms and standards prevalent in the countries of advanced modernity; on the other, it seeks to root the adaptive process in a native discourse (managed and interpreted, of course, by the regime) while refusing to succumb to traditionalist insularity. This dualism characterizes most democratic institutions and processes in Russia and provides the framework for the dual state. The Putin strategy for political and economic modernization could not depend on the strata or institutions traditionally relied on by modernizing regimes, such as the army or Western-educated elites, and while forced in part to adapt to the social milieu in which it finds itself, it feared above all being absorbed by that milieu, in particular the social forces created by the transition process itself (notably, the oligarchs). By the end of the first decade of the twenty-first century it was clear that new forces were emerging, notably a more active class of citizens who demanded inclusion in the political system on an equal and universal basis. Even before the political mobilization provoked by the flawed elections in December 2011 and March 2012 there had been clear manifestations that the Putinite system of tutelary politics was becoming increasingly dysfunctional.

Putin's modernizing technocratic regime became more isolated, bereft of substantive support from abroad and unable to rely on the emerging sociopolitical structures domestically (above all, the rising class of entrepreneurs, intelligentsia, and service workers). Instead, it became reliant on traditional sources of power, above all the security apparatus and the bureaucracy, both of which were oriented to the power system itself. The existence of this bureaucratic mass provided scope for innovation since it furnished critical support to the modernizing leadership, but at the same time it subverted the development of the autonomous agents of a genuinely modern society. The striving for regulation and control by the *securitistas* threatened liberty itself. The room for maneuver of the centrist regime was rapidly declining. The fundamental choice facing Putin in his third presidency is whether to strengthen the constitutional state and with it enhanced political pluralism, free and fair competitive elections, and the consolidation of independent courts, or whether to turn to administrative regulation, micromanagement of politics, manipulation of the state-owned media, and a combative foreign policy.

CONCLUSION: THE POWER OF CONTRADICTION

Putin appealed to the principles of stability, consolidation, and the reassertion of the prerogatives of the state. However, the concepts of consensus, centrism, and the appeal to "normal" politics were beset by a number of fundamental contradictions. These contradictions are reflected in the central problem facing any analysis of Putin's leadership: the nature of his statism. Putin came to power promising to restore the state after the depredations of the Yeltsin years, yet his focus from the first was on building up the resources of the administrative regime. He did not entirely neglect the state, undertaking a liberal reform of the judicial system in his early years and ensuring that government workers were paid on time, and that the army and security apparatus received increased funds. But instead of letting the state, together with its broader representative institutions such as parliament, get on with its business, his leadership constantly intervened in manual mode to ensure that his centrist administration could govern and perpetuate its power. The regime sought to insulate itself as far as possible from ideological and popular pressure, but by the same token it began to lose touch with popular aspirations.

Putin's centralism carried both a positive and a negative charge. The normative resources of the constitutional state were balanced against the arbitrariness of the administrative regime managed by a security-minded centrist authority. Putin emphasized "the dictatorship of law," and thus encouraged the development of a genuine rule of law state, but it did not subordinate itself to the pluralistic political process enshrined in the constitution. Once again traditions of the "revolution from above" were perpetuated, and patterns of lawlessness and arbitrariness were replicated. Putin insisted that the 1993 constitution established a viable framework for the development of a new governmental order, but his leadership was characterized by the absence of the spirit of constitutionalism, and this in turn undermined faith in the evolutionary potential of the constitution. There were few restraints on presidential power, and parliament and society were unable to call the authorities to account. Medvedev sought to overcome the gulf between the constitutional (normative) state and the administrative regime, but his halfhearted (although far from negligible) reforms were unable to achieve not rule by law but the rule of law.

It is not difficult to identify tensions in the "project" espoused by Putin, but, paradoxically, these tensions themselves became the source of much of his power. Putin was able to appeal to a variety of constituencies, many of whom would be exclusive if his ideas were enunciated more clearly. The essence of Putin's centrism was the ability to reconcile antagonistic and contradictory social programs. He transcended narrow party politics and affiliation with either left or right not by evasion, but by a distinct type of political praxis that was itself transcendent of the classic political cleavages of the age of modernity. It would be hard to label Putin's policies as president, prime minister, and once again president as either "left" or "right," and the same applies to Medvedev. The latter declared himself a "conservative," while Putin has been described as a "liberal conservative," an oxymoron that typifies the contradictory nature of his leadership. In an age when politics is based less on interests or ideologies than on identities and values, Putin reconciled policies and groups that in an earlier period would have been in conflict. Putin's style was antipolitical, although as a leader confronted by the need to reconcile conflicting interests and views, he proved a highly adept politician. The self-constitutive character of democracy in Russia imbued political processes with a contradictory dynamic. These contradictions are now becoming increasingly exposed, forcing Putin in his third presidential term to find new ways of ruling.

The characteristic feature of modernity is the emergence of autonomous civic actors accompanied by attempts by the state to manage various transformative projects that entail the management and reordering of society. In this respect Putin reflected the larger contradiction within modernity. It is a contradiction exacerbated in Russia by the clear tension between liberal democratic aspirations and the state's inability to act as a coherent vessel in which these aspirations can be fulfilled. It is for this reason that a strong state is often seen as an essential precondition for the development of liberalism,[28] while others continue to see it as the greatest threat to those liberties. However, it is more dangerous when the state is challenged by an administrative system that it can barely constrain, and when power is exercised by a technocratic, but often corrupt, elite that sees its own perpetuation as synonymous with stability, security, and development. At that point only the evolutionary but rapid consolidation of the constitutional state may avert the onset of a renewed era of revolutionary upheavals. There appears to be a natural cycle to leadership, and with Putin's return to power for a third term it appears that the country is entering another terminal phase. It would be the supreme test of his leadership to prove his critics wrong.

SUGGESTED READINGS

Lynch, Allen C. *Vladimir Putin and Russian Statecraft*. Washington, DC: Potomac Books, 2011.

Sakwa, Richard. *Russian Politics and Society*. 4th ed. London: Routledge, 2008.

———. *The Crisis of Russian Democracy: The Dual State, Factionalism and the Medvedev Succession*. Cambridge: Cambridge University Press, 2011.

Treisman, Daniel. *The Return: Russia's Journey from Gorbachev to Medvedev*. London: Simon & Schuster, 2011.

White, Stephen. *Understanding Russian Politics*. Cambridge: Cambridge University Press, 2011.

White, Stephen, Richard Sakwa, and Henry Hale, eds. *Developments in Russian Politics 7*. Basingstoke: Palgrave Macmillan, 2009.

NOTES

1. Martin Malia, *Russia under Western Eyes: From the Bronze Horseman to the Lenin Mausoleum* (Cambridge, Mass.: Belknap, 2000), 411–12.

2. Ernst Fraenkel, *The Dual State: A Contribution to the Theory of Dictatorship*, translated from the German by E. A. Shils, in collaboration with Edith Lowenstein and Klaus Knorr (New York: Oxford University Press, 1941; reprinted by The Lawbook Exchange, Ltd., 2006).

3. Andrew Wilson, *Virtual Politics: Faking Democracy in the Post-Soviet World* (New Haven, Conn.: Yale University Press, 2005).

4. The "Plan" encompassed all eight of Putin's state-of-the-nation addresses, as well as his "Russia at the Turn of the Millennium" article of December 30, 1999, his February 10, 2007, speech to the Munich security conference, and some other key speeches. They are in *Plan prezidenta Putina: Rukovodstvo dlia budushchikh prezidentov Rossii* (Moscow: Evropa, 2007).

5. "Vystuplenie na vneocherednom s'ezde Assotsiatsii iuristov Rossii," January 29, 2008, www.medvedev2008.ru/live_press_01_29_law.htm.

6. "Vystuplenie na V Krasnoyarskom ekonomicheskom forume 'Rossiia 2008–2020: Upravlenie rostom,'" www.medvedev2008.ru/live_press_15_02.htm.

7. Dmitry Medvedev, "Rossiia, vpered!" www.gazeta.ru/comments/2009/09/10_a_3258568.shtml.

8. "Dmitry Medvedev Spoke at the St Petersburg International Economic Forum: The President Gave an Assessment of the Current State of Russia's Economy and Outlined the Main Modernization Priorities," June 17, 2011, eng.kremlin.ru/news/2411.

9. "Stenograficheskii otchet o soveshchanii po voprosam zashchity prav sobstvennosti sub'ektov malogo i srednego predprinimatel'stva," July 31, 2008, www.kremlin.ru/transcripts/995.

10. See, for example, Mark R. Thompson, "Whatever Happened to 'Asian Values,'" *Journal of Democracy* 12, no. 4 (2001): 154–63.

11. Samuel P. Huntington, "Democracy's Third Wave," *Journal of Democracy* 1, no. 2 (1991): 12–34. The argument was developed at length in Samuel P. Huntington, *The Third Wave: Democratization in the Late Twentieth Century* (Norman and London: University of Oklahoma Press, 1991).

12. Ernest Gellner, *Conditions of Liberty: Civil Society and Its Rivals* (New York: Viking, 1994).

13. On the size and role of the *siloviki* in Putin's administration, see Olga Kryshtanovkaya and Stephen White, "Putin's Militocracy," *Post-Soviet Affairs* 19, no. 4 (2003): 289–306; and for updated figures, Ol'ga Kryshtanovkaya and Stephen White, "Inside the Putin Court: A Research Note," *Europe-Asia Studies* 57, no. 7 (2005): 1065–75.

14. See William Tompson, "Putin and the 'Oligarchs': A Two-Sided Commitment Problem," in *Leading Russia: Putin in Perspective*, ed. Alex Pravda (Oxford: Oxford

University Press, 2005), 179–202; also William Tompson, "Putting Yukos in Perspective," *Post-Soviet Affairs* 21, no. 2 (2005).

15. Vladimir Gel'man, "Political Opposition in Russia: A Dying Species?" *Post-Soviet Affairs* 21, no. 3 (2005): 242.

16. Pavel Isaev, "Ob'edinennaia partiia vlasti vystraivaet svoiu regional'nuiu vertikal' so skandalom," *Rossiiskii regional'nyi biulleten'* 4, no. 6 (2002).

17. For an overview, see Harley Balzer, "Managed Pluralism: Vladimir Putin's Emerging Regime," *Post-Soviet Affairs* 19, no. 3 (2003): 189–227.

18. See kremlin.ru/text/appears/2005/04/87049.shtml; *Rossiiskaia gazeta*, April 25, 2005.

19. For example, Masha Gessen, "The Dictator," *New York Times*, May 21, 2012.

20. See Richard Sakwa, "Two Camps? The Struggle to Understand Contemporary Russia," *Comparative Politics* 40, no. 4 (2008): 481–99.

21. M. Steven Fish, *Democracy Derailed in Russia: The Failure of Open Politics* (New York: Cambridge University Press, 2005), 1.

22. For example, Peter Reddaway and Dmitri Glinski, *The Tragedy of Russia's Reforms: Market Bolshevism against Democracy* (Washington, DC: The United States Institute of Peace Press, 2001).

23. See Harley Balzer, "Vladimir Putin's Academic Writings and Russian Natural Resource Policy," *Problems of Post-Communism* 53, no. 1 (2006): 48–54, with Putin's article "Mineral Natural Resources in the Strategy for Development of the Russian Economy" at 49–54.

24. For earlier discussions, see Richard Sakwa, "The Regime System in Russia," *Contemporary Politics* 3, no. 1 (1997): 7–25; Richard Sakwa, *Russian Politics and Society*, 3rd ed. (London and New York: Routledge, 2002), 454–58; Richard Sakwa, *Putin: Russia's Choice* (London and New York: Routledge, 2004), 86–88.

25. Malia explains Alexander I's position as follows: "Hemmed in by his position as one of the chief architects and guarantors of the Vienna system, and increasingly frustrated by his failures to effect reform at home, [Alexander] became ever more preoccupied with preserving 'legitimacy' and the established order throughout Europe." Malia, *Russia under Western Eyes*, 91.

26. Malia, *Russia under Western Eyes*, 167.

27. The theme of partial adaptation is explored in my "Partial Adaptation and Political Culture," in *Political Culture and Post-Communism*, ed. Stephen Whitefield (Basingstoke: Palgrave Macmillan, 2005), 42–53, from which this paragraph draws.

28. For example, Marcia A. Weigle, *Russia's Liberal Project: State-Society Relations in the Transition from Communism* (University Park, Pa.: Penn State University Press, 2000), p. 458, where she talks of the need for a "state-dominated liberalism."

2

Parliament and the Dominant Party Regime

Thomas F. Remington

One of the most important constitutional reforms in Russia after the end of the communist regime was the establishment of the principle of separation of powers. Article 10 of the 1993 constitution stipulates: "State power in the Russian Federation shall be exercised on the basis of the separation of the legislative, executive and judiciary branches. The bodies of legislative, executive and judiciary powers shall be independent." The reason this provision is so significant is that under the Soviet system, constitutional theory held that state power was "fused" in the soviets and that there could be no separation between the branches of state power: "all power to the soviets" meant that state power was unitary. All state power, though exercised through multiple instruments, derived from a single source and served a common purpose. In reality, state power did not flow from the soviets, of course; it was exercised by the Communist Party in the name of the soviets. But the party and state officials nonetheless adhered to the doctrine of the unity of state power, itself a legacy of tsarist absolutism. For this reason, the doctrine of constitutional separation of power represented a revolutionary break from the traditional model of Russian state power.

Under Boris Yeltsin, there was some separation of powers in fact. To a large degree this was due to the weakness of the executive and the fact that the opposition forces were well represented in the legislature. The president's inability to impose control over all parts of the executive and to enforce his will throughout the regions (in part because of the sharp divisions within the political elite) permitted opposition forces to exert influence over policy through parliament. It also allowed the Constitutional

Court a degree of independence in adjudicating disputes arising between the other branches.[1] At one point in 1998, in fact, President Yeltsin backed down in the face of adamant opposition from the Duma to his proposed candidate for prime minister and chose a figure more acceptable to the Duma. Therefore, there is no starker contrast between the Putin and Yeltsin presidencies than in the steady aggrandizement of presidential power at the expense of legislative and judicial autonomy under Putin. The severe centralization of power continued during the four years of Dmitry Medvedev's presidency but, as noted below, there are reasons to question whether it will continue long into the future.

Under the constitution, Russia's parliament, the Federal Assembly, has two chambers. The lower chamber is the State Duma and the upper is the Federation Council. In the State Duma, the authorities have achieved total dominance on the basis of a strong majority of seats controlled by the loyal United Russia (UR) faction. In the Federation Council, the Kremlin's managers have seen to it that only individuals loyal to the president are selected as members of the chamber and potential opponents are co-opted or intimidated. Similarly, the independence of the judiciary has been sharply restricted by the overwhelming concentration of administrative power in the hands of the presidential administration, so that no significant measure of the president is blocked by the courts. Like the parliament, the courts have become instruments for the endorsement of presidential prerogatives and the suppression of political opposition.

This chapter will concentrate on two closely related developments: the subjugation of parliament and the creation of a party system in which United Russia dominates regional and federal elections while opposition parties are sidelined. During the Yeltsin and Putin eras, Russia's political system evolved from one in which "super-presidentialism" tended to undermine incentives for politicians to form competing programmatic parties to one in which politicians have a strong incentive to join the dominant pro-Kremlin party, United Russia.[2] The model resembles that of Mexico's political system in the 1950s and 1960s, when the dominant party, PRI, was intertwined with all institutions of government, which it used to maintain its dominance. The PRI's organizational strength and large majority in the legislature ensured that any laws submitted by the president were rubber-stamped; opposition parties faced a variety of legal and extralegal forms of repression but were allowed to win minor electoral victories for the sake of preserving the façade of democracy; and the country's president headed a system of patron-client networks through which he dispensed rewards and punishments intended to keep him and his supporters in power. Such a system can be stable for decades. Since Putin left the presidency to become prime minister, the dominant party regime model is becoming still more entrenched. The regime appears intent on consolidating United Russia's position as the premier political institution linking executive and legislative branches, and central government with government in the regions.

Putin's team created this configuration of power through a succession of skillful institutional maneuvers and the intimidation of opposition forces. Moreover, Putin benefited from a spike in world oil prices that began almost at the same time he became president and continued through mid-2008; like the oil prices, his domestic popularity reached extremely high levels (especially impressive in view of Russians' generally cynical view of their leaders). His strategy for taming parliament and building a dominant "party of power" had four elements.

First, beginning in January 2000, when he became acting president, Putin worked to create a loyal majority in the Duma that would ensure passage of any legislation he proposed. He was relatively successful in the Third Duma (2000–2003), when the pro-Putin parliamentary faction Unity formed an alliance with three other factions and gained control over the agenda. He was spectacularly successful with the Fourth Duma, which convened following the December 2003 parliamentary election. The Fifth Duma elected in December 2007 continued the same pattern. The Sixth Duma elected in December 2011 gave Putin a reduced but still absolute majority for United Russia. (See table 2.1 on page 55.)

Second, Putin established direct control over the upper chamber of parliament, the Federation Council, through a reform of the way its members were chosen. The reform, enacted in summer 2000, removed the regional governors from the chamber and replaced them with permanent representatives appointed by the regional governors and legislators. The Kremlin oversaw the appointments process, ensuring that the new members would be faithful to the president's wishes. Since then, the Federation Council has voted by overwhelming margins for all of the president's initiatives.

Third, Putin moved to make United Russia the dominant party throughout the political system, controlling not only the State Duma in Moscow but regional parliaments as well. He did this through a series of legislative acts making it more difficult for other quasi-party structures (such as governors' or oligarchs' machines) to enter the political arena, by pressuring officials at all levels to affiliate with United Russia, and by dividing and diverting the followings of rival parties, such as the communists. These moves gave United Russia a resounding advantage in Duma elections in 2003, 2007, and 2011. The authorities also used a great deal of fraud and manipulation to ensure the desired outcomes of elections. With United Russia enjoying solid majorities in the Duma and manifesting tight party discipline, the president and government did not need to ally with any other forces in the Duma to exercise full control over the agenda and the outcome of all voting.

Finally, Putin created a set of consultative bodies that paralleled some of parliament's deliberative functions. These diverted policy-making expertise from the parliament to structures that the president can consult or ignore at his pleasure. To the extent that the president grants these "parallel parliaments" the right to advise him on a particular policy matter and to develop policy proposals, the Federal Assembly loses its constitutional monopoly on lawmaking and executive oversight and simply becomes one more consultative body lending the president political support. Among these parallel structures are the State Council (formed in 2000 as part of the reform of the Federation Council) and the Public Chamber (formed in 2005 as one of the reforms Putin proposed following the Beslan incident). In addition, Putin sometimes also uses the Security Council, a constitutional body that advises the president on national security matters, as a vehicle to draft policy measures in a wide range of areas.

Taken together, these steps reflect a coherent strategy to ensure that the president can exercise power unchecked by parliament or by opposition forces. Let us examine in more detail what Putin has done with the power he accumulated so successfully and discuss the continuation of the Putin system under President Dmitry Medvedev. We will conclude by asking whether it is likely that this system will continue under Putin 3.0.

PRESIDENT AND PARLIAMENT

Although the Russian constitution gives the president far-reaching political prerogatives, he must nonetheless obtain the consent of parliament if he seeks to pass legislation. In all cases, the Duma must approve draft legislation before it can be signed into law. There are certain categories of legislation that the Federation Council must consider, and it can consider any bill if it takes it up within two weeks of passage by the Duma. The Federation Council's vetoes of legislation, however, can be overridden by the Duma. The two chambers can also override a presidential veto by a concurrent two-thirds vote. Therefore, if the president wants to enact a law, he must obtain the consent of a majority of the Duma members. The president can enact measures by edict if a law is not already in force, but even then, experience has shown that a law is more stable and therefore more authoritative than a decree, which can be more easily reversed. Putin and Medvedev have preferred to operate by the normal legislative process, in contrast to President Yeltsin, who often relied on presidential decrees (*ukazy*) to enact important policy changes, particularly in 1992–1994. Under Putin, the number and importance of presidential decrees continued to decline. Most presidential decrees tend to concern appointments or classified issues such as military procurement rather than policy.

Thanks to a reliable base of support in the Federal Assembly, Putin and Medvedev have enacted a comprehensive body of legislation, some of it aimed at stimulating economic growth and some at restricting the political rights of potential opposition. Putin's success in enacting his legislative agenda is due not only to his control over lawmaking in parliament but also to his ability to control the policy development process as bills are drafted.

One of Putin's first steps as acting president was to institute a more orderly process for developing policy than had been the case under Yeltsin. The loose and fragmented nature of policy making in the Yeltsin regime meant that many interests, both inside the state's official bodies and outside them, initiated policy. For instance, well-connected business tycoons occasionally pushed through presidential decrees or pieces of legislation, and often presidential initiatives were successfully blocked by powerful but anonymous resistance from within the government bureaucracy.

Putin demanded a much more centralized approach to policy development, and in his first term, he used it to advance a far-reaching agenda of economic and institutional reform. In his first message to parliament in July 2000, Putin listed several ambitious policy measures that he wanted to enact into law. These included a flat income-tax rate, lower taxes on profits, a lower social tax, firm protections on property rights, less intrusive regulation of business, banking reform, property rights in land, labor relations, reform of the customs regime, and a new law on political parties. In his April 3, 2001, message he called for new legislation on federal relations and criminal and civil procedure, administrative reform, reducing the regulatory burden on business, further tax cuts, reform of the pension system, a system of mandatory federal health insurance, a new labor code, and intellectual property rights protection.

His 2002 message was still more ambitious. He called for legislation that demarcated the jurisdictions of the federal government and federal territorial subjects, reform of local government, a series of judicial reforms (including delineation of the jurisdictions of general and arbitration courts, reform of the criminal code, new codes of civil and arbitration court procedure, a law on arbitration tribunals [*treteiskie sudy*], amendments to the law on the procuracy, and penal reform), reform of the structure of the state bureaucracy and the rules governing state employment, reform of banking, reform of bankruptcy law, a law allowing the sale of agricultural land, and legislation harmonizing Russian trade law with WTO standards. Moreover, he advocated breaking up the large natural monopolies (the gas industry, electric power, and railroads) and for reform of the housing and utilities sector. This was the most ambitious program of his first term.

Then, beginning in the spring and summer of 2003, there was a marked slowdown in the pace of economic reform and a turn to a more state-oriented economic policy. The president's 2003 message made very little mention of new legislative priorities, calling only for acceleration of the development of reforms of the state administration and development of a new law on citizenship. A few months later, in summer 2003, the campaign to destroy Yukos began. Putin's 2004 and 2005 messages likewise touched only lightly on economic and institutional reform and emphasized instead the need to improve state services in health, education, and other spheres of social policy. Thus, even as his control over the legislative process grew, his interest in using it to advance a radical reform agenda decreased. The "liberal" phase of Putin's presidency, therefore, ended even before his first term was over. As many observers have pointed out, the shift away from a liberal agenda coincided with a period of high world oil prices, which reduced the pressure on the government to encourage competition, innovation, and investment.

Still, in his first term, Putin won some significant victories in enactment of the liberal agenda. The first several bills of his package of tax reform passed by the end of the spring 2000 term. In the spring 2001 term alone, the Duma passed in at least the first reading the land code; the first of a series of pension reform bills; a new labor code; comprehensive tax reform, including a low flat income-tax rate, a unified tax for all social assistance funds, a lower excise tax, a lower profits tax, a lower rate on transactions in hard currency, a new sales tax, and a lower tax on production-sharing agreements; the first bill in a package of judicial reform legislation; part 3 of the civil code, liberalizing inheritance rights; a set of reforms lowering the regulatory burden for business, including laws on the registration of businesses, licensing of businesses, regulation of stock companies, money laundering, and three laws on banking reform; and a law on the regulation of political parties. The spring 2002 term was similarly productive from the standpoint of the government. The Duma passed legislation on standards and on bankruptcy, elimination of the last remaining turnover tax, reduced taxes on small businesses, a new code of procedure for arbitration courts, and a law on sales of agricultural land. All of this legislation would have been difficult if not impossible to pass in the Yeltsin-era Duma. Putin's success reflected both the changed balance of political forces in the parliament and the Kremlin's skillful management of its relations with parliament in building majorities for its policy program.

On the other hand, Putin's early reform efforts were not always successful. Resistance came not from the parliament, however, but from the state bureaucracy, which has long experience in quietly torpedoing initiatives aimed at increasing its efficiency and accountability. For example, reform of the state bureaucracy was a theme emphasized in Putin's 2002 message, but eventually the impetus for a major overhaul of the organizational structure of the state bureaucracy died completely. A presidential commission worked for two years to come up with an ambitious plan to restructure the federal executive, eventually dusting off an old reform scheme originally developed under Yeltsin. This plan, called "administrative reform," was implemented in March 2004. Rather than the sweeping overhaul of procedures for recruiting, training, and promoting federal civil servants, enforcing discipline and accountability within the bureaucracy, and rationalizing the organizational structure of the executive branch by eliminating redundancies, the new plan simply reshuffled responsibilities of officials at the top. Observers noted that although the ostensible purpose of the reform was to make the executive branch more streamlined and efficient, it instead increased the number of federal-level executive bodies from fifty-seven to seventy-two. This reorganization plan is widely recognized to have caused confusion to the participants and embarrassment to its sponsors. Since then, Putin has quietly shelved the project of administrative reform.

The key to Putin's success in enacting his legislative agenda is his control over the United Russia Party. The members of its parliamentary faction depend heavily on Kremlin support for their spots on the party list; disloyalty to the party is punished by exclusion from the faction, the consequence of which is the loss of the member's seat in parliament. Under these circumstances, United Russia deputies prefer to air their demands in the intimate settings of party discussions rather than to defect from the party line in voting on the chamber floor. Duma deputies who belong to United Russia certainly lobby hard for the interests of the firms and regions that support them, but, much like British MPs, they vote cohesively once the party's position has been decided. The sharpest policy debates therefore occur among ministries in the government rather than in parliament.

REMAKING THE FEDERATION COUNCIL

As Putin was maneuvering to win control of the Duma, he also took steps to take control of the Federation Council. Although Putin's strategy for the Federation Council was quite different from that used to tame the Duma, it was equally effective. The law that he succeeded in getting passed in both chambers in the summer of 2000, which overhauled the method by which the members of the Federation Council are chosen, had the result of giving him a secure base of support in the upper house. Under the new procedure, the Federation Council comprised members chosen by the chief executives and the legislatures of the territorial subjects of the federation.[3] Previously, the chamber's members were the chief executives and chief legislative officials of the regions, who held their seats ex officio.

In 2009, under former president Medvedev, the law on forming the Federation Council was revised yet again. The new law provided that Federation Council members must be elected to local councils in the region in which they represent in the Federation Council, ostensibly a democratic measure. However, the new provision made little difference in fact— elections to local councils were easily arranged for those individuals whom the Kremlin wished to see as members of the Federation Council, and the Kremlin could still ensure that no one was named whom it opposed. A widely held view is that some way must be found to allow Federation Council members to be popularly elected. The problem is that under the constitution, the two senators from each region must represent the executive and legislative branches of the regional government. No one has yet found a way satisfactory to all sides to reconcile the principle of direction election of senators with adherence to the rule that they represent the executive and legislative branches of their regions.

Federation Council members closely follow the direction of the presidential administration. Tight coordination between the Kremlin and the chamber is achieved through the weekly meetings between the chamber's first deputy chair and the committee chairs. At these meetings, the Kremlin's position on pending legislation is communicated, and the chamber's position is established. As a result, the chamber votes with remarkable efficiency to back the Kremlin on almost every issue: the chamber meets only one day every two weeks, speeding through dozens of bills each time and providing large, lopsided majorities on almost every bill. Moreover, even on matters where many governors have registered their dissatisfaction or overt opposition, the Kremlin's influence is sufficient to ensure that members faithfully follow the president's line. Although members can be and sometimes are recalled and replaced, most governors appear to accept the political expediency of allowing their representatives to vote the president's line in the Federation Council as the price for giving them policy influence through lobbying on more particularistic issues. This system has succeeded in guaranteeing overwhelming majorities for almost every piece of legislation that the Kremlin supports.[4]

Thus, in both chambers, Putin helped to engineer the formation of standing majorities through which the presidential administration and government could obtain support for their major legislative priorities, trading off privileged access to the Kremlin in return for reliable voting support. The number of bills that the president vetoes dwindled in the latter half of the 2000s to almost zero.

BUILDING A PARTY OF POWER

In the 2000–2003 Duma, the political party Unity was the pivotal member of nearly every winning coalition. It delivered the president and government a string of victories, but at a price. The government had to make concessions on a number of policy issues in order to win passage of its highest-priority legislation, such as the modifications to the annual budget, and tax reform. On land reform, for example, the government simply dropped the provisions that would have legalized the buying and selling of agricultural land as a condition for winning passage of this landmark law. The separate bill dealing specifically with agricultural land then passed the following year, in 2002. The convergence of interests of the government and the key pro-government factions in the Duma led to their efforts to create a more durable alliance structure that would lower the bargaining costs of building a majority.

Putin's team moved methodically to create a permanent coalition supporting Putin and the government in the Third Duma consisting of Unity and three allied factions. In spring 2001, this coalition formed an organizational structure for coordinating positions on major legislation, although they faced continuing difficulty in imposing voting discipline. Unity, which boasted a high level of voting discipline even in comparison with other party factions, sometimes had a difficult time holding its coalition partners in line on divisive votes.[5] Forming majorities for individual pieces of legislation required ad hoc bargaining and concessions—a costly and inefficient procedure from the president's standpoint. Putin's parliamentary managers looked for more direct methods to give Unity a political monopoly. The next step therefore was for Unity to swallow the Fatherland/All-Russia party and its parliamentary faction and become, under the new name United Russia, the dominant party in Russia.

From the Kremlin's point of view, there were three main benefits from using a dominant party as an instrument of rule. First, it would ensure solid, consistent, reliable majorities in legislative voting, both in the Duma and in regional legislatures. Instead of having to cobble together piecemeal majorities for each bill, the Kremlin could instruct its party followers in the legislature how to vote and could let the party deploy the necessary sticks and carrots to enforce party unity on the floor. Second, the party would be the Kremlin's face to the country at election time, advertising the party as a team of politicians faithful to the popular President Putin and devoted to the country's well-being. Success in mobilizing the electorate would discourage the party's opponents, symbolize the party's popularity, and reveal which local officials were not performing up to expected standards. Finally, the party helped to manage the careers and ambitions of politicians. It would decide which politician would get which spot on the party list, who would run for governor, mayor, or local legislator, and who would not be given a party endorsement. A dominant party in an authoritarian regime can be a useful instrument for exercising power, even though the rulers have to give up some of their prerogatives in order to attract sufficient commitment from other interests.[6]

In order to make United Russia into a dominant party, the Kremlin sponsored a series of legislative measures that made it difficult for governors' machines or big business to sponsor candidates and further squeezed small parties to the margins of the system. Putin put through legislation raising the requirements for registration of parties, so that a party must have 50,000 members (later reduced to 40,000) and branches in at least half the regions of the country to be legally registered. Moreover, only registered parties (and not other kinds of public organizations) were given the right to run candidates in elections. These provisions made it harder for small parties to compete. The tough registration requirements also give federal and local authorities more legal grounds for denying parties access to the ballot. Parties that support the authorities are routinely registered in regional and local elections; opposition parties find signatures on their petitions disqualified or their candidates removed from the ballot for various alleged administrative violations. The new rules resulted in a massive drop in the number of parties. There were over forty registered parties in 2003, but by January 2006, only thirty-three parties remained. As of January 1, 2007, when the new legislation took force, sixteen more parties were disqualified. By September 2008, only fourteen parties remained. The number continued to fall as minor parties either lost their registration or merged with others to remain viable.

In addition, legislation passed in 2005 eliminated single-member district seats from the Duma, so that all 450 seats in the 2007 election were filled by party lists. Parties had to collect large numbers of signatures or put down sizable deposits to qualify to run, and they had to win at least 7 percent of the vote to win seats. As a result, in the December 2007 election, only four parties cleared the threshold to representation; seven parties (including all the democratic parties) fell below it. The same outcome occurred in the December 2011 election: once again, the "big four" parties cleared the election threshold and won seats in the Duma, and their smaller rival parties all fell below the 5 percent threshold. It is unclear, however, whether this result is more a reflection of the voters' preferences or the many direct and indirect ways in which the authorities rigged the election. Table 2.1 shows the current breakdown of parties in the Duma elected in 2011.

Administrative restrictions pressuring small parties to dissolve or merge into bigger ones are not the only methods by which the regime works to ensure a dominant position for United Russia. Recent elections have seen large-scale manipulation as well, including highly unequal access to the media for parties, court decisions that disqualify particular candidates from running, pressure on business to support United Russia materially, administrative pressure on various groups of the population (such as military service members, government employees, students, farmers, and others) to

Table 2.1.   Official Vote Totals and Parliamentary Seats, Sixth Duma (2012–2017)

	Vote share (%)	Seats awarded	Seat share (%)
United Russia	49.32	238	53
Communist Party of the Russian Federation	19.19	92	20
Liberal Democratic Party of Russia	11.67	56	12
A Just Russia	13.24	64	14
Total	93.42	450	100

vote the right way, and in a growing number of regions, outright falsification of results.[7] The election process is thus a mixture of electoral mobilization techniques plus coercion and fraud, all to ensure that United Russia wins by large margins in national and regional races.

The ascendancy of United Russia transformed the way the Duma is run. Previously, factions had shared power in steering the Duma and setting its agenda roughly proportionally to their voting strength on the floor. Starting in 2004, United Russia took full control of the governance of the Duma. It named UR members to all of the committee chairmanships and cut staff positions for committees but increased the staff for factions and the central staff, greatly expanding its control over the flow of legislation. It gave committees greater power to kill bills to reduce members' agenda rights.

Yet for all United Russia's power in the Duma, it has virtually no influence over the president; the presidential-parliamentary relationship is asymmetric. United Russia contributed almost no members to the new government in 2004, 2008, and again in 2012. The oddity of the situation is made even more piquant by the fact that Vladimir Putin headed the party's list in the December 2007 election—thus contributing his own popularity to the party—but never joined the party. As soon as Putin announced that he would head the party list in October 2007, the party's approval rating rose 6 percent. He publicly stated on several occasions that he wanted United Russia to win a large victory so that the parliament would be capable of working effectively to pass the laws the country needed. As prime minister, he said he needed a solid majority of support in parliament. Finally, in April 2008, as he was preparing to step down from the presidency, Putin agreed to become party chair—still without formally joining the party!—and thus attached his prestige and stature to the party in the eyes of the political elite and electorate.

The asymmetry between party and Putin was clear again when in September 2011 Putin announced at a United Russia congress that he intended to return to the presidency and make Medvedev his prime minister. He claimed they had agreed on this arrangement years before. (This was unlikely to be true, considering the truly miserable expression on Medvedev's face when Putin made the announcement.) In keeping with the logic of this "castling move," as Russians dubbed it, Putin declared that Medvedev, not Putin, would head the party list for the December 2011 election and then would replace Putin as party leader. The party publicly welcomed these proposals, although privately, party leaders were dismayed that they would lose their close association with the still-popular Putin. As prime minister, Medvedev went on not only to become the party's leader but even, in stark contrast to Putin, chose to join the party. Thus Putin as president enjoys the freedom of being unaffiliated with any party, while United Russia has to accept whatever terms Putin offers for the relationship.

PATRONAGE AND POWER

As noted above, Putin's legislative agenda changed beginning in 2003, concentrating on centralizing power in the executive branch at the expense of civil society and other branches of government, and he created a number of new structures and programs increasing state social spending and state control over the economy. Taken together, these measures had the effect of giving the government and United Russia more opportunities to cultivate patronage relations with regional governments and big business, and to tighten the Kremlin's control over the political system.

Among the measures Putin and the government sponsored, and the parliament passed, were increased subsidies to mothers for having children, a higher minimum wage, ceilings on rate increases for power and heating utilities for homes, higher pensions, new special economic zones, higher spending on the "national projects,"[8] increased spending on highway construction and maintenance, and creation of new state corporations in aviation, shipbuilding, nuclear power, nanotechnologies, and other fields, as well as the establishment of large new state investment funds to direct public funds into promising new fields. The steady, large increases in federal budget revenues—which owed to soaring world oil and gas prices—allowed the Putin regime to raise spending in a number of politically beneficial ways. Parliament, and United Russia, shared in the general glow of public good feeling. Putin's own approval ratings rose steadily.

In effect, Putin and the Duma entered into an implicit exchange: the Duma approved a range of initiatives expanding executive power at the expense of the legislature, the media, parties, governors, and opposition forces in return for lucrative patronage opportunities to spread state resources around to their own client groups.[9]

President Putin took the occasion of the Beslan incident in September 2004[10] to propose several pieces of legislation further centralizing power in the state and in the executive branch; the Duma duly enacted all of it, some of it virtually without debate. Included was a proposal to eliminate direct popular election of regional governors in favor of a system whereby the president would nominate candidates who would be confirmed by the regional legislatures. Second, he proposed changing the law on elections of Duma deputies by eliminating all single-member district seats, another measure intended to strengthen the role of political parties in elections, and United Russia in particular. Finally, he proposed forming a new body, the Public Chamber, to serve as a forum for public discussion of policy and oversight of the bureaucracy.

All three of these measures had the direct or indirect effect of weakening parliament's role in the political system. The new system of appointed governors eliminated regional executive elections, which gave national parties some opportunity to participate in regional politics. The end of the mixed electoral system for the State Duma meant that no deputies in the Duma would represent single-member districts. This reduced the representation of local interests in the parliament and therefore much of the autonomy that Duma had had vis-à-vis the executive branch by virtue of their local bases of support. Finally, the creation of a Public Chamber as a forum for the representation of state-sanctioned nongovernmental organizations (NGOs) effectively weakened parliament's role in deliberating on matters of national policy. None of these specifically addressed the challenge of Islamic terrorism or Chechen separatism. Moreover, they had been discussed before the Beslan incident and were consistent with Putin's policy of strengthening presidential power, imposing strict regulation on party competition, weakening the autonomy of governors, and co-opting civil society. For that reason, it is clear that Beslan provided a politically opportune moment to advance them but that political centralization rather than fighting terrorism was their actual goal.

Beslan also spurred other legislation aimed at fighting terrorism. Security legislation was at the top of the priority list when United Russia drew up the legislative agenda for the fall session. The heads of four Duma committees (security, defense, legislation, and state organization) agreed to propose new legislation to strengthen security at sites where large numbers of people congregated and to tighten rules on immigration, residency registration in cities, and registration of automobiles. United Russia introduced a comprehensive new counterterrorism bill, prepared by the Federal Security Service (FSB), giving the police wider powers to prevent acts of terrorism.[11] If they believed that an act of terrorism was about to be committed, the FSB could declare a "regime of terrorist threat" and place the media and society under control, using wiretapping and mail intercepts, limiting travel, and prohibiting meetings and strikes.

Putin also used Beslan and the terrorist threat as a rationale for other bills that limited political freedom and expanded the discretionary rights of the security services. For instance, in December 2005 Putin defended a bill sharply limiting the autonomy of NGOs as being necessary "to secure our political system from interference from outside, as well as our society and citizens from the spread of terrorist ideology." Still another law authorized the president to send armed agents abroad to fight terrorism on foreign soil; this legislation was used as the basis for an operation to find and kill those responsible for killing four members of the Russian embassy staff in Iraq.

The global economic crisis struck Russia hard in fall 2008. Total GDP in 2009 fell almost 8 percent, more than in any other country of the G20. Putin, as prime minister, oversaw a vigorous set of measures to ameliorate the effects of the crisis. He drew down the sizable reserve funds that the high oil prices of the previous years had allowed Russia to accumulate and used them to inject infusions of working capital into banks and large enterprises, as well as to raise salaries for public sector workers and pensions for retirees. These measures allowed Russians to ride out the recession with much less hardship than in the 1990s and let Putin take credit for saving Russia from the worst consequences of the recession—which of course he blamed on the West. The fact that Russia's economy was highly vulnerable to the crisis due to its heavy dependence on high world oil prices was a point he tended to leave to others to emphasize.

MEDVEDEV AS PRESIDENT

Commenting on his stormy relationship with his domineering chancellor, Otto von Bismarck, German emperor Wilhelm once complained that it was not easy being emperor under such a chancellor. President Medvedev undoubtedly felt somewhat the same way about Putin. Despite ostensibly enjoying all the extensive formal and informal powers of the president, Medvedev, by virtue of temperament and the realities of the situation, was clearly subordinate to his prime minister during the four years of his presidency. Putin continued to shape the domestic and foreign policy agenda, allowing Medvedev only to make modest changes at the margin. Despite many bold pronouncements about the need for major reforms, Medvedev's actual policy achievements were extremely modest. Real policy-making power was in the hands of Putin, who used his control over the Duma through United Russia to shape Russia's response to the economic crisis and decide on specific reforms in social and economic policy. For example, although Medvedev repeatedly called for dismantling the large state corporations created under Putin that swallowed up large sectors of the economy, not one was broken up. To fight corruption, Medvedev passed legislation requiring all state officials and their family members to publish annual statements of their incomes and property. However, Medvedev himself acknowledged that this law had been impotent to reduce corruption. Medvedev tried to overhaul the corrupt and inefficient Ministry of Internal Affairs, which oversees the police. He sponsored a law reforming the police, which passed after extensive public debate. In the end, the only real change the law made was to rename the police *politsiia* in place of its former name, *militsiia*. Many of Medvedev's proposed reforms were of the same sort, that is, minor and cosmetic changes to the existing system instead of serious fundamental reforms. Medvedev regularly complained that his decrees and orders were ignored, but he lacked the means to alter the situation. Medvedev generally succeeded in passing his reforms through parliament, but only after they had been watered down by bureaucratic interests that were represented in the government. Thus, the basic relationship between the executive and legislative branches remained unaltered under Medvedev.

PRESSURE FROM BELOW FOR REFORM

This chapter has described a set of arrangements in which Vladimir Putin dominates the political system, using his control over United Russia and his command of the means of coercion to ensure electoral victories and solid legislative majorities to back his policy agenda. Efforts by Medvedev to introduce democratizing reforms into the political system largely failed to make any lasting impression. The success of the "castling move" by which Putin and Medvedev exchanged jobs in spring 2012 only underlined Putin's firm control over the regime. Yet there are serious reasons to question whether the Putin system is durable.

First, a large-scale protest movement has sprung up opposing Putin's manipulation of formally democratic institutions in Russia. It had been building as local activists in many cities mounted protests against local abuses of power (for example, they launched Internet campaigns against destruction of the environment or demanded justice for officials who tried to avoid prosecution for crimes). But the simmering discontent of the socially networked, politically savvy urban classes came to a head when Putin announced in September 2011 that he would return to the presidency, and then boiled over when Putin resorted to heavy election fraud and manipulation in the December 2011 and March 2012 elections. In Moscow, St. Petersburg, and dozens of other cities around the country, large-scale demonstrations were held against Putin and demanding fair elections: upward of 100,000 people marched on a few occasions in Moscow, numbers not seen since the late 1980s and early 1990s. The protesters organized a large-scale election observers' movement, which registered tens of thousands of people to monitor the parliamentary and presidential elections and report violations of the law. The authorities, remarkably, allowed many of these protests to pass without massive arrests and beatings, lending confidence and a sense of momentum to the protesters. The protest movement has no formal leaders or structure, but a number of well-known bloggers, writers, artists, and television celebrities have given a personal face to the movement.

Second, among former president Medvedev's formal reforms of the political system was a law drastically easing the requirements to register new political parties. Previously, a party had to prove that it had 40,000 members. Now it only needs 500. In response, many dozens of new parties are seeking registration. Some of these are undoubtedly "Trojan horse" parties created by the authorities to draw off support from serious opposition parties. But others are likely to form and win seats in local and regional legislatures. The new party law may well increase the degree of political competition in the country and give the democratic opposition movement new openings for participation. It is not impossible that when the next Duma elections are held in December 2017, new parties may break through the cartel enjoyed by the "big four."

Finally, another of the measures former president Medvedev enacted was one restoring the direct popular election of governors. The authorities came to recognize that appointed governors were no more effective in governing than elected ones and were less effective than elected governors in cultivating ties with voters and developing capable electoral organizations. Consequently, Medvedev's law returns to a system under which regional chief executives will be elected. But, evidently to ensure that there are no unwelcome surprises, the law inserted a set of "filters" into the selection of candidates. The filters require that candidates for gubernatorial elections be approved by a certain percentage of local deputies (regions can choose a percentage between 5 and 10). Given United Russia's dominance in regional and local councils, this means that opposition candidates may have a hard time receiving a nomination. Still, like the new law on parties, it is another step toward a more open and competitive system.

Taken together, the emergence of a large-scale protest movement organized through the social media and coupled with institutional opportunities to participate formally in the political system make it unlikely that we will see a full return to the Putin system of the 2000s. Serious policy challenges loom: Russia cannot maintain its current level of spending on pensions and other social entitlements, plus its high defense spending, without either sizable tax increases or very high world oil prices. Spending cuts and tax increases are painful in any country. In a country lacking a firm basis of popular consensus for policy change such as Russia, any cuts in entitlements for powerful organized interests are likely to result in a new surge of political protest. The United Russia Party, as we have seen, is capable of delivering reliable majorities in parliament but lacks the deep roots in society that would be needed to preserve public order through a period of major upheaval. Thus the Putin system, which was durable through the first decade of the 2000s, may need to give way to a more open and competitive system in the second decade.

SUGGESTED READINGS

Fish, M. Steven. *Democracy Derailed in Russia: The Failure of Open Politics*. New York: Cambridge University Press, 2005.

Gel'man, Vladimir. "From 'Feckless Pluralism' to 'Dominant Power Politics'? The Transformation of Russia's Party System." *Democratization* 13, no. 4 (2006): 545–61.

Hale, Henry. *Why Not Parties in Russia? Democracy, Federalism, and the State*. Cambridge: Cambridge University Press, 2006.

McFaul, Michael. *Russia's Unfinished Revolution: Political Change from Gorbachev to Putin*. Ithaca, N.Y.: Cornell University Press, 2001.

Remington, Thomas F. "Majorities without Mandates: The Federation Council since 2000." *Europe-Asia Studies* 55, no. 5 (2003): 667–91.

———. "Patronage and the Party of Power: President-Parliament Relations under Vladimir Putin." *Europe-Asia Studies* 60, no. 6 (2008): 965–93.

———. *The Russian Parliament: Institutional Evolution in a Transitional Regime, 1989–1999*. New Haven, Conn.: Yale University Press, 2001.

Reuter, Ora John, and Thomas F. Remington. "Dominant Party Regimes and the Commitment Problem: The Case of United Russia." *Comparative Political Studies* 42, no. 4 (2009): 501–526.

NOTES

1. Michael McFaul, *Russia's Unfinished Revolution: Political Change from Gorbachev to Putin* (Ithaca, N.Y.: Cornell University Press, 2001); Michael McFaul, "The Fourth Wave of Democracy and Dictatorship: Noncooperative Transitions in the Postcommunist World," *World Politics* 54, no. 2 (2002): 212–44.

2. Henry Hale, *Why Not Parties in Russia? Democracy, Federalism, and the State* (Cambridge: Cambridge University Press, 2006); M. Steven Fish, *Democracy Derailed in Russia: The Failure of Open Politics* (New York: Cambridge University Press, 2005).

3. There were eighty-nine such territorial units at the point that Russia adopted the new constitution in 1993. By fall 2008, a series of mergers of smaller units into larger ones reduced the total to eighty-three, where it has remained since then.

4. Thomas F. Remington, "Majorities without Mandates: The Federation Council since 2000," *Europe-Asia Studies* 55, no. 5 (2003): 667–91.

5. Thomas F. Remington, "Presidential Support in the Russian State Duma," *Legislative Studies Quarterly* 31, no. 1 (2006): 5–32.

6. Ora John Reuter and Thomas F. Remington, "Dominant Party Regimes and the Commitment Problem: The Case of United Russia," *Comparative Political Studies* 42, no. 4 (2009): 501–26.

7. Mikhail Myagkov, Peter C. Ordeshook, and Dimitri Shakin, *The Forensics of Election Fraud: Russia and Ukraine* (Cambridge: Cambridge University Press, 2009).

8. The national projects were spending programs initiated by President Putin to improve the state of health care, education, housing, and agriculture. By 2008, they were rolled into regular budget spending.

9. Thomas F. Remington, "Patronage and the Party of Power: President-Parliament Relations under Vladimir Putin," *Europe-Asia Studies* 60, no. 6 (2008): 965–93.

10. The Beslan crisis occurred in September 2004 when a band of Islamist terrorists held hostage an entire school with schoolchildren and teachers inside. On the third day of the crisis, Russian security forces stormed the school, resulting in massive loss of life on the part of the hostages. Nearly all the terrorists were killed. The incident had an impact on public consciousness in Russia comparable to that of September 11, 2001, in the United States.

11. The FSB (Federal Security Service) is a successor agency to the Soviet KGB (Committee on State Security).

3

Regional Politics

Nikolai Petrov and Darrell Slider

Vladimir Putin's return to the post of Russian president offers mixed signals about "stability" in the area of center-region relations. Starting in mid-2011 there were some moves in the direction of returning some of the power concentrated in the center toward the regions, culminating in a return of elections for governors in 2012. At the same time, there is reason to question whether he and his circle can bring themselves to commit to redesigning a system that they have expended so much effort to create.

When Vladimir Putin was first elected president in 2000, one of the areas he identified for immediate attention was the relationship between Russia's regions and the central government. The weakness of the Yeltsin regime, both politically and financially, forced him to make considerable concessions to the regions. Regional leaders increasingly took on responsibilities that would normally be carried out by federal agencies, and they used these opportunities to entrench themselves in power while often willfully flouting federal laws and presidential decrees.

Putin came to the Kremlin after having spent the early part of the 1990s as a regional government official. He witnessed the extent of regional-center problems from a different perspective when he supervised Russia's regions for Yeltsin from March 1997 to July 1998. At that time Putin was head of the department within the presidential administration (called the Main Oversight Department, or *glavnoe kontrol'noe upravleniie*) that gathered evidence on violations of federal laws and policies in the regions. Interestingly enough, Putin's predecessor as head of the department was Aleksei Kudrin, who was elevated to minister of finance and deputy prime minister, and his successor was Nikolai Patrushev, who became head of the FSB (which had replaced the KGB) and was later promoted to head the Kremlin's Security Council in 2008. Both men were key figures in implementing elements of Putin's policy toward the regions. All three, not coincidentally, were from Russia's second city, St. Petersburg.

This chapter examines the policies toward regional leaders. Center-region relations continued to be a key area of concern in Putin's second term and during the Medvedev presidency. Instead of attempting to develop or refine federalism in the Russian context, Putin aggressively pursued an antifederal policy designed to take away or circumscribe many powers exercised by regional leaders. His goal was to establish a unitary, centralized state under the guise of "restoring effective vertical power in the country," to use Putin's own description of his intentions. In keeping with Putin's background in the KGB (the secret police in Soviet times and early post-Soviet Russia), the main emphasis was on discipline and order. These institutional and personnel choices, however, produced a number of negative consequences. As early as 2005, some Russian officials began to propose what might be described as "re-decentralization" in order to correct some of the deficiencies in a centralized model. The period of joint rule by Medvedev and Putin from 2008–2012 did not respond seriously to these challenges, and the centralized model was further entrenched. By mid-2011 the Kremlin appeared to be shifting toward a path that would restore elements of a federal system, though reluctantly and with as many braking mechanisms as the political situation permitted.

BEFORE PUTIN: FEDERALISM BY DEFAULT

Even after the other fourteen former Soviet republics became independent, Russia remained the world's largest country; thus, it is perhaps inevitable that there would be serious problems in administering its far-flung territories. This was true both before and after the establishment of the Soviet state. The traditional approach of Russian rulers was to tighten control from the center. Despite some outward trappings of federalism (the Russian republic, for example, was called the RSFSR—Russian Soviet Federative Socialist Republic), the Soviet Union was in essence a unitary state supplemented by parallel hierarchies—the Communist Party of the Soviet Union (CPSU) and an extensive state bureaucracy. Even under Stalin, however, "family circles" or cliques based on personal relations and patronage ties arose in the regions, insulating local politics from Moscow and allowing regional elites a free hand in many matters.[1]

In many of the former communist states of Eastern Europe—particularly in countries whose leaders embarked on a reformist agenda—a comprehensive redrawing of subnational administrative boundaries took place. In

Poland, the Czech Republic, the former German Democratic Republic, Hungary, and Croatia, communist-era regional entities were eliminated or replaced with new ones. In part this was done to meet European Union (EU) entry requirements, but often another important motivation was to break up political and economic power at the regional level that had emerged under communist rule.[2] No radical redrawing of the political boundaries took place in Russia, with the consequence that political-economic elites of the communist era remained intact at the regional level. Russia's administrative structure closely mirrored that of the Russian republic under communism. Republics within Russia, designated "autonomous republics" in the Soviet period, received elevated status because they were home to a non-Russian ethnic group. Most often, though, Russians were the largest ethnic group even in republics; the exceptions were Dagestan, Chuvashia, Chechen-Ingushetia, Tuva, Kabardino-Balkaria, North Ossetia, Tatarstan, and Kalmykia. The most numerous administrative entities were *oblasts* (provinces) and *krais* (territories). The cities of Moscow and St. Petersburg also had the status of "subjects of the federation." Starting in the first Putin presidency, smaller autonomous *okrugs* (districts) located within the territory of other entities began to be merged with larger entities; this was done for the purpose of simplifying control from the center. As a result, Russia went from having eighty-nine administrative entities in 2000 to eighty-three by 2008.

Russian and Soviet history had never seen an attempt to apply a federal model as the basis for organizing the relationship between national and regional authorities. In this regard, Yeltsin's policies represented a revolutionary break from past methods of rule. The Yeltsin constitution of 1993 made federalism a core component of the Russian political system. Article 71 of the constitution defines the areas of federal jurisdiction, Article 72 defines joint jurisdiction, and Article 73 grants all other functions to the regions. Many of these relationships remained to be defined by legislation, however, and Yeltsin did not take the goal of developing federal principles seriously. What prevented Yeltsin from building a more balanced system of federalism was the center's political and economic weakness. This weakness was exploited by republic presidents and governors to carve out substantial autonomy. By the time Yeltsin resigned from office, Russia's federal system remained very much a work in progress, the result of an improvised series of steps and compromises.

In the late Soviet period the regions became an arena for political struggle. In 1990–1991 there was the battle that took place over the fate of the Soviet Union. Both Gorbachev and Yeltsin sought the support of regional elites, particularly those in the ethnically based autonomous republics within the fifteen union republics that became independent in late 1991. It was in the context of the struggle with Gorbachev for the loyalty of republic leaders that Yeltsin in 1990 famously encouraged them to "take as much sovereignty as you can swallow." In most of the republics, local leaders followed Yeltsin's lead and created the popularly elected post of president, thus giving them a status and legitimacy lacked by heads of Russia's other regions at that time.

Almost immediately after the collapse of the Soviet Union in 1991, Yeltsin faced a new and lengthy conflict—this time with the Russian legislature. Their disputes covered a wide range of issues but centered on the relative powers of the parliament versus the president and on the strategy of economic reform that the country should pursue. In this struggle, Yeltsin sought the support of regional executives—the governors whom he had the right to appoint and dismiss—and the republic presidents. Ruslan Khasbulatov, the speaker of the Russian parliament who became Yeltsin's nemesis, appealed to the regional legislatures in an effort to build an alternative national power base. Since republic leaders had more independence than governors, Yeltsin rewarded the republics with larger budget subsidies and greater relative autonomy.[3] These concessions were often codified in the form of bilateral agreements signed by Yeltsin and individual leaders. The most generous terms were granted to Tatarstan, Bashkortostan, and Yakutia, the republics with the most potential leverage because of their economic assets.

This battle culminated in the events of September–October 1993, when Yeltsin issued a decree dissolving the parliament. When Khasbulatov and Alexander Rutskoi, Yeltsin's appointed vice president, resisted and attempted to seize power by force, Yeltsin responded by having tanks shell the building. The new political context led to fundamental changes in regional politics.

First was the drafting of the 1993 constitution that enshrined the concepts of federalism, including the creation of a new legislature with an upper house to represent the regions—the Federation Council—with the right to veto laws passed by the lower house—the State Duma. A second consequence of the 1993 events was the dissolution of regional legislatures (though not in the republics) that had been elected in 1990. As a third consequence, political power in the regions shifted dramatically toward the executive branch of government. Executive power in the regions was further strengthened in the mid-1990s when Yeltsin gave in to the demand by regional executives for popular elections of governors. Yeltsin's last set of appointments to the post of governor took place in late 1995–early 1996, when he appointed thirteen.[4] After that, all governors were elected to office. This gave governors added legitimacy and made their removal by Yeltsin almost impossible.

In 1994–1995, new regional legislatures were elected. The new assemblies were smaller in size than the soviets of 1990, and their powers were substantially reduced. With just a few exceptions, the new deputies tended to be local officials, employees from sectors funded by the government (education and health care), or the regional economic elite—all groups that were dependent on the executive. Only a small proportion of deputies were full-time legislators, and in their legislative role they were both unwilling and unable to challenge the region's governor or president. Very few legislatures had more than token representation by national political parties.[5]

A year after the October 1993 attack on parliament, Yeltsin once again attempted to use force to solve a political problem—this time in Chechnya. Unlike republics such as Tatarstan and Bashkortostan, Chechnya refused to enter into a dialogue with the Kremlin and instead pressed for full independence. Under the leadership of General (and President) Dzhokhar Dudayev, Chechnya created its own military forces and expelled representatives of virtually all central Russian ministries, including the FSB and the Ministry of Finance. It should be said, however, that the Russian leadership did not make a serious attempt to achieve a negotiated solution to Chechnya's complaints, which contributed to the Chechens' resolve to secede. In December 1994, Yeltsin ended several years of neglect of the Chechen problem and ordered Russian Army and Interior Ministry troops into Chechnya in hopes of a quick military victory. The result was a disaster: the army was ill-prepared for a guerrilla war and suffered many casualties while directing much of its military might against the civilian population.

The war in Chechnya and ineffective policies in a number of other areas threatened defeat for Yeltsin in the 1996 presidential election, and he again turned to regional leaders (as well as the business elite) for help. With the help of regional "administrative resources" such as control over the local press, government workers, and simple vote fraud in some cases, Yeltsin came from behind to win reelection in 1996. Following his victory, Yeltsin further strengthened the status of regional leaders by initiating a change in how the Federation Council was formed. From 1996 to 2000, governors and the chairs of regional legislatures would automatically have seats in the Federation Council.

These serial political crises took place against a background of persistent economic emergencies that were stabilized in the mid-1990s only by resorting to "virtual" economics and financial trickery. These schemes eventually collapsed in the August 1998 devaluation and default. One common mechanism to formally balance tax receipts and expenses, which was used both by central agencies and regional governments, was sequestering funds—in other words, reducing expenditures by not paying salaries and not meeting obligations to suppliers of goods and services. In this way, the federal government effectively lost control of many of its agencies in the regions. Shortfalls in tax collection and nonpayment meant regional leaders were almost forced to step in to provide funds or in-kind payments (office space, transportation, heat, hot water, electricity, and even food) in order to support the continued operation of federal institutions such as the criminal police, tax police, prosecutors, courts, and even Yeltsin's presidential representatives (created in 1991 to serve as his "eyes and ears" in the regions). Inevitably, federal entities in the regions shifted their loyalty from the center to the regions. Even the Russian military became increasingly dependent on regional leaders for logistical support. The result was "a sustained trend towards increasing compartmentalization and regionalization of military structures, driven primarily by the shortage of resources and underfinancing."[6] It should be emphasized that this was not a power play by regional leaders. In the face of the failure by the Kremlin to carry out its responsibilities, the regions were simply trying to cope. The result was federalism by default.

Another feature of Yeltsin's policies toward the regions was the personalized and bilateral nature of many of the center-region relationships. This was in many ways a continuation of the informal operation of regional lobbying of the central institutions during the Soviet era; both Yeltsin and most regional leaders had practical experience dating back to the Brezhnev era. Some of this bilateralism was formally institutionalized in treaties negotiated between the Yeltsin administration and regional leaders. The first of these agreements was with republics; it provided a set of exceptions and exemptions that went far beyond what other regions were allowed under the "1992 Federation Treaty" and the 1993 constitution. In the mid-1990s over twenty new bilateral treaties with *oblasts* and *krais* were signed. These agreements had the effect of making Russian federalism extremely asymmetrical, but in a way that was unsystematic and nontransparent.[7] Much of the enabling documentation at the ministerial level was kept secret. Later, most *oblasts* and *krais* also negotiated bilateral treaties with the center, though under less favorable terms. The personalization of politics meant that Yeltsin often turned a blind eye to violations in a region as long as its leader demonstrated loyalty to him in federal elections.

Overall, the institutional framework and dynamics of "federalism, Russian style" had a number of dysfunctional elements and allowed regions control over other areas of federal responsibility that were atypical of a normal federal system.[8] The nature of federal relations also undermined efforts to democratize the political system as well as efforts to marketize the Russian economy. Governors and republic presidents obstructed the development of a national party system and used their powers to harass political opponents and independent news media. In an effort to protect local industries and markets, regional leaders created barriers to free trade between regions. They also preserved an economic climate that was hostile to outside investment and the rise of small business.[9]

PUTIN'S RECENTRALIZATION

In contrast to Yeltsin, Putin began his first term with the advantages of both firm control over central political institutions and an economy that was beginning to prosper. The improvement of the Russian economy after the August 1998 crisis cannot be overestimated in this regard. Growing oil revenues, the result of skyrocketing prices on the world market, provided Putin with resources to remold Russian government structures. This led to enhanced tax collection and greater budgetary resources that could be used to pay off past debts and to finance federal institutions. Putin's election to the presidency was closely linked to the second Chechen war (1999–2004), which eventually restored federal control over that region by brute force. At the same time, he began a more sophisticated, multipronged strategy to restore central control over all Russian regions. One early change was in budgetary policy. Since the center had easy access to a larger revenue stream, it quickly revised the tax code to increase the center's share, from roughly a 40/60 split in favor of the regions to 60/40 in favor of the center. As a result, regions became much more dependent on the central authorities for budgetary allocations—a factor that greatly increased their vulnerability to pressure from the Kremlin.

Federal Districts and Presidential Representatives

The first major institutional change adopted by Putin was the creation of a new level of administration between the center and the regions in the form of seven federal administrative districts (*federal'nye okruga*) headed by specially appointed presidential representatives. Each of these "super-regions" was headed by a presidential envoy, called the "plenipotentiary presidential representative"—*pol'nomochnyi predstavitel' prezidenta*, or *polpred* for short. The ultimate purpose of this new structure was not to replace existing regions, but rather to increase the ability of the center to coordinate the operation of federal agencies in the regions through a framework that was totally controlled by Putin's Kremlin. The federal districts were not drawn anew based on any particular political or administrative purpose; they corresponded completely to the regional command structure of the Soviet/Russian Interior Ministry troops.[10] The "capital" or administrative center of each district in every case corresponded to the location of the headquarters of the corresponding Interior Ministry district.

The term *polpred* had been used by Yeltsin in 1991 to designate his personal representative in each region. Putin abolished this post in the regions, replacing them with "chief federal inspectors" who would be directly subordinate to (and appointed by) the presidential representative for the corresponding administrative district. The decree creating presidential envoys provided for their direct accountability to the president. Yeltsin had initially given the same degree of access to his representatives, but later they were subordinated to a department within his administration.[11] In practice, though, while Putin appointed each of his representatives, they did not report solely to the president. The *polpreds* were still part of the presidential administration, which meant they were supervised by the head of Putin's staff. This was a source of consternation among the presidential representatives, since they wanted to be closer to the ultimate source of authority at the top of the administrative ladder. A symbolic indicator of the status of the seven representatives was Putin's decision to give each a seat on his Security Council, a body that has been important in establishing strategic priorities in government policy, both foreign and domestic. The *polpreds* were also allowed to participate in the regular meetings of the Russian government chaired by the prime minister.

Putin's "magnificent seven," as they were initially referred to with some irony in the media,[12] were drawn for the most part from the *siloviki* or "power ministries": FSB, military, police, and prosecutors (the FSB is the successor to the KGB). The contrast with the early Yeltsin period could not be more vivid. Many of Yeltsin's *polpreds* were drawn from the ranks of radical democrats who had worked with Yeltsin in the Soviet and Russian parliaments. In effect, the early Yeltsin appointees to this post were the type of people that several of the Putin appointees had worked to put in prison camps or psychiatric wards! Later though, Yeltsin replaced his initial appointees with career bureaucrats, including several FSB officials, a trend accelerated by Putin on becoming acting president in January 2000.

From the beginning, presidential envoys were denied many of the instruments of real power to control developments in the regions—the right to direct financial flows from the center, for example, or the power to appoint federal officials in the regions. Depending on their skills and resourcefulness, many presidential representatives found other ways to attain leverage. *Polpreds* worked to expand their links with important regional actors, such as the business community. *Polpreds* influenced personnel decisions by federal agencies and the president in their district through their recommendations for promotions. Over time, they were able to create a web of cadres in the district that facilitated the center's "penetration" of the regions.

Much of the work performed by presidential representatives was secret; as a result, their actual role remained hidden.[13] The functions of the office changed over time. An early assignment to the *polpreds* was to restore the preeminence of federal law. They devoted considerable effort to overseeing the process of bringing regional legislation (including republic constitutions and regional charters) into conformity with federal law and the Russian constitution. Given that Russia has yet to address seriously the problem of establishing the rule of law, a massive effort to improve the content of laws appeared to be premature. Russia, and this is even truer of the regions, is a country where the letter of the law often counts for little in the face of arbitrariness, incompetence, politicization, and corruption in the judicial system and in the bureaucracy.

Another task the Kremlin assigned the *polpreds* was to redivide powers between the center, regions, and local government to the advantage of the center. Starting in the latter part of 2001, a major effort was undertaken to standardize relationships between center and regions. Part of this initiative was to diminish the role of the bilateral treaties that had been signed between regions and Yeltsin. Cities and rural districts, the third level of government, were also subjected to increasing restrictions on their autonomy in the interest of restoring top-down control. Under Yeltsin, the constitution had proclaimed "local self-management," which meant that popularly elected mayors enjoyed considerable powers, often leading them into conflicts with governors. Putin's 2003 "Law on Principles of Organizing Local Self-Management" increased the control of regional authorities over local officials, gradually pushing mayors into the "vertical of authority." Many mayors of big cities resigned their posts, frustrated both by these changes and inadequate budgetary resources. For those who didn't get the message, prosecutors began targeting mayors with corruption charges in an apparent campaign of intimidation. Another innovation introduced under Putin replaced elected mayors in favor of "city managers" chosen by city councils—bodies that were more easily manipulated by governors and the Kremlin. By 2011 the capital cities of over half of all regions had shifted from popularly elected mayors to appointed city managers.

Over time, the accretion of other Kremlin-initiated policy instruments to control regional decision making changed the functions and the status of the *polpred*. In general, the power and prestige of the office varied depending on the degree to which the Kremlin viewed a region as problematic. The lack of progress in bringing stability to the North Caucasus led President Medvedev to create a new, eighth, federal *okrug* in January 2010 that encompassed the non-Russian republics of the North Caucasus along with the predominantly Russian Stavropol region. A high-ranking official, Alexander Khloponin, former governor of Krasnoyarsk with previous business experience in the metals industry, was appointed *polpred*. Khloponin was given additional powers to coordinate federal activities by virtue of a joint appointment as deputy prime minister. In contrast to earlier *silovik* appointments to this post, his mandate was primarily to facilitate improved governance and economic development in the region. Similarly, the Kremlin appointed a long-term former governor, Viktor Ishaev of Khabarovsk, to serve as *polpred* in the Far East region in 2009. The region was stagnating economically and dramatically losing population. In May 2012 the Kremlin enhanced Ishaev's status by creating a new ministry for him to head, the

Ministry for Development of the Far East. This will give him a large staff both in Moscow and Khabarovsk and his own budget, to supplement the political and coordinating functions that are typically performed by *pol-preds*. Like Khloponin, it is assumed that Ishaev will be given the powers needed to coordinate the activities of federal ministries in the region.

The prominence and level of experience of other appointees to the position of *polpred* declined over time, reflecting a drop in prestige and power. By the beginning of Putin's third term in 2012, the status of the position had fallen so low that Putin felt comfortable naming a total novice, Igor Kholmanskikh, as *polpred* for the Urals region. Kholmanskikh had been a foreman at the Uralvagonzavod tank factory in Nizhnii Tagil. He gained national prominence in December 2011 when he told Putin on a televised call-in program that he and "his boys" were ready to come to Moscow to break up anti-Putin demonstrations. Putin brought him into his reelection campaign, and the appointment appeared to be Putin's way of thanking a supporter. Kholmanskikh had no previous administrative or political experience.

Parallel Vertical Structures

An important element of Putin's centralization was the expanded role of central government and political institutions in regional decision making. The idea was to coordinate and optimize federal agencies' activity in regions "from above" rather than allowing federal officials to be "captured" by governors. A key element was regaining control over appointing and monitoring personnel in federal agencies in the regions. The strategy was to strengthen the vertical chain of command from the Moscow-based ministries or agencies to the federal district agencies and from there to ministry officials in the regions. This process of centralization was accompanied by a massive expansion in the number of federal officials in the regions. Between 2001 and 2006, the number of federal executive-branch employees in the regions (not including law enforcement agencies) grew from 348,000 to 616,000, according to the Russian statistical agency.

New territorial structures were established in the seven federal districts by the most important federal agencies and ministries—in all, about twenty federal agencies. To illustrate, within a year of Putin's reform, there were nineteen federal agencies represented in the Volga federal district. These included the prosecutor's office, the Ministry of Justice, the Tax Police, the Federal Tax Service, the Federal Agency on Governmental Communication, the Ministry of the Interior for Internal Troops, the Federal Criminal Police, the Federal Service on Financial Restructuring and Bankruptcy, the State Courier Service, the Committee on State Reserves, the Federal Securities

Commission, the Property Ministry, the Federal Property Fund, the Ministry on Publishing and TV and Radio Broadcasting, the Ministry of Natural Resources, the Pension Fund, the Ministry of Transportation, the Health Ministry, the State Committee on Statistics, and the Ministry of Anti-Monopoly Policy (the latter two had other regional branches within which they established federal district departments).[14]

First priority was given to returning central control over military, police, and security organs. This had been largely accomplished by 2002. Central control was rapidly increased over other federal organs in the regions including courts, prosecutors, election commissions, and even the mass media. Some of the most important changes in administrative subordination took place in the Ministry of Internal Affairs (MVD). When Putin came to power, there was a symbiosis between police generals and regional leaders that seemed to be unbreakable. Putin employed chesslike maneuvers to reassert dominance over this key lever of control. A change in the law in June 2001 eliminated governors' effective veto on appointments of regional MVD chiefs. Instead of immediately appointing his own men as the top police official in each region, he began by establishing a new intermediate level that separated the regional bottom from the central top. Seven MVD district directorates were created, headed by high-ranking police officials who were directly subordinate to the minister of internal affairs and appointed by decrees issued by Putin.[15] It took a year of personnel transfers at the regional level to disentangle existing networks of relationships, with the *polpreds* providing a mechanism for restoring control by the central ministry over regional police chiefs. In subsequent years, Putin and Medvedev maintained these gains by forcing high rates of turnover among regional police heads, regularly moving officials from region to region.

It should be emphasized that none of the heads of the new district agencies were subordinate to the *polpred*. While such a change would make sense from the standpoint of a clear and single vertical chain of command, it would represent a major assault on the prerogatives of the Moscow-based ministries. Ever since Khrushchev's attempt to undermine the ministries and transfer their powers to regional economic councils (the *sovnarkhozy*), the ministries have effectively fought reorganizations that would decentralize power to the district or regional level. The *polpred* typically could not order the federal agencies in his district to do anything, though he could complain to Putin if they ignored his advice.

The FSB was one of the few federal ministries that did not create a new territorial structure based on the federal districts. However, in February 2006, Putin announced the creation of a new federal structure, the National Anti-Terrorism Committee, headed by the FSB chair. Each region's antiterrorism committee (none were created at the federal district level) would be headed by the governor or president of the region. The result was a new "anti-terror vertical." On matters concerning terrorism and its prevention, which can be broadly construed, governors were subordinate not just to Putin but also to the chairman of the FSB. In each region, the local FSB head (also subordinate to the FSB chief, not the regional leadership) served as the head of the operational staff for antiterror operations and preparations. In 2007, an "anti-drug vertical" was added as well, under the State Committee to Combat Narcotics. It paralleled the antiterror vertical, and some analysts concluded that it was designed to act as a counterweight to the FSB or at least allow Putin to monitor its regional activities.

Another vertical hierarchy established to increase central control over the regions was the new political party that Putin helped found, United Russia. While it got off to a slow start in many regions, United Russia rapidly expanded its regional party structures after 2004. Following the pattern of its predecessor "parties of power," United Russia was spread into the regions by recruiting key officials at all levels. It was not accidental that the party was called United Russia. The party was highly centralized, always under the control of Putin loyalists, and designed as a kind of straitjacket to bring under control what had been autonomous or governor-controlled regional political institutions. There was virtually no intraparty democracy; major party personnel decisions were made by the party's curators in the Kremlin. Putin himself served as chairman of the party from 2008–2012 while prime minister; Medvedev took over as party leader in May 2012.

Political parties that had significant support among regional elites were undermined or forced from the playing field. As a result of the 2001 law on political parties, regionally based parties were not allowed to register and compete in national elections, thus reducing the role of governor-dominated political organizations. In 2003, the Kremlin changed the rules on electing regional legislatures to require that at least half the deputies be chosen by a proportional representation system—by party list. *Polpreds* and federal officials provided United Russia with enormous advantages in elections. This mobilization of "administrative resources" allowed United Russia to establish a dominant role in most regional legislatures by 2006 and in virtually all regions by 2010.

The popular election of governors gave them a status that was difficult for the Kremlin to overcome. In some cases before 2005, the Kremlin succeeded in preventing incumbent governors from winning reelection. Methods included exerting influence on elections by instructing or pressuring the election commission or the local courts to remove a candidate from the ballot. In some cases, *kompromat* (compromising material) gathered on regional leaders was employed to persuade them not to seek another term in office. In 2003–2004, for the first time, serious criminal investigations were launched against a number of sitting governors, most typically those the Kremlin labeled as weak and ineffective. While none of these cases were brought to trial, they helped Putin establish his primacy in the period before he began appointing regional leaders. Over one-third of Russia's regional leaders were replaced during Putin's first term. (See table 3.1 on page 77.)

A critical component of Putin's policy restoring central control over regions was the decision to end direct popular elections of regional leaders. This occurred in the aftermath of the terrorist attack in Beslan, North Ossetia, in September 2004. Rebels, mostly from the neighboring republic of Ingushetia, took over a school on the opening day of classes, and the poorly coordinated effort to save the hostages resulted in over 300 deaths.

In order to deflect criticism that Russia was abandoning democratic principles, the appointment process was fitted with a veneer of democratic choice. Three candidates had to be nominated, initially by the presidential envoy in the federal district in which the region was located, and they were expected to consult with major political forces in the region. From the beginning the authenticity of the process was brought into question when outsiders who were unknown in the region ended up as nominees and then governors. Another element of formal democracy was that the president's choice, once nominated, had to be approved by the regional legislature. In every case, however, regional legislatures ratified the president's choice. If they did not, the law provided for the dissolution of the legislature and new elections. After Putin began appointing governors, most of those who had not yet become members of United Russia rushed to join. By the time of the 2007 Duma elections, almost all governors had become members of the party, and they had a direct interest in ensuring the best possible performance for United Russia in subsequent regional and national elections. Governors who organized massive vote fraud were rewarded for their actions and never faced punishment.

Perhaps because of his dependence on regional leaders who could produce the electoral results he needed, Putin was extremely cautious in his dealings with strong, popular regional leaders. During his second term, governors and republic presidents who had been elected to their posts prior to 2005 and were perceived to be "loyal" were allowed to remain in power. A procedure was adopted that allowed governors to seek Putin's "vote of confidence," most often through a personal meeting with him, prior to the end of their term in office. In the vast majority of cases, Putin responded favorably without even considering other candidates and submitted the current governor's name to the regional assembly for reappointment. An important consequence of the end of elections was the de facto suspension of term limits for Russia's regional leaders. There was some speculation that this was the main purpose of the change: it would permit the reappointment of leaders viewed by the Kremlin as hard to replace.

With appointments replacing elections, a new mechanism for evaluating regional performance was instituted in January 2006. Regular sessions of the government would review socioeconomic conditions in a different region each month. At these meetings the governor or republic president was brought before assembled government ministers and provided an overview of his or her region and its problems. On the one hand, governors could use this opportunity to lobby for special projects for their regions with the chief decision makers all in attendance. At the same time, the sessions allowed Putin to assess the performance of governors and hold them to account for failings in their work. Starting in April 2008, regions that were developing at a slow pace or underperforming compared to other regions became the chief focus of these sessions. A system of detailed statistical reporting was developed as well to assess the performance of governors. The system comprised forty-three socioeconomic indicators, among which were economic output totals, new housing construction per capita, education expenditures per pupil, crime rates, and the percentage of the population that engages in physical exercise or sports. Polls would also be conducted to determine the level of satisfaction with education, health care, and the performance of regional government, including access to information. Meetings between Putin and governors continued after Putin moved into the post of prime minister. They were often characterized by detailed reports and questions about which indicators showed progress and which were lagging in a particular region. In effect, the purpose was to provide an accountability mechanism that would substitute for popular election—only now accountability was to the Kremlin rather than to the voters.

As president, Dmitry Medvedev introduced a change in the system for nominating candidates for governor that provided further gloss to the democratic veneer. Starting in 2009 the nomination of the three candidates was transferred from the *polpred* to the largest party in the regional assembly. This meant turning the nomination process over to United Russia, since it had become the largest party in every regional parliament. Given the Kremlin's leverage over all these political actors, the charade that unfolded was obvious to all. Each of the actors in the spectacle would dutifully follow the Kremlin's script, and nominees became candidates who became governors. As a rule, the decisions about who would be nominated and who would be approved were made by the internal politics department of the presidential administration in the Kremlin.

It was Medvedev who presided over the most significant change in the corps of Russia's regional leaders. The so-called regional heavyweights who had won election many years earlier and had consolidated control over regional political and economic institutions were systematically targeted for removal starting in 2009. The victims included some of the most prominent figures on the Russian political scene, including Yegor Stroev, Orel *oblast* leader since 1985, Mintimir Shaimiev, who had led Tatarstan since 1989, and Murtaza Rakhimov, head of Bashkortostan since 1989. Most governors quickly saw the writing on the wall and agreed to resign quietly. The exception was the powerful mayor of Moscow, Yury Luzhkov, who resisted efforts to force him out in October 2010. Luzhkov, who had been mayor since 1992, was relieved by Medvedev with the formulation that he had "lost confidence" in Luzhkov. Later, Medvedev would claim that a number of the governors had been removed because of evidence against them of corruption, though none were subjected to criminal prosecution. Many had held leadership positions in United Russia until the end and had repeatedly demonstrated their loyalty to the Kremlin.

Massive popular protests in the aftermath of elections to the Duma in December 2011 led Putin and Medvedev to reverse themselves on the issue of popular elections of governors. Only a couple of years earlier, Medvedev had said that gubernatorial elections would not be reinstated even in "a hundred years." A law was quickly passed in early 2012 that again made the post an elected one. Almost immediately, though, steps were taken to minimize the impact of the new law. One provision, the "municipal filter," required that candidates get signatures of support from as many as 10 percent of the deputies in local legislatures. Given the high percentage of local deputies affiliated with United Russia, the chances for opposition candidates to qualify were severely limited. In most regions, only a candidate supported by the Communist Party could easily pass through this "filter." Another tactic demonstrating the Kremlin's fear of regional elections was the flurry of new appointments made in early 2012 (see table 3.1). The new law on elections went into effect on June 1, 2012, but by appointing new

Table 3.1. Replacement Rates of Governors and Regional Police Chiefs (MVD), percent of total

Year	Governors (%)	Police chiefs (%)
2000	17	11
2001	7	25
2002	7	18
2003	8	27
2004	10	10
2005	15	23
2006	5	23
2007	13	19
2008	10	14
2009	11	7
2010	22	33
2011	7	42
2012	20	5

Source: www.president.kremlin.ru/acts
Note: 2012 data are as of June 1, when new law on electing governors went into effect.

governors or reappointing old ones ahead of schedule, elections could be delayed in those regions for another five years. As a result, the number of elections that were scheduled to take place in the fall of 2012 dropped from eleven (based on the initial timetable of governors' terms in office) to only four regions—Amur, Belgorod, Novgorod, and Briansk. In each region, none of which is considered critically important, the Kremlin was reasonably sure it could manage the outcome to prevent an opposition candidate from winning.

IS REFORM POSSIBLE UNDER PUTIN?

The state of center-region affairs under Yeltsin was not sustainable—the regions had become too strong at the expense of the center. But Putin swung the pendulum too far in the opposite direction. His policies curtailed both federalism and democratic development in Russia.

The methods used by Putin and his team were in large part derived from the standard operating procedures of the KGB and its successor organization, the FSB. These included gathering compromising materials against "targets," using this information to blackmail the targets in order to gain their cooperation, planning and carrying out extralegal operations with a maximum degree of secrecy, and using diversions and feints to direct attention away from the real purpose of an operation. In the case of the shift of powers to the federal districts, a part of Putin's strategy seemed to be to create new institutions that at first seem merely to duplicate functions of existing institutions, but that could later take their place. The emphasis on discipline, carrying out orders without question, and strict hierarchical relations also reflects the internal ethos of the KGB. The Putin approach to the regions seemed to suffer from a set of limitations that reflected his life experiences and background. There is a Soviet-era joke about a machinist from a defense plant who made Kalashnikovs (machine guns). When he retired from the factory, he decided to make toys for the children in his neighborhood. But whatever he tried to make, whether it was a rocking horse, a doll, or a model ship, it always came out looking like a Kalashnikov! Putin's choice of instruments and personnel made it almost inevitable that his policies for dealing with the regions would end up "looking like a Kalashnikov," a recentralized, unitary system.

Russia's leaders from the outset had only a hazy notion of what constitutes federalism or liberal democracy. To an extent this paralleled Soviet-era misunderstandings about the nature of a market economy. The absence of a planned or command system for allocating resources was equated with chaos and anarchy. Democracy and an effectively operating federal system rely on political institutions for resolving disputes with an emphasis on transparent, lawful action and the use of methods such as negotiation, persuasion, and compromise. If one sets aside the obvious exception of Chechnya, the Yeltsin presidency relied heavily on compromise and negotiation to achieve settlements with the regions. Putin, with much higher levels of public support, an effective working majority in the Duma, and a much more favorable economic and budgetary situation, could dispense with democratic procedures and still get results. Putin preferred to use his strength to force the changes he wanted largely without bargaining and without employing constitutional mechanisms.

How did Putin's policies work in practice? The evidence is contradictory. On the one hand, the new policies did remove some gubernatorial control over the military, police, and federal agencies that rightfully belonged under federal jurisdiction. On the other hand, there was little recognition among Putin's inner circle that this strategy could go too far, or that excessive centralization was one of the weaknesses of the Soviet system. It is clear from Putin's statements on "restoring" vertical power that his main reference point was the USSR. To someone who was a product of the Soviet system, the elimination of checks and balances appears to increase the manageability and effectiveness of the political system. This may have been true in the short run, but there was a serious downside. A highly centralized system runs the risk of collapsing in the face of a crisis or rapidly changing conditions.

A high degree of centralization is problematic in any political system, but this was especially true of a country as diverse as Russia. Natalia Zubarevich has argued that there are in effect four different Russias.[16] First there is the Russia of big cities (from 21 to 36 percent of the total population), where the middle class is concentrated and where skilled, white-class professions dominate. Second is what remains of industrial Russia (around 25 percent of the population), where regions are dominated both by blue-collar workers and *budzhetniki*—pensioners, teachers and others dependent on the federal and regional budgets. This Russia includes an important subset of "monocities," dominated by one large factory or industry, that are especially vulnerable to changes in state contracts or subsidies. The third Russia (about 38 percent of the population) is poor, peripheral, and mostly rural. It is less dependent on government policy and survives on the natural economy. Finally, a fourth Russia is made up of the poorest republics of the North Caucasus and southern Siberia (Tuva, Altai). Dominated by clans, these regions are highly dependent on direct transfers from the federal budget.

One could argue that the default option for the Kremlin was to create a set of policies designed to respond to the worst-case scenario in the regions; in practice, this meant the North Caucasus republics. This region suffered from serious economic and political difficulties, such as low levels of development, high unemployment, inequality, and poor governance. At the same time, there was an active insurgency under way that threatened a collapse of the entire system. One could make the case that Putinism in regional policy was an attempt to bring to the entire country the "successful" lessons learned from dealing with Chechnya after the war there[17]: forgoing elections to put in place a hand-picked regional leader (Ramzan Kadyrov) who restored order by dealing ruthlessly with his opponents, demonstrated total loyalty to the Kremlin, shamelessly manipulated election results to the advantage of United Russia, and implemented a state-dominated reconstruction program financed both from central and local resources. Yet, centralized policy making was simply not capable of formulating policies that would be effective in the varied settings that comprise the Russian Federation. It was proving more difficult to mobilize voters under the banner of United Russia. Chechnya-type policies applied in Moscow in 2010 and 2011 alienated a significant stratum of the population, producing massive anti-Putin demonstrations starting in December 2011.

What are the prospects that Putin, as he enters his latest term as president, could adopt policies that would begin the process of returning the pendulum in center-region relations back toward the regions? Dmitry Medvedev, who played the role of a loyal protégé of Putin as president, only gave lip service to the need for political reform as an element in modernizing the country. It took until mid-2011 for part of the ruling elite to begin to recognize that overcentralization was a serious problem that could threaten its hold on power. There were several signs that a reassessment was under way. Working groups headed by two of the most important officials tasked with regional policy, deputy prime ministers Dmitry Kozak and Alexander Khloponin, headed commissions to develop proposals that would reallocate government functions and budgetary resources from the center to the regions. In the run-up to the December 2011 Duma elections, United Russia began to reduce the centralized nature of the nomination process through more participatory "primaries" that provided greater input from regional elites. Other measures to democratize United Russia, proclaimed as a goal by Medvedev in May 2012, could further address some of the overcentralization of regional politics, as could the return to elected governors. Reforms were also proposed in the methods through which the Duma and Federation Council would be formed, in order to provide greater opportunities for regional representation in the national parliament. Ultimately, though, to make a difference, these changes and proposed changes will need to be accompanied by a rethinking of the entire model that has guided Putin's policies toward the regions.

SUGGESTED READINGS

Evans, Alfred B., and Vladimir Gel'man, eds. *The Politics of Local Government in Russia*. Lanham, Md.: Rowman & Littlefield, 2004.

Gill, Graeme, and James Young, eds. *Routledge Handbook of Russian Politics and Society*. London: Routledge, 2011.

Golosov, Grigorii. *Political Parties in the Regions of Russia: Democracy Unclaimed*. Boulder, Colo.: Lynne Rienner, 2004.

Reddaway, Peter, and Robert W. Orttung. *The Dynamics of Russian Politics: Putin's Reform of Federal-Regional Relations*, vols. 1 and 2. Lanham, Md.: Rowman & Littlefield, 2004 and 2005.

Ross, Cameron. *Local Politics and Democratization in Russia*. London: Routledge, 2009.

Ross, Cameron, ed. *Russian Regional Politics under Putin and Medvedev*. London: Routledge, 2011.

Ross, Cameron, and Adrian Campbell, eds. *Federalism and Local Politics in Russia*. London: Routledge, 2009.

NOTES

1. See Graeme Gill, *The Origins of the Stalinist Political System* (Cambridge: Cambridge University Press, 1996); and Gerald Easter, *Reconstructing the State: Personal Networks and Elite Identity in Soviet Russia* (Cambridge: Cambridge University Press, 1996).

2. Peter Jordan, "Regional Identities and Regionalization in East-Central Europe," *Post-Soviet Geography and Economics* 42, no. 4 (2001): 235–65.

3. Daniel Triesman, "The Politics of Intergovernmental Transfers in Post-Soviet Russia," *British Journal of Political Science* 26, no. 3 (1996): 299–335; and Daniel Triesman, "Fiscal Redistribution in a Fragile Federation: Moscow and the Regions in 1994," *British Journal of Political Science* 28, no. 1 (1998).

4. Michael McFaul and Nikolai Petrov, *Politicheskii Al'manakh Rossii 1997*, vol. 1 (Moscow: Carnegie Center, 1998), 149.

5. Darrell Slider, "Elections to Russia's Regional Assemblies," *Post-Soviet Affairs* 12, no. 3 (1996): 243–64.

6. Pavel K. Baev, "The Russian Armed Forces: Failed Reform Attempts and Creeping Regionalization," *Journal of Communist Studies and Transition Politics* 17, no. 1 (2001): 34.

7. Steven Solnick, "Is the Center Too Weak or Too Strong in the Russian Federation?" in *Building the Russian State*, ed. Valerie Sperling (Boulder, Colo.: Westview, 2000).

8. Alfred Stepan, "Russian Federalism in Comparative Perspective," *Post-Soviet Affairs* 16, no. 2 (2000): 133–76.

9. Darrell Slider, "Russia's Market-Distorting Federalism," *Post-Soviet Geography and Economics* 38, no. 8 (1997): 445–60.

10. Nikolai Petrov, "Seven Faces of Putin's Russia: Failed Districts as the New Level of State Territorial Composition," *Security Dialogue* 33, no. 1 (2002): 219–37.

11. Mathew Hyde, "Putin's Federal Reforms and Their Implications for Presidential Power in Russia," *Europe-Asia Studies* 53, no. 5 (2001): 719–43.

12. The reference is to the movie *The Magnificent Seven*, which was one of the first American films to be widely shown in the Soviet Union during the Cold War. The film, a western about seven gunslingers hired by a poor Mexican village to protect it from bandits, was extremely popular in the 1960s when Vladimir Putin was growing up.

13. The most detailed examination of the early role of the federal districts and *polpreds* is Peter Reddaway and Robert W. Orttung, *Putin's Reform of Federal-Regional Relations*, vol. 1, *The Dynamics of Russian Politics* (Lanham, Md.: Rowman & Littlefield, 2004). The second volume of this study (2005) shows the impact of Putin's federal reforms on law enforcement, the courts, Federation Council, local government, political parties, and business.

14. An additional eighteen federal agencies had regional offices in another location, while forty-three had no intermediate structures between their central headquarters and regional branches. "Federal Agencies on the Territory of Nizhniy Novgorod *Oblast*," chart prepared by the Volga federal district administration (2001).

15. The number of staff (150) assigned to the federal district MVD offices was greater than that assigned to the staff of the *polpred*.

16. Natalia Zubarevich, "Chetyre Rossii," *Vedomosti*, December 30, 2011. Her statistical report monitoring regional social and economic trends, at www.socpol.ru, is an important resource.

17. See Robert Ware, "Has the Russian Federation Been Chechenised," *Europe-Asia Studies* 63, no. 3 (2011): 493–508.

4

The Role of Law

Kathryn Hendley

Law has had a checkered history in Russia. The rule of law, as evidenced by an independent judiciary that applies the law in an even-handed manner to all who come before it, has been mostly absent. During the Soviet era, the leaders of the Communist Party used law in a blatantly instrumental fashion. This began to change in the late 1980s, when Gorbachev put forward the goal of a *pravovoe gosudarstvo* or a "state based on the rule of law."[1] The leaders of post-Soviet Russia have reiterated this goal, yet their actions reflect ambivalence. The heavy-handed prosecutions of political opponents of the Kremlin suggest that the willingness to use law as a weapon to achieve short-term goals is a vestige of Soviet life that lives on in post-Soviet Russia. Though these prosecutions have become the most well-known feature of the Russian legal system, both domestically and internationally, they do not tell the whole story. They have occurred within a legal system that has undergone remarkable institutional reforms over the past two decades.

The contemporary Russian legal system is best conceptualized as a dual system, under which mundane cases are handled in accordance with the prevailing law, but under which the outcomes of cases that attract the attention of those in power can be manipulated to serve their interests.[2] To put it more simply, justice is possible and maybe even probable, but cannot be guaranteed. This lack of predictability is unfortunate, but does not make Russia unique. Law is inherently messy. Many countries aspire to the rule of law, but none has yet achieved it in full measure. Articulating the rules is always easier than applying them to concrete circumstances. Some gap between the law on the books and the law in practice is inevitable. The efforts to bridge this gap in Russia are the subject of this chapter.

HISTORICAL OVERVIEW

The role of law in any society is not dependent solely on written law and formal legal institutions, but is also influenced by how these laws and institutions are understood and by how they are used (or not used) by both the powerful and the powerless within that society.[3] These attitudes, often referred to as legal culture, are neither uniform nor consistent. They are influenced by many factors. Primary among them are the common perceptions of the responsiveness of law and legal institutions to the interests of society. For some, these perceptions are shaped by their own experiences. But in Russia, much as in the rest of the world, the vast majority of citizens have had no firsthand encounters with the formal legal system. For them, their attitudes toward the legal system are influenced by beliefs about how law has worked in the past as well as by mass media accounts about how the legal system is presently functioning and/or anecdotal accounts of the experiences of friends or family. As a result, making sense of the role of law in contemporary Russia requires some knowledge of what came before.

The Soviet Union is often referred to as a lawless society. Taken literally, this was not true. The Soviet Union possessed all the elements of a typical legal system.[4] It had a complex body of statutory law as well as a series of constitutions. It had a hierarchy of formal courts that mirrored what would be found in any Western democracy, as well as a well-developed system of alternative dispute resolution that allowed for neighborhood mediation in so-called comrades' courts. But all of these institutions were firmly under the thumb of the Communist Party. Though the constitution prominently proclaimed their commitment to the principle of judicial independence, the absence of judicial review made the constitution largely symbolic. The legislature, though composed of representatives who were ostensibly popularly elected, operated as a rubber stamp for decisions made by party leaders. Likewise, judges tended to toe the party line.[5] All understood that anyone who diverged would not be invited to stand for reelection, and the short five-year terms ensured that judges were kept on a short leash. At the same time, this should not be taken to mean that party officials dictated the outcomes of all cases. Judges were left alone to resolve many (perhaps most) of the cases they heard in accord with the law and their consciences.[6] But judges knew that at any moment the telephone might ring and they might be told how to decide a specific case. The specter of "telephone law" hung over all cases and gave rise to a culture of dependency within the judiciary. Over time, fewer and fewer calls were needed as judges developed an instinct for what the party wanted. Not surprisingly, ordinary citizens grew skeptical of the power of the law to protect their interests. This legal culture of distrust persists to some extent to the present day and has stymied efforts to reform the legal system. Whether Russians are firmly committed to a governmental structure in which the courts enjoy full institutional independence is unclear. Recent public opinion polls indicate that only about a quarter of those surveyed believe that the courts should be totally free from the influence of the executive branch.[7]

Gorbachev was the first Soviet leader to make a systematic effort to change the role of law.[8] He regularly invoked the goal of creating a rule-of-law-based state or *pravovoe gosudarstvo* in his public statements. Moreover, he took concrete actions to that end. His reforms to the electoral system brought an end to the era of the rubber-stamp legislatures. Under his tenure, the judicial selection system was overhauled, eliminating the Communist Party's stranglehold and granting judges life tenure. Though these reforms were certainly necessary to achieving judicial independence, they were far from sufficient. Judges could not shake off the mantle of dependency so easily. Citizens were likewise slow to abandon their skepticism regarding the capacity of judges to rule in an even-handed manner without clear proof of a shift in judicial behavior. Along similar lines, Gorbachev introduced the principle of judicial review to Russia for the first time. He created the Committee on Constitutional Supervision, which, while not a full-fledged constitutional court, was empowered to review acts of the executive and legislative branches, making it an early (albeit feeble) attempt at checks and balances. Its impact was largely symbolic. How far Gorbachev would have pushed the legal reform had he not lost power is unknowable.

Reform to the legal system was less of a marquee issue under Yeltsin, but continued throughout the 1990s. In some ways, the challenges were mitigated by the disintegration of the Soviet Union. No longer did reformers have to concern themselves with how reforms would play out in all the republics, which became independent countries in 1992, but the immense size of Russia as well as the wholesale nature of the transformation left reformers with their hands full. Yeltsin's decision to abandon the halfway reforms that characterized *perestroika* and to embrace the goals of creating a democracy and a market economy meant that comprehensive reforms were needed. The institutional infrastructure both for democracies and markets is grounded in law. Much of the Soviet-era legislation and legal institutions were inadequate to the task. Russian reformers turned to Western advisors for assistance in writing the new laws and creating the necessary institutions. Many of these advisors approached Russia as if it was a *tabula rasa*, disregarding what existed on paper as well as the prevailing legal culture. Almost no area of law was left untouched by the legislative whirlwind of the 1990s. The top-down nature of these reforms and the unwillingness to pay attention to the needs of those who would be impacted felt familiar to Russians, who recognized the *modus operandi* from their Soviet past, albeit

under a new banner.[9] The result was a continued skepticism toward the usefulness of law; a sentiment that was only deepened as the new institutions
were rocked by a series of corruption scandals.

Snapshots of the judicial system taken at the beginning and end of the
1990s would reveal dramatically different pictures. Though the basic court
system remained intact and continued to handle the bulk of cases, other
more specialized courts were introduced. The most well-known is the
stand-alone Constitutional Court, which represented a dramatic break with
Russia's autocratic tradition. Through its power of judicial review, the court
could declare legislative and executive acts unconstitutional, thereby making the judicial branch an equal partner for the first time in Russian history.
In its early days, the court took some highly controversial positions, most
notably siding with the legislature against Yeltsin in the lead-up to the
October Events of 1993.[10] Yeltsin disbanded the court during this crisis and,
when it was reconstituted in early 1994, the justices, having learned their
lesson, shied away from disputes with political overtones. Less well-known,
but essential to the development of a market economy, was the emergence
of the *arbitrazh* courts in 1992. These courts were not created out of whole
cloth, but were built on the foundation of the Soviet-era system for resolving disputes between state-owned enterprises. Critical changes were made
in terms of the status of the decision makers (raised from arbiters to judges)
and jurisdiction (expanded to include disputes involving private firms as
well as bankruptcy), but the *arbitrazh* courts represent a creative adaptation
of Soviet-era institutions to serve the needs of the new Russia.[11]

In addition to the structural innovations, the depoliticization of the judicial selection process was consolidated under Yeltsin.[12] The constitution,
approved by popular referendum in December 1993, provides that judges
be appointed by the president, with the proviso that nominations to any
of the top courts be confirmed by the Federation Council. The seemingly
unchecked power of the president to select lower-level judges might seem
to be an example of the expansive powers granted to the president by this
constitution. In reality, however, it constituted the final step in a system
designed to preference competence over political reliability, a noteworthy
reversal from the previous system in which judges served at the pleasure of
the Communist Party. Under the new system, open positions were publicized, and anyone with a law degree who was at least twenty-five and had
five or more years of work in the legal profession could apply. Their applications were assessed by judicial qualification commissions (JQCs), who
forwarded their recommendations up the bureaucratic chain. Though the
president was entitled to reject these recommendations, he rarely did.[13]
After an initial three-year probationary period, judges received life tenure,
subject to a mandatory retirement age of sixty-five. Allegations of judicial
corruption and other malfeasance were handled by the JQCs, which had

the power to sanction and remove judges. This basic procedure persists to the present day.

Yeltsin's successors, Vladimir Putin and Dmitry Medvedev, came to the presidency with legal training, though neither ever worked as a lawyer. Their attitude toward law was undeniably shaped by their work experiences. Putin's years in the KGB seemed to have taught him the importance of discipline and predictability. Not surprisingly, he has consistently espoused a philosophy of "supremacy of law" (*gospodstvo zakonnosti*) that complements the "power vertical" and emphasizes the importance of law and order over the protection of human rights.[14] Medvedev, by contrast, spent several years on the law faculty at St. Petersburg State University, and has a subtler view of law. While president, he proved more willing to meet with rights activists, and his rhetoric was notably less bombastic than Putin's. In terms of action, however, Medvedev rarely challenged Putin.

LEGISLATIVE REFORMS IN THE TWENTY-FIRST CENTURY

Putin's consolidation of power within the Duma and his emasculation of the Federation Council allowed for legislative reforms that had eluded Yeltsin. During the 1990s, a number of key pieces of legislation had stalled due to opposition within the Duma. As a result, those affected had to hobble along using either the stopgap presidential decrees or Soviet codes, which had been amended so many times that they had come to resemble a patchwork quilt. Not only did this undermine the predictability of law by making it difficult to discern what the rules were, but it also left the guiding principles of the Soviet era in place, at least on paper. During Putin's first two terms, this legislative logjam was broken. The manner in which they were passed may signal a return to the Soviet style of rubber-stamp legislatures. Under both Putin and Medvedev, United Russia (the Kremlin-affiliated party) was able to take advantage both of its numbers and the ability of its leaders to enforce party discipline and build coalitions to enact the Kremlin's legislative agenda.

The criminal procedure code in effect when Putin took office was originally passed under Khrushchev. A new code, which enhanced the rights of judges at the expense of the police, got bogged down in the Duma in the latter years of Yeltsin's tenure. This new code was finally passed and came into effect in 2002.[15] Under its terms, the police are required to obtain warrants for investigative activities that previously could be carried out without judicial supervision. The code also limits the circumstances under which the accused may be kept in pretrial detention. Whether all of these procedural niceties are being observed in practice is a different question. The question of whether judges do a better job of safeguarding individual rights has also come into question. The Khodorkovsky case, in which the Yukos chief was jailed while awaiting trial on fraud charges despite not meeting the prerequisites of the code, shows that the rules regarding pretrial detention can and will be disregarded when inconvenient for the Kremlin.[16] Judging a system solely on high-profile cases can be dicey. The extent to which the state lives up to its obligations in more mundane cases is unclear, but the strong culture of backdoor dealings between judges and procurators (or prosecutors) creates grounds for suspicion. The procuracy is a uniquely Russian component of the legal system that is charged not only with prosecuting crime, but also with supervising justice more generally. It has stubbornly held out against numerous reform efforts aimed at making its activities more transparent.[17]

Under both Putin and Medvedev, a Soviet-era tactic of drafting laws with intentionally vague language reemerged. Such legislation offers maximum flexibility to officials and minimal predictability to citizens. Examples of this practice include the 2005 NGO law, which set up murky requirements for registration. It mandated reregistration, a tactic familiar from the Soviet era, when it was used as a way to purge undesirables from the Communist Party. The fear of NGO activists that reregistration would be used as a pretext to get rid of those NGOs that were distasteful to the authorities was realized when the law went into effect. Likewise the law on extremism, which was passed in 2002 to fight terrorism, has been used to outlaw political parties not in sync with the Kremlin. The seemingly innocuous requirement that candidates submit the petitions supporting their candidacy as well as for permits authorizing demonstrations have been used to stymie opponents of the Kremlin. These actions demonstrate the Kremlin's willingness to use law instrumentally.

JUDICIAL POLITICS IN THE
TWENTY-FIRST CENTURY

Judicial Selection and Supervision

The method of selecting judges and supervising them once they are on the bench has profound implications for the independence of the judicial system. Ideally, judges should look only to the law in resolving disputes; politics should not factor into their decisions. But when judges feel beholden to a political benefactor for their appointments, their impartiality can be compromised. Lifetime tenure is a potential solution, but runs the risk of creating a judicial corps detached from society, answerable to no one. Judges, even those with lifetime appointments, must be held accountable for misbehavior. Some oversight is necessary. Yet it requires a delicate touch; otherwise it risks undermining independence. As this suggests, the mechanics of maintaining an independent judicial system is excruciatingly difficult and highly political. Striking an acceptable balance between independence and accountability can be elusive.

Locating this equilibrium point in post-Soviet Russia has proven to be particularly vexing. Under Putin's leadership, concerns about the lack of judicial accountability gave rise to subtle but important changes in the selection system.[18] The composition of the judicial qualification commissions (JQCs) was altered. Judges no longer enjoyed a monopoly, but still made up two-thirds of the membership of the JQCs at all levels. In theory, opening JQC membership to nonjudges might seem to be democratic, in that it creates an avenue for societal concerns to be expressed. Judges saw it differently, fearing an effort by the Kremlin to exert more control over the courts. While it is true that the change allows other voices into the decision-making process, it is also true that most other European countries with organs analogous to the JQCs include a mixture of judges and laypeople. Russian civil society activists have complained bitterly about their lack of influence in the judicial selection process.

In addition to selecting judges, the JQCs have sole responsibility for disciplining judges. This brings some level of accountability into the mix. Possible sanctions range from private reprimands to dismissals. Such decisions are made in two contexts. Russian judges receive life tenure only after successfully completing a three-year probationary period, and the decision as to whether to retain these newcomers is made by the JQCs. Such decisions are supposed to be based on job performance, but some contend that JQCs are using this opportunity to purge the judicial corps of anyone who rocks the boat politically. The paucity of reliable data makes such allegations difficult to substantiate. Once judges have gotten over this hurdle, complaints about their behavior are referred to the JQCs. The number of complaints has grown by over 50 percent between 2005 and 2009. Although litigants raised almost 37,000 complaints before JQCs in 2009, this represented less than .02 percent of the cases brought before Russian courts.[19]

In contrast to the U.S. judicial system, in which legal professionals go onto the bench after a fairly lengthy career in some other legal arena, becoming a judge in Russia is a career choice made at a much earlier stage of life. Those interested in becoming a judge typically go to work for the courts as an assistant to a judge immediately after completing their legal education in order to gain the necessary experience to apply for a judicial post. Once they get onto the bench, most stay for their entire work life. The gender makeup of the Russian judiciary has shifted from being primarily female during the Soviet era, to being more evenly divided.[20] Though the prestige of the judiciary has risen considerably since the demise of the Soviet Union, it remains lower than in the United States. This is not unique to Russia, but is a common feature of countries with a civil law legal tradition.[21] Recognizing that status is linked to salary and workload, both Putin and Medvedev consistently pushed for increased funding for the courts. Even so, recruiting a sufficient number of judges to staff the courts remains difficult. Institutional efforts aimed at enhancing the status of the judiciary represent a starting point, but are effective only if accompanied by societal trust. This has been slow to develop, as evidenced by public opinion polls indicating that a majority of Russians distrust the courts.[22]

As part of an effort to build legitimacy for the courts, a law was passed mandating that, as of July 2010, all courts create websites on which judicial decisions as well as schedules for hearings are posted. Such websites have been created, though their quality varies widely.[23] Notwithstanding the fact that court decisions do not constitute binding precedent, some litigants have made active use of the information posted to investigate how the judges assigned to their cases have ruled in previous analogous cases. They believe that compiling this information helps them to persuade judges to be consistent in their rulings.

Constitutional Court

The Constitutional Court is a post-Soviet innovation. Its purpose is to ensure that the constitution remains the preeminent legal authority in Russia. To that end, it is empowered to invalidate legislative and/or executive acts as unconstitutional. From a technical legal point of view, the Constitutional Court stands on equal footing with the Supreme Court and the Higher *Arbitrazh* Court (see figure 4.1), but it is unlike them in several important respects. First, it does not stand at the apex of an elaborate hierarchy of courts that stretch across Russia. It is a stand-alone court.[24] Second, it is a much smaller court, with only nineteen judges, who are organized into two chambers for working purposes. The background of these judges is quite different from that of their counterparts on the other two top courts, most of whom have worked as judges for their entire careers. By contrast, many members of the Constitutional Court are drawn from the top ranks of legal scholars and come to the bench only after several decades of working in universities or research institutes. This means that they are free of the legacy of dependence that hangs over the rest of the Russian judiciary. Because they mostly come from a scholarly background, their opinions are longer and more literate, providing a clearer window into their thinking than is possible with opinions from the other courts. This is facilitated by the fact that only this court enjoys the right to write dissenting opinions. Finally, the decisions of the Constitutional Court constitute a source of law and, as such, are binding on the other branches of government as well as on other courts. As is the norm in other European countries

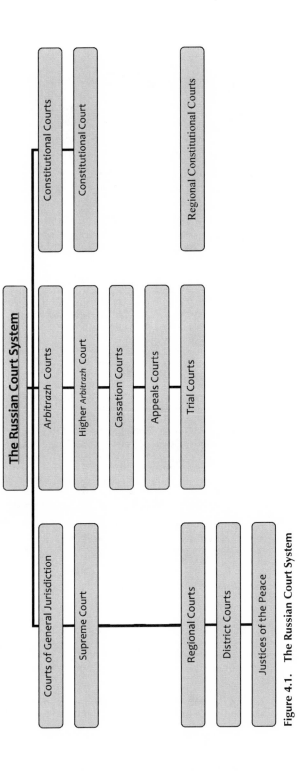

Figure 4.1.   The Russian Court System

that share Russia's civil law legal heritage, the decisions of the courts of general jurisdiction and the *arbitrazh* courts are typically binding only on the parties to the specific cases.[25]

Between 2007 and 2011, the number of petitions sent to the Constitutional Court ranged between 16,000 and 20,000 per year.[26] Almost all come in the form of individual complaints centering on alleged violations of constitutional rights. The remaining cases stem from claims initiated by the president, a group of legislators (at least 20 percent of the members of either chamber), or regional governments. Its decisions take several forms. Not all involve an up-or-down vote on the constitutionality of a particular law or regulation. Many of its rulings lay out the justification for legal norms' constitutionality. These so-called authoritative interpretations can have the effect of rewriting the law under the guise of ensuring its constitutionality. They have given the court tremendous influence in many areas of law (including tax, contracts, and social benefits) that would not appear to fall under its jurisdiction. The court has further expanded its jurisdiction by issuing rulings that declared contested legal norms "noncontradictory to the constitution," but their interpretations of these laws are considered binding on all Russian courts.[27]

Since its reconstitution following the October Events, the Constitutional Court has been reluctant to immerse itself in political controversy. Its ability to do so has been institutionally constrained by the decision to limit its jurisdiction to cases brought to it; the court can no longer take up cases on its own initiative. The court has also adopted a more deliberative pace for resolving cases. In contrast to the chaotic practices of the early 1990s, when decisions were sometimes issued on an overnight basis, cases now take eight or nine months to wind their way through the system, allowing time for the sorts of back-and-forth discussions among the judges that is familiar to students of the U.S. Supreme Court.[28] In terms of the substance of its decisions, the Constitutional Court has consistently been supportive of Putin's agenda to curtail regional power, including the elimination of popular elections for governors.[29] Even when the regions prevail, as in the March 2003 case brought by the legislatures of Bashkortostan and Tatarstan, the court is careful to note that regional governments are entitled to expand their powers only to the extent that they do not infringe on the federal system. The court seemed to feel emboldened by the Kremlin to bring the regions to heel. One member of the court noted, "We struck down the key clauses of 7 constitutions of the republics in June 2000 only after President Putin announced his crackdown on recalcitrant regions; we would not have been brave enough to do this under Yeltsin."[30]

Getting its decisions enforced is a problem that the Constitutional Court shares with the courts of general jurisdiction and the *arbitrazh* courts. Enforcing judgments is not just a problem in Russia; it is a problem that plagues courts everywhere. For the most part, litigants are expected to live up to the obligations imposed by the courts out of a combination of respect for the institution and a fear of being identified as noncompliant and shamed. The lack of societal trust in courts turns these assumptions upside down in Russia. Flouting judicial orders brings no disgrace. The Constitutional Court has attempted to remedy the problem by creating a department charged with monitoring its decisions. But the small size of the department (four people) and intransigence of the underlying political issues have hampered efforts at improving the record on implementation.

The Courts of General Jurisdiction

The courts of general jurisdiction are the workhorses of the Russian judicial system. Any case that is not specifically allocated to the Constitutional Court or the *arbitrazh* courts lands in their lap. In 2011, the workload of these courts, constituting almost 19 million cases, was more than eighteen times greater than that of the *arbitrazh* courts. They handle all criminal cases as well as any civil or administrative case that affects an individual (rather than a firm). The number of cases heard by these courts more than tripled between 1995 and 2010. The increase has been driven by civil cases; the number of criminal cases has actually decreased in recent years. The rise in civil claims is particularly intriguing given that these are cases brought by individuals. Whether this reflects a fundamental shift in attitudes toward the legal system, namely a greater willingness on the part of Russians to use the courts to protect their interests, is unclear.[31]

The courts of general jurisdiction can be found in every administrative district, making them the most accessible of the Russian courts. This has only increased under Putin with the introduction of a new layer of court, the justice of the peace (JP) courts (see figure 4.1). The JP courts were first authorized in late 1998, and were intended to provide a way to siphon off simple cases, thereby alleviating the burden on the already-existing courts.[32] Creating thousands of new courts proved to be easier said than done. When Putin took over, none existed, but by 2009, JP courts could be found in every part of Russia. From an institutional perspective, they have lived up to their promise. In 2010, almost all (95 percent) administrative cases, 76 percent of civil cases, and 46 percent of criminal cases originated in these courts.[33] Thanks in large measure to this, delays throughout the entire system have been lessened.[34] The JP courts have also benefited litigants by making courts more accessible, both geographically and in terms of the simplified procedure. As figure 4.1 indicates, those dissatisfied with the JP courts are entitled to appeal the judgment to a higher court.

Most cases that have not been diverted to the JP courts originate in the district courts, which are located in each rural or urban district. More serious matters are heard for the first time by the regional courts (which also serve as courts of appeal for the district courts).[35] The court of last resort for this system is the Supreme Court of the Russian Federation. In addition to its pure judicial function of reviewing individual cases, the court is also charged with overseeing the general development of judicial practice. To this end, it periodically issues guiding explanations of legislation that has been interpreted in contradictory fashion by lower courts. These explanations are binding on the lower courts. Ironically this gives the Russian Supreme Court greater institutional latitude than that enjoyed by the U.S. Supreme Court, though few would argue that the political clout of the Russian court approaches that of its American counterpart.

Putin's control of the legislature allowed for thorough reforms of the three procedural codes (administrative, civil, and criminal) that govern the day-to-day operations of the courts of general jurisdiction. Some of the innovations of the new criminal procedure code have been discussed above. The code also changed the operation of the courts by institutionalizing jury trials throughout Russia. Defendants charged with serious felonies can opt for a jury trial, and have been doing so with increasing frequency. Jury trials accounted for 16.5 percent of such trials in 2010, compared with 8.3 percent in 2003.[36] Defendants tend to fare better with juries than with judges. While in 2010 fewer than 1 percent of defendants were acquitted in bench (nonjury) trials, over 14 percent of defendants in jury trials were acquitted.[37] Jury verdicts, including acquittals, have been subject to appeal from the outset. After the Kremlin was embarrassed when juries acquitted defendants in several politically sensitive cases, the law was changed in 2008 to eliminate the right to a jury trial in cases of espionage, treason, terrorism, and other crimes against the state.

The broader impact of the availability of jury trials on Russians' attitudes toward the legal system is unclear. Elsewhere, juries have been justified on the grounds that they allow defendants to be judged by their peers and that they provide jurors with hands-on experience in how a democratic system operates. The relatively small number of Russians who have served on juries undermines any argument that they are building support for democracy. Russians themselves seem ambivalent about their merits. A series of public opinion surveys fielded in 2004, 2007, and 2011 suggests that Russians' confidence in juries is declining. In 2004, 34 percent saw juries as fairer and more independent than judges, whereas 29 percent viewed them as less knowledgeable and experienced than judges and more likely to be influenced by the parties. By 2011, these results had flipped. (The remainder of respondents saw little difference between having cases decided by judges or juries.)[38]

The *Arbitrazh* Courts

The jurisdiction of the *arbitrazh* courts is threefold: (1) disputes between firms (irrespective of ownership structure), (2) disputes between firms and the state, and (3) bankruptcies. At the outset, almost all cases fell into the first category, but, over time, the docket has shifted. Comparing the case distributions for 1997 and 2011 illustrates the point well. In 1997, disputes between firms dominated the docket, constituting over 80 percent of the cases decided by these courts. By 2011, however, the tables had turned. These disputes made up less than half of the cases decided, and the number of cases involving the state had increased dramatically. This change can be partially explained by the general economic recovery under Putin, which has led to fewer debt collection cases. Given that the vast majority of cases involve tax disputes, this shift also indicates that citizens are becoming less tentative about suing the state and that the state is becoming more aggressive in collecting what is owed to it. As plaintiffs, both taxpayers and the state generally prevail, suggesting that *arbitrazh* judges may be guilty of a pro-petitioner bias, but contradicting the common wisdom that they are in the pocket of the state.

The number of cases brought to the *arbitrazh* courts grew by over 300 percent from 1997 to 2011.[39] The willingness of economic actors to submit their disputes to the court is driven by the comparatively low costs and speed of the process. This is not to say that litigation is the only or even the preferred mechanism of resolving disputes. For Russian managers, much as for their counterparts elsewhere, turning to the courts is a last resort, used only when efforts at negotiation have failed. Rather, the point is that litigation is a viable option for commercial disputes in Russia.

The reworking of the *arbitrazh* procedural code in 2002 demonstrates the pragmatic character of the Putin-era reforms. This new code made a multitude of changes aimed at streamlining the work of the courts, such as limiting the number of cases requiring a three-judge panel at the trial level. The prior code had empowered single judges to resolve interfirm disputes on their own, and the new code expands this to include most cases involving the state. Bankruptcy cases still require a three-judge panel. While this change will allow cases to be processed more quickly, it may have the unintended consequence of facilitating corruption, in that one judge is easier to bribe than three. The new code also clarifies that disputes involving competing claims to stock ownership are within the *arbitrazh* courts' jurisdiction. Because the prior code had denied access to the *arbitrazh* courts to individuals (nonfirms), disputes involving both individual and corporate shareholders ended up being brought simultaneously in the *arbitrazh* courts and the courts of general jurisdiction, and sometimes led to inconsistent outcomes, which undermined the public's faith in the courts. The decision to assign all these cases to the *arbitrazh* courts reflects a respect for their greater expertise.

The European Court of Human Rights

With Russia's accession to the Council of Europe in 1996 and its ratification of the European Convention on Human Rights in 1998, it now falls within the jurisdiction of the European Court of Human Rights (the ECHR) in Strasbourg. Were Russians as nihilistic about law as is typically assumed, this would have made no difference. But Russians have flocked to the ECHR in record numbers. More petitions to the ECHR originated from Russia than from any other country.[40] This tells us that Russians still believe justice is possible and that they are searching out ways of holding their courts and government to account. At the same time, the fact that fewer than 1 percent of these Russian petitions are declared admissible reveals that Russians remain unclear about the precise function of the ECHR. Moreover, a 2008 public opinion survey revealed that only 7 percent of respondents would appeal to Strasbourg if their rights were violated.[41]

The Russian government has a mixed record at the ECHR. When the decisions have gone against it, they have been accepted and paid without question. But when the court calls for changes in policy, Russia's record is less impressive, as the many cases brought to challenge Russian policy in Chechnya illustrate.[42] On the other hand, the availability of recourse to the ECHR has undoubtedly affected judicial behavior. Russian judges, worried that their opinions will become the subject of appeals to the ECHR, are taking more care to live up to their procedural obligations. Though it might be more gratifying if such behavior stemmed from a commitment to the rule of law, fear of public humiliation can be a powerful stimulant, and perhaps the behavior will become habitual over time. Regardless of the incentive for the behavioral change, it inures to the benefit of litigants and the legal system.

THE POLITICS OF THE LEGAL PROFESSION IN TWENTY-FIRST-CENTURY RUSSIA

In many countries, lawyers are potent catalysts for legal reform. Their comprehensive knowledge of the law makes them well-qualified to identify where changes are needed. Such changes may be either iterative or fundamental. Their willingness to embrace these changes and to operationalize them through their clients can have a profound impact. Merely passing a law is only a first step. More difficult is integrating new norms into daily life. Lawyers can be integral in this process.

The legal profession in Russia has not traditionally performed this sort of role. The reasons are complicated. As in other countries with civil law traditions, lawyers tend to act more as technicians than as social activists. The divided nature of the profession in such countries also contributes to its political passivity. In Russia, for example, there is no single organization that speaks for lawyers, nor is there any uniform system for licensing lawyers. This inevitably gives rise to a fragmented profession. The Soviet heritage, under which lawyers were heavily regulated and their independence was constrained, has only deepened this natural instinct.

Most of the state regulations governing lawyers were eliminated and/or ignored in practice during the initial transition. The traditional distinction between litigators (*advokaty*) and business lawyers (*iuriskonsl'ty*) broke down during the 1990s. Private law firms, which had been outlawed during the Soviet era, sprang up and included both varieties of lawyers. Courts treated them similarly. This permissiveness was viewed with dismay by many *advokaty*, who had long viewed themselves as the elite of the legal profession. Admission to the *advokatura* had always been a rigorous and selective process, in contrast to becoming a *iuriskonsul't*, which simply required advanced legal education. *Iuriskonsul'ty* took advantage of the laxness of the regulatory regime to establish themselves as experts in business law, a specialization that had been more-or-less nonexistent during the Soviet era and an area of law not much exploited by *advokaty* (who tended to focus on criminal defense work). Prosecutors and judges are separate categories of lawyers. The disaggregated nature of the legal profession makes it impossible to determine the total number of Russian lawyers. The number of *advokaty* has been increasing by 1,300 per year, and by 2012 there were approximately 60,000 Russian *advokaty*.[43] This reflects the growing popularity in legal education, as evidenced by a tenfold increase in the number of law schools over the past two decades.[44]

Drafts of a law that would restore the *advokaty* to their preeminent role were floated, but never passed during the 1990s. Under Putin, this state of affairs changed. His legislative dominance allowed for the passage of a law dealing with the legal profession in 2002. Though the law did not create a monopoly on courtroom practice, as desired by *advokaty*, it certainly made them the default option. In criminal cases, for example, defendants must use an *advokat* unless being represented by a family member. The law also established a standard process for gaining entry to the *advokatura*. Much like judges, prospective *advokaty* must satisfy the requirements of a qualifications commission, which include an oral exam. Though the questions come from a preapproved list, some have argued that the subjective nature of evaluation leaves the door open for preferential treatment and for discrimination.[45] The law takes an important step toward institutionalizing the independence of the legal profession by establishing a privilege for attorney-client communications.[46]

CONCLUSION

This review of the role of law in contemporary Russia illustrates that easy conclusions are not possible. The reasons for criticism of Putin's regime on this score are obvious. Under both Putin and Medvedev, the Kremlin's leg-islative agenda was pushed through with a heavy hand and often had the result of curtailing human rights. Putin's willingness to use the courts as a weapon for punishing his political opponents quite rightly calls their inde-pendence into question. Such policies would be troubling in any context, but are particularly disquieting in post-Soviet Russia. They are disturbingly reminiscent of problem-solving tactics employed by Soviet leaders that would seem to have been renounced as part of the transition to a rule-of-law-based state (*pravovoe gosudarstvo*). On the other hand, the post-Yeltsin era brought critical institutional innovations. The introduction of the JP courts increased the responsiveness of courts to citizens and eased the strain on the district and regional courts. The use of courts has continued to grow, suggesting a societal willingness to turn over disputes to the courts.

These seemingly contradictory indicators make sense only when the Rus-sian legal system is analyzed as a dualistic system. The institutional progress cannot be dismissed as mere window dressing. After all, the vast majority of the millions of cases heard each year within the Russian judicial system are resolved on the basis of the law on the books, as interpreted by the judge, and without any interference from political authorities. Justice is not out of reach in Russia; it is the likely outcome in most cases. But the contin-ued willingness of those with political power to use law in an instrumental fashion to achieve their short-term goals means that justice can sometimes be out of reach. It also means that the commitment to the basic principle of the rule of law, namely that law applies equally to all, irrespective of their power or connections, is not yet complete. A gap between the law on the books and the law in practice exists in Russia, as in all countries. Surely it has receded from the chasm it was during the Soviet era. But whether it will increase or decrease as time goes on remains to be seen.

SUGGESTED READINGS

Burnham, William, and Jeffrey Kahn. "Russia's Criminal Procedure Code Five Years Out." *Review of Central & East European Law* 33, no. 1 (2008): 1–93.

Henderson, Jane. *The Constitution of the Russian Federation: A Contextual Analysis.* Portland, Ore.: Hart Publishing, 2011.

Kahn, Jeffrey, Alexei Trochev, and Nikolay Balayan. "The Unification of Law in the Russian Federation." *Post-Soviet Affairs* 25, no. 4 (2009): 310–46.

Maggs, Peter B., William Burnham, and Gennady Danilenko. *Law and Legal System of the Russian Federation.* 4th ed. New York: Juris Publishing, 2009.

Solomon, Peter H., Jr., and Todd S. Foglesong. *Courts and Transition in Russia: The Challenge of Judicial Reform.* Boulder, Colo.: Westview Press, 2000.

Trochev, Alexei. *Judging Russia: Constitutional Court in Russian Politics, 1990–2006.* Cambridge: Cambridge University Press, 2008.

NOTES

1. For background on the meaning of *pravovoe gosudarstvo*, see Harold J. Berman, "The Rule of Law and the Law-Based State *(Rechsstaat),*" *The Harriman Institute Forum* 4, no. 5 (May 1991): 1–12.

2. The conceptualization of the Russian legal system as dualistic was first suggested by Robert Sharlet with regard to the Stalinist system. "Stalinism and Soviet Legal Culture," in *Stalinism: Essays in Historical Interpretation*, ed. Robert C. Tucker (New York: W.W. Norton, 1977), 155–56. He, in turn, was drawing on the ideas of Ernst Fraenkel, *The Dual State: A Contribution to the Theory of Dictatorship* (London: Oxford University Press, 1941). For more on the dualistic nature of the contemporary Russian legal system, see Kathryn Hendley, " 'Telephone Law' and the 'Rule of Law': The Russian Case," *Hague Journal on the Rule of Law* 1, no. 2 (2009): 241–64.

3. For an overview of the rule of law, see Lon L. Fuller, *The Morality of Law* (New Haven: Yale University Press, 1965), and Phillipe Nonet and Philip Selznick, *Law and Society in Transition* (New York: Harper & Row, 1978).

4. Harold J. Berman, *Justice in the U.S.S.R: An Interpretation of Soviet Law* (Cambridge, Mass.: Harvard University Press, 1963).

5. George Ginsburgs, "The Soviet Judicial Elite: Is it?" *Review of Socialist Law* 11, no. 4 (1985): 293–311.

6. George Feifer, *Justice in Moscow* (New York: Simon and Schuster, 1964).

7. A majority of those surveyed in 2006 and 2010 responded that courts should either be completely (30 percent) or somewhat (30 percent) controlled by the executive branch. www.levada.ru/archive/sudebnaia-sistema/kak-vy-schitaete-kontroli ruetsia-li-organami-ispolnitelnoi-vlasti-deiateln (May 20, 2012).

8. Kathryn Hendley, *Trying to Make Law Matter* (Ann Arbor, Mich.: University of Michigan Press, 1996), 34–45.

9. Kathryn Hendley, "Legal Development in Post-Soviet Russia," *Post-Soviet Affairs* 13, no. 3 (1997): 228–51.

10. In addition, the court famously took on the question of the legality of the Communist Party, giving rise to a lengthy and rather bizarre trial. David Remnick, *Lenin's Tomb: The Last Days of the Soviet Empire* (New York: Vintage Books, 1994), 494–530. The text of the court's decision is available in *Vestnik Konstitutsionnogo Suda*, no. 4/5 (1993): 37–64.

11. Kathryn Hendley, "Remaking an Institution: The Transition in Russia from State Arbitrazh to Arbitrazh Courts," *American Journal of Comparative Law* 46, no. 1 (1998): 93–127.

12. Peter H. Solomon Jr. and Todd S. Foglesong, *Courts and Transition in Russia: The Challenge of Judicial Reform* (Boulder, Colo.: Westview Press, 2000).

13. In 1997, only 2 percent of the recommendations forwarded to the president were rejected. Solomon and Fogelsong, *Courts and Transition in Russia*, 30.

14. There are two words for "law" in Russian: *pravo* and *zakon*. The former conveys a notion of law that incorporates human rights, while the latter invokes a more positivistic notion of statutory law. Although the phrases used to capture the goals of legal reform in Russia used by Gorbachev (*pravovoe gosudarstvo*) and Putin (*gospodstvo zakonnosti*) seem similar on the surface, they actually capture very different notions of the role of state and society.

15. William Burnham and Jeffrey Kahn, "Russia's Criminal Procedure Code Five Years Out," *Review of Central & East European Law* 33, no. 1 (2008): 1–93.

16. Mikhail Khodorkovsky was arrested in the fall of 2003 on charges of fraud, tax evasion, and theft of state property in the course of privatization. At every stage of the process, the authorities skirted on the edge of legal proprieties, typically obeying the literal letter of the law (though not always), but trampling on its spirit. Equally troubling was the treatment of Sergei Magnitsky. He was the lawyer for a Western hedge fund who uncovered a massive scheme of corruption among Russian officials. He was arrested and detained for months, during which he died as a result of being denied medical care. Both cases have become *cause célèbre* among the international human rights community, and tend to confirm the common wisdom about the dysfunction of the Russian legal system. For background on these cases, see Richard Sakwa, *The Quality of Freedom: Khodorkovsky, Putin and the Yukos Affair* (Oxford: Oxford University Press, 2009).

17. Gordon B. Smith, "Putin, the Procuracy, and the New Criminal Procedure Code," in *Public Policy and Law in Russia: In Search of a Unified Legal and Political Space*, ed. Robert Sharlet and Ferdinand Feldbrugge (Leiden: Martinus Nijhoff Publishers, 2005), 169–85.

18. Alexei Trochev, "Judicial Selection in Russia: Towards Accountability and Centralization," in *Appointing Judges in an Age of Judicial Power: Critical Perspectives from Around the World*, ed. Peter H. Russell and Kate Malleson (Toronto: University of Toronto Press, 2006).

19. "Obzor rezul'tatov deiatel'nosti za 2006 god," www.vkks.ru/ss_detale.php?id=856 (July 20, 2008).

20. According to the data of the United Nation's Economic Commission for Europe, about 60 percent of Russia's judicial corps is comprised of women. This has held constant since 2000, though the total number of judges has increased dramatically due to the need to staff the JP courts. w3.unece.org/pxweb/quickstatistics/readtable.asp?qs_id=32 (May 15, 2012). By contrast, only 14 percent of the members of the Russian parliament are women.w3.unece.org/pxweb/quickstatistics/readtable.asp?qs_id=20 (May 15, 2012).

21. On the differences between common law and civil law legal traditions, see John Henry Merryman, *The Civil Law Tradition: An Introduction to the Legal Systems of Western Europe and Latin America*, 2d ed. (Stanford: Stanford University Press, 1985).

22. In a series of polls conducted between 2006 and 2011, Russians were asked whether a fair trial was possible in Russia. The results were remarkably consistent. Fewer than 5 percent felt certain that a fair trial was possible. A quarter of those surveyed thought it might be possible. But most were less sanguine. Around 40 percent said it was unlikely, while about 20 percent were quite sure it was impossible. www.levada.ru/25-05-2011/o-sude-prisiazhnykh-i-dele-ob-ubiistve-s-markelova (May 15, 2012).

23. The Fund for Freedom of Information, a St. Petersburg–based nongovernmental organization, has been monitoring these websites since their creation. Each year, they rank the court websites according to clearly stated criteria. Several court administrators have contacted the researchers to find out how they could improve their rankings, indicating that officials are paying attention. www.svobodainfo.org/ru/node/6 (May 15, 2012).

24. The fifteen regional constitutional courts are not institutionally linked to the Russian Constitutional Court. Alexei Trochev, "Less Democracy, More Courts: The Puzzle of Judicial Review in Russia," *Law & Society Review* 38, no. 3 (2004): 513–38.

25. The role of judicial opinions as binding precedent is in flux in Russia. Both the Russian Supreme Court and the Higher *Arbitrazh* Court have asserted their right to have their decisions treated as precedent. William Pomeranz and Max Guthrod, "The Push for Precedent in Russia's Judicial System," *Review of Central and East European Law* 37, no. 1 (2012): 1–30.

26. www.ksrf.ru/Treatments/Pages/Statistic.aspx (May 14, 2012).

27. Trochev, *Judging Russia*, 122–23.

28. Trochev, *Judging Russia*, 120–21.

29. Trochev, *Judging Russia*, 139–59.

30. Alexei Trochev, "The Zigzags of Judicial Power: The Constitutional Court in Russian Politics, 1990–2003" (PhD dissertation, Department of Political Science, University of Toronto, 2005), 177.

31. Kathryn Hendley, "The Puzzling Non-Consequences of Societal Distrust of Courts: Explaining the Use of Courts in Russia," *Cornell International Law Journal* 45, no. 3 (2012).

32. Peter H. Solomon Jr., "The New Justices of the Peace in the Russian Federation: A Cornerstone of Judicial Reform?" *Demokratizatsiya* 11, no. 3 (2003): 380–96.

33. "Obzor sudebnoi statistiki o deiatl'nosti federal'nykh sudov obshchei iurisdiktsii i mirovykh sudei v 2010 godu," www.cdep.ru/index.php?id = 5 (January 26, 2012).

34. Solomon and Foglesong report that in the mid-1990s, the statutorily imposed deadlines for resolving cases were not met in more than 25 percent and 15 percent of criminal and civil cases, respectively. *Courts and Transition in Russia,* 118–19. The 2010 caseload data indicate that about 60 percent of civil and criminal cases are resolved within three months of filing. www.cdep.ru/index.php?id = 79 (May 21, 2012). Even so, delays remain a serious concern. Litigants are entitled to seek compensation from the court when cases are unreasonably delayed. In extreme instances, parties can take their complaints to the European Court of Human Rights.

35. In 2007, only 0.4 percent of criminal cases and a tiny (less than 0.001 percent) portion of civil cases originated in the regional courts.

36. "Obzor deiatel'nosti federal'nykh sudov obshchei iurisdiktsii i mirovykh sudei za 2010 god," *Rossiiskaia iustitsiia,* no. 9 (2011): 56; "Obzor deiatel'nosti federal'nykh sudov obshchei iurisdiktsii i mirovykh sudei v 2004 godu," *Rossiiskaia iustitsiia,* no. 6 (2005): 29. When taken as a percentage of the total criminal cases, the share of cases heard by juries is infinitesimal.

37. "Obzor deiatel'nosti federal'nykh sudov," 56–58.

38. www.levada.ru/25-05-2011/o-sude-prisiazhnykh-i-dele-ob-ubiistve-s-mark elova (May 15, 2012).

39. "Osnovanye pokazateli raboty arbitrazhnykh sudov v 1996-1997 godakh," *Vestnik Vysshego Arbitrazhnogo Suda,* no. 4 (1998): 21–23; "Analiticheskaia zapiska k statisticheskomu otchetu o rabote arbitrazhnykh sudov Rossiiskoi Federatsii v 2011 godu," Spravka osnovanykh pokazatelei raboty arbitrazhnykh sudov v 2006-2007

godakh," arbitr.ru/_upimg/758C971D400EDE3EE299C1A078E77811_2.pdf (May 15, 2012).

40. "European Court of Human Rights: Analysis of Statistics 2010," www.echr .coe.int/NR/rdonlyres/OA35997B-B907-4A38-85F4-A9311A78F10/0/Analysis_of_ statistics_2010.pdf (May 16, 2012). When the data are analyzed on a per capita basis, Russia's share of the docket is less extreme, but the sheer number of cases (which made up almost 30 percent of cases in 2010) risks overwhelming the court.

41. Results reported at wciom.com/archives/thematic-archive/info-material/sin gle/9815.htm l (October 1, 2008).

42. Julia Lapitskaya, "ECHR, Russia, and Chechnya: Two Is Not Company and Three Is Definitely a Crowd," *NYU Journal of International Law & Politics* 43, no. 3 (2011): 479–574.

43. www.fparf.ru/fpa/fpart.htm (May 17, 2012).

44. www.alrf.ru/dynamic/press/2012-01-23-07-31-29 (May 20, 2012).

45. Eugene Huskey, "The Bar's Triumph or Shame? The Founding of Chambers of Advocates in Putin's Russia," in *Public Policy and Law in Russia: In Search of a Unified Legal and Political Space*, ed. Robert Sharlet and Ferdinand Feldbrugge (Leiden: Martinus Nijhoff Publishers, 2005), 149–67.

46. For an analysis of the challenges associated with inculcating professional ethics among Russian lawyers, see Katrina P. Lewinbuk, "Perestroika or Just Perfunctory? The Scope and Significance of Russia's New Legal Ethics Laws," *Journal of the Legal Profession* 35, no. 1 (2010): 25–80.

5

Civil Society and Protest

Alfred B. Evans Jr.

Scholars in the social sciences think of civil society as the sphere of activity that is initiated, organized, and carried out primarily by citizens, and not directed by the state. Larry Diamond, for example, characterizes civil society as "the realm of organized social life that is voluntary, self-generating, at least partially self-supporting, autonomous from the state, and bound by a legal order or set of shared rules."[1] Diamond's definition suggests that organizations in a civil society accept common norms and operate under the rule of law.[2] We also may see civil society as located between the family and the state, and as distinct from the sector of businesses that are oriented primarily toward making a profit. The principal reason for scholars' interest in that subject is the widespread acceptance of the argument that a thriving civil society exerts a favorable influence on the growth and consolidation of democratic political institutions.[3] In other words, civil society is generally regarded as a crucial part of the structures supporting a democratic political system. The purpose of this chapter is to examine the development of civil society in Russia today. In particular, because the right and ability to protest governmental action is a key aspect of civil society, considerable attention will be given to protest movements in Russia.

HISTORICAL BACKGROUND

The political regime of the Soviet Union was hostile toward the idea of civil society because its leaders saw any independence of organized groups as threatening their monopoly of power. Russian historians have confirmed that even during the earliest years of the Soviet system, the Communist Party wanted to eliminate independent groups, and that the party intensified its control of social organizations from the 1920s to the 1930s.[4] By 1932, official policy called for consolidating multiple existing societies in each area of activity, such as creative writing, art, composing, or filmmaking, into one unified society. By the height of the Stalin period civil society had been suppressed in the Soviet Union. After Stalin's death, during the 1950s and 1960s, a variety of informal and unofficial social groups did come into existence quietly, and there are reports that the number of groups that were not sponsored by the Communist Party increased during the 1970s and early 1980s.[5] A dissident movement voiced open criticism of the Soviet regime by the 1960s, often at great personal cost for its members, but the active participants in that movement were a tiny minority of the intelligentsia in the USSR. It seems likely that most people in the Soviet Union who had heard of the dissenters were indifferent or even hostile toward them, so that dissidents "failed to strike a responsive chord among the masses at large."[6]

Most Soviet citizens satisfied their daily needs under a highly authoritarian political regime, not by openly challenging authority, but by working their way around it. Under the surface of a monolithic system there was a complex, officially unrecognized society in which people exerted remarkable ingenuity and energy in solving the key problems that they encountered in everyday life. For Soviet citizens the constraints imposed by detailed regulations and institutionalized privileges were relieved by the opportunities presented by informal relationships of mutual benefit. An enormously important factor in the unofficial society was *blat*, which was defined by Hedrick Smith in the 1970s as "the influence or connections to gain the access you need."[7] Alena Ledeneva has skillfully explored the meaning and uses of *blat* in Soviet society.[8] She points out that reliance on informal contacts was necessitated by the shortages of goods and services created by the centrally planned economy of the USSR.[9] For the exchange of favors a person could turn to people in two circles: first, that of family members and close friends, and second, those contacts who would provide assistance on a pragmatic basis, with the awareness of the implicit potential that such favors might be reciprocated. As Ledeneva puts it, "*Blat* articulated private interests and 'human' needs against the rigid constraints of the state order, allowed people to meet harsh conditions, to maintain their social comfort, and enjoy a sense of 'beating the system.'"[10] Since such informal connections and exchanges not only made the command economy more tolerable for citizens but also made it possible for it to function, they were a source of stability for the Soviet system, in a sense. Yet at the same time the prevalence of such unofficial practices made it clear to people that the ideology of the system did not correspond to daily reality, so that the exchange of favors exerted a subversive influence on the level of political culture.[11]

After he came to power as head of the Communist Party of the Soviet Union, Mikhail Gorbachev opened the way for a major shift in the relationship between the state and society. Part of his program of radical reform, or *perestroika*, allowed citizens to create "informal" groups (*neformalye*), which were not controlled by the Communist Party. The number of those groups grew very rapidly; in 1988 the party newspaper *Pravda* estimated that there were about 30,000 informal groups in the USSR, and in 1989 that newspaper reported that around 60,000 of those groups had come into existence.[12] Those groups were devoted to a wide range of activities, but many of them asserted demands for change in the policies of the state, and some called for change that was more basic than Gorbachev had wished. Soon some Western scholars spoke very optimistically about the emergence of civil society in the Soviet Union, even suggesting that the shift in power between society and the state could not be reversed.[13]

CIVIL SOCIETY IN POST-SOVIET RUSSIA

Assessments of civil society in Russia several years after the collapse of rule by the Communist Party and the breakup of the USSR painted a more negative picture than one might have expected before 1991. Among Russian and Western scholars there was a consensus that the boom in civil society organizations under *perestroika* had been followed by a slump in the activity of such organizations in post-Soviet Russia in the 1990s.[14] It had become apparent that the legacy of the Soviet system on the level of political culture was the source of major problems for organizations that sought to unite groups of Russian citizens for the pursuit of common interests. Ken Jowitt contends that the experience of living under communist rule led citizens to see a dichotomy between the official realm and the private realm.[15] In the unofficial culture of such citizens, the sphere of political life was regarded as "suspect, distasteful, and possibly dangerous,"[16] and sharply distinct from the sphere of private life, the only area where intimacy could be found and ethical conduct was possible.[17] In consistency with that thesis, Marcia Weigle reports that post-Soviet Russians have a high level of distrust for public figures and public life.[18] She adds that the lack of legitimacy of the public sphere has reinforced the importance of "a network of informal relations as the dominant form of social integration." Nongovernmental organizations are seen as part of the public sphere, since all social organizations in the Soviet Union were subjected to control by the Communist Party and were expected to mobilize citizens to assist in achieving the goals of the political regime. On the basis of an extensive analysis of data from surveys,

Marc Morjé Howard reached the conclusion that "most people in post-communist societies still strongly mistrust and avoid joining any kind of formal organizations,"[19] and showed that the rate of membership in voluntary associations is lower in postcommunist countries than in the older democracies, or in postauthoritarian countries that had not been under communist control.[20] In Russia during its first postcommunist decade, as Sarah Henderson puts it, many citizens "viewed NGOs with hostility, mistrust, and—at best—indifference."[21]

Another serious problem for social organizations in the post-Soviet period in Russia was a result of the deep dislocation in the economy of that country during the 1990s.[22] Because of interruptions in the payment of wages and pensions and a high rate of inflation, most people in Russia were preoccupied with the struggle for economic survival, and did not have the means to offer financial support for nongovernmental organizations, even if they had wanted to do that. Thus it is not surprising that most of those organizations did not even attempt to engage in raising funds by expanding the ranks of their dues-paying members or soliciting donations from potential supporters. Valerie Sperling's research on women's organizations in Russia in the 1990s found that few of those organizations had tried to expand the number of their members or to carry out fund-raising drives, in sharp contrast with familiar activities of NGOs in Western countries.[23] In surveys, the leaders of nongovernmental organizations in Russia often said that their biggest problem was a lack of financial support for their activities.[24] During the 1990s a few of those organizations received grants from foreign sources, but that kind of support had mixed effects, on the one hand raising the level of professional competence of the leaders of the organizations, but on the other hand, discouraging the leaders of such groups from seeking to build a base of support among groups in their society.[25] In summary, civil society in Russia was weak, on the whole, by the end of the 1990s, and the two main reasons for the marginal condition of the vast majority of organizations in civil society were found in a culture of distrust of the public sphere and unfavorable economic circumstances for social organizations.

CIVIL SOCIETY UNDER PUTIN

State-based obstacles were not among the major barriers to the growth of organizations in civil society in post-Soviet Russia while Boris Yeltsin was president in the 1990s. The political regime no longer prevented the creation of independent groups in society, since the Communist Party of the Soviet Union, the force that had controlled all social groups for several decades, had disappeared, and the state no longer prohibited the founding of organizations that challenged a particular ideology. After Vladimir Putin became president of Russia in 2000, however, he pursued a change in strategy, deliberately consolidating control over the political system and subordinating the parliament, regional governments, political parties, and television networks to domination by the national executive leadership. Within a few years Putin turned his attention to bringing civil society into an integrated system of support for the centralized state that he headed.[26] While his speeches frequently mentioned the importance of civil society, they made it clear that he envisioned social groups as assisting the state in addressing tasks that serve the needs of the whole nation.[27] Putin is suspicious toward nongovernmental organizations in Russia that receive funding from abroad, especially if those organizations are at all involved in politics. In his address to the parliament in May 2004, he charged that for some social organizations the priority is "obtaining funding from influential foreign or domestic foundations," and for others it is "servicing dubious group and commercial interests."[28] In 2006 the parliament passed changes in legislation on the framework of regulations for NGOs. Some groups complained that the requirements for registration and reporting under the new laws were onerous, but it is not clear whether the new procedures actually have forced any genuinely active organizations to close down.[29] There did seem to be a consensus that some of the procedures mandated by that legislation were burdensome, and those regulations were revised in 2009.[30]

Putin also enhanced positive incentives for organizations in civil society to provide the kinds of services that the state considered most valuable. In 2006 the federal government began to award grants to Russian NGOs through a competitive process, offering an alternative to Western funding.[31] The political regime also took the initiative in forming groups that some scholars have called "government-organized nongovernmental organizations," or GONGOs. Perhaps the most prominent of those were a series of state-sponsored youth groups on a national scale, the best known of which currently is *Nashi* (Ours),[32] which has been distinguished by its adulation for Putin, its contempt for his critics, and its tendency toward outbursts of xenophobia. Another innovation of the Putin leadership that was intended to ensure a closer relationship between the state and civil society was the Public Chamber of the Russian Federation.[33] In 2004 Putin proposed the establishment of a public chamber, "as a platform for extensive dialogue, where citizens' initiatives could be presented and discussed in detail,"[34] and a law adopted by the parliament made it possible for that body to begin functioning in early 2006. The president plays a major role in appointing the members of the Public Chamber, who are said to be representatives of organizations in civil society. Though some of the members of that body have spoken out as individuals on some controversial issues, over time there has not been enough of a consensus among the members to make it possible for them to attempt to exert influence on the resolution of any major question that has aroused excitement in the nation. It does not appear that Vladimir Putin's conception of civil society as consisting of organizations that support the work of the state in service to the nation has been institutionalized in a way that has brought dramatic change in Russian society on a practical level. It is likely, however, that the leaders of many nongovernmental organizations sense that there is an implicit threat of repression if they challenge the regime. It seems likely that since Putin first took office as president in 2000, economic and social changes that have been partly due to the policies of his leadership have been far more important in contributing to the potential for change in civil society.

THE ANTI-MONETIZATION PROTESTS OF 2005

There were protests in Russia during the 1990s, which were similar to some that had taken place during the last years of the Soviet system. Scholars disagree on the level of protest activity in Russia during the 1990s. Most analysts have depicted the population of Russia as politically passive in that period, in terms of a low level of participation in strikes, demonstrations, and other acts of protest, despite the economic hardships suffered by most Russians during those years.[35] However, some other scholars contend that relatively large numbers of Russians took part in protests in the 1990s, mostly in connection with strikes by workers in reaction to wage arrears.[36] Graeme Robertson reports that there was a sharp decline in protests in Russia in 1999, and that the level of protest in that country remained low during Vladimir Putin's first term as president, from 2000 to 2004.[37]

The situation was to change dramatically, however, in early 2005. The protests that erupted on a startling scale at that time arose in response to change, or "reform" in certain social benefits, or *l'goty*, to large numbers of Russians. The *l'goty* that had been inherited from the Soviet system and expanded under Boris Yeltsin were entitlements that guaranteed their recipients certain services, such as public transportation, medicines, housing, and utilities, either free of charge or at reduced rates.[38] Those benefits were provided for people in certain categories, including pensioners, veterans, the disabled, single parents, and orphans, altogether comprising about one-quarter of the population of the country. The Putin administration proposed to eliminate those entitlements and replace them with cash payments to those who had been eligible for the *l'goty*. The legislation instituting that change was adopted by the federal parliament in August 2004 after little debate, and came into effect on January 1, 2005.[39] Those who had been eligible for such entitlements lost their access to free transportation and medications, and lost the subsidies for housing and utilities, on the first day of 2005, but they would not receive cash payments until the end of January. In addition, the funding that the federal government allocated for assistance to the regional governments was only a fraction of that which would have been sufficient to compensate individual recipients for expenses that they would now have to pay, and the regional governments did not have the means to cover the difference.

The result was an explosion of discontent and anger, coming mainly from elderly Russians, which rapidly took on alarming proportions. Protest meetings were held in and around Moscow and St. Petersburg on January 9 and 10 and almost immediately took place in other cities. The first protests were largely spontaneous, organized by elderly citizens themselves, and political parties were caught by surprise by those protests.[40] In the assessment of Susanne Wengle and Michael Rasell, "What was surprising about these events was their grassroots and uncoordinated organization; opposition parties and movements only became involved in the protests at a later stage."[41] Within a few weeks similar protests had broken out in eighty of Russia's eighty-nine regions. The number of Russians who took part in those protest actions cannot be known, but it consisted at least of tens of thousands of people, and probably hundreds of thousands. There is a consensus that the demonstrations of discontent against the replacement of entitlements were the largest protests to take place since Putin had become president, by a wide margin,[42] and the first on a nationwide scale under Putin.[43] In many places the protesters blocked traffic on streets or highways, and in some cities there were physical clashes with bus drivers who refused to allow pensioners to ride for free.[44]

The intensity of the reaction to the replacement of *l'goty* seemed to catch the authorities by surprise. It was reported that, generally, local police forces responded passively to the protests, as they did not attempt to hinder the movements of protesters, even when they blocked streets, or to break up their demonstrations.[45] In his first speech after the protests began, President Putin defended the benefits reform in principle, but criticized the government for its alleged mishandling of the reform and tried to shift the blame to regional and local leaders.[46] He also began to offer concessions to the opponents of the reform, calling for the acceleration of an increase in pensions and the allocation of additional funds to regions for compensation payments.[47] Many regional leaders also offered concessions that were intended to placate the protesters. Officials of the federal government and broadcasts on national television networks alleged that a few "instigators" or "provocateurs" had been behind the demonstrations, and had manipulated the masses in the streets to serve particular political objectives.[48] Though police refrained from using force to disperse demonstrations, after some protests indictments for administrative violations were issued to the organizers of the events.[49] The political elite also mobilized thousands of its followers to march in the streets in support of the monetization of social benefits. By the middle of March 2005, the wave of protest actions had largely subsided.[50]

Even though the spontaneous gatherings of citizens in January and February of 2005 were driven by powerful emotions, they did not leave a substantial organizational legacy.[51] Nonetheless, those protests did leave a distinct imprint in the memory of members of Russian society. Many thousands of ordinary people had risen up to take part in a bold, angry confrontation of the political authorities. The regime had not carried out massive repression of the protesters; most of those who took part in those public rallies returned safely to their homes afterward. In addition, when it was confronted with vehement discontent, the political leadership had backed down, making concessions in an effort to placate those who expressed their rage in public protests. Maria Lipman of the Carnegie Center in Moscow said in January 2005, "The people have got it; you just blockade a highway and the authorities will cave in."[52] Though that clearly was an oversimplification, the adaptation of policies had given partial rewards for those who had poured into the streets to join in demonstrations. The example of the protests against the monetization of social benefits in early 2005 has served as a model for many groups that have resorted to public protests to urge changes in policies on various levels in Russia since that time.

The protest movement of early 2005 concentrated consistently on concrete, specific policy demands, centering on the goal of repeal of the reform of entitlements. During the first protests, *RFE/RL's Newsline* reported that the "chief demand" of retired people taking part in rallies in diverse cities across Russia was "that free public transportation be reinstituted."[53] An article in *Izvestiia* pointed out that the "main demands" of protesters in St. Petersburg were the immediate suspension in that city of the federal law converting *l'goty* into monetary allowances, and the preparation of a legislative initiative to rescind that law throughout Russia.[54] Protesters demanded the restoration of the benefits that they had enjoyed before, especially the free use of local public transportation.[55] In other words, demonstrators "called for a return to the old system of in-kind benefits."[56] At rallies in various cities, prominent slogans urged the government to bring back the benefits that people had received before the reform.[57] The policy-related demands of the protest movement were narrowly focused and reflected a fundamentally defensive orientation. They were conservative in nature, in the sense that they sought a return to a previous state of affairs that was viewed as having been normal, predictable, and acceptable.[58]

PROTEST MOVEMENTS FROM 2005 TO 2011

The importance of public protests obviously has grown in Russia during the last several years, reflecting a trend that has been evident roughly since the beginning of Vladimir Putin's second term as president.[59] Since most Russian citizens in the postcommunist period have been reluctant to take part in activities in the public realm, it may be surprising that a substantial number of citizens have been willing to take part in protests. Yet, after the beginning of 2005, the Russian press reported on many examples of protest activity. In 2010 the Ministry of the Interior of Russia said that the number of protests in that country had grown and the number of people taking part in protests had increased during 2009–2010.[60] That trend was raised to another level when unusually large crowds assembled for protests in Moscow in December 2011 and February 2012 over the December 2011 Duma election and in March and May of 2012 in protest action that was related to the presidential election. Smaller groups took part in demonstrations in the streets of other cities in Russia on the same days. Clearly, protests have become a more common means of expressing the demands of groups of Russian citizens, posing open challenges for the political regime. The mass protests in December 2011 and early 2012 received considerable attention in the Western media, but there is a prehistory that is much less well-known. This section discusses some protest movements in the years leading up to 2011–2012.

Evgeniia Chirikova and her husband own a small business and have two daughters. They live in the city of Khimki, a suburb of Moscow. In 2007 she learned that the federal government planned to build a new highway between Moscow and St. Petersburg, whose route would go through the forest near their town. Ms. Chirikova objected vigorously to that plan, since it would require cutting down large numbers of trees in the Khimki Forest.[61] After sending letters to officials, she took the lead in forming a movement of the defenders of the forest. In August 2008 the Defenders of the Khimki Forest set up a camp in the proposed route for the highway, to protest against the planned removal of trees. When work crews began cutting down trees in July 2010, the events in the Khimki Forest attracted a great deal of attention from the mass media in Moscow. In August a rally was held in Moscow to support the defenders of the forest, with Yury Shevchuk, a famous rock singer, as the main performer. On August 26 the United Russia Party, the majority party in the national parliament, asked President Dmitry Medvedev to suspend the construction of the highway through the Khimki Forest.

Medvedev ordered the suspension of the clearing of the route through the forest, and said that public hearings would be held and experts would be consulted on possible routes for the highway to St. Petersburg. Evgeniia Chirikova thought that the president's statement signaled "a great victory," but her sense of triumph would not last for very long. In December 2010 a commission headed by deputy prime minister Sergei Ivanov published its report, which recommended that the new highway follow the route through the Khimki Forest, as had been planned before August. President Medvedev's office promptly announced that he had approved that recommendation. At the same time Ivanov disclosed that some measures would be taken to mitigate the highway's impact on the environment, such as making the area to be cleared narrower than previously planned, installing sound barriers along the highway through the forest, and planting 500 hectares of new trees to compensate for the trees that would be cut down. Some of those who had supported the cause of the defenders of the forest regarded the government's decision as a significant compromise that included "substantial concessions." The leaders of the movement to block the route through the forest said that they had been betrayed, however, and Ms. Chirikova promised that she would carry on with the struggle to defend Khimki Forest. Soon she began to take part in demonstrations calling for the removal of the political leadership of Russia, including Medvedev and Prime Minister Vladimir Putin.

Another movement that engaged in protests against a decision by government officials came into existence in Russia's second largest city, St. Petersburg. Gazprom, Russia's giant natural gas monopoly, planned to build a new office center in that city, to be called the Okhta Center, with a tower over 400 meters high. The government of the city had relaxed the regulation that had been in effect for many years that had restricted the height of buildings to no more than forty meters, in order to allow the construction of Gazprom's skyscraper. Some residents of the city were angered by that change, since they believed that the new tower would have a negative effect on the architectural character of that historic city. They used public protests, among other means, to call for a reversal of the decision by the government of St. Petersburg. In May 2010 Medvedev's office sent a message to the governor of St. Petersburg, Valentina Matvienko, urging that she consider the recommendation by UNESCO's World Heritage Committee that all work on the project be suspended. In December 2010 the governor disclosed that Gazprom's tower would not be built in the location that had been selected earlier. Later Gazprom announced that its new office complex would be erected in another location, much farther from the center of St. Petersburg. Even though the new plan called for the tower to be even taller—500 meters—and there were complaints about that feature, there was a feeling that the opposition to the Okhta Center had won a victory.

In 2009 groups of owners of automobiles in Russia began to express their indignation about the large number of cars of government officials and business executives that were equipped with blue lights (*migalki*) on the roof, allowing their drivers blatantly to violate the laws of the road and bypass vehicles that were moving slowly or stuck in traffic jams. The members of the Blue Buckets movement taped plastic blue buckets, designed as toys for children, to the roofs of their cars, in protest against the use of privileges of those whose cars had genuine *migalki*. Protests by drivers in that movement took the form of processions of cars with blue buckets, moving slowly on the major streets of Moscow and other cities. The police usually have not greatly impeded such demonstrations, and when penalties have been imposed on any of the drivers in such protests, only small fines have been involved. A poll in Moscow in 2010 showed that 68 percent of those surveyed approved of the blue bucket demonstrations. In May 2012 Vladimir Putin as president of Russia signed an order sharply reducing the number of officials' cars that are allowed to have blue lights.[62]

Many groups in Russia have used protest tactics since the anti-monetization movement arose in 2005. The protests that have been mentioned here are only a few of those that have been covered in the national press in Russia since 2005, and those are probably only a small fraction of many others that have taken place in various localities around the country. I suggest that the recent protest movements that have been most successful in winning support from their potential base in a social group, or from the majority of the members of Russian society as a whole, have been influenced by the example of the protest movement of early 2005.[63] When citizens in Russia have been moved to protest against a decision, it has been evident time and time again that they usually have objected to a change that threatened to disturb a situation that previously had seemed to be stable and acceptable. In each case the demands of the protesters with respect to government policies have been concrete and specific, and in each case the orientation of the protest movement has been essentially defensive, in the sense that the movement sought to return to a state of affairs that had existed before a change was initiated and to restore benefits that people had assumed they enjoyed as a matter of right.

Thus, I conclude that the anti-monetization movement of 2005 left a legacy that has influenced many groups that have carried out protests in Russia in recent years. Typically, such groups have not called for the radical transformation of Russian political institutions; instead, they have sought to defend features of their existence that they have regarded as normal. We should be aware, however, that some other movements that have engaged in public protests in Russia in recent years have supported goals that would entail more fundamental changes in their country's political system in accordance with liberal democratic values. Yet experts on Russian society and politics point out that the organizations that have carried out demonstrations on behalf of broad, abstract political principles, such as freedom of speech or the right to assemble, have a very narrow base of support among the people of Russia. Denis Volkov of the Levada Center for the study of public opinion has said that demonstrations by those organizations "do not come into the field of view of the basic mass of the population."[64] Even though Maria Lipman has been a persistent critic of the Putin leadership, she acknowledges that in Russia "today there is a shortage of public demand" for such principles as freedom of the press and the accountability of government, and she argues that the majority in the country "does not care much about human rights violations or compromised democratic procedures."[65] The organizations that have not accepted the general outlines of the master frame of protest movements that emerged from the anti-monetization movement of early 2005 have not really sought a broad base of support within Russian society.[66]

In contrast, the groups engaging in protests that have inspired support from wide circles of the public have focused on issues that are relevant to the everyday lives of most people, and usually are grounded in the self-interest of average citizens. Denis Volkov stresses that for ordinary Russians it is important to feel that "someone is ready to be occupied with their problems."[67] Former ambassador James Collins agrees that in Russia in recent years, "successful activists have seized on local issues that have affected people personally and left them feeling that government has exceeded the bounds of decency."[68] The latest annual report of Russia's Public Chamber affirms that the mass inclusion of citizens in protests "is observed when restrictions or infringements of rights directly touch on their lives or interests."[69] There is reason to believe that the frame that emerged during the anti-monetization protests has resonated very well with the culture of Russian society. As we have seen, most Russians distrust the public sphere, which includes not only the state but also social organizations, and they are profoundly skeptical about the possibility of transforming the basic features of the operation of the political system of their country. Most of them do not believe that any form of popular participation in politics could produce fundamental improvement in the working of political institutions. Though they see themselves as powerless to bring changes in the larger public sphere, they have developed strategies of coping with the challenges of everyday life, which include reliance on informal networks of family members and friends. When the authorities intervene in a way that threatens the effectiveness of citizens' strategies for survival, the average people are likely to feel that an informal social contract has been violated. When that happens, as Maria Lipman and Nikolai Petrov have phrased it, "an invasion of 'the citizens' space' is perceived as a violation of a secret treaty of nonaggression" between the state and society.[70] The examples of many protest movements show that Russians can be moved into action when the state takes actions that damage their interests, and that they are likely to sympathize with fellow citizens of their country who try to defend themselves against abuse. We may conclude that the themes of the anti-monetization protests of 2005 resonated strongly with the values and attitudes of most Russians, which helps to explain why the frame that was shaped by those protests has left a strong impression on the outlook of many protest movements that have followed.

THE LATEST WAVE OF PROTESTS, FROM DECEMBER 2011 TO MAY 2012

In December 2011 protests in Russia rose to a new level of magnitude, in terms of the number of people taking part in them, and perhaps in terms of their political impact. Certainly they presented more serious challenges to the national political regime than any previous protests since Vladimir Putin had first become president of Russia. The demonstrations that began after the parliamentary elections of December 4, 2011, which attracted several thousand participants, focused on the charge of election fraud and demanded new elections.[71] What was more surprising was that on December 10, tens of thousands took part in a demonstration in favor of "honest elections" (*chestnye vybory*) on Bolotnaia Square, which is near the center of Moscow and not far from the Kremlin.[72] The consensus of the press was that the crowd that assembled on December 10 was the largest that had attended any protest in Russia since the early 1990s. Even larger crowds gathered for protest rallies in the capital on behalf of the same cause on December 24, 2011, and February 4, 2012.[73] For years, each rally protesting against infractions of democratic political principles drew a small number of people, often fewer than fifty, and at best around two hundred. Thus it was startling that from 40,000 to 80,000 people attended each of those three protests in Moscow in favor of fair elections during the winter of 2011–2012, with smaller numbers of people taking part in protests that were held by that movement in other cities across Russia on the same days. After the presidential election was held in early March 2012, the number of people taking part in demonstrations decreased greatly, and some commentators thought that the movement for fair elections was running out of steam, until a large crowd came together in Moscow again for a protest on May 6, 2012, on the eve of Putin's inauguration.[74] Events on that day and on the days that have followed have shown that the protests have not gone away, and that they can change form in unexpected ways.

In some ways the themes of the new wave of protests were similar to those of the protests that had concentrated on social and economic issues from 2005 to 2011. The protesters' characterization of themselves as victims of illegitimate treatment by leaders in government, their voicing of anger and contempt toward key leaders in positions of authority, their accusation of a betrayal of trust, and the demand that responsible officials (such as the head of the federal election commission and Vladimir Putin) leave office closely resembled the major themes in the frames of movements that had engaged in protests over policy issues in Russia since the time of the anti-monetization protests of 2005. What then was new? The answer is that the demonstrations that began in December 2011 brought the same themes to bear on an issue in the political realm—the question of fairness in democratic elections—even though that issue did not have a direct impact on the delivery of social benefits, the protection of a forest, the location of a skyscraper, the behavior of the drivers of the vehicles of the elite, or other matters that have an obvious effect on people's daily lives. Now the words and actions of a large number of people communicated that they regarded fraud in elections as an unacceptable violation of an unwritten contract between the political regime and the people.

It was evident that the "fair elections" movement gave voice to the frustration that a feeling of powerlessness had generated among a substantial segment of the population of Russia. Many of those who took part in protests said that they had been reminded of their utter lack of control over the future of their country in September 2011 when it was announced that Vladimir Putin would run for president in 2012, on the basis of an arrangement that had been made with Dmitry Medvedev. In an instant it was clear that the crucial decision about the selection of a president had already been made, and might have been made several years earlier. Since everyone was aware that if Putin would be the candidate of the United Russia Party, which seemed quite certain, it could be taken for granted that Putin would serve as president until 2018, and it was possible that he might stay in that post until 2024. So even before the parliamentary elections were held, a substantial number of citizens of Russia felt that they had been treated with implicit contempt. During the parliamentary election in early December 2011 many people believed that irrefutable evidence of fraud had been shown, in large part through the use of digital cameras and smartphones at polling places, furnishing visual images that were disseminated very rapidly through the Internet. Many Russians said that the impact of those images intensified their feeling that they had been treated with blatant disrespect. Though fraud in elections was not new, a critical mass of resentment had gathered enough force to send tens of thousands of Russians into the streets to express their anger over the perceived violation of their sense of dignity.

It was clear that those who took part in the protests in favor of honest elections had certain characteristics. Surveys reported in the Russian press showed that a majority of the protesters were young adults who had higher education, lived in large cities, and worked as professionals (though older people also were present in the protest rallies).[75] Since December 2011 there has been much discussion in the Russian media about the mood and the wishes of the "angry urbanites" (*rasserzhennye gorozhane*). Most of the participants in the large-scale protests also use the Internet, which gives them access to reporting of news that does not come from the national television networks, which are controlled by the government and are the main source of news for most Russians. Many of the protesters also are plugged into social media such as Facebook, VKontatke, and Twitter, which makes it possible to inform large numbers of people almost instantaneously about events that have just been planned, and makes it easier to assemble large crowds for protests.[76] The stereotype of the participants in the new wave of protests, which of course is oversimplified, is that they belong to the iPhone and Facebook movement. As that information implies, another large segment of the population of Russia is quite different in terms of its sources of information and its attitudes, and the base of support for Putin is found mainly in that part of the people, which consists particularly of those with lower levels of education and those who live outside the largest cities in the country.

CONCLUSION

It is true that the new wave of protests in Russia that began in December 2011 was an immediate response to violations of the law in the most recent parliamentary elections. However, the announcement of Putin's candidacy in September 2011 and the Duma election in December 2011 were only the precipitants of the explosion of discontent that followed. The manipulation and falsification of elections were nothing new; in fact, those techniques had been used in Russia on a regular basis since the 1990s. Why was it suddenly unacceptable to many citizens that they had no say on the question of who would govern them? The answer to that question must be found in conditions that had changed over time in Russian society. We should recall that at the end of the 1990s, when Boris Yeltsin's term as president was nearing an end, civil society in Russia was weak, disappointing the hopes of some observers. Earlier in this chapter we learned that one of the main reasons for the weakness of organizations in civil society at that time was the desperate condition of Russia's economy during the 1990s. When most people in that country found themselves on the verge of poverty if not actually in it, very few of them had the capacity to offer financial support for organizations that were dedicated to goals that would benefit groups of citizens.

We should be aware, however, that economic conditions in Russia have changed greatly since the end of the 1990s, when Vladimir Putin was rising to ascendancy in the county's political system. There was a high rate of economic growth in Russia from 1999 to 2008, and by 2010 into 2011 the economy seemed to recover from the financial meltdown of 2008–2009. Thus, since 2000 the incomes of most Russians have risen dramatically,[77] and the proportion of the population with incomes above the subsistence level has increased. A growing number of Russians no longer feel themselves to be in a struggle for economic survival. Among those who have higher levels of education and are fairly comfortable economically (whom the newspaper *Moskovskie novosti* has called the "new intelligentsia"), some not only are able to give modest financial support to social organizations, but also show changed attitudes, including greater confidence, independence, and assertiveness. Many citizens in that segment of Russian society (who are still a minority but are growing) are ready to place higher demands on the political system, and are willing to be more confrontational if their demands are not satisfied, as has been reflected by the "honest elections" movement and a number of other movements that have carried out protests.

We should realize, though, that the growth in the number of groups engaging in protests in Russia in recent years should not be viewed simply as the result of changes in economic conditions and social structure. The recent large-scale protests in Russia also should be seen as the product of a pattern of learned behavior. Since 2005, each group that has carried out protests has been able to draw on the experience of other groups that have employed similar tactics, and in turn it has provided another example for groups that have come later. In most of those cases, people united on behalf of a common cause and became willing to confront political authority only when they were forced to break out of a passive stance because their interests were directly threatened. As we have seen, most protests in Russia from 2005 to the present have expressed defensive reactions to incursions by those in power. It may be true that in a society in which distrust of the public sphere is pervasive, one of the best ways to motivate people to cooperate in the pursuit of common interests is to arouse them to defend themselves from an immediate threat. Yet Russian newspapers now are printing more stories about charitable organizations, which suggests that a growing number of Russian citizens can be persuaded to support such organizations, implying an increase in the capacity to combine with others in efforts to assist people who are in need. Some of the leaders of charitable organizations have joined the "fair elections" movement, while others have remained politically neutral, and still others endorsed Putin's latest candidacy for president. That brings up the point that social activism in Russia is advancing in various ways at the same time, though perhaps not at the same rate in all those forms.

The current protests calling for fair elections seem to express the attitudes of a minority of Russians. For that minority to win broader support, it needs to appeal to groups that are skeptical about the possibility of fundamental political change. We might suggest that in any society culture usually changes more slowly than economic conditions, and major elements of culture are carried over from one period of history to another. Also, cultural change is likely to move faster among some groups in the population than others. In Russia today those who are most dissatisfied with the Putin regime have not yet linked up with the majority of the Russian people. We should recall that one feature of the old intelligentsia of tsarist Russia was its lack of interest in winning support from the *narod*, the less educated mass of the population. That tendency of the intelligentsia carried over into the Soviet period and beyond.[78] If there is any chance that the protests of the "new intelligentsia" can strike a responsive chord among other groups that make up a majority of the people of Russia, the protesters of the intelligentsia probably would have to make a common cause on behalf of goals that are important in the lives of citizens in those groups. Some commentators have argued that if the energy of the larger demonstrations of the past winter is to be sustained, and if it is to have a lasting political impact, it will have to support efforts to address specific, local problems that are important in people's everyday lives.[79] Undoubtedly those commentators know that in recent decades, Russians of a wide variety of groups in society, including retired people, factory workers, residents of small towns, and young urban professionals, have used protests to try to defend their interests. If the activists from the recent large-scale protests can identify issues that are important in the eyes of the majority of their fellow citizens, that will be an indication of the degree of change in the outlook of the intelligentsia. We may be confident that the political and economic elites of Russia are so determined to defend their privileges and so arrogant in their disdain for the majority of citizens that many such issues will arise.

SUGGESTED READINGS

Cook, Linda J., and Elena Vinogradova. "NGOs and Policy-Making in Russia's Regions." *Problems of Post-Communism* 53, no. 5 (2006): 28–41.

Evans, Alfred B., Jr., Laura A. Henry, and Lisa McIntosh Sundstrom, eds. *Russian Civil Society: A Critical Assessment.* Armonk, N.Y.: M. E. Sharpe, 2006.

Henderson, Sarah L. "Civil Society in Russia: State-Society Relations in the Post-Yeltsin Era." *Problems of Post-Communism* 58, no. 3 (2011): 11–27.

Henry, Laura A. *Red to Green: Environmental Activism in Post-Soviet Russia.* Ithaca, N.Y.: Cornell University Press, 2010.

Johnson, Janet Elise. *Gender Violence in Russia: The Politics of Feminist Intervention.* Bloomington: Indiana University Press, 2009.

Sperling, Valerie. *Organizing Women in Contemporary Russia: Engendering Transition.* Cambridge: Cambridge University Press, 1999.

Sundstrom, Lisa McIntosh. *Funding Civil Society: Foreign Assistance and NGO Development in Russia.* Stanford, Calif.: Stanford University Press, 2006.

NOTES

1. Larry Diamond, *Developing Democracy* (Baltimore: Johns Hopkins University Press, 1999), 221.

2. Marcia A. Weigle, *Russia's Liberal Project* (University Park: Pennsylvania State University Press, 2000), 28, includes those elements explicitly in her definition of civil society.

3. Laura A. Henry and Lisa McIntosh Sundstrom, "Introduction," in *Russian Civil Society: A Critical Assessment*, ed. Alfred B. Evans Jr., Laura A. Henry, and Lisa McIntosh Sundstrom (Armonk, N.Y.: M. E. Sharpe, 2006), 4.

4. Alfred B. Evans Jr., "Civil Society in the Soviet Union?" in *Russian Civil Society: A Critical Assessment*, ed. Alfred B. Evans Jr., Laura A. Henry, and Lisa McIntosh Sundstrom (Armonk, N.Y.: M. E. Sharpe, 2006), 30.

5. Evans, "Civil Society?" 42.

6. Walter D. Connor, *Socialism's Dilemmas: State and Society in the Soviet Bloc* (New York: Columbia University Press, 1988), 45. See also Evans, "Civil Society in the Soviet Union?" 43.

7. Hedrick Smith, *The Russians* (New York: Ballantine Books, 1976), 8.

8. Alena V. Ledeneva, *Russia's Economy of Favours: Blat, Networking, and Informal Exchange* (Cambridge, UK: Cambridge University Press, 1998).

9. Ledeneva, *Russia's Economy of Favours*, 36.

10. Ledeneva, *Russia's Economy of Favours*, 46.

11. Ledeneva, *Russia's Economy of Favours*, 85–87, 103.

12. Evans, "Civil Society," 45.

13. Evans, "Civil Society," 45.

14. Alfred B. Evans Jr., "Recent Assessments of Social Organizations in Russia," *Demokratizatsiya* 10, no. 3 (2002): 322–42.

15. Ken Jowitt, *New World Disorder: The Leninist Extinction* (Berkeley: University of California Press, 1992), 287. Jowitt believes that his generalization applies to all countries that have been under "Leninist," or communist, rule.

16. Jowitt, *New World Disorder*, 293.

17. The annual report of Russia's Public Chamber for 2011 confirms that Russians typically see the "circle of trust" as extending only to family members and close friends. Obshchestvennaia Palata Rossiiskoi Federatsii, *Doklad o sostoianii grazhdanskogo obshchestva v Rossiiskoi Federatsii za 2011 god* (Moscow: Obshchestvennaia Palata Rossiiskoi Federatsii, 2012), 9.

18. Weigle, *Russia's Liberal Project*, 49.

19. Marc Morjé Howard, *The Weakness of Civil Society in Post-Communist Europe* (Cambridge: Cambridge University Press, 2003), 26.

20. Howard, *The Weakness of Civil Society*, 63.

21. Sarah L. Henderson, "Civil Society in Russia: State-Society Relations in the Post-Yeltsin Era," *Problems of Post-Communism* 58, no. 3 (2011): 16. Linda J. Cook and Elena Vinogradova, "NGOs and Social Policy-Making in Russia's Regions," *Problems of Post-Communism* 53, no. 5 (2006), 38, argue, "The limits of civil, legal, and political culture in Russia constitute a deeper reason for the relatively poor development of NGOs and participatory politics."

22. Evans, "Recent Assessments."

23. Valerie Sperling, *Organizing Women in Contemporary Russia: Engendering Transition* (Cambridge: Cambridge University Press, 1999), 46, 171–72.

24. Even as recently as early 2012, the annual report of Russia's Public Chamber said that NGOs in Russia "for the most part are extremely weak economically and often are barely surviving." Obshchestvennaia Palata, *Doklad o sostoianii grazhdanskogo obshchestva*, 18.

25. Sarah L. Henderson, *Building Democracy in Contemporary Russia: Western Support for Grassroots Organizations* (Ithaca, NY: Cornell University Press, 2003), 154–55, 165; Lisa McIntosh Sundstrom, *Funding Civil Society: Foreign Assistance and NGO Development in Russia* (Stanford, Calif.: Stanford University Press, 2006), 99–101; Jo Crotty, "Making a Difference? NGOs and Civil Society Development in Russia," *Europe-Asia Studies* 61, no. 1 (2009): 91.

26. Alfred B. Evans Jr., "Putin's Design for Civil Society," in *Russian Civil Society: A Critical Assessment*, ed. Alfred B. Evans Jr., Laura A. Henry, and Lisa McIntosh Sundstrom (Armonk, N.Y.: M. E. Sharpe, 2006), 149.

27. Evans, "Putin's Design," 149; Henderson, "Civil Society in Russia," 18.

28. Evans, "Putin's Design," 149.

29. Henderson, "Civil Society in Russia," 21; Debra Javeline and Sarah Lindemann-Komarova, "A Balanced Assessment of Russian Civil Society," *Journal of International Affairs* 63, no. 2 (2010): 173–75.

30. The latest annual report from Russia's Public Chamber characterizes the process of registration of social organizations as "complicated and long." Obshchestvennaia Palata, *Doklad o sostoianii grazhdanskogo obshchestva*, 15.

31. Henderson, "Civil Society in Russia," 20; Lindemann and Komarova, "A Balanced Assessment," 176–80. We also should point out that since the 1990s funding for grants to NGOs in Russia from Western governments and foundations has decreased substantially, not because of actions of the government of Russia, but because of changes in the priorities of the funding agencies and foundations.

32. Julie Hemment, "Soviet-Style Liberalism? *Nashi*, Youth Voluntarism, and the Restructuring of Social Welfare in Russia," *Problems of Post-Communism* 56, no. 6 (2009): 36–50.

33. Alfred B. Evans Jr., "The First Steps of Russia's Public Chamber: Representation or Coordination," *Demokratizatsiya* 16, no. 4 (2008): 345–62; James Richter, "Putin and the Public Chamber," *Post-Soviet Affairs* 25, no. 1 (2009): 39–65. Public chambers also have been established in most regions of Russia and in some cities.

34. Evans, "Putin's Design," 151.

35. Debra Javeline, *Protest and the Politics of Blame: The Russian Response to Unpaid Wages* (Ann Arbor: University of Michigan Press, 2003), 2, 7, 8, 50; Linda J. Cook, *Postcommunist Welfare States: Reform Politics in Russia and Eastern Europe* (Ithaca, N.Y.: Cornell University Press, 2007), 71.

36. Graeme B. Robertson, *The Politics of Protest in Hybrid Regimes: Managing Dissent in Post-Communist Russia* (Cambridge: Cambridge University Press, 2011), 41.

37. Robertson, *The Politics of Protest*, 128, 148.

38. Cook, *Postcommunist Welfare States*, 179; Susanne Wengle and Michael Rasell, "The Monetization of *L'goty*: Changing Patterns of Welfare Politics and Provision in Russia," *Europe-Asia Studies* 60, no. 5 (2008): 740.

39. Cook, *Postcommunist Welfare States*, 179; Wengle and Rasell, "The Monetization of *L'goty*," 740.

40. Robertson, *The Politics of Protest*, 180.

41. Wengle and Rasell, "The Monetization," 745. See also Cook, *Postcommunist Welfare States*, 181.

42. *RFE/RL Report*, "Russians Continue to Protest Social Reforms," January 16, 2005.

43. Cook, *Postcommunist Welfare States*, 181.

44. Wengle and Rasell, "The Monetization," 745.

45. Vladimir Aleksandrov, Ol'ga Gorbunova, and Viktor Troianovskii, "Glas naroda: Vresh', l'gota, ne uidesh'!" *Gazeta*, January 31, 2005.

46. Steven Lee Myers, "After Wide Protests, Putin Softens on His Policy of Cutting Benefits," *New York Times*, January 18, 2005.

47. Cook, *Postcommunist Welfare States*, 182; Wengle and Rasell, "The Monetization," 746.

48. Robertson, *The Politics of Protest*, 179.

49. Robertson, *The Politics of Protest*, 179.

50. Ol'ga Nikitina, "Playing the Blame Game: Reforms Leave Officials and the Public Looking for a Scapegoat," *Russia Profile*, March 28, 2005.

51. That is, they did not produce many new organizations that continued to exist after the first few months of 2005. Of course, a number of organizations that had already existed and that had allied themselves with the protesters in early 2005, including political parties, labor unions, and other social organizations, survived after that time.

52. Fred Weir, "What Russia's Pensioners Want—and How They're Starting to Get It," *Christian Science Monitor*, January 21, 2005.

53. *RFE/RL, Newsline*, January 14, 2005.

54. Elena Rotkevich, "Governor Matvienko 'Has Received Many Thanks from Pensioners.'" *Izvestiia*, January 18, 2005, in *Current Digest of the Post-Soviet Press* 57, no. 3 (February 16, 2005).

55. Larisa Nikitina, Aleksandr Klimovich, Nikita Korablev, and Ekaterina Gordeeva, "It's their Last Stand," *Vremia novostei*, January 24, 2005, in *Current Digest of the Post-Soviet Press* 57, no. 4 (February 23, 2005).

56. Global Newswire, "Russia: Benefits Reform Protests Continue, Grow in Scale," January 26, 2005.

57. Oksana Yablokova, "Pensioners' Protests Spreading," *Moscow Times*, January 13, 2005; Andrei Bondarenko and Sergei Migalin, "Pensioners Have Lost Faith in Benevolent Government," *Nezavisimaia gazeta*, February 1, 2005, in *Current Digest of the Post-Soviet Press* 57, no. 5 (March 2, 2005).

58. Compare with Robertson's observations in *The Politics of Protest*, 42, 59, 50, concerning the demands of protests in Russia in the late 1990s. That implies a great deal of continuity between the protests of the Yeltsin years and those of 2005, which suggests that to some extent the frame created by protests of early 2005 did draw on examples from previous years.

59. Robertson, *The Politics of Protest*, 186; Alfred B. Evans Jr., "Protest and Civil Society in Russia: The Struggle for Khimki Forest," *Communist and Post-Communist Studies* 45, no. 3 (2012).

60. Paul Goble, "Window on Eurasia: Russian Protests, Sanctioned and Not, Increase Dramatically in 2010, Interior Ministry Says," *Johnson's Russia List*, no. 106 (June 1, 2010).

61. Evans, "What Protests Can Tell Us." That article gives a more extensive list of sources for the information in this part of this chapter.

62. Ivan Pirogov, "'Migalki' poshli na sokrashchenie," *Kommersant*, May 19, 2012; Iuliia Kotova, "Putin utverdil spisok mashin s 'migalkami,'" *Vedomosti*, May 19, 2011. The Federation of Automobilists of Russia (FAR) also, and perhaps equally, played a role in agitating against the *migalki*.

63. Of course, there are also other measures of the success of a movement, in addition to winning popular support. For instance, another measure that most movement organizations with political goals consider important is bringing changes in a government's policies. Whether a movement is successful in reaching that goal will depend on a number of factors, including the nature of the issue that is involved and the interests that have a stake in that issue.

64. Denis Volkov, "Golos 'molchalivogo bol'shinstva,'" *Gazeta.ru*, October 7, 2010.

65. Maria Lipman, "Freedom of Expression without Freedom of the Press," *Journal of International Affairs* 53, no. 2 (2010): 163–64.

66. Jason M. K. Lyall, "Pocket Protests: Rhetorical Coercion and the Micropolitics of Collective Action in Semiauthoritarian Regimes," *World Politics* 58, no. 3 (2006), describes a movement in Russia whose organizational culture "dictates the use of tactics and slogans that have little mass appeal (379)," and whose "patterns of protest reinforce group solidarity but do not appeal to a broader audience" (400).

67. Elina Bilevskaia and Ivan Rodin, "Protestnye nastroeniia ne rastut," *Nezavisimaia gazeta*, September 27, 2010.

68. Kathy Lally, "Trying to Save a Forest, and Change Russia," *Washington Post*, October 17, 2010.

69. Obshchestvennaia Palata, *Doklad o sostoianii grazhdanskogo obshchestva*, 62.

70. Maria Lipman and Nikolai Petrov, "Obshchestvo i grazhdane v 2008–2010 gg," *Moskovskii Tsentr Karnegii, Rabochie Materialy*, no. 3 (2010): 5. They immediately added: "In distinction from that, the expansion of power in the political space, whether on the federal or regional level, does not arouse popular resistance, since the majority of citizens do not perceive that space as 'their own.'"

71. Alexander Bratersky, "50,000 Protest Duma Election Results," *Moscow Times*, December 6, 2011; Fred Weir, "Chanting 'Russia without Putin,' Flash Mobs Roil Moscow," *Christian Science Monitor*, December 7, 2011; Kseniia Zav'ialova, "Ne zabyli vkiuchit' televizor," *Kommersant*, December 10, 2011.

72. Ellen Barry, "Rally Defying Putin's Party Draws Tens of Thousands," *New York Times*, December 10, 2011; Kseniia Zav'ialova, "Dukh perepostmodernizma," *Kommersant*, December 10, 2011.

73. For large crowds, the estimates of the number of participants have differed every time, with the police estimating the number as much smaller than that stated by those who organized the event. "Tens of Thousands Gather in Fresh Russia Vote Protest," *Moscow News*, December 24, 2011; Fred Weir, "Huge Protest Demanding Fair Russian Election Hits Moscow," *Christian Science Monitor*, December 24, 2011;

Ellen Barry, "Young and Connected, 'Office Plankton' Protesters Surprise Russia," *New York Times*, December 24, 2011; Andrei Kozenko, "Pokhody vykhodnovo dnia," *Kommersant*, February 4, 2012; Dmitrii Vinogradov, "Poklonnaia prevzoshla Bolotnuiu na 18 tysiach chelovek," *Moskovskie novosti*, February 4, 2012; Eileen Barry and Andrew E. Kramer, "Protesters Throng Frozen Moscow in Anti-Putin March," *New York Times*, February 4, 2012. Weir and Barry both estimated the crowd on December 24 as numbering 50,000 or more. Barry and Kramer said that the crowd on February 4 was larger than that on December 24, and that statement fits the consensus of journalists reporting on the events.

74. Kseniia Zav'ialova, "'Marsh millionov' zakonchilsia massovoi drakoi i zader-zhaniiami," *Kommersant*, February 6, 2012; Ezekiel Pfeifer, Jonathan Earle, and Rachel Nielsen, "On Eve of Inauguration, Mass Protest Ends in Violence," *Moscow Times*, May 7, 212.

75. Alina Lozina, "Yuppies Comprise Core of Election-Rights Protesters," *Moscow News*, December 27, 2011; Iuliia Khomchenko, "Zrelyi protest," *Moskovskie novosti*, December 27, 2011; *Novaia gazeta*, "Kto vyshel na prospekt Sakharova 24 Deka-bria?" December 28, 2011; Viacheslav Riabykh, "Portret gospodina Demonstranta," *Novye Izvestiia*, December 28, 2011; Boris Dubin, "Iakimanka i Bolotnaia 2.0. Teper' my znaem, kto vse eti liudi!" *Novaia gazeta*, February 9, 2012.

76. Roland Oliphant, "Social Networks Strained at Rallies," *Moscow Times*, December 28, 2011; Georgii Il'ichev, "Dekabristy-2011. Sotiologi izmerili kaches-tvo protestnogo dvizheniia," *Novaia gazeta*, December 28, 2011.

77. From 2000 to 2009 the median income of Russians rose from under 3,000 rubles per month to about 12,000 rubles per month (in current rubles). During the same period, the mean personal income increased even more. Thomas F. Reming-ton, "The Russian Middle Class as Policy Objective," *Post-Soviet Affairs* 27, no. 2 (2011): 102–3.

78. Sarah E. Mendelson and Theodore P. Gerber, "Activist Culture and Transna-tional Diffusion: Social Marketing and Human Rights Groups in Russia," *Post-Soviet Affairs* 23, no. 1 (2007): 56–58.

79. Elena Borovskaia and Aleksandr Gazov, "Deep-Sixing of Protests Turns Out to Have Been Premature," *Osobaia bukva*, April 8, 2012, *Johnson's Russia List*, no. 66 (April 10, 2012); Viktoriia Musvik, "Pravoshchitnaia deiatel'nost' protivorechit interesam srosshikhsia biznesa i vlasti," *Moskovskie novosti*, April 11, 2012; Vera Moslakova, "They Could and They Did," *Novye izvestiia*, April 19, 2012, *Johnson's Russia List*, no. 72 (April 19, 2012). The idea that in the field of social policy it might be possible to create "the basis for the future development of civil society, of links between an activist 'core' and the mass of the population," was suggested several years ago by Cook and Vinogradova, in "NGOs and Social Policy-Making in Russia's Regions," 37.

6

The Media and Political Developments

Maria Lipman

International organizations such as Freedom House or Reporters Without Borders have invariably rated freedom of the press in Putin's Russia as very low. Based on elaborate criteria, the assessments made by these internationally recognized organizations provide a general idea of the Russian media environment, in which media outlets operate in an essentially authoritarian polity and journalists face serious constraints.[1] But Russia's score on the Freedom of the Press Index (by Freedom House), moving from seventy-fifth in 2007 to eightieth in 2012, does not fully reflect the media environment in Russia.[2] While Russia's political system is based on tight controls and on constraining political and civil rights, the Russian media has become more vibrant in the past two or three years.

This chapter focuses on media outlets operating in, or broadcasting from, Moscow. Moscow is the center of Russia in more ways than most national capitals: it is a powerful magnet for anyone with ambition, whether it be making money, a career in government or management, academic or artistic pursuits, in literature, or in fashion. Media is no exception.[3] In recent years the media has had an impact—if not on the government policies directly, then at least on the public mindset; it has helped shape public opinion and abetted civic organization. It may be argued that the nongovernment media—greatly amplified by the wide penetration of the Internet and the spread of social networks—has contributed to the reemergence of a public realm that had been suppressed during the earlier years of Putin's governance.

PUBLIC/PRIVATE SPHERES IN
POSTCOMMUNIST RUSSIA

After the collapse of Soviet communism and the establishment of an independent Russian state, President Boris Yeltsin's reforms created new opportunities for independent political, social, and economic activity. The new Russian media were developing professionally and commercially, guided by Western editorial standards of independence, objectivity, and accuracy as well as business factors, such as ownership, competition, and advertising revenues. As they remember the early days of the post-Soviet media, their founders and top editors commonly mention the aspiration to inculcate Western media standards on Russian soil.[4] In the early stages, however, commercial viability was often of lesser concern than the principles of editorial freedom or the emulation of the best Western editorial models. Insufficient concern about solid business models made it much harder for the media to sustain their independence in the early postcommunist period.[5] *Kommersant*, originally a weekly paper, was the only outlet that from the start relied on commercial viability as a basis of editorial independence.[6]

The 1990s witnessed a largely unconstrained press, though the causes of this freedom were many. During the political turmoil of the last years of the Soviet Union, Yeltsin evolved as a fierce anticommunist, and this turned him into a proponent of an independent press. He did not intervene to mute criticism of himself or the exposure of abuse of authority by government. Very early in his tenure, Yeltsin's government succeeded in passing a very progressive law on mass media.[7] In addition, during the years leading up to the 1996 presidential campaign, Yeltsin and the press were allies against a common threat—a comeback by the Communist Party.[8] But the Yeltsin government was also weak. Fighting many political and economic battles simultaneously, the Russian state simply did not have the capacity to control the media.

THE RISE OF PRIVATELY OWNED MEDIA

Market reforms initially helped to stimulate the growth of media outlets not controlled by the government, including, first and foremost, television.[9] NTV, the first private television network, was started in 1993 by one of Russia's first-generation business tycoons, Vladimir Gusinsky.[10] NTV emerged as a source of independent information that reached beyond Moscow.[11] NTV quickly earned its credentials as a serious news organization when it provided critical coverage of the first Chechen war (1994–1996). This coverage shaped the Russian public opinion of the war in much the same way that the coverage of the Vietnam War shaped opinions of the U.S. audience.

Every day, the horrible scenes from Chechnya appeared on television screens in Russian homes and generated broad antiwar sentiments. In the end, Yeltsin was forced to initiate a peace process with Chechnya; otherwise, he had no chance for reelection in 1996. NTV also produced the puppet show *Kukly*, a political satire that spared no one. Yeltsin's chief of staff called NTV managers to ask them to stop *Kukly*, but they would not listen. NTV quickly achieved a new level of post-Soviet professionalism, quality, and style that the rival state channels Ostankino and RTR lacked. Evgeny Kiselev, NTV's cofounder and host of *Itogi*, a Sunday-night wrap-up show on politics, became a national celebrity.

Before starting NTV, Gusinsky already had launched his own daily newspaper, *Segodnia* (Today). He also bought a stake in a popular radio station, *Ekho Moskvy*, and in 1995 founded a weekly magazine, *Itogi*, published in partnership with *Newsweek*, making his company, Media-Most, a media powerhouse. Other financial tycoons followed Gusinsky, believing that the media, especially television, were an important political tool.[12] Through an inside deal arranged by the Kremlin, Boris Berezovsky acquired part ownership and de facto control of Ostankino, Russia's largest television network, which was renamed ORT (*Obshchestvennoe Rossiiskoe Televidenie*, Russian Public Television).[13] Since there was no law on public television, this "public" status hardly meant anything, except the emergence of another powerful media tycoon and another national television asset under private control. Berezovsky also obtained a major stake in a smaller channel, TV-6. Russia's small group of financial houses and oil and gas companies also gobbled up most of the Moscow-based, mainstream daily newspapers.[14]

Adherence to the high principles professed by editors and journalists was problematic in the Russian media environment of the 1990s. Russia's media tycoons who emerged during Yeltsin's presidency were not consistent advocates of a free and independent press. Rather, they were profit seekers with questionable business ethics and controversial political agendas. As a result, media outlets were not unbiased, and the new tycoons would use them to pursue their own political and business goals. Yet the very fact that they were owned or controlled by nonstate actors endowed those post-Soviet media with immense importance: after the decades of tight ideological control by the state they could offer alternative coverage, not guided by the interests of the government. Besides, tycoons were permanently engaged in fierce rivalry because their interests were different. So if the media environment of the 1990s did not meet high democratic and ethical principles, at least it ensured pluralism of coverage and opinion.[15]

However, in the aftermath of Russia's unprecedented transition from a centralized economy to market capitalism, the "private" ownership of the media was shaky, and formal rules and institutions were weak or missing.

As a result, Russia's early entrepreneurs operated in largely unchartered territory, and they took advantage of the new opportunities of enrichment in ways similar to those of the nineteenth-century American robber barons, not of their contemporaries in Western market democracies. Their questionable practices yielded huge profits, but made the new magnates potentially vulnerable to government oversight. The state—or more aptly in Russian, *vlast'* (the power)—may have been dramatically weakened after the political turmoil following the collapse of the USSR and the ensuing economic meltdown, but it retained some leverage in different strategic sectors, including the media. For example, the Russian federal government remained the majority shareholder in ORT and owned 100 percent of RTR, while regional administrative leaders still controlled the major television networks in their territories and subsidized most local print media. In 1998, as the Kremlin was preparing for the election cycle of 1999–2000, the government began to slowly reclaim the media territory it had lost to the oligarchs in the 1990s. The first major step was the creation of a government agency in charge of the media and a consolidation of state broadcasters under federal auspices. In 1998, regional TV stations, which until then had been controlled by local governors, were brought together and subordinated to VGTRK (All-Russian State Radio and Television Company), whose main asset was the national channel RTR, renamed *Rossiia* in 2001.[16]

RECONSOLIDATION OF THE STATE

When Vladimir Putin emerged as Russia's new president in 2000, his primary goal was to reassert the power of the state; this implied, first and foremost, reinstating the dominant authority of the nation's top leader. In his book of interviews, Putin said, when referring to the 1990s, "At some point many people decided that the president was no longer the center of power. I'll make sure that no one ever has such illusions anymore."[17] During his presidency, he effectively fulfilled his pledge. Since the outset of Putin's presidency, all political power has been steadily concentrated at the top of the executive branch, and government decision making was sealed from the public eye.

As for the media, state-owned television was strengthened organizationally and financially for the upcoming election cycle of 1999–2000. The oligarchic media played a very significant role in the political campaign of 1999–2000. But unlike the 1996 presidential election when Gusinsky and Berezovsky combined their TV resources in the effort to get Yeltsin reelected,[18] this time the two media tycoons ended up on different sides. Berezovsky committed his channel, ORT, to support the Kremlin.[19] Gusinsky's channel, NTV, however, would not support the Kremlin's hastily masterminded party *Edinstvo* (Unity) in the parliamentary race, nor would it back Yeltsin's anointed successor, Vladimir Putin, in the March 2000 presidential election.

The Kremlin defeated its rivals. The pro-Kremlin *Edinstvo* outperformed the party of the Moscow mayor Yury Luzhkov and former prime minister Evgeny Primakov, and Putin was elected president. This made Berezovsky the winner (and Putin's kingmaker) and Gusinsky the loser. But the consequences for their media properties, as well as for themselves, were not dissimilar. Soon thereafter, both ended up in exile, stripped of most of their media assets.

THE CAMPAIGN AGAINST OLIGARCHIC MEDIA

Expanding state control over mass-audience media was one of Putin's major goals; his campaign against privately owned national television was launched within days of his inauguration in May 2000. Gusinsky and his media holdings were occasionally attacked as early as 1999, but it was after Putin's inauguration that attacks were launched in full force.[20] The Kremlin, however, carefully avoided harassing or persecuting journalists or editors. Instead, the campaign was mostly disguised as business litigation against Gusinsky's businesses. Finally, in the spring of 2001, Gusinsky's media company was taken over by the state-controlled giant Gazprom. Media-Most, once the biggest privately owned media group in Russia, was dismantled. Eventually, though not immediately, the editorial line of NTV was taken under control and kept firmly in line with the Kremlin's political goals.

Putin's goal with regard to the media was much more ambitious, however, than eliminating a defiant tycoon and taming his media (in late 2000, Gusinsky was forced to flee abroad and never came back). The longer-term objective was to bring under state control all national television networks with political broadcasting. This task was greatly facilitated by the fact that the majority of the Russian public would not see the attack at NTV/Media-Most as a threat to freedom of the press, and, more generally, was not opposed to the reinstatement of the government control undertaken by Putin.[21] Neither would the journalistic community show solidarity with their Media-Most colleagues.[22]

ORT, the channel controlled by Berezovsky, was reclaimed by the state at about the same time as NTV. Ironically, it may be argued that Berezovsky's significant role in Putin's election was one of the reasons Putin wanted to get rid of him. Putin likely wanted no powerful kingmaker by his side. Besides, some of Putin's first steps were not to Berezovsky's liking, and he tried to oppose the new president's moves. Regaining control over ORT took much less time than the takeover of NTV and was mostly hidden from the public eye. There were many rumors about the way Berezovsky was stripped of his television asset, but it was not until litigation in the High Court of London in 2011 between two major Russian tycoons, Boris Berezovsky and Roman Abramovich, that the story was finally revealed to the public. According to testimony at the hearings, Berezovsky was pressured to sell his 49 percent stake in ORT. Those who testified in High Court differed only in the degree of pressure, but nobody denied that the sale was not Berezovsky's own desire. Berezovsky had already left Russia, so Putin's emissary had to travel to Europe to negotiate the terms of the deal with the exiled tycoon. At some point Putin himself also traveled abroad to meet (for five minutes) with Berezovsky. The whole transaction was kept secret; the appointed buyer was Roman Abramovich. Abramovich did special, secret, and costly favors for Putin, and therefore could count on protection against unwelcome scrutiny of his own business deals. Buying ORT on Putin's, or the Kremlin's, behalf was one of such favors. Berezovsky was paid at least $150 million for his stock in ORT. Abramovich did not claim control over the channel, so the Kremlin could use this political resource as it saw fit.[23]

In 2001–2002, there were two failed attempts to launch new, privately owned, national television channels. Through various techniques, the Kremlin made sure that both projects would be short-lived.[24] In 2002 the highly popular political satirical show *Kukly* was closed. By the middle of 2003, the Kremlin had virtually full control over political coverage of all major national television networks whose programming included news coverage. In 2004, government control was further tightened: several popular hosts were barred from television; among other steps was the closure of *Svoboda Slova* (Freedom of Speech), the only political talk show that was still broadcast live on the air.[25] Federal channels, whose outreach far surpasses all other Russian media, were turned into a political tool of the government.[26]

MANAGED TELEVISION COVERAGE

The coverage of three tragedies—the 2000 sinking of the submarine *Kursk*, the 2002 terrorist siege of a Moscow theater, and the 2004 terrorist attack on a school in Beslan—illustrates the Kremlin's expanded control over television broadcasting. Back in 2000, the media, including national television, tried their best to cover the sinking of the *Kursk*, which took the lives of all 118 sailors on board. Russian officials, both uniformed and civilian, sought to cover up the inefficiency of the rescue operation and the poor condition of the Russian Navy. Their public statements conflicted with each other. Russian journalists undertook thorough investigations to report what the government sought to hide. Putin was furious: he lashed out at "people in television" who "over the past ten years have destroyed that same army and navy where people are dying today."[27] Yet no steps were taken against reporters or TV stations. Instead, Putin took over ORT as a whole.[28]

In 2002, a group of terrorists seized a Moscow theater with over 800 people inside. In a badly bungled rescue operation, at least 129 hostages were killed, almost all of them by the poisonous gas used by the rescuers. This time, federal television was mostly tame, but the journalists of NTV, though taken over by Gazprom the previous year, still retained their professional instincts. They tried to produce professional coverage of the tragic developments, even as government officials instructed the channel's top manager to temper the journalists' investigative zeal. Once again, Putin was infuriated.[29] Within three months of the event, the NTV top manager was fired.

In September 2004, over 1,100 people, most of them children, were taken hostage in a school in Beslan, in the Caucasus region of North Ossetia-Alania (in southern Russia). During the siege and subsequent attack on the terrorists, at least 334 hostages were killed. The rescue operation left serious doubts about the competence of those in charge. By 2004, however, the government had secured full control over all three major federal television channels. For top managers, cooperation with the government had become a much higher priority than professional skills or ethics.[30] As soon as the rescue operation was over, a lid was put on their coverage. No eyewitness accounts, independent experts, survivors, or victims' relatives appeared on the screen. In the aftermath, Putin made no remarks about the coverage or TV reporters' performance.

TIGHTENED CONTROL OVER POLITICAL AND PUBLIC SPHERES

The government used the tragedy at Beslan as a pretext to tighten controls, launching what eventually amounted to full-blown political reform that endowed the Kremlin with an unlimited capacity to bar any unwelcome force or figure from Russian political life.[31] With all government institutions radically weakened or eviscerated, the Kremlin had the ability to make the rules, oversee their implementation, and exercise selective enforcement in order to get rid of unwanted political actors.

The end of 2004 was also marked by the Orange Revolution in Ukraine, which deeply alarmed the Kremlin, and Putin in particular. Events in Ukraine were perceived as a Western plot to install a pro-Western regime on Russia's border with the help of foreign-funded NGOs fomenting antigovernment sentiments. In addition, Putin had become personally involved in Ukraine's presidential campaign in an attempt to achieve a desired election result, only to see his effort dramatically fail. The frustration over this failure further aggravated the sense of alarm. Putin and his inner circle feared that the spirit of the Orange Revolution would reach Russia and challenge their power. The Russian government's rhetoric following the final victory of the "orange coalition" bordered on hysteria. Kremlin officials and loyalists spoke about Russia as a "besieged fortress," about "the enemy at the gate," and "the front line running across every house and every yard."[32] The "orange scare" pushed the Kremlin to further tighten its grip on power: to expand control to the public realm. The primary target of this campaign was NGOs, especially those sponsored from abroad. The campaign drew on a range of methods from co-optation to marginalization or discrediting. Only in rare cases did the government resort to harassment or repression.

By the middle of Putin's second term, his power reached a monarchical scope. He stood at the top of a radically deinstitutionalized political system; he did not have to worry about political competition or public accountability; his authority was unchallenged and unchecked. In the public realm, the government sent a clear message that autonomous public activism was unwelcome. By the 2007–2008 election cycle, any remaining independent political groups and activists were scarce, fragmented, or marginalized, and generally reduced to political irrelevance. Putin's approval rating hovered around 80 percent.[33]

The dominant mood of the people was that of quiescence. The state-society relationship that took shape during Putin's presidency and especially during his second term may be described as a tacit pact: the government delivers better living standards, and the people stay loyal and support the government by their vote.[34] For the more modernized minorities—the better educated and the entrepreneurial—the government offered another deal, that of nonintrusion: you do not meddle in government affairs, and we do not interfere with your individual pursuits, whether in making money, creative or academic professions, or other forms of self-fulfillment. This constituency was granted the opportunity of critical expression limited to smaller-audience media. But political *action* or organization opposing the government was strongly discouraged. Both pacts, the broader one with the majority and that of nonintrusion for the minority, were almost universally accepted. Both constituencies assumed that government officials were corrupt, self-seeking, and commonly abused their authority; both agreed that they shouldn't bother because there is nothing they can do about it anyway.[35]

CONTROLLED TELEVISION AS A TOOL OF POLITICAL CONTROL

Controlled national television constituted a major element in the political system and the pattern of state-society relations that Putin built. The mass-audience channels, especially Channel One (ORT was renamed Channel

One in 2002) and *Rossiia*, as well as NTV, have been effectively used as tools to shape public perceptions in a way best suited to the Kremlin's goals. The political and public affairs coverage of the federal channels mostly targeted the less urban, conservative majority that constituted the electoral base of Putin's political regime.[36]

The 2003 State Duma election, which further consolidated the Kremlin's control, was criticized by the Organization for Security and Cooperation in Europe (OSCE) monitoring mission, which pointed to biased media coverage favoring the incumbent.[37] Putin's reelection in 2004 was a heavily manipulated affair with a preordained result: Putin won handily, with 71 percent of the vote.[38]

As the 2007–2008 election cycle approached, Putin faced no challengers—nobody came even remotely close to him in popularity. But the election was to be a challenge in a different way. Putin was not eligible to run for a third consecutive term unless he changed the constitution, something that he stated he did not favor. But he had to stay in charge because in the deinstitutionalized political system that he created, Putin stood as the only safeguard of stability. He had presided over a major redistribution of power and property, and he alone was recognized as the arbiter by the competing power-and-property clusters. If politics is about reconciling conflicted interests, Putin *was* Russian politics.

The trick that Putin figured out so he would stay in charge even after he had vacated the presidential post came to be called a "tandem." Before he formally stepped down in the spring of 2008, Putin had handpicked a successor, his protégé Dmitry Medvedev. Because he had enjoyed considerable influence over Russia's political life, Putin had Medvedev easily voted into the presidency, and the latter promptly nominated Putin as prime minister, who was then approved by a quiescent Duma. Thus emerged a ruling tandem that shared Putin's uncontested and unchecked political authority. Though technically his position was inferior to Medvedev's, in fact Putin remained the most powerful man in Russia. Like in previous national campaigns, state-controlled national TV networks played an essential role in Medvedev's smooth election and in the transition to the tandem rule.[39]

The coverage of the three major TV channels was deftly adjusted to tandem rule. Their main political message was: whatever problems Russia may be facing, the tandem leadership is firmly in charge, and any political alternative is inconceivable. This TV operation helped maintain high approval ratings for both leaders. From October 2008 through February 2010 Medvedev's approval rating never dropped below 68 percent; Putin's stayed between 76 and 86 percent—despite the ongoing economic crisis.[40] During the tandem rule the three major channels continued to shape public opinion by boosting, playing down, or ignoring issues, figures, or groups, and maintaining the general mindset of quiescence and political nonparticipation.[41]

What made this operation especially effective is that national television was a successful business model. While the three federal broadcasters did not compete in news coverage—generally bland and hardly different channel to channel—the competition for viewers and thus for advertisers' ruble was fierce. Channels sought to win audiences by offering a broad choice of entertainment shows, some of them high quality, some playing to lowly tastes. Viewers were glued to the screens and stayed on the same channels for the news coverage shaped in a way that best fit the government goals. Advertisers attracted to large audiences eagerly committed their budgets to government-controlled TV. Federal TV channels, as a key element in the structure of state power, are subsidized by the state.[42]

ECONOMIC RISE

In the 2000s Russian media was declining as a public institution, but as an industry and as lucrative business it flourished. In order to impose state control over the media, Putin had drawn on redistributing the assets, so major media would be either state owned or held in loyal hands. The redistribution, launched in the early 2000s as Putin's political stratagem, continued as market-driven developments and greatly intensified in the following years.

The growing price of oil boosted economic growth and eventually led to a steady rise of the advertising market (it reached R131 billion in 2011),[43] making media a promising and prestigious property.[44] Russian media groups perfected their business models and expanded to include movie production, printing and distribution businesses, and telecommunications.[45] Channel One and *Rossiia* were by far the largest in terms of advertising revenues and capitalization. In 2010 these two major federal television channels received about 40 percent of all the TV advertising revenues in Russia. Gazprom's media subsidiary, Gazprom-Media, evolved as one of the largest media holdings in Europe—with the third biggest national TV channel, NTV; a unique political radio talk show, *Ekho Moskvy*; as well as other TV channels, magazines, and radio stations.

While Putin's government took pride in ridding Russia of oligarchic media, media assets amassed during Putin's tenure were enormous and substantially exceeded those held by Vladimir Gusinsky or Boris Berezovsky in the 1990s. The difference, however, is that media magnates of today can be trusted by Putin to be fully loyal; some belong to his close inner circle. Among the media magnates who came to the fore under Putin is banker Yury Kovalchuk. Numerous press reports indicate that he and Putin have long-term personal ties. Kovalchuk's National Media Group includes two national media channels (REN TV and Channel Five) and an entire range of print and Internet resources. In early 2011 he vastly increased his holdings by purchasing a 25 percent share in Channel One.[46] In addition to media assets, Kovalchuk has taken an active interest in advertising. In 2010 his affiliated business interests became 100 percent owners of Video International, a major company that sells advertising on TV and, in particular, on Channel One.[47]

BEYOND DIRECT CONTROL, BUT AT THE KREMLIN'S DISCRETION

The critically minded, modernized audiences commonly dismiss news coverage of national TV broadcasters as heavy-handed propaganda, but they have an array of alternative sources of information on which to draw. Government control over media beyond the federal television channels remains much less tight. A range of outlets—print, radio, Internet, and smaller-audience television channels—pursue relative editorial independence. The list of such outlets includes dailies such as *Kommersant*, *Vedomosti* (a business daily published jointly by the *Wall Street Journal* and the *Financial Times*), and *Novaia Gazeta*; weeklies, such as *The New Times*, *Vlast'*, or *Russian Newsweek* (closed on the initiative of its German publisher in 2010); and the radio station *Ekho Moskvy*. A variety of websites offer a combination of news, analysis, and opinion unconstrained by censorship or other modes of state control (the Internet in Russia remains free). REN TV, a channel with a sizable audience, has a relatively independent voice, especially in comparison with mass-audience state-controlled channels. These and other outlets run reportage, opinion pieces, and blog posts criticizing the government operation. Some journalists even engage in investigative reporting and expose abuses of offices by high-ranking government officials. The picture of Russia from those outlets is entirely different from the image offered by federal TV channels.

The problem with media freedom in Putin's Russia is therefore not the absence of alternative sources of information. In the system of securely controlled politics, the Kremlin can afford not to stifle every voice. In fact, the media that pursue editorial independence may even be useful for the Kremlin as a safety valve that helps the critically minded to let off steam, and as an element of the nonintrusion deal. In a more open political environment, some of the stories reported by those relatively independent media would become the subject of a parliamentary discussion or probe; others would generate political scandals. But Putin's Russia has no competitive politics, the legislature has turned into an arm of the executive, judicial rulings bend to the Kremlin's will, and autonomous public activism is thoroughly marginalized. In these conditions, existing elements of free media cannot make a difference in policy making but instead remain politically irrelevant.[48]

Political apathy by the public is another serious obstacle to having a political impact: the nonintrusion pact remains intact. Further, as the critically minded audiences read media reports about the latest abuses by state officials, with habitual cynicism they shrug their shoulders—"What else is new?"[49] The lack of impact is a discouraging factor for many journalists. Some opt for nonpolitical beats or even other occupations; others adjust to the controlled political environment and engage in self-censorship.[50]

The Kremlin tolerates a degree of free expression, but it has an array of tools to crack down on the media, thereby keeping the relatively independent outlets vulnerable. The Kremlin makes sure that the nongovernment media stay marginal. First and foremost, the nongovernment media are insulated from mass-audience television. Stories by smaller-audience media are not picked up by federal TV broadcasters. Nongovernment print, Internet, and radio reporters are barred from federal TV news shows.

The government also exercises control over lawmaking and law enforcement. For example, shortly before the 2007–2008 election cycle, new amendments infringing on the operation of the media were made in the antiextremism and antiterrorism legislation. These amendments enabled the government to suspend media outlets or even shut them down. Though the antiterrorism legislation is infrequently used against media, nobody can feel secure, and media that dare to challenge government policies are aware that if they go too far, the Kremlin may move against them.[51]

Russia has a substantial degree of media freedom to convey uncensored messages, report news, or voice opinions. It appears to be more appropriate, however, to describe this as *freedom of expression*. But freedom of expression is different from *freedom of the press*, if the latter implies a network of democratic institutions that helps citizens hold the government accountable.

TANDEM RULE: GROWING PERMISSIVENESS AND A BROADENING OF FREE EXPRESSION

By the end of Putin's second term, the media that exercised relative editorial independence, jointly with their critically minded constituencies, formed "islets" or "ghettos," insulated and divorced from the government or from broader Russian audiences. They shared limited free expression, modernized attitudes, and independent life pursuits. They resided in their intellectually comfortable ghettos and didn't seem to mind that they remained unrepresented and made no difference in the political or public affairs.[52]

Things began to change with the transition to tandem rule. Though Dmitry Medvedev remained inferior to his mentor Putin and was hardly seen as an independent figure (the more cynical even regarded him as merely a "soft face" to Putin's authoritarian regime), Medvedev's liberal rhetoric, his enthusiasm for gadgets and the digital world, and the very fact that there were two men at the top instead of just one, loosened the system a bit and emboldened some of the marginal opponents of the regime.[53] The phrase "political thaw" entered the political lingo of the tandem's early period.[54] "The new reality legalized in part by Medvedev began to live its own life," a Russian political commentator wrote in late 2010.[55]

The new permissiveness unleashed more criticism by the media.[56] Even federal television began to look just a little less bland. The TV content targeting older and conservative audiences had become too stale, and TV managers were concerned about losing their viewership. New humor shows began to emerge that reacted to current events and treated them in a light, funny fashion. "Very seldom and very carefully [this show] sounds ironic even with respect to president Medvedev and prime-minister Putin," a prominent TV critic wrote about one such new show in March of 2010.[57]

The slight softening notwithstanding, TV remained fully under state control. It may be suggested, however, that the television community was not happy to be seen as servile hands of the regime. Beyond their everyday operation on federal TV, a mild degree of audacity could be found. For instance, annual TV awards were repeatedly granted to "non grata" TV journalists who had been barred from television, or to those from smaller-audience TV channels who had retained a relatively independent voice. At the award ceremony in 2010 Leonid Parfyonov, a top TV star forced out of NTV in 2004, gave a speech in which he harshly denounced federal broadcasters:

> For a correspondent of federal television the top government executives are not newsmakers but the bosses of their bosses . . . a correspondent is not a journalist, he is a bureaucrat guided by the logic of allegiance and subordination. . . . Nothing critical, skeptical or ironic about the president or the prime minister can be aired on federal channels.[58]

Tandem rule was also marked by the emergence of new media outlets, or the politicization of those that heretofore remained largely nonpolitical. *Kommersant*, which since its inception back in 1990 had become a well-established (mostly print) media holding, in 2010 launched a radio station, *Kommersant* FM. Drawing on the vast journalistic resources of the print holding, the radio station quickly rose to prominence as well-informed news radio. TV *Dozhd'*, a small operation started in 2010 as an Internet-TV outlet, has been included in cable packages and increased its outreach. It has eagerly invited political and public figures whom federal channels kept on their "black lists." Over the past years several thick glossies, such as *GQ*,

Citizen K, or *Esquire* have also turned to political themes (some made this choice even earlier)—apparently responding to the shift among their wealthy, well-traveled, Westernized audiences who were increasingly interested in politics. *Bolshoi Gorod* (Big City), a biweekly magazine about Moscow city life, has been reformatted and offers strongly politicized, sometimes angry coverage. *Afisha* (Billboard) magazine originally focused on arts and culture, but now has developed a defiant political voice. Though television remains the main (or only) source of news for a majority of Russians, a growing number (mostly in big urban centers) draw on the Internet. In 2012, 24 percent of Russians relied on the Internet for news,[59] up from 11 percent less than one year earlier.[60]

The newly energized media realm is filled with reportage, critical policy analysis by experts, as well as angry opinion and poisonous jokes. A weekly radio/video/Internet project called *Grazhdanin Poet (Citizen Poet)* was launched in spring 2011 that offers biting satire on the latest political events. Satirical verse from Dmitry Bykov and performances by actor Mikhail Yefremov were appreciated by a vast and admiring audience every Monday for almost one year. Neither the author nor the performer treated their political characters, including Putin and Medvedev, with the slightest reverence.[61]

It was also during the tandem period that most major print and radio outlets rapidly developed Internet platforms; Web, print, audio, and video are also merging. Advanced Web users in greater numbers have switched to Facebook to search for references to the media publications. The use of social networks is increasing dramatically, with the number of users growing faster in Russia than anyplace else in Europe.[62] The Internet is awash with reports, submitted by professional reporters or ordinary citizens, of egregious lawlessness, injustice, or abuse by government or police authority. The number of bloggers has increased, some gaining huge popularity and becoming voices of authority for tens of thousands of regular readers. The popularity of social networks facilitated the exchange of information, social linkages, and promoted interest in civic causes. The late 2000s were, therefore, a time of rising civic initiatives.[63] Thus, fragmented "islets" have been merging into something of an archipelago, but while the Russian civil society was on the rise, political causes left people mostly indifferent. For instance, the fraudulent Moscow city Duma election in the fall of 2009 left Muscovites fully indifferent. Polls showed that people *assumed* that the election would be rigged, so when it indeed turned out to be falsified, it was a nonevent.[64]

MASS PROTESTS AND POLITICIZATION OF SOCIETY

The fall of 2011 marked the end of political quiescence. An upsurge in public anger was stirred by Putin's comeback to the presidency orchestrated as a "trading-places" trick. Medvedev announced that he wouldn't run for a second term, abdicating in Putin's favor. When Medvedev mentioned that the two of them had made that decision a long time ago, this trick was seen as the government's utter contempt for the people. The ensuing unfair campaign and fraudulent parliamentary election in December 2011 became a trigger that transformed angry mood into action. People in Moscow (to some extent also in other cities) took to the streets protesting against election fraud, the government's manipulative politics, lies, falsehood, and lawlessness. What began as a demand for a new, free, and fair election evolved into an anti-Putin movement; the protesters carried signs such as "Putin, Go!" or "Russia without Putin." By the time Putin was inaugurated in May 2012, the nonintrusion pact was beyond repair. At least a part of Russian society was repoliticized and determined to make a difference. In June 2012, tens of thousands of Muscovites took to the street on Independence Day, some carrying signs that said "Russians against Putin." The Internet and social networks were useful in disseminating information and organizing the mass rallies. The new media network covered the protests and broadcast live online sessions of the rallies' organizing committee. Social networks became the venue for heated discussions of the tactics and strategy of the protest movement.

CONCLUSION

With tens of thousands of people in the streets of Moscow, federal TV channels could no longer ignore the rallies. The coverage was cautious, restrained, and frequently biased, but at least TV audiences all over Russia could see their Moscow compatriots carrying signs: "Russia without Putin." Similar small-scope political actions in previous years had been simply ignored by national TV.

In another permissive move, many of the "blacklisted" figures barred from TV were invited to talk shows. Only a few remained non grata, apparently deemed too dangerous by the Kremlin; first and foremost of these was Aleksei Navalny. A couple of shows, such as NTV's *Tsentralnoe Televidenie* (Central Television), launched in 2010, or *Nightly Urgant* (modeled after the Late Night Show), launched in 2012, were broadcast live and offered political and public affairs reportage that differed in facts, tone, and style from the filtered coverage of the national television.

But loosening the grip does not amount to freer television. The national TV channels still had the Kremlin's interests as their unquestioned priority, and while there was more permissiveness on some talk shows, in others the same people who participated in televised political discussions would be shamelessly smeared in "documentaries" that portrayed them as immoral agents of the evil West.

With the presidential election behind him, Putin's new government has launched a counteroffensive against the newly politicized and defiant Russian citizenry. Rumors were circulating that the *Tsentralnoe Televidenie* show had become too bold and may soon be tamed.[65] The editor-in-chief of *Bolshoi Gorod* was forced to resign, and a top executive of *Kommersant* also left his post. They were not fired directly by the Kremlin. The respective companies' formal explanations cited business reasons, but it was broadly assumed that politics was involved. The editor of *Bolshoi Gorod* made this clear in his comments made to *Vedomosti*.[66]

It is likely that Putin's government will continue to crack down, but the new societal shifts are unlikely to go away, and the mood of quiescence will not return. The former "islets" and "ghettos" have merged, held together in part by Facebook and other social networks in which "consumption of information is closely linked to action and participation. Participation is what turns news into public and political events. Thus emerges a media model diametrically opposite to the one built by the Kremlin whose goal ever since Putin came to power was to use television to stimulate the non-participation."[67] For the first time in Putin's Russia, the previously tame opposition has put up resistance to the Kremlin. The repoliticization of the society is still in its very early stages, but in the coming years the new media are bound to play a significant role in the revitalization of Russia's civil society.

SUGGESTED READINGS

Federman, Adam. "Moscow's New Rules." *Columbia Journalism Review*, January–February 2010. www.cjr.org/feature/moscows_new_rules.php?page = all.

Fossato, Floriana. "The Russian Media: From Popularity to Distrust." *Current History* 100, no. 648 (2001): 343–47.

Gorbachev, Aleksandr, and Ilya Krasil'shchik, eds. *Istoriia russkikh media 1989–2011*. Moscow: Afisha, 2011.

Kachkaeva, Anna. "Glamurny totalitarizm: Televizionnaia industriia v epokhu stabil'nosti (2004–2007)." In *Teleradioefir: Istoriia i sovremennost'*. Moscow: Elitkomstar, 2008.

———. "Transformatsiia Rossiiskogo TV." In *Sredstva Massovoi Informatsii Rossii*. Moscow: Aspekt, 2006.

Lipman, Maria. "Freedom of Expression without Freedom of the Press." *Journal of International Affairs* 63, no. 2 (2010): 153–69.

———. "Svoboda pressy v usloviakh upravliaemoi demokratii." *Carnegie Moscow Center Briefing Paper* 8, issue 2 (2006).

———. "The Media in Russia—Freedom of Expression under Conditions of Political Monopoly." In *The Medvedev Presidency—A Wasted Effort*. The EU–Russia Centre Review, Issue 19, October 2011. www.eu-russiacentre.org/wp-content/uploads/2008/10/EURC_review_XIX_ENG.pdf.

Zubarevich, Natalia. "Sovremennaia Rossiia: Geografiia s arifmetikoi." *Otechestvennye zapiski*, no. 1 (2012).

NOTES

1. One of the key factors for Russia's low press-freedom score is an appalling record of assassinations of journalists. The Kremlin is not directly responsible for these murders (www.cpj.org/killed/europe/russia). The highest risk for journalists is not to challenge the political system or its Kremlin masterminds, it is to encroach on powerful interests who resort to contract assassinations in order to get rid of rivals, adversaries, or overinquisitive journalists. The Kremlin should be blamed not for contracting murders, but for creating an atmosphere of lawlessness where clout and money easily override the law, and where contractors and perpetrators of killings get away with impunity.

2. www.freedomhouse.org/report-types/freedom-press. Russia is currently sandwiched between Tajikistan and Ethiopia.

3. For example, Aleksandr Gorbachev and Ilya Krasil'shchik, eds., *Istoriia russkikh media 1989–2011* (Moscow: Afisha, 2011), does not mention a single media outlet based outside of Moscow.

4. See, for instance, chapters about newspapers *Kommersant, Nezavisimaia Gazeta*, and TV-channel TV6 in *Istoriia russkikh media*.

5. Floriana Fossato, "The Russian Media: From Popularity to Distrust," *Current History* 100, no. 648 (2001): 343–47.

6. Gorbachev and Krasil'shchik, *Istoriia russkikh media*, 9–14.

7. The Russian law on mass media, adopted in December 1991, was preceded by a Soviet media law framed the previous year by the same group of liberal experts, which was inspired by a desire to legally enforce the idea that media be independent of the state. See www.medialaw.ru/e_pages/laws/russian/massmedia_eng/massmedia_eng.html.

8. Michael McFaul, *Russia's 1996 Presidential Election: The End of Polarized Politics* (Stanford, Calif.: Hoover Institution Press, 1997).

9. Ellen Mickiewicz, *Changing Channels: Television and the Struggle for Power in Russia* (Oxford: Oxford University Press, 1997).

10. Gorbachev and Krasil'shchik, *Istoriia russkikh media*, 87–90. See also the chapter about Vladimir Gusinsky in David E. Hoffman, *The Oligarchs: Wealth and Power in the New Russia* (New York: Public Affairs, 2002), chap. 7.

11. On the channel's creation, see the detailed account by Hoffman, *The Oligarchs*, chap. 7.

12. Floriana Fossato, "Russia: Changes Sweep through Two TV Networks," *Radio Free Europe/Radio Liberty*, November 5, 1997.

13. Russian Public Television (ORT) gained control of the first national television channel in Russia through a presidential decree (no. 2133) on November 29, 1994, and began broadcasting on April 1, 1995. In the company's charter, organizations listed as shareholders included state institutions, as well as private companies such as Menatep, National Kredit, and Stolychny banks; Gazprom; and Berezovsky's

own company, Logovaz. See *Russian Public Television: Collection of Constituent Documents* (Moscow: ORT, 1995), 18. The private companies purchased 49 percent of the new company and faced no competition for their purchase. Berezovsky's Logovaz owned 8 percent of the shares, while the share of the state owners totaled more than 50 percent. Nonetheless, Berezovsky used side payments and bribes to gain control of the company's operations and editorial policy. See Paul Klebnikov, *Godfather of the Kremlin: Boris Berezovsky and the Looting of Russia* (New York: Harcourt, 2000), 159–61.

14. Mark Whitehouse, "Buying the Media: Who's Behind the Written Word?" *Russia Review*, April 21, 1997, 26–27; and Oleg Medvedev and Sergei Sinchenko, "The Fourth Estate—Chained to Banks," *Business in Russia* 78 (June 1997): 38–43.

15. On the distorting influences of private ownership on editorial lines, see Laura Belin, "Political Bias and Self-Censorship in the Russian Media," in *Contemporary Russian Politics: A Reader*, ed. Archie Brown (Oxford: Oxford University Press, 2001), 323–44.

16. Anna Kachkaeva, "Transformatsiia Rossiiskogo TV," in *Sredstva Massovoi Informatsii Rossii* (Moscow: Aspekt, 2006), 303.

17. Natalia Gevorkyan, Natalia Timakova, and Andrei Kolesnikov, *Ot pervogo litsa: Razgovory s Vladimirom Putinym* (Moscow: Vagrius, 2000), 172–73. See also an English version: Vladimir Putin, *First Person* (New York: Public Affairs, 2000).

18. Hoffman, *The Oligarchs*, chap. 13.

19. The 1999 parliamentary election turned out to be Russia's last truly competitive national election, and the competition was fierce and at times ugly. The operation of Berezovsky's television was shocking even by Russian standards. The use of television as a tool for smearing the Kremlin's political rivals was driven to grotesque proportions by TV journalist Sergei Dorenko, hired to fulfill this mission by Boris Berezovsky. See Hoffman, *The Oligarchs*, 464–70.

20. For more detail about the campaign against Gusinsky and his media, see Maria Lipman and Michael McFaul, "Putin and the Media," in *Putin's Russia: Past Imperfect, Future Uncertain*, 2nd ed., ed. Dale R. Herspring (Lanham, Md.: Rowman & Littlefield, 2005), 59–64; and Hoffman, *The Oligarchs*, 442–85.

21. Though the campaign against NTV caused public protest and two large protest rallies were held in Moscow, national polls suggested that "only 4 percent of the public regarded the NTV takeover as a government attempt to limit media freedom." Fossato, "The Russian Media," 343.

22. Russian society in general is strongly fragmented, and journalists are no exception. Even assassinations of journalists have mostly failed to bring the journalistic community together. When Anna Politkovskaia was murdered, hundreds of thousands took to the streets of European capitals, but not in Moscow. www.vedomosti.ru/opinion/news/1847924/opyat_promolchim-ixzz1xylyjHJI. It should be remembered that the Kremlin campaign against the oligarchic media targeted the tycoons and wisely refrained from attacking journalists. This way the Kremlin ensured that journalists would not come together and stand up for their colleagues at Media-Most/NTV.

23. "Tainaia zapis': Abramovich i Berezovsky o Putine," BBC Russian, November 9, 2011, www.bbc.co.uk/russian/russia/2011/11/111108_abramovich_berezovsky_

tape.shtml; Berezovsky vs Abramovich: Abramovich kupil ORT za $10 mln (www
.gazeta.ru/business/2011/11/07/3825378.shtml1/2).

24. The fates of two channels, TV-6 and TVS, are discussed in more detail in Lipman and McFaul, "Putin and the Media," 64–67.

25. Susan B. Glasser, "Russian Talk Show Faces Shutdown," *The Washington Post*,
July 8, 2004, www.washingtonpost.com/wp-dyn/articles/A35389-2004Jul7.html.

26. According to Russia's leading TV expert, Anna Kachkaeva, "Fast development
of cable TV and the Internet notwithstanding . . . Russia still remains a country of
traditional . . . television. Almost 90 percent of the Russian population watch TV
every day." Anna Kachkaeva, "Glamurny totalitarizm: Televizionnaia industriia v
epokhu stabil'nosti (2004–2007)," in *Teleradioefir: Istoriia i sovremennost'* (Moscow:
Elitkomstar, 2008), 41.

27. Peter Baker and Susan Glasser, *Kremlin Rising: Vladimir Putin's Russia and the
End of Revolution* (New York: Lisa Drew/Scribner, 2005), 89. See his even more emo-
tional statements quoted in *Kommersant-Vlast'*, August 29, 2000.

28. According to the testimony in the above-cited litigation between Abramovich
and Berezovsky, the coverage of Kursk disaster by ORT was the final reason why
Putin demanded that Berezovsky relinquish control of the largest national TV channel. Putin was cited as saying that he would be personally in charge of ORT.

29. Baker and Glasser, *Kremlin Rising*, 174–75.

30. Baker and Glasser, *Kremlin Rising*, 34–35.

31. For a detailed description of the electoral reform see Nikolai Petrov, "Kakaia
vlast'—takie i vybory, kakie vybory—takaia i vlast' (ob itogakh izbiratel'nogo tsykla
2007–2008 gg.)," *Carnegie Moscow Center Briefing Paper* 10, issue 2 (2008).

32. See interview with Vladislav, www.kp.ru/daily/23370/32473.

33. According to Levada-Center's polls Putin's approval rating in 2007–2008 was
79–88 percent. See www.levada.ru/indeksy.

34. Masha Lipman, "Russia's No-Participation Pact," March 30, 2011, www
.project-syndicate.org/commentary/russia-s-no-participation-pact.

35. Over 80 percent of Russians respond in polls that they make no difference
in political affairs. See Levada-Center's 2011 yearbook: *Obschestvennoe mnenie–2011*
(Moscow: Levada-Center, 2012), 34.

36. See, for instance, Natalia Zubarevich, "Sovremennaia Rossiia: Geografiia s
arifmetikoi," *Otechestvennye zapiski*, no. 1 (2012).

37. The head of the Long-Term Observation Mission deployed by the OSCE
Office for Democratic Institutions and Human Rights stated, "We have serious concerns regarding the lack of media independence. State media failed to provide balanced coverage of the campaign." See www.osce.org/item/7974.html.

38. Maria Lipman, "In Russia It's No Contest," *Washington Post*, December 1,
2004, www.carnegieendowment.org.

39. When Medvedev was picked as Putin's anointed successor, he was immediately featured on television almost as prominently as Putin. This way the nation
learned for whom it should vote, and the Russian people did not fail the Kremlin.
In the March 2008 presidential election, candidate Medvedev received 70 percent of
the vote.

40. "Rankings of Russian leaders and the situation in the country," Levada Center, March 4, 2010, www.levada.ru/press/2010030404.html. See also Mikhail Fishman and Konstantin Gaaze, "Efir dlia dvoikh," *Russian Newsweek*, August 4, 2008;

Maria Lipman, "Freedom of Expression without Freedom of the Press," *Journal of International Affairs* 63, no. 2 (2010): 153–69.

41. For example, in recent years Russian television promoted anti-Ukrainian, anti-Georgian, and anti-American sentiments. It ran "documentaries" smearing Mikhail Khodorkovsky (once Russia's richest man, whom Putin and some in his close circle deemed a dangerous rival; they had him prosecuted and sentenced to two jail terms), and Mikhail Saakashvili (president of Georgia) as ultimate villains. It presented foreign-funded NGOs as agents of a hostile West. It vilified Moscow mayor Yury Luzhkov, who wouldn't resign at the Kremlin's request. In late 2011 national television was useful in waging a harsh anti-American campaign that accompanied the parliamentary and the presidential races, and in discrediting the organizers and participants of mass political protests.

42. For instance, signal transmissions to smaller cities (under 200,000 residents) are subsidized by the state. Fishman and Gaaze, "Efir dlia dvoikh."

43. See www.akarussia.ru/node/2085.

44. On media as business, see Kachkaeva, "Glamurny totalitarizm"; Maria Lipman, "La scène médiatique en Russie: Déclin des institutions et montée en puissance de l'industrie," *Outre-Terre*, no. 19 (2007), 2.

45. Consider a few examples illustrating the scale of the Russia media market. In 2006, $2 billion was spent in transactions on the media market. A Russian media company, Prof-Media, owns holdings in a publishing house, movie theaters, Rambler Media, a film production company, entertainment radio, and TV. In 2011 the entertainment channel TNT bought a controlling stake in the Russian company Comedy Club Production (CCP) that produces popular TV shows. The CCP was estimated to be worth $450 million.

46. Konstantin Gaaz, "Otdel'no vziatiy telekanal," February 9, 2011, www.forbes.ru/ekonomika-opinion/vlast/63087-otdelno-vzyatyi-telekanal; Aleksandr Polivanov, "Perviy plyus pyatiy," February 11, 2011, www.lenta.ru/articles/2011/02/10/first/.

47. Ksenia Boletskaya, "Who owns Video International," *Vedomosti*, June 29, 2010; also lenta.ru/articles/2011/02/10/first/.

48. Maria Lipman, "Constrained or Irrelevant: The Media in Putin's Russia," *Current History* 104, no. 684 (2005): 319–24; and Maria Lipman, "Svoboda pressy v usloviakh upravliaemoi demokratii," *Carnegie Moscow Center Briefing Paper* 8, issue 2 (2006).

49. Valery Panyushkin, "Was It Something I Wrote?" *New York Times*, May 21, 2011, www.nytimes.com/2011/05/22/opinion/22panyushkin.html?pagewanted=all; Gorbachev and Krasil'shchik, *Istoriia russkikh media*, 295–97.

50. Gorbachev and Krasil'shchik, *Istoriia russkikh media*, 295–97.

51. For example, radio *Ekho Moskvy* repeatedly was threatened when its coverage angered Putin. See David Remnick, "Echo in the Dark," *New Yorker*, September 22, 2008; and Philip P. Pan, "In Wake of Georgian War, Russian Media Feel Heat," *Washington Post*, September 15, 2008. In 2012 *Ekho Moskvy* was once threatened. See Maksim Ivanov, "My vsegda na krychke," *Kommersant*, March 30, 2012. As of this writing, however, the station continues its broadcast and its editorial policy does not seem to have changed.

52. Masha Lipman, "Barack Obama in Russia's Liberal Ghetto," *Washington Post,* July 9, 2009.

53. Medvedev's liberal rhetoric was reflected by his famous saying that "freedom is better than nonfreedom."

54. Vladimir Gelman, "Treschiny v stene," *Pro et Contra,* nos. 1–2 (2012).

55. Kirill Rogov, "Na boevom blog-postu," *Novaia Gazeta,* November 21, 2010, www.novayagazeta.ru/politics/743.html.

56. Masha Lipman, "Novaia slovesnaia vol'nost," *Ezhednevniy Zhurnal,* February 12, 2010, www.ej.ru/?a = note_print&id = 9875.

57. Arina Borodina, "Mikhail Prokhorov podnyal reiting 'ProzhektorPerisKhilton,'" *Kommersant,* March 17, 2010.

58. See Parfyonov's address at www.kommersant.ru/doc/1546420. Not unexpectedly, the coverage of the TV awards ceremonies censored out the unwanted lines.

59. See www.levada.ru/20-03-2012/chislo-polzovatelei-interneta-rastet.

60. On the rift between the more and less modernized constituencies, including the difference in Internet usage, see Lev Gudkov, "Sotsial'ny kapital i ideologicheskie orientatsii," *Pro et Contra,* no. 3 (2012).

61. www.echo.msk.ru/programs/citizen/. Thirteen million views on YouTube, February 2012.

62. Olga Razumovskaya, "Social Networks See Big Bucks in Inmates and Spirits," *The Moscow Times,* March 24, 2011.

63. See, for instance, Masha Lipman, "Quashing Rallies May Not Stave Off Discontent in Russia," *Washington Post,* August 9, 2010.

64. See Moscow city Duma elections monitoring by Levada-Center: www.levada .ru/press/2009122501.html.

65. Arina Borodina's commentary on Kommersant FM Radio, www.kommersant .ru/doc/1951814.

66. www.vedomosti.ru/companies/news/1827716/filipp_dzyadko_po kidaet_ bolshoj_gorod.

67. Kirill Rogov, personal communication with author.

II

THE ECONOMY AND SOCIETY

7

Population Trends

Timothy Heleniak

With recent economic growth and stability, Russia's steep post-Soviet demographic decline seems to be ending. However, this is not a reason for optimism, as the population of Russia continues to have a number of demographic problems that belie its status as an upper-middle country. These unfavorable demographic indicators will continue to affect the Russian economy and society and its standing in the world into the foreseeable future. The population of Russia peaked in 1993 at 148.6 million and declined by nearly 7 million to a nadir of 141.9 million in 2009 before increasing by over a million to 143.0 million at the beginning of 2012.[1] In the post-Soviet period, deaths have exceeded births by 13.4 million and net immigration into Russia of 6.7 million has only partially compensated for the excess of deaths over births. The recent stabilization and actual increase in the total population is due to a combination of an increase in the number of births, decrease in the number of deaths, and an increase in immigration. Deaths began to exceed births in 1992, and it is only coincidental that that was the first year of Russia's independence. A combination of declining fertility, high mortality, and an aging population has contributed to negative natural increase. The fertility rate has increased recently though remains far below the replacement level of 2.1 children per woman that a society needs to retain a stable population size. Part of the recent increase in the number of births is the result of a temporary demographic dividend of a larger cohort of women moving into the peak childbearing ages. Life expectancy has increased considerably in recent years though remains below the levels of the late Soviet period and far below levels of countries at similar income levels. Part of the recent population increase is due to increased immigration (or better counting of immigrants), though Russia remains wary of large numbers of non-Russian, non-Slavic populations.

Deaths exceed births in a number of other countries in Eastern and Western Europe. In Russia, however, the amount by which deaths exceed births is the largest in the world. The trends of natural decrease and net immigration insufficient to stem population decline are expected to continue into the future, pointing to the demographic dilemma that Russia faces. To avoid the decline, Russia needs to raise fertility, lower mortality, or increase immigration, while some question whether attempting to reverse population decline is even the wisest policy to pursue. The term *population decline* can refer to many different phenomena: a decline in the size of a population; a decline in the rate of growth or the fertility rate; an aging of the population; a decline in the proportion of the majority or dominant ethnic group; or a decline in attributes often attributed to a growing population, such as innovation, mobility, risk taking, and optimism, for which are substituted conservatism, immobility, risk aversion, and pessimism.[2] Russia is hardly the first country to fear population decline, nor is this the first time that Russia has worried about declining or negative rates of growth.

This chapter has several aims. The first is to analyze Russian demographic trends from the late Soviet period through the first decade of the twenty-first century and into the future. The second goal is to determine what these demographic trends herald for Russia's political and economic future. The third task is to assess the effectiveness of population policy in Russia. The chapter examines fertility, mortality, composition of the population, migration, and the spatial distribution of the population in Russia, ending with a discussion of population projections and population policy.

FERTILITY

By the 1960s, Russian women had completed the fertility transition and adopted the two-child family as the norm. The total fertility rate declined to replacement level in the early 1960s and stayed at that level throughout the Soviet period.[3] In 1989, of the cohort of women who had just completed their childbearing, only 3.5 percent had never married and only 7.9 percent were childless.[4] Thus, fertility in Russia at the beginning of the transition period was characterized by nearly universal marriage and childbearing, both of which occurred at relatively young ages. Because of these trends of early marriage and childbearing, there was a much larger contribution of younger cohorts to total fertility than in Western countries, where women delayed childbearing while pursuing education or careers. Russian women typically had children relatively early and then relied on abortion for future fertility regulation, as contraceptive rates were rather low.

The number of births fell from a recent peak of 2.5 million in 1987, during a period of pro-natalist policies, to a low of 1.2 million in 1999, then increased to 1.8 million in 2011 (see figure 7.1). The mortality increase in Russia has been well publicized, but the fertility decline actually has had the largest numerical impact. The fertility rate in Russia also peaked during the pro-natalist period in 1987 at 2.194 children per woman, the last time it was above the replacement level. Thereafter, it declined sharply, reaching a low of 1.157 in 1999 before increasing to 1.537 in 2009, only partially influenced by a package of pro-natalist measures put into place by the government. Even the recent rise is quite minuscule and foreshadows continued population decline. The fertility rate in Russia places it among what demographers refer to as "lowest-low" fertility, along with a group of countries in Western and Eastern Europe that includes a number of other former Soviet states with fertility rates below 1.3.[5] Most analysts believe that lowest-low fertility is not likely to be merely a short-term phenomenon in Russia and other Central and East European states.

As the trade-off between children and education/careers shifts in favor of the latter, the fertility pattern in Russia is shifting toward that seen in Europe, where the highest fertility rates are among women ages 25 to 29 and overall rates are lower. Between 1989 and the nadir of fertility in Russia in 2000, women at all ages had fewer children, with the largest decline

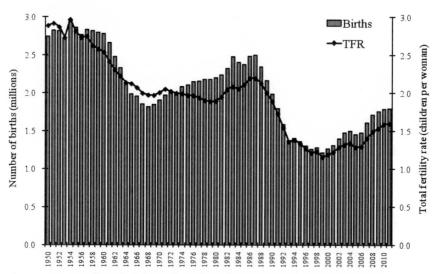

Figure 7.1. Number of Births and Total Fertility Rate in Russia 1950–2011
Source: Rosstat, *Demograficheskii ezhegodnik* (various years)

among women ages 20 to 24. Three-quarters of the increase since then is attributable to increased births among women ages 25 to 34, with the fertility of women ages 20 to 24 further declining. The mean age at childbearing increased from 24.6 in 1994 to 27.4 in 2009.[6] Changes in annual total fertility rates can reflect changes in the average number of births, which is known as the quantum effect, or they can reflect shifts in the timing of births, which is known as the tempo effect. The main factor driving the decline in Russia is the reduction in the quantum of fertility, in particular the low propensity to have a second child, as studies show evidence of a shift to a one-child family norm in Russia.[7] During the transition period in Russia, there was a rapid increase in the returns to education, which played a role in the fertility decline.[8] The number of children that Russian women had at each level of education stayed roughly the same between the 1989 and 2002 censuses. What explains much of the decline in fertility is the increase in the number of women pursuing higher education, with the largest increases among young women aged 16 to 29, which are prime fertility ages.

One issue that Russia will confront is that the smaller cohorts of women born in the late 1980s will soon enter their peak childbearing years. The number of women of childbearing age peaked in 2003 at 40 million and is expected to fall to 32 million by 2020. More crucial is that the number of women aged 20 to 29 peaked at the end of the 2000s at 12 million and will decline to 7 million by 2020. In Russia, women of these ages give birth to 65 percent of the children who are born. Without a massive increase in fertility levels, the number of births in Russia will decline from its current level of 1.6 million to less than one million per year in 2025.

Demographers have identified four determinants that account for the majority of the differences in fertility levels among societies and within societies over time: the share of women who are married or in a union; the prevalence of contraceptive use; abortion rates; and level of postpartum breast-feeding.[9] Social and economic factors work through these determinants to influence the fertility rate. In Russia, this includes the steep income declines in the 1990s and increases in the direct costs of children during the transition period.

The annual number of marriages fell from 1.4 million in the late 1980s to a low of 850,000 in 1999 before increasing to 1.3 million in 2007. The ratio of divorces to marriages has also recently fallen. Both factors increased the share of women who are married and the length of marriage, when they are engaging in regular intercourse and may become pregnant. This is important for fertility levels because of the continued importance of marital fertility to the overall fertility level in Russia. From the peak of fertility in 1987, the annual number of marital births fell by 1.1 million while the contribution of nonmarital births increased by only 114,000. Though marriage and childbearing are no longer as synonymous as they once were, the decline in the number of marriages in Russia can still explain a significant portion of the overall fertility decline.

With the economic transition and the opening of the Russian economy, the levels of contraceptive use have increased considerably. The contraceptive prevalence rate went from 31.5 percent in 1990 to 73 percent in 1999.[10] The bulk of this increase was greater use of more effective, modern contraceptive methods (e.g., the pill, IUDs, condoms, sterilization). Soon after the Bolsheviks took power, abortion was legalized. Over time, an abortion industry emerged, and abortion became the cheapest and most readily available form of fertility regulation. From 1960 to 1990, the abortion ratio (number of abortions per 100 births) averaged about 220.[11] The abortion ratio fell from 205 in 1989 to 107 in 2006.[12] However, the historical legacy of reliance on abortion remains, as this ratio means that over half of all conceptions are terminated in abortion. Legislation enacted during the 1990s further increased the grounds under which a woman could obtain an abortion upon request. Russia continues to have among the highest abortion rates in the world, and abortion remains a major fertility-inhibiting factor.[13]

Like other low-fertility countries, Russia would prefer to raise fertility rates rather than increase the flow of migrants. Starting in January 2007, a new package of pro-natalist policies was introduced, designed to halt or reverse the steep decline in Russia's birth rate. The package included large child benefits of $113 a month for a second child, longer maternity leaves of eighteen months at 40 percent salary, and a payment of $9,000 to each woman who had a second child.[14] Russian women are increasingly reluctant to leave the labor force to have and care for children, and the policy has clauses to guarantee reentry into the labor market. There are also components that seek to address the poor social status of parents, to make having children more desirable. The long-term effectiveness of these policies remains to be seen, but the leadership should be commended for adopting positive measures rather than negative ones, such as reduced access to contraception or restrictions on abortion. However, empirical evidence has shown that pro-natalist programs typically encourage couples to have children sooner but not to increase the overall number of children born.[15]

MORTALITY

The mortality situation in Russia has received considerable attention and for good reason. Mortality levels and patterns of death and disease in Russia are far out of line for a country at its level of development. Russia is a literal "point off the curve" in combining relatively low child mortality levels with very high adult mortality levels.[16] It is the exceptionally high working-age mortality where Russia differs, with mortality three to five times that for males and twice for females among countries with similar income levels.[17] Studies have shown that the key factor driving increases in mortality during the transition period in Russia is acute psychosocial stress, brought about when individuals are called upon to adjust to new situations for which they have few coping mechanisms.[18] This is evidenced in the pattern of causes of death: increases in deaths due to cardiovascular diseases, suicides and accidents, and ulcers and cirrhosis of the liver. The transition period in Russia and the other transition countries was marked by unemployment, rapid labor turnover, job insecurity, family instability, distress migration, and increased social stratification. Less-educated and more socially marginalized groups tended to have much higher mortality levels, as there was widening of the life expectancy gap during the 1990s between those with high and low levels of education. Most studies have demonstrated that absolute deprivation, the collapse of the health-care system, and environmental pollution were not major contributing factors.[19]

There was a temporary decline in deaths during the antialcohol campaign of the late 1980s, which saved an estimated 930,000 lives over the years 1985 to 1992 (620,000 male lives and 310,000 female lives).[20] There was a sharp upturn between 1990 and 1994, when the number of deaths increased from 1.7 million to 2.3 million, at the time the Soviet Union was breaking up and the economic transition began. There was a decline after this until 1998, the year of the financial crisis, when deaths increased again, peaking in 2003. Since 2004, there has been a steady decline in the number of people dying in Russia.

Life expectancy in Russia rose from quite low levels in the first part of the twentieth century, and levels approached those of the United States and other developed countries in the mid-1960s (see figure 7.2). After that time, life expectancy in Russia remained stagnant (for females) or declined slightly (for males), while in the rest of the world it continued to rise. One noticeable feature that keeps overall life expectancy in Russia low is the large female advantage. Globally, women live three years longer than men, but in Russia they live thirteen years longer.[21] Aside from the antialcohol period of 1986 to 1988, the highest life expectancy that Russian males achieved was in 1964. Following the peak in 1988, when life expectancy was 64.9 years for males and 74.4 for females, it plunged for both to lows in 1994 of 57.5 for males and 71.1 years for females, at which time the female-male gap reached its apex of 13.6 years. After 1994, life expectancy rose to 1998 and then fell following the ruble crisis. If there is any hopeful sign, it is that with the recent period of economic growth, life expectancy

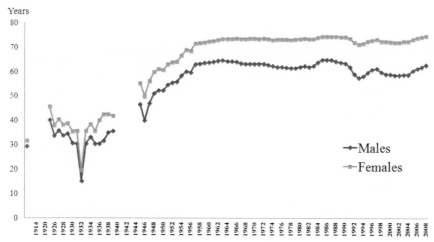

Figure 7.2.   Life Expectancy at Birth in Russia, 1897–2009
Source: Rosstat, *Demograficheskii ezhegodnik* (various years)

has increased by nearly four years since 2003 and the female-male gap has narrowed slightly.

More so than in other countries, life expectancy in Russia seems influenced by short-term fluctuations in economic and social currents. Long-term mortality trends in Russia are influenced by cardiovascular disease, while external causes (suicides, murders, accidents, and poisonings) tend to be responsible for short-term fluctuations.[22] Periods of mortality increase in Russia are marked by increased deaths from heart and circulatory system diseases and external causes among working-age males, while during periods of decrease, deaths from these causes among males decline the most. The fluctuations for working-age females are usually somewhat less than for males, and females typically have larger increases in deaths from circulatory system causes and less from external causes. Death rates among children and the elderly account for very little of the fluctuation in life expectancy in Russia. Infant mortality has steadily declined from 21 infant deaths per 1,000 births in 1985 to 7 per 1,000 in 2011. While Russia does not have anywhere near the lowest infant mortality rate in the world, it is not high enough to have a very significant impact on overall mortality levels, though the poor health of newborns and children affects the population later in life. The improved education and health of Russian children is critical to developing the well-educated and skilled human capital needed for Russia's economic and social development.

Poor diets with an abundance of protein-rich, fatty foods with high cholesterol content have increasingly marked the Russian diet since the

1970s.[23] High blood pressure, high cholesterol, and tobacco account for 75 percent of all deaths in Russia. Low fruit and vegetable consumption, high body-mass indexes, alcohol consumption, physical inactivity, and urban outdoor air pollution are other leading risk factors. Noncommunicable diseases and injuries account for the ten leading causes of death in Russia. There are substantial gains to be made, both demographic and economic, from reducing these causes of death.[24]

In a country where 54 percent of physicians continue to smoke, the anti-tobacco movement in Russia lags far behind that of the West. Russia is one of a handful of countries that has not signed the Framework Convention on Tobacco Control. The tobacco lobby in Russia has hampered measures that have been effective elsewhere, such as advertising limits, price increases, warning labels on cigarette packages, bans on marketing to children, and restrictions on public smoking. Russian females rank twenty-seventh of 131 countries in terms of smoking prevalence, while Russian males have the highest smoking rates in the world.[25] The smoking rates among teenagers thirteen to fifteen also place Russia among the top 20 countries in the world, a sign that the problem of smoking and smoking-related morbidity and mortality show no signs of abating soon.

High and increased levels of consumption of alcohol have played a major role in explaining changes in mortality levels in Russia over time and between Russia and other countries, as Russia ranked fifth in the world in levels of alcohol consumption.[26] A substantial portion of the increase in mortality in the early 1990s can be attributed to alcohol.[27] Alcohol consumption in Russia is characterized by high levels of binge drinking, drinking large amounts of high-alcohol-content *samogon*, and higher levels of consumption of spirits. Three-quarters of alcohol-caused deaths were either binge drinking or alcoholic cardiomyopathy—chronic long-term abuse of alcohol leading to heart failure.

HIV-AIDS came late to Russia, but over the past few years, Russia has had among the highest incidence rates in the world. According to official data from the Russian Federal AIDS Center, at the end of 1995, there were barely 1,000 reported HIV-AIDS cases in the country and only 364 deaths from the disease.[28] By mid-2008, the number of persons living with HIV-AIDS had skyrocketed to 433,827 and the number of reported deaths was 27,341, while other estimates put the true prevalence level at 940,000 to 1.3 million.[29] There is a different epidemiology of transmission of HIV-AIDS in Russia, with intravenous drug use becoming a major mode of transmission in the late 1990s. This helped fuel a major increase in the incidence rate in Russia in 1996. The epidemic is now growing among the non–drug-using heterosexual population, and over 80 percent of those infected are under age thirty.[30]

Many attribute at least part of the health problems in Russia to an inadequate response of the health-care system, stemming from the legacy of the output-oriented Soviet health-care system. The health-care system plays a role in explaining differences between Russia and Western European countries, but it cannot explain a majority of the differences. With infusions from the National Priority Health Program, spending levels have now risen to pretransition levels. But even with increased health spending, the system is very inefficient, with too many resources aimed at hospitalization and too few devoted to primary and preventative care. Estimates are that in 2005, 150,000 deaths could have been prevented by referrals to primary prevention.[31] There have also been increased funds available for HIV-AIDS prevention, including a twentyfold increase in spending since 2006, targeted in part toward scaling up access to antiretroviral drugs. A World Bank policy note on the Russian health situation suggested four key interventions: controlling excessive alcohol consumption, controlling tobacco consumption, promoting changes in diet and physical activity, and improving road safety. In addition to the quantitative decline of the population acting as a deterrent to economic growth, the qualitative decline in terms of poor health is also a factor.

COMPOSITION OF THE POPULATION

While the quantitative aspects of Russia's demographic situation are important, so is the qualitative. This section examines four important aspects of Russia's population: sex ratios, age structure, educational levels, and ethnic composition.

Sex Ratios

In the 2010 census, there were 76.7 million females versus 66.2 million males, a difference of 10.5 million and a slight increase over the 1989 and 2002 censuses, when females outnumbered males by 9.6 million caused by the increasing female-male gap in life expectancy during the 1990s. A large excess of females over males has persisted in Russia for quite some time. Males suffered the brunt of the devastating losses during World War II, and at the end of the war the sex ratio was 74.7 males per 100 females, among the lowest ratios ever recorded for a sizable population. The sex ratio gradually increased to a peak of 88.4 males per 100 females in 1995, before declining again to 86.1 males per 100 females in 2010, making it among the lowest in the world.[32] There are more males than females until age thirty-three, so there is limited effect on the marriage market. From that age onward, higher male mortality continues to pull down the sex ratio, so that over age eighty-five, there is only one male per every five females.

There are several implications of this unequal sex ratio for Russian society and the economy. The primary one is that the population would obviously be a lot higher if not for the large male mortality. The effects of Russia's unbalanced sex ratio are akin to a country involved in war or experiencing large-scale emigration of males. One study examining the effects of war on Russian women who were in their twenties during World War II found that women in cohorts or regions with lower sex ratios had lower rates of marriage and fertility, and higher rates of out-of-wedlock births and abortions than those less affected by the war.[33] While current male mortality in Russia is not at levels found during wartime, it is extremely high, which might impact marriage and fertility decisions, as Russian women can expect to spend much longer portions of their lives as widows.

Age Structure

As in many countries, the population of Russia is aging, though Russia does not appear on a list of the world's oldest countries because so many Russians, especially male, do not live long enough to be classified as old age. Because fertility was at or above replacement for most of the twentieth century, the size of the working-age population was growing as a share of the total population, contributing to overall economic growth.[34] As the smaller cohorts of the past two decades replace larger cohorts that are retiring, the size of the working-age population peaked in 2007 and will continue to decline, acting as a brake on economic growth. The size of the labor force will decline from its peak of 90.4 million to 74.8 million in 2025, a drop of 15.6 million. To maintain economic growth, labor productivity will have to match or exceed this labor force decline. Further exacerbating this problem is that even within the working-age population there is aging; 95 percent of the decline in the working ages of 11 million persons between now and 2025 will be in the fifteen-to-thirty-nine age group. Thus, to avoid further declines, labor participation rates will have to increase among those in the older working ages, or among other groups with traditionally lower participation rates.[35] The challenges will be to sustain economic growth through improved productivity and to manage the fiscal costs associated with aging.

A recent World Bank study labeled the demographic transition of rapidly aging and shrinking populations in Russia as the "third transition," after the political and economic transitions that have taken place. What makes Russia unique is that the demographic transition is going on at the same time as the other two. This will lead to further economic decline unless productivity and labor-force participation are raised and health care, elder care, and pension expenditures are reduced. Because of aging, Russia's challenges are more complex and less demographically deterministic than suggested by conventional wisdom. First, the impact of aging on total expenditures in health is low, as many drivers of increased expenditures are technological, independent of aging. Second, aging is one factor that affects level of pension spending, but so do pension-system parameters. One suggestion is to equalize retirement ages between men and women and to perhaps increase them, as the duration of working careers are four years less than in countries of the Organization for Economic Cooperation and Development (OECD). With women living much longer than men in Russia, there is little reason other than tradition for maintaining this. The study's conclusion is that changes in population size and composition are not highly influential factors in overall health-care expenditures over the medium and long runs.

In the age-sex structure of the Russian population in October 2010 what is important for future population change is the very narrow base at the bottom, with nearly every cohort from age twenty to age five being smaller than the one above it (see figure 7.3). This is the major factor contributing to the declining Russian population in the recent past and in the future. In the last few years, there has been a moderate increase in cohort size from

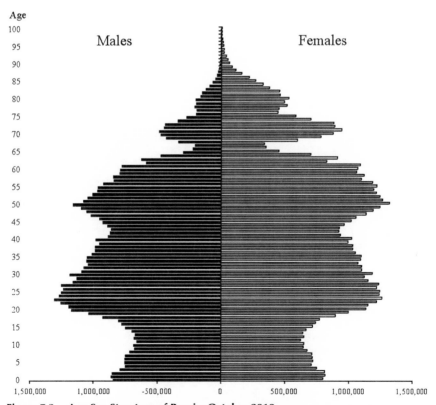

Figure 7.3.   Age-Sex Structure of Russia, October 2010
Source: Rosstat, *Results of the All-Russian Population Census* 2010, volume 2, table 1

a combination of actual fertility increases and the larger size of cohorts a generation earlier.

One area where the decline in births will be felt most keenly is the military, where current plans seem to be at odds with demographic reality.[36] Since the mid-1980s the decline in male births has reduced the conscription pool by one-half, at a time when the government plans to maintain the armed forces at 1.1 million. Simultaneously, the plans call for reducing the term of conscription from two years to one year, which implies doubling the number of conscripts annually. A number of the current deferment categories are to be abolished, but this will not likely matter much, since at present about 70 percent of recruits are rejected at the medical-board stage. It appears that the change to a one-year conscription will cause a manpower crisis of an unprecedented scale and a host of security, social, economic, and policy consequences.

Educational Levels

At the beginning of the transition period, Russia could be rightly proud of the achievements of its education system. As part of the education reforms in Russia, there has been a move away from rote learning toward problem solving and lifelong learning. There has been a decreased demand for technical training in vocational schools and engineering at higher levels, and an increased demand for courses in the humanities, economics, finance, languages, and other skills needed for new labor markets. The wage structure under the Soviet economic system was rather narrow but has widened considerably under market conditions, causing a large increase in returns to education.[37] The increasing returns to education brought about by the economic changes of the transition period are evident in the increased shares of the population obtaining higher-level degrees. Those with a higher or graduate degree increased from 11.3 percent in 1989 to 16.0 percent in 2002. Between 1989 and 2002, the share of the population with higher degrees (higher, secondary professional, or primary professional) increased from 34 to 59 percent of the population aged fifteen and older.[38] However, there are worrying signs that while overall levels of education are rising, outputs as measured by scores on standardized tests are declining. Russia's scores in mathematics and science in the Program for International Student Assessment (PISA) for grade 8 students declined between 1995 and 2003. And its scores declined in both absolute and relative terms on the Trends in International Mathematics and Science Study (TIMSS) assessment between 2000 and 2003.

Nationality Composition

The complex ethnic mosaic that was the Soviet Union was always difficult to manage and played a part in its demise. There were fears before the last Soviet census that Russians would lose their demographic majority, but they just managed to cling to it as they made up 50.8 percent of the population in 1989.[39] One of the fears of population decline is the decline of the titular ethnic group, but according to official census data, the ethnic Russian population only declined from 81.3 to 80.9 percent of the population between 1989 and 2010, a share that has not changed much since the first Soviet census in 1926 when Russians made up 78.0 percent of the population.[40] Russia has always had an uneasy relationship with the Muslim world of which it is part by virtue of having a larger and growing Muslim population of its own, and having Muslim states along its southern periphery, which figure prominently into Russia's internal and foreign policy agenda. The Muslim population in Russia increased from 7.9 to 10.2 percent of the total population between the 1989 and 2002 censuses.[41] Russia already has troubled ethnic and religious tensions, and if it needs to recruit non-Russians from the other states of the former Soviet Union and beyond to compensate for its demographic shortfall, this will only exacerbate the situation.[42]

INTERNATIONAL MIGRATION

The breakup of the Soviet Union added 28 million persons to the world stock of migrants, and Russia, with 12 million, has the second largest stock of migrants after the United States.[43] There was actually an increase in the percentage of "foreign born" in Russia between the 1989 and 2002 censuses, from 7.8 to 9.3 percent of the population, due to continued immigration of nonnative groups and a natural decrease of ethnic Russians.[44] International migration has become a major internal issue for population and economic growth as well as social cohesion in Russia. It is also an external issue in Russia's relations with other former Soviet states, as the treatment of migrants is often seen as a form of soft power that Russia exerts over its neighbors. The sheer number of migrant workers from Central Asia and the Caucasus seeking work in Russia has forced these other former Soviet states to maintain contacts with what had been the imperial center.[45]

Net migration into Russia rose from 115,000 in 1989 to a peak of 810,000 in 1994 then declined to just 39,000 in 2003 before increasing again to 320,100 in 2011.[46] The first decade after the breakup of the Soviet Union was a period of porous borders with visa-free travel among the Commonwealth of Independent States (CIS). Most of what is recorded in migration statistics are movements for permanent migration, and a considerable portion of the movement into Russia is temporary and quasi-legal. One problem that Russia confronts in formulating migration policy is that it has not fully developed a migration statistics system adequate for the new flows that are taking place.[47] The broad pattern of migration by country for Russia is one of net immigration from the other former Soviet states and net emigration to countries outside the former Soviet Union. The bulk of the net immigration from within the former Soviet states has come from Central Asia and the Caucasus. Most emigration to outside states has been toward Germany, Israel, and the United States.

One issue facing Russian migration policy is that current migration into the country, both documented and undocumented, is extremely ethnically homogenous. Since 1989, ethnic Russians made up two-thirds of the recorded migration into Russia.[48] If undocumented migration were included, the majority would be non-Russian. In the immediate post-Soviet period, many of the migration movements across the post-Soviet space were ethnically motivated, people returning to their ethnic homelands or fleeing ethnic violence. More recently, the motivations have been economically motivated, driven by the large income disparities between Russia and the non-Russian former Soviet states. For persons from the low-income former Soviet countries, the returns to migration are large. Moldova, Tajikistan, and Armenia are among the top countries in the world in terms of remittances as a share of GDP, most earned in Russia.[49] The shares of the labor forces of some non-Russian states of the former Soviet Union working permanently or seasonally in Russia are quite significant, with estimates ranging from 10 to 30 percent of the labor forces of Moldova, Armenia, Azerbaijan, Georgia, Tajikistan, Kyrgyzstan, and Uzbekistan.[50] Current estimates put the number at four to five million illegal workers in Russia.[51] As in other migration magnet countries, a dual labor market is developing in Russia, with migrants occupying large sectors of the workforce in trade, construction, transport services, and agriculture, and working quite separate from local residents. Being illegal or quasi-legal, these migrants are subject to the same abuses and exploitation as in other migrant-destination countries, perhaps more so in Russia with its history of discrimination against "others."

The first formative phase of Russian migration policy during the years 1992 to 1994 was characterized by assistance toward involuntary migrants from the other former Soviet states, the establishment of the Federal Migration Service, passage of key migration and refugee laws, abolishment of the *propiska* system, and the signing of key international migration and refugee conventions. The second half of the 1990s saw further passage of key migration legislation such as laws on labor migration. This period of more liberal attitudes toward migrants ended in 2000 when the Federal Migration Service was abolished and its functions transferred to the Ministry of Internal Affairs, and the overall thrust of migration policy became one of combating illegal migration. In 2002, a somewhat restrictive Citizenship Law was passed. Russia quit the Bishkek Agreement allowing visa-free travel among the former Soviet states and began to negotiate entry and labor migration on a bilateral basis. The years after 2006 have seen a shift in migration policy and legislation toward a realization of the inevitability of migration into Russia and its possible benefits both demographically and economically. There was also the realization that efforts were needed to better regulate and protect those migrants who were in the country. Regulations have been passed to increase enforcement of policies toward illegal migrants but also to make the process of registering for work permits easier. As a result, there was a surge in the number of work permits issued in 2007, to four times that of the previous year.[52]

This policy shift is partially the result of the increased necessity for "replacement migration," the use of migration to compensate for declining populations or labor forces. According to a set of UN simulations of replacement migration, for Russia to maintain the same population size over the first half of the twenty-first century, there would have to be a net migration of 25 million people, and to maintain the same labor-force size, there would need to be a net migration of 36 million. This would require immigration levels to exceed those of the 1990s, when there was a net immigration of 4.5 million.[53] For centuries, and most of the Soviet period, Russia was a major sending state and is making an uneasy transition to being a major migration destination.

SPATIAL DISTRIBUTION OF THE POPULATION

Just as the rise in GDP disparities among the former Soviet states was a major driver of post-Soviet migration among the states, rising income disparities among Russian regions drove internal migration patterns. The Soviet Union attempted to equalize incomes among all regions through centrally administered wages, prices, and subsidies that made disparities lower than what they would have been under market conditions. Between 1990 and 2002, the ratio of regions with the highest gross regional product per capita to the lowest rose from five to thirty-six.[54] The restructuring of the regional economic geography of Russia has caused two major internal movements. The first is out of Siberia, the Far East, and the North toward central Russia, and the second is movement up the urban hierarchy (see figure 7.4).

Between 1989 and 2009, there was an out-migration of 17 percent of the population from the regions that make up the Far North.[55] At the extreme were the two regions in the far northeast, Magadan and Chukotka, which respectively had net out-migration of 57 and 74 percent of their populations. According to Hill and Gaddy, the overpopulation of Siberia and the North was one of the mistakes of Soviet central planners when it came to determining the spatial allocation of population and economic activity.[56] Among others were the lack of medium-size cities, which are often the engines of

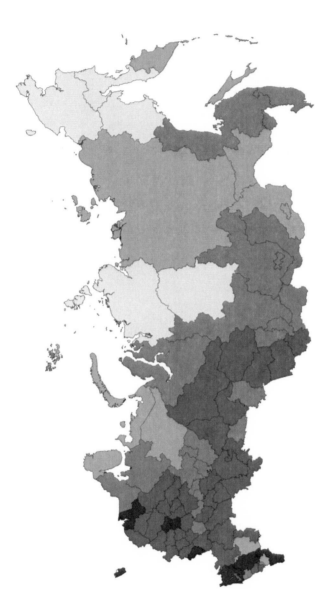

Net migration, 1989 to 2008 (percent of 1989 population)

11.1 to 28.6	0.1 to 11.0	-15.2 to 0.0	-39.6 to -15.3	-74.2 to -39.7

Figure 7.4. Net Migration by Region, 1989–2008 (percent of 1989 population)
Source: Rosstat, *Demograficheskii ezhegodnik* (selected editions)

economic growth, and the lack of connectedness among urban centers. Since the transition, Moscow has grown from 8.9 to 11.5 million persons, and from 6.0 to 8.1 percent of the population in 2008.[57] This trend of population growth in the primate city during the period of economic transition also occurred across many of the former Soviet Union and Eastern European countries. Within Russia, there has been a trend of population concentration into the *oblast* centers and the dying out of many smaller villages, as the cost of living in smaller and more distant settlements has became prohibitively expensive with the withdrawal of subsidies on transport.

POPULATION PROJECTIONS
AND IMPLICATIONS

Population projections for Russia are routinely done by four different agencies: Rosstat, which is the state agency for statistics in Russia,[58] the United Nations Population Division,[59] the World Bank,[60] and the U.S. Census Bureau.[61] The projections done by the latter three agencies extend to the year 2050. All expect that Russia will continue to have a negative natural increase where deaths exceed births, and that Russia will continue to be a net immigration country. Deviations from replacement-level fertility of 2.1 children per woman greatly influence rates of population change. For Russia and other low-fertility countries, there is no expectation that fertility will ever rise again to replacement level. Projections of the fertility rate for Russia in 2050 range from 1.21 to 2.21 children per woman. It is these differing assumptions regarding future fertility levels that explain much of the difference among the projections of Russia's future population size by different organizations and among the different variants. Similar to fertility, assumptions are made regarding the future levels of life expectancy and the age distribution of mortality. The general assumption is that with improvements in wealth, health care, and technology, life expectancy will continue to rise. All agencies project improvements in life expectancy for Russia, albeit to different levels. The range of projections of life expectancy in 2050 is from 68.5 to 72.3 years for males and from 77.9 to 80.2 years for females. However, little in Russia's recent demographic past or current social policy points toward improvements in life expectancy of the magnitudes embedded in the projections.

The impact of HIV-AIDS on Russian population change, economic growth, and society has been the subject of considerable speculation. The modeling work done at the U.S. Census Bureau is one careful study of AIDS, which uses adjusted data on the disease to produce likely scenarios based on paths of transmission seen elsewhere in the world.[62] The study starts with an infected population of 1.3 million in 2004 and projects that the number of infected persons will peak at about 2.6 million between

2010 and 2015 before gradually declining to 870,000 in 2050. HIV-AIDS-related deaths will increase to 250,000 annually in 2015 before declining to about 100,000 annually in 2050. Overall, HIV-AIDS is expected to account for 8.6 million deaths in Russia in the first half of the century and 8.3 percent of total deaths. The study concludes that HIV-AIDS will have a relatively minor impact on the Russian population and that the disease will not be as catastrophic as in some parts of Africa, though its impact will not be insignificant.

Migration is the most volatile and difficult-to-project component of population change because it involves so many exogenous economic, political, and social factors. It is also the component that could have the most significant impact on the Russian economy and society and Russia's relations with its neighbors. Since the breakup of the Soviet Union, net migration into Russia has averaged 360,000 annually. The UN projects that net migration into Russia will remain positive at 50,000 persons a year from 2005 to 2050, and the World Bank projects a similar level of immigration. The Rosstat low, medium, and high migration scenarios project an annual average immigration into Russia of 220,000, 415,000, and 840,000 from 2005 to 2025. Barring unforeseen political events, economic differentials between Russia and its neighbors will determine future levels of migration into the country, as well as rates of population growth.

In 1946, after the devastation of World War II, Russia's population was 97.5 million, rising steadily to a peak of 148.6 million in 1993 before declining. The three different Rosstat projections range from 125.0 million to 146.7 million in 2026, the latter being the only one of the eight scenarios to project a population increase.[63] The three different UN projections range lower than the three Rosstat projections, from a low of 119.4 million to a high of 135.2 million in 2026. The low UN projection scenario shows the largest decline of any, indicating a population decline of 23 million or 16 percent in just two decades. Projecting further out to midcentury, the three UN projections bracket those of the World Bank and U.S. Census Bureau and range from a low of 89 million to a high of 130 million, with a medium scenario of 108 million.

GLOBAL IMPLICATIONS
OF POPULATION DECLINE

For the last several centuries, the Russian Empire or the Soviet Union was the third largest country in the world in terms of population size, behind China and India, and just ahead of the United States. When the Soviet Union broke apart, Russia became the sixth most populous country in the world; by 2008, it had fallen to ninth.[64] Russia is expected to fall to twelfth in 2025 and to fifteenth by midcentury.[65] Population size is just one determinant of a state's capabilities. Others include size of economy, territory, technological level, size and equipment of armed forces, and qualitative attributes such as organizational effectiveness and morale, as well as location, climate, and topography.[66] The relative weights of these factors change over time, and having a large territory is less important than factors such as size of economy and technological capability. Classifying countries as a function of the size of territory, population, and GDP, the Soviet Union/Russia has fallen out of the category of super-giants where it had been during the Soviet era (others were Britain, China, and the United States), and is now classed as a sub-giant, with the United States and China being the only remaining super-giants.[67] This is not just because Russia has declined in population rank but more because its economic size has fallen from second to tenth in the world. One source, speculating broadly on global trends in the first half of the twenty-first century, notes that Russia has an unmatched treasure trove of energy resources, but its current weaknesses, including overall population decline and decline in ethnic Russian majority, might keep it on the sidelines of the great-power game.[68]

One study identified six security implications of global population change, many of which apply to Russia.[69] These include disproportionate growth in large and Muslim countries, shrinkage in population in EU and former Soviet states, differential age structures between developed and developing countries and increased migration between those groups, and the impact of AIDS. As the report points out, given these trends, leaders of affected countries, including Russia, must concentrate on mitigation measures, none of which will be easy.

Russia seems destined to fall to about fifteenth place among the world's populations by midcentury, when it will have a population just one-quarter the size of the United States. How Russia deals with this new demographic reality and how well it deals with the other elements of state power and national wealth will determine its future place among great powers.

CONCLUSION

During the 1990s, demographic issues were largely ignored by the Russian government, but in his 2006 state of the nation address, Putin identified the demographic decline as the country's largest problem. His speech addressing population policy is without parallel by a European head of state.[70] He laid out programs to lower the death rate, increase the birth rate, and more effectively manage migration. Following that speech, Putin issued a decree to adopt the "Concept on Demographic Policy of Russia until 2025."[71] The program was implemented during 2008–2010 and comes at a time when Russia has the financial resources to commit. It is too early to fully measure the effectiveness of these policies, but it is a positive sign that the government is taking the dire demographic situation seriously and taking concrete steps to address them.

Not surprisingly, new president Putin is likely to continue the demographic policy agenda laid out by him in his first administration and expanded upon by former president Dmitry Medvedev. In his first state of the nation address in November 2008, Medvedev reemphasized the importance of increased education, healthy lifestyles, ethnic tolerance, internal mobility, and regulation of immigration, including recruitment of those highly skilled.[72] However, there is only so much a government can do to affect fertility, mortality, and migration trends. The federal government, regional governments, business, the media, and most importantly, the population itself all must contribute, and success depends on social and economic factors outside government control. Empirical evidence has shown that there is a two-way relationship between economic growth and improved health.[73] Russia needs to use its recent economic prosperity to improve its dire demographics, lest it fall into a spiral of demographic and economic decline.

SUGGESTED READINGS

Chawla, Mukesh, Gordon Bethcherman, and Arup Banerji. *From Red to Gray: The "Third Transition" of Aging Populations in Eastern Europe and the Former Soviet Union.* Washington, DC: World Bank, 2007.

Eberstadt, Nicholas. *Russia's Peacetime Demographic Crisis: Dimensions, Causes, Implications.* Seattle, Wash.: The National Bureau of Asian Research, 2010.

Ivakhnyuk, Irina. *The Russian Migration Policy and Its Impact on Human Development: The Historical Perspective.* United Nations Development Research Paper 14. New York: United Nations Development Program, 2009.

United Nations Development Program. *National Human Development Report, Russian Federation 2008: Russia Facing Demographic Challenges.* Moscow: United Nations, 2009.

United Nations in Russia. *Demographic Policy in Russia: From Reflection to Action.* Moscow: United Nations, 2008.

World Bank. *Dying Too Young: Addressing Premature Mortality and Ill Health Due to Non-Communicable Diseases and Injuries in the Russian Federation.* Washington, DC: World Bank, 2005.

NOTES

1. Rosstat website, www.gks.ru (accessed May 5, 2012).

2. Michael S. Teitelbaum and Jay M. Winter, *The Fear of Population Decline* (San Diego: Academic, 1985), 10–11.

3. The total fertility rate is the number of children per woman, with 2.1 children per woman considered replacement level.

4. CIS Statistical Committee, *1989 USSR Population Census CD-ROM* (Minneapolis, Minn.: Eastview, 1996).

5. United Nations Population Division, *World Fertility Patterns 2007* (New York: United Nations, 2008).

6. Rosstat, *Demograficheskii ezhegodnik Rossii* (Moscow: Rosstat, 2010), 164.

7. A. Avdeev, "The Extent of the Fertility Decline in Russia: Is the One-Child Family Here to Stay?" paper presented at the IUSSP Seminar on "International Perspectives on Low Fertility: Trends, Theories and Policies," Tokyo, March 21–23, 2001.

8. Louise Grogan, "What Caused the Post-Transition Fertility Decline in Central and Eastern Europe and the former Soviet Union?" Discussion Paper no. 2002–5, University of Guelph, September 18, 2002.

9. John Bongaarts, "A Framework for Analyzing the Proximate Determinants of Fertility," *Population and Development Review* 4, no. 1 (1978): 105–32; John Bongaarts, "The Fertility Inhibiting Effects of the Intermediate Variables," *Studies in Family Planning* 13, nos. 6/7 (1982): 179–89.

10. U.S. Bureau of the Census, "International Data Base," www.census.gov/ipc/www/idb/; U.S. Department of Health and Human Services, *Reproductive, Maternal, and Child Health in Eastern Europe and Eurasia: A Comparative Report*, April 2003, 62.

11. Henry P. David, ed., *From Abortion to Contraception: A Resource to Public Policies and Reproductive Behavior in Central and Eastern Europe from 1917 to the Present* (Westport, Conn.: Greenwood, 1999), 232–33.

12. UNICEF Innocenti Research Centre, *TransMONEE 2008 Database*, released May 2008, www.unicef-irc.org.

13. United Nations Population Division, *World Abortion Policies 2007* (New York: United Nations, 2007).

14. Elizabeth Brainerd, "The Baby Decision amid Turmoil: Understanding the Fertility Decline in Russia of the 1990s," National Council for Eurasian and East European Research Working Paper, February 2007.

15. Central Intelligence Agency, *Long-Term Global Demographic Trends: Reshaping the Geopolitical Landscape* (Washington, DC: CIA, July 2001).

16. Christopher J. L. Murray and Jose Luis Bobadilla, "Epidemiological Transitions in the Formerly Socialist Economies: Divergent Patterns of Mortality and Causes of Death," in *Premature Death in the New Independent States*, ed. Jose Luis Bobadilla, Christine A. Costello, and Faith Mitchell (Washington, DC: National Academy Press, 1997), 184–219.

17. United Nations in Russia, *Demographic Policy in Russia: From Reflection to Action* (Moscow: United Nations, 2008), 28.

18. Giovanni Andrea Cornia and Renato Paniccia, eds., *The Mortality Crisis in Transitional Economies* (New York: Oxford University Press, 2000), 27–34.

19. Cornia and Paniccia, *The Mortality Crisis in Transitional Economies*, 27–34; Charles M. Becker and David Bloom, eds., *World Development, Special Issue: The Demographic Crisis in the Former Soviet Union* 26, no. 11 (1998): 1913–2103; Bobadilla, Costello, and Mitchell, *Premature Death in the New Independent States*.

20. Vladimir M. Shkolnikov and Alexander Nemtsov, "The Anti-Alcohol Campaign and Variations in Russian Mortality," in *Premature Death in the New Independent States*, 239–61.

21. Population Reference Bureau, *2008 World Population Data Sheet* (Washington, DC: PRB, 2008).

22. Vladimir M. Shkolnikov, France Mesle, and Jacques Vallin, "Recent Trends in Life Expectancy and Causes of Death in Russia, 1970–1993," in *Premature Death in the New Independent States*, 34–63.

23. Renato Paniccia, "Transition, Impoverishment, and Mortality: How Large an Impact?" in *The Mortality Crisis in Transitional Economies*, 105–26.

24. Patricio Marquez, Marc Suhrcke, Martin McKee, and Lorenzo Rocco, "Adult Health in the Russian Federation: More than Just a Health Problem," *Health Affairs* 26, no. 4 (2007): 1040–51.

25. World Health Organization, *World Health Statistics 2007*, www.who.int/tobacco/global_data/en/index.html.

26. World Health Organization, *WHO Global Status Report on Alcohol 2004*, www.who.int/globalatlas/default.asp.

27. Becker and Bloom, eds., *World Development, Special Issue: The Demographic Crisis in the Former Soviet Union*, 1913–2103.

28. Russian Federal Scientific-Methodological Center for the Prevention and Treatment of AIDS, //hivrussia.org.

29. United Nations in Russia, *Demographic Policy in Russia*, 35.

30. U.S.-Russia Working Group against HIV/AIDS, *On the Frontline of an Epidemic: The Need for Urgency in Russia's Fight against AIDS* (New York: Transatlantic Partners, 2003).

31. United Nations in Russia, *Demographic Policy in Russia*, 38.

32. United Nations Population Division, *World Population Prospects: The 2004 Revision and World Urbanization Prospects: The 2003 Revision*, //esa.un.org/unpp.

33. Elizabeth Brainerd, *Uncounted Costs of World War II: The Effects of Changing Sex Ratios on Marriage and Fertility of Russian Women*, National Council for Eurasian and East European Research Working Paper, October 2007.

34. Working ages are sixteen to fifty-nine for males and sixteen to fifty-four for females.

35. Mukesh Chawla, Gordon Betcherman, and Arup Banerji, *From Red to Gray: The "Third Transition" of Aging Populations in Eastern Europe and the Former Soviet Union* (Washington, DC: World Bank, 2007), 110.

36. Kier Giles, *Where Have All the Soldiers Gone? Russia's Military Plans versus Demographic Reality*, Russia Series 06/47 Defence Academy of the United Kingdom, October 2006.

37. Yuriy Gorodnichenko and Klara Sabirianova Peter, *Returns to Schooling in Russia and Ukraine: A Semiparametric Approach to Cross-Country Comparative Analysis*, IZA Discussion Paper Series no. 1325, September 2004.

38. Rosstat, *All-Russian Census of Population 2002, vol. 3, Education*, www.gks.ru.

39. Goskomstat SSSR, *Natsional'nyi sostav naseleniia SSSR* (Moscow: Finansy i statistika, 1991).

40. Rosstat, *All-Russian Census of Population 2002*, www.gks.ru.

41. Timothy Heleniak, "Regional Distribution of the Muslim Population of Russia," *Eurasian Geography and Economics* 47, no. 4 (2006): 426–48.

42. "The CIA Director on Demographics and Security," *Population and Development Review* 34, no. 3 (2008): 593–94.

43. United Nations Population Division, *Trends in Total Migrant Stock: The 2005 Revision,* //esa.un.org/migration.

44. *1989 USSR Population Census* and Rosstat, www.gks.ru.

45. Sebastein Peyrouse, *The Russian Minority in Central Asia: Migration, Politics, and Language,* Kennan Institute Occasional Paper no. 297 (2007), 1.

46. Rosstat, *Demograficheskii ezhegodnik Rossii* (annual editions) and Rosstat, www.gks.ru.

47. Yuri Andreinko and Sergei Guriev, *Understanding Migration in Russia,* CEFIR Policy Paper no. 23, Center for Economic and Financial Research at the New Economic School, November 2005.

48. Timothy Heleniak, "Migration of the Russian Diaspora after the Breakup of the Soviet Union," *Journal of International Affairs* 57, no. 2 (2004): 99–117.

49. Ali Mansoor and Quillin Bryce, eds., *Migration and Remittances: Eastern Europe and the Former Soviet Union* (Washington, DC: World Bank, 2007).

50. Leonid Rybakovsky and Sergey Ryazanstev, *International Migration in the Russian Federation* (New York: UN Population Division, 2005).

51. Natalia Voronina, "Outlook on Migration Policy Reform in Russia: Contemporary Challenges and Political Paradoxes," *Migration Perspectives Eastern Europe and Central Asia,* ed. Roger Rodriguez Rios (Vienna: International Organization for Migration, 2006), 71–90.

52. "FMS to Discuss Priorities of Migration Policy for 2008," *ITAR-TASS (Russia),* January 31, 2008, www.itar-tass.com/eng/.

53. United Nations Population Division, *Replacement Migration: Is It a Solution to Declining and Ageing Populations?* (New York: United Nations, 2001).

54. Goskomstat Rossii, *Regiony Rossii* (Moscow: Rosstat, various years).

55. Timothy Heleniak, "Migration and Population Change in the Russian Far North during the 1990s," in *Migration in the Circumpolar North: New Concepts and Patterns,* ed. Chris Southcott and Lee Huskey (Edmonton, Alberta, Canada: Canadian Circumpolar Institute Press, University of Alberta, 2009).

56. Fiona Hill and Clifford Gaddy, *The Siberian Curse: How Communist Planners Left Russia out in the Cold* (Washington, DC: Brookings Institution Press, 2003).

57. Rosstat, www.gks.ru.

58. Rosstat, *Predpolozhitel'naia chislennost' naseleniia Rossiskoi Federatsii do 2025 goda: Statisticheskii biulleten* (Moscow: Rosstat, 2005).

59. United Nations Population Division, *World Population Prospects: The 2006 Revision,* //esa.un.org/unpp.

60. World Bank, *World Development Indicators CD-ROM 2007* (Washington, DC: World Bank, 2007).

61. U.S. Census Bureau, *International Data Base,* www.census.gov/ipc/www.

62. Dennis Donahue, "HIV Prevalence in the Russian Federation: Methods and Estimates," paper presented at the 2004 annual meeting of the Southern Demographic Association, Hilton Head Island, South Carolina, October 14–16, 2004.

63. Rosstat, *Demograficheskii ezhegodnik* (Moscow: Rosstat, 2005), 41; and Rosstat, www.gks.ru.

64. U.S. Census Bureau, "International Database," updated June 18, 2008, www .census.gov/ipc/www/idb.

65. U.S. Census Bureau, International Data Base, www.census.gov/ipc/www.

66. Geoffrey McNicoll, "Population Weights in the International Order," *Population and Development Review* 25, no. 3 (1999): 411–42.

67. Andrei Treyvish, "A New Russian Heartland: The Demographic and Economic Dimension," *Eurasian Geography and Economics* 46, no. 2 (2005): 123–55.

68. Vaclav Smil, "The Next 50 Years: Unfolding Trends," *Population and Development Review* 31, no. 4 (2005): 605–43.

69. Jack A. Goldstone, "Flash Points and Tipping Points: Security Implications of Global Population Changes, 2005–2025," paper prepared for the Mackinder Forum, Minster Lovell, UK, March 14–15, 2006.

70. "Vladimir Putin on Raising Russia's Birth Rate," *Population and Development Review* 32, no. 2 (2006): 385–89.

71. United Nations in Russia, *Demographic Policy in Russia: From Reflection to Action* (Moscow: United Nations, 2008).

72. Dmitry Medvedev, "Address to the Federal Assembly of the Russian Federation," November 5, 2008, www.kremlin.ru/eng/.

73. Patricio V. Marquez, *Better Outcomes through Health Reforms in the Russian Federation: The Challenges in 2008 and Beyond* (Washington, DC: World Bank, December 2007).

8

Economic Policy

Pekka Sutela

The decade of the 1990s was not kind to the Russian economy. During the decade, the economy contracted up to 50 percent in industrial output, and another 40 percent of agricultural production was lost. In all, from 1990 to 1995, Russia's GDP declined by an estimated 50 percent. Unemployment and labor unrest spiked. Russia experienced mass poverty. Inflation peaked at 2,509 percent in 1992, when most consumer prices were freed, and declined thereafter but failed to reach single digits during the remainder of the decade. The Russian government ran up enormous debt. The federal budget deficit fluctuated between 5 and 10 percent of GDP. As the decade wore on, budget deficits were financed by issuing short-term ruble-denominated government debt (GKOs). Due to the size of the financial need, together with political and economic uncertainty, the GKOs could only be sold with very high yields, which ultimately reached 100 percent annually. The debt spiral was clearly unsustainable. Worse, about one-third of GKOs were held by foreigners. The litany of economic troubles culminated in the ruble crisis of August 1998, when the state had to announce a partial default on its debt, and the ruble collapsed against foreign currencies. The ruble crisis had two main effects. First, Russia's credibility as a borrower was lost. Second, the crisis changed the framework for Russia's macroeconomic policy. A political consensus for macroeconomic stabilization had been reached in principle by 1995, though views on proper rate of inflation and the exchange rate regime continued to vary.

The 1998 crisis marked an end to one phase in Russia's economic transformation. Thereafter, a new consensus emerged on economic policy. The new approach was introduced by the leftist Primakov-Masliukov government in 1998–1999 (against their early announcements), and continued

173

to the end of the Yeltsin period. The new economic consensus had several ingredients, which defined the political economy of Putin's Russia.[1] The purpose of this chapter is to examine the elements of the post-1998 economic stabilization consensus.

TASKS FOR THE 2000s

The first task facing the new Putin regime was that the budget had to be balanced. Continued accumulation of debt was not only potentially destabilizing but also in conflict with the goal to attain economic sovereignty. Russia needed to do away with the need to finance its debt from external lenders. The only way to do that in the short term was to reduce expenditures, in particular the complex and nontransparent web of subsidies that had emerged behind the veil of economic liberalization in the 1990s at the federal, regional, and local levels. From 1997 to 2001 a fiscal adjustment of some 10 percent of general government balance was enacted, primarily by cutting expenditures, especially subsidies to companies.[2] In the short term there was little alternative to this fiscal shock, as a return to monetizing deficits was excluded by the bitter experiences of the early 1990s. There was still a fiscal deficit of 4 percent of GDP in 1999, but thereafter the country experienced surpluses until the financial crisis of 2008–2009. Public foreign debt shrank from 66.8 percent of GDP in 1999 to 2.7 percent in 2007; total public debt remained less than 10 percent of GDP after 2006.[3] Russia, one of the grandest fiscal failures of the 1990s, emerged as a model for fiscal conservatism in just a few years. Necessity caused by failure was turned into virtue.

Russia's quest to balance the budget was helped by traditional export commodities—oil, gas, minerals, and later, agricultural production. Exporters reaped great benefits from the cheap ruble and later from high prices, although their export volumes were often constrained by production and transport capacity. Russia was able to increase exports of oil and some minerals while exports of pipeline-tied gas stagnated. The world had an unprecedented golden period of economic growth during 1992–2008. Russia, with its newly privatized companies, was at last able to join booming global markets. From the trough of early 1998 to the peak in summer 2008 the export price of oil increased by ten times. Russia's other export commodities also increased, though generally not as much. Gaddy and Ickes estimate that in the second half of the 2000s the oil windfall alone reached up to 30 percent of GDP annually.[4] The price of oil was important for Russian incomes and budgets, but Russia was not able to live on oil revenue alone. Distributing the revenue windfall became a key policy issue that had not existed in the 1990s because of low oil prices.

The second task was to fix the tax system. The state had fought a losing battle for more effective company taxation in the 1990s, especially under finance minister Boris Fyodorov. The true state of company finances was hidden in nonmonetary exchanges and webs of implicit subsidies, especially at the regional level. It is estimated that only one-fifth of all transactions in and around the domestic energy sector were conducted in rubles. Even the state routinely accepted nonmonetary clearing of tax obligations. A construction company could have its tax arrears offset by contributing to a public construction project. What prices were used in calculating a proper offset remained unclear. With a ballooning export revenue windfall, this situation could no longer be accepted. Oligarchs, regional governors, and others had to be subordinated to an emerging "power vertical," to use Putin's words.

The share of the federal center in tax revenue was increased, and most regions became dependent on tax transfers from the Moscow center. A stiff oil revenue taxation regime was introduced: the average tax rate rose to 60 percent, and the marginal tax rate even surpassed 90 percent.[5] The former figure is not exorbitant in international comparison, but the latter one is and leaves hardly any incentives to increase upstream oil production.

The state also needed to decide what to do with the tax revenue from the energy sector, which had reached one-half of all federal tax revenue. Logically—and in Russian debates—there were three alternatives. The first alternative was that monies could be distributed among the population, to be used for consumption or private investment as households wished. In view of the income decline and hugely increased income differentials in the 1990s this would have been a politically popular solution, but it was abandoned by the regime as populism. Many resource-rich countries had shown evidence of the "Dutch Disease" due to using high export revenue to increase money and wealth of the population presumably for the general good, but actually leading to high inflation, an overvalued exchange rate, and lost competitiveness in nonresource production. The Putin regime was politically strong enough to avoid this alternative.

The second alternative had stronger political support and suggested to use oil-sector tax revenue for investment in the economy at large. Though investment ratios were very high under Soviet socialism, evidence showed that much of the money used by the state had actually disappeared in hidden inflation, with little if any impact on actual production capacity. Russia thus inherited a capital stock that was smaller, older, and more worn out than official statistics claimed. What had been inherited from the Soviet Union was not what the emerging market economy needed. In addition, while official GDP had dropped by almost one-half in the 1990s, the collapse of investment was even steeper, some four-fifths. The country badly needed high real investment to grow in a sustainable way. Moreover, there was a need to close plants in and around the military sector, which produced very little of what was needed in a market economy. This side of capitalist creative destruction was, however, hardly raised in Russian debates. Protecting existing jobs has always been a priority that constrained economic choices in the Putin regime. One key question for the future is whether this basically conservative attitude will continue.

Because there was little optimism that foreign investment was sufficient to fund modernization, a decision was made that export revenue windfall should be invested into the economy, not only in roads, railways, and airports, but also in health, education, housing, innovation, and other such purposes that were seen as the responsibility of the state. This argument for development was made, not surprisingly, by the Ministry of Economic Development. Investment in the economy was to receive a major boost by the introduction of four "national programs" that took effect in 2006 with great fanfare, in health, housing, education, and agriculture. Dmitry Medvedev, as first deputy prime minister, was responsible for their implementation. Looking not at the budget plans but at their actual implementation, however, shows that the national programs' share as a proportion of all state expenditures never increased.

The third alternative proved the winner of policy debate. Russia opted for a fiscal conservative strategy of maintaining a budget surplus, paying back most public debt, and accumulating reserve funds. This course was pursued by Alexei Kudrin, the longtime finance minister. The decisive voice for fiscal conservatism was that of Vladimir Putin. Steep taxation of oil export revenue was in place by 2004. Accumulation of a stabilization fund was started the same year. By the end of 2007 it amounted to $156.8 billion and a year later to $225.1 billion.[6] The growth is stupendous. As part of the official reserves of the country—peaking at just over $600 billion in mid-2008— these monies had a key role in combating the 2008 crisis. Just before the crisis the stabilization fund had been divided into a reserve fund (for stabilizing fiscal revenue) and a national welfare fund (mostly for supporting the pension system).

The reason for the conservative option was that the 1997–1998 Asian financial crisis had shown that resource-dependent countries that have either consumed or invested their export revenue are vulnerable to external shocks. When any international slowdown causes oil and other resource prices to drop, these countries lack a buffer for maintaining previous spending levels. Usually, only a resource-rich small country like Norway can accumulate large reserve funds that help to maintain posthydrocarbon welfare levels. The International Monetary Fund expects that in resource-rich countries with a small population—Kuwait, Qatar, and Saudi Arabia— current account surpluses will vary from around 30 to 40 percent of GDP;

even in Norway the surplus is around 15 percent of GDP. The corresponding level of surplus for Russia is around 5 percent (and for China only about 2 percent).[7] Populous countries with voluminous imports often find it difficult to build up large welfare funds, but a stabilization fund for evening out fiscal revenue fluctuations will be useful for them as well. As a consequence, many resource-dependent countries decided in the 2000s to accumulate reserve funds.

The third task was that Russia had to be transformed from an economy based on barter to one based on rubles; in other words, the economy had to be monetized. A monetized economy increases the productivity of labor compared to an economy based on barter. In Russia, barter chains could have a number of participants, and the transaction costs involved in establishing and maintaining such chains were great. Barter has little transparency, exchange pricing could be arbitrary, avoiding taxation was easy, and the whole barter economy was prone to corruption. When barter was used in lieu of taxation, the efficiency of public finance obviously suffered. Goods obtained in barter can only be used for limited purposes. On the other hand, money facilitates risk control, saving for investment, and economic growth. There is considerable evidence that monetary and financial systems contribute to economic growth. Berkowitz and DeJong show that financial development was the key domestic driving force for Russia's economic growth in the 1990s.[8]

States usually wish to have complete or at least shared (in currency unions) control over the money circulating within their borders. It is a matter of prestige—sovereign currency being one of the defining features of a state—but more important is the economic benefit. Beyond that, sovereign currency opens up the possibility of monetary policy; its scope depends on foreign trade and trade payments. Russia liberalized its foreign trade in the early 1990s, but capital mobility was officially announced as a major achievement of economic policy only in 2006.

There was some speculation in the 1990s that Russia's nonmonetary market economy was nationally specific, an outcome of the Soviet economy. However, as predicted by standard economic theory, the Russian economy monetized and de-dollarized quickly as inflation was brought under control and the exchange rate stabilized. At peak, in late 1998 barter accounted for 61 percent of manufacturing turnover. In a few years the ratio normalized to about 10 percent.[9] Correspondingly, Russian financial indicators show extremely fast ruble growth since 2001 (see table 8.1).

Table 8.1 shows no correlation between ruble growth and inflation. The ruble had lost much of its credibility in the early 1990s, and continued high inflation made it difficult to reestablish. Savings held in rubles were lost in 1992, to some degree in 1994 and again more widely in 1998. Dollars remained for a few years rare in Russia, but the share of foreign currency

Table 8.1.   Russian Monetary Indicators 2003–2011 (in percent, end of year)

	2003	2004	2005	2006	2007	2008	2009	2010	2011
Consumer price inflation	12.0	11.7	10.9	9.0	11.9	13.3	8.8	8.8	6.1
Broad monetary (M2) growth	50.5	35.8	36.8	48.8	47.5	1.2	16.3	28.5	22.6

Source: BOFIT Russia Statistics, www.suomenpankki.fi/bofit_en/seuranta/venajatilastot/Pages/default.aspx (accessed June 11, 2012).

deposits as a percentage of all deposits peaked at more than 40 percent after 1998.[10] From 1999 to 2007 deposit dollarization declined gradually, especially after 2003 when the ruble began to appreciate due to high export revenue. In early 2008 deposit dollarization hit the minimum of 12 to 13 percent, but with the crisis it temporarily increased, only to soon start falling again.[11]

MONETARY POLICY

Russia's transformation into a money-based economy was one of the major positive changes of the early 2000s. However, Russian financial markets still remain small and underdeveloped relative to the size of the economy, which has implications for the conduct of monetary policy.

Inflation

Turning first to inflation, table 8.1 indicates that inflation was on a downward trend, from 12 percent in 2003 to 9 percent in 2006. In 2007 and 2008 it again increased. Some of the increase may be explained by external factors: the global economy was in overdrive, global food prices increased, and though Russia is among the three biggest exporters of grain, it imports many other foodstuffs. There was also domestic overheating with excess demand for skilled city-based labor and construction materials in particular. Fiscal policy was procyclical, as it targeted the budget surplus. As revenue was increased by higher export tariff incomes, expenditures increased as well. The ruble devaluation of fall 2008 raised import prices.

After 2008 inflation continued to decline, reaching 8.8 percent in 2009 and 2010, and then declining to 6 percent in 2011. In the twelve months from March 2011 to March 2012 inflation was, for the first time, less than 5 percent, reaching only 3.7 percent. Russian authorities explained this by the postponement of hikes in gas, electricity, and railway tariffs from early to midyear 2012. Many Russians blame inflation on the monopolized structure of the economy, but that is a valid explanation only if monopoly profits increase continuously or the efficiency of monopoly producers keeps declining.

While avoiding direct inflation targeting, the Central Bank was until 2006 able to keep inflation on a downward trend. As export revenue kept increasing, the Central Bank increased ruble supply, as shown in table 8.1. Ruble supply should preferably have been sterilized, that is, withdrawn from the market by selling government or Central Bank bonds. As bond markets remained very small—and the state did not need them for financing budget deficits—this option did not work. The Central Bank did issue its bonds, but not so much to sterilize as to offer an asset in which to park excess liquidity. There has been no distinct effect on the financial markets stemming from Central Bank issuance of bonds.[12]

The Central Bank of Russia has shifted its strategy to inflation targeting and full exchange rate flexibility as longer-term goals. The shift to inflation targeting implies a shift from rough policy instruments like reserve ratios to more market-based policy instruments like interest rates. Peculiarly for a country that has announced introduction of a managed peg exchange rate regime, due to segmented markets, lack of trust, and excess liquidity in the banking system, Russia does not yet have the conditions for interest-rate-based monetary policy. Existing studies offer little if any evidence on the effectiveness of Central Bank policy so far. Were the existing managed float regime severely tested by markets, the reaction of the authorities would be difficult to foresee. Importantly, there has been no discussion so far of an eventual use of capital controls under any future circumstances. The introduction of full capital mobility in 2006 is seen as such an important policy achievement of the Putin regime.

Exchange Rate Policy

Turning to exchange rate policy, until 2009 the Central Bank chose to maintain a stable nominal exchange rate first pegged to the dollar and to a bicurrency basket that reflects the structure of Russia's foreign trade—55 percent USD/45 percent euro. Exchange rate stability was maintained by interventions in foreign exchange markets. There was pressure on the ruble to appreciate, as much of the ballooning export revenue was exchanged into rubles, thus strengthening demand for domestic currency. The Central Bank sold rubles and bought foreign currency. There is no hard evidence that the ruble was overvalued in 1998, but it was clearly undervalued after the devaluation. As no country with an open economy can choose a real exchange rate of its liking, real appreciation of the ruble was inevitable in the 2000s. As the nominal exchange rate was kept stable, real appreciation had to happen through domestic inflation that was higher than abroad.

Targeting the nominal exchange rate was understandable given Russia's history of dollarization and the goal of de-dollarization. Shifts in asset allocation between the ruble and foreign currencies have been sensitive to the real exchange rate between currencies, a matter of rational market behavior. Targeting the exchange rate may also have been inevitable as the Central Bank did not have a monetary policy channel through which to choose suitable money supply. There was a lot of uncertainty about demand for money. Fine-tuning money supply was also impossible as the behavioral patterns of the small but fast-growing banking sector were largely untried. The Russian Central Bank has mostly concentrated on fighting money laundering and other violations of regulation, in the process learning little of actual bank behavior. There has been a target for annual money growth, but that has been traditionally missed by wide margins with no negative consequences for the Central Bank. Nor could the Central Bank easily use interest rates to regulate demand for money. With little market for interest-bearing assets, real interest rates were negative, and the interest rate channel has been of little importance. Therefore, there is really no overall liquidity of the market that could be regulated by the Central Bank.

Beginning in 2009 the Central Bank gradually withdrew from foreign exchange markets, and the current exchange rate policy moved to a managed float. The Central Bank has, as a policy rule, an exchange rate corridor of 55 percent dollars and 45 percent euros. Within the corridor the exchange rate is allowed to move freely. If it approaches one or another of the set borders of the corridor, the Central Bank intervenes. If a change in markets is deemed permanent, the corridor itself will be shifted. Whether Russia will go all the way to a free currency float remains to be seen. The ruble exchange market volatility has indeed increased since 2009. Monetary policy has also been made more transparent as the fluctuation corridor and the rules of managing the ruble were published in late 2011.

FISCAL POLICY

Taxation

Before 2010 the main responsibility for fighting inflation remained with fiscal policy. Most windfall oil export revenue was and still is taxed by the state. As noted above, energy sector taxation—including export tariffs and natural resource exploitation payments—has accounted roughly for about one-half of federal fiscal revenue. Russia is dependent on energy for exports and tax revenue, but not directly for jobs. Less than 2 percent of all Russian jobs are in extracting and transporting basic energy.[13]

Taming the oil sector for taxation has been a major challenge. Oil companies have been able to minimize their taxation by using such vehicles as
transfer pricing and on- and offshore tax havens. As a consequence, many
analysts have estimated that the true share of GDP from the energy sector
has been grossly underestimated in official statistics. The actual share has
not been less than 10 percent, as in official statistics, but rather somewhere
between 20 and 30 percent.[14] Part of highly taxed energy sector income has
been hidden in more leniently taxed transportation and trade or has been
transferred totally out of the reach of the taxman. Tax authorities have even
been unable to trust the bookkeeping values and profits of oil companies.
Company taxation has therefore not been based on profits but on trade
turnover.

Taxation of oil and oil companies is also complicated by the changing
structure of production. As long as almost all production was in basically
similar conditions in the traditional Western Siberian super-giant fields, the
taxation system did not matter too much. Production must now increasingly move into high-cost and widely differing far eastern and northern
conditions. Taxation by turnover discriminates severely against investment
in such fields, which are needed for maintaining national production levels.
Consequently, both oil and gas producers have received tax exemptions,
first in the Far East and in the North as well. Turnover-based taxation that
was supposed to be similar for all has thus given way to negotiated taxation,
a certain recipe for influence-peddling and outright corruption in the heart
of Russia's export and tax revenue.

Contrary to most advanced market economies, Russia receives only a little revenue from the taxation of personal income, accounting for only a
couple of percent of GDP; most government revenue comes from foreign
trade, commodity taxes, and profit tax, as well as from social security contri-
butions. Income tax avoidance has traditionally been rife. To take a somewhat exotic example, all major Moscow banks seemed in the 2000s to be
engaged in the same tax-avoidance scheme. Employees were not paid a salary but were extended major loans, which were then deposited back into
the bank. The interest paid for the deposit was the employee income—
nontaxable, as it happens. Russia did not engage in a huge fiscal risk when
it was one of the first Central and Eastern European countries to introduce
a flat tax of 13 percent on all income in 2001. The goal was to decrease tax
avoidance. Studies show that the impact on tax avoidance was much greater
than that on labor supply.[15] Flat income tax is seen as one of the major
economic policy achievements of the Putin regime. Introducing progressive
income taxation regularly figures in further tax reform proposals, especially
in those coming from experts with a European egalitarian value orientation. The prospects for abandoning the flat income tax remain weak. It is a
feature of Russian capitalism to remain.

Regional Revenue

Russia is according to the 1993 constitution a federation. Since 1992, relations between the center and regions have changed thoroughly. During the Yeltsin years, regions were much more independent and less beholden to the center. In the 1990s regional revenues as share of total state revenues increased from 40 percent in 1992 to about 55 percent in 1997–1998.[16] One might have expected the regions to do their utmost to widen the tax base by promoting new entrepreneurship. Instead, incumbent plants captured the state. Both regional and local authorities tended to protect existing jobs through taxation, regulation, and corruption.[17] This was partly due to the importance of several hundreds of one-company towns, usually based on military industrial companies that had little future. Simultaneously, regional expenditures as a share of total expenditures also rose from less than 30 percent to about 55 percent.

The relationship between center and regions changed in many ways. Putin took several steps to reestablish the primacy of centralized power beginning in 2000. Establishing "the vertical of power," the Putin regime aimed at controlling regional political and economic elites. The share of regional expenditures declined only slightly, to about one-half of total expenditures. In contrast, the share of regional revenues fell significantly, to about 35 percent.[18] On average, therefore, regions became dependent on transfers from the center. Only a few so-called donor regions remained relatively independent: Moscow and a few resource-rich regions. Thus, building the power vertical was largely successful, although in practice the division of revenue between the center, regions, and municipalities remained an issue for negotiations. Lobbying power in Moscow once more came to dominate in the outcomes. "Loyal" regions often received preferential treatment.

The traditional thinking is that fiscal revenue will rise simultaneously with other revenue. Budget expenditures increase when the economy is booming. This was clearly the case in Russia in the 2000s.

As shown in table 8.2, budget expenditures contributed to the overheating of the economy during the second half of the decade. The International

Table 8.2.   Russian Central Government Financial Indicators (percent of GDP)

	2003	2004	2005	2006	2007	2008	2009	2010	2011
Revenue	19.5	20.1	23.7	23.4	23.6	22.3	18.8	18.7	20.9
Expenditure	17.8	15.8	16.3	16.0	18.1	18.2	24.7	22.7	20.1
Balance	1.7	4.4	7.5	7.4	5.4	4.1	−5.9	−4.1	0.8

Source: BOFIT Russia Statistics, www.suomenpankki.fi/bofit_en/seuranta/venajatilastot/Pages/default.aspx (accessed June 11, 2012).

Monetary Fund has argued that fiscal policy should be based on maintaining a constant "non-oil" deficit, defined as expenditure minus revenue, assuming some "normal" oil price and ensuing revenues. Before the 2008 crisis Russia did in fact adopt a medium-term non-oil deficit target of 4.7 percent of GDP. The "normal" oil price was defined as the average for the preceding ten years. The 2008 crisis, however, intervened and the actual non-oil deficit surged to almost 14 percent of GDP in 2009, and is expected to remain above 10 percent of GDP at least until 2013.[19]

Current expenditure decisions often imply longer-term spending commitments. Basing expenditure decisions on temporarily high, but intrinsically volatile, oil revenue is fiscally irresponsible. The argument in favor of using a non-oil deficit constraint on expenditure commitments is thus a strong one. The simplicity of the non-oil deficit concept is, however, deceptive. In spring 2012 Russian authorities debated whether the "normal oil price" should be the average of the past ten years (as the fiscally conservative Ministry of Finance argued), or the past three years (as preferred by the high-spending Ministry of Economic Development). This seeming technicality does not have a self-evident answer, but implies huge differences in expenditure levels, as the average oil price of 2010–2012 is much higher than that of 2001–2012. An even weightier difference in interpretation lurks behind the number of years to look at. The fundamental argument in favor of using the non-oil deficit concept is based on the supposed volatility of oil price in the future. An IMF Working Paper argues that the price of oil may almost double within the next decade.[20] Thus, the issue is whether high and even higher oil prices are here to stay or not. On prudency grounds one might wish to use a conservative assumption of high and low oil prices that continue to alternate in the future as they have done in the past. But if we have entered a world of permanently high oil prices, a huge transfer of income will be given to the next Russian generation.

THE 2008–2009 CRISIS

The global financial crisis that started in late 2008 and extended through 2009 affected the Russian economy in three ways. The first impact was on export prices, led by oil and followed by minerals and then gas. When the crisis hit, there was a lot of uncertainty among international economists about the coming pattern of the crisis. Although some economists expected a fast dip followed by an equally fast global recovery (a V-form crisis), the majority opinion in Russia, as elsewhere, foresaw a long recession (a U-form crisis). Amidst the uncertainty, the collapse of global commodity prices occurred faster and deeper than was justified, in retrospect. When fears of a

U-form recession gave way to optimism on a V-form, global oil prices also recovered quickly.

The second impact was on Russia's export volumes. For example, steel exports were cut in half practically overnight, as European construction activity was curtailed. More important for the long run, in the beginning of 2009 Russia and Ukraine got involved in another dispute over gas prices, transit tariffs, and the settlement of accumulated Ukrainian debt for gas. Four-fifths of Russian gas exports to Europe cross Ukrainian territory, and supplies to Central Europe were disrupted exactly at the time when relatively cheap liquefied natural gas (LNG) was entering markets in large amounts. Russia's reliability as gas supplier was compromised, and its gas export prices seemed inflated. The final impact on Russia's role in European gas markets still remains to be seen.

The third and arguably most important impact was that global investors started pulling their monies out of all peripheral markets. Russian public and private entities were not deep in debt, but existing debt was short term, it had increased quickly, and investors grew pessimistic about Russia's overall economic prospects since they tended to see them through the prism of oil prices. Foreign short-term finance had maintained what existed as interbank markets, and now that it was withdrawn the wheels of Russian finance were fast slowing down. Another full-scale financial crisis was threatening Russia, and were financial markets to stall, the impact on production, incomes, and employment would be drastic as well.

After an initial period of uncertainty about which way the crisis would go, Russian authorities took three sets of measures that have been praised by the international financial community as being swift, significant, and appropriate. Like elsewhere, the first priority was to pump liquidity into the financial markets. Russia had the reserves to do that, and although its financial markets did not function well, the main state-controlled banks could be told to act as vehicles in order to channel money into the economy. Second, the ruble had appreciated quickly in the 2000s. As export prices had collapsed, there was no alternative to depreciating the ruble. The alternative preferred by experts was a one-off devaluation, but it was difficult to determine the proper degree of devaluation, as everything in the economic environment was in turmoil. The other alternative was to let the currency float. The problem, even more than in the one-off devaluation case, was that an unpredictable exchange rate might cause a new round of dollarization, something Russian authorities strongly wished to avoid. In the end, Russia opted for a highly unorthodox alternative—step-wise devaluation. Over the course of many weeks the exchange rate was devalued in small steps, without any target level being announced. Households, companies, and banks alike were given ample time to shift their assets from rubles into foreign currency. There was no market panic, and when this path was capped with a 10 percent one-off devaluation in January 2009, tranquility returned to markets.

This was an expensive policy alternative: some $200 billion of official reserves had been used to satisfy demand for foreign currencies. But this money did not just disappear. Some of it was used to service private foreign debt, which declined by about $100 billion dollars during the fall.[21] The remainder of the reserves that were expended was privatized, shifted from public reserves into private assets. Most important, devaluation did not lead into a continuous spiral fed by further expectations of further devaluation, as experts in general had expected. What had failed elsewhere somehow succeeded in Russia.

The third step taken by Russia was that it supported both the financial sector and real economy, similar to other countries. According to IMF estimates, Russia pledged 7.7 percent of 2009 GDP as financial sector support, but because a banking crisis did not emerge, it only had to use 3.1 percent. The G20 average was 4.0 percent of GDP pledged and 2.4 percent utilized.[22] Contrary to advanced countries with large troubled financial industries, Russia pledged no resources for guarantees, asset swaps, or purchase of financial assets. In contrast, Russia used its financial resources for supporting what were regarded as strategic industries and companies, often located in the hundreds of one-company towns created by Soviet industrialization. The Medvedev-Putin regime, with an eye toward the elections cycle of 2011–2012, chose defending incumbent jobs over economic creative-destruction. Moreover, as the majority of voters are either pensioners or public sector employees, their incomes were raised during the crisis. The average pension was increased by more than one-half.[23] Not only did the non-oil deficit widen to almost 15 percent of GDP, large commitments were left as a fiscal burden for future years.

CONCLUSION: TOWARD RUSSIA IN 2020

By 2006, Russia's leadership became convinced that Russia's economic development could not be based on oil and gas. Experts projected that production would increase little, if at all. Maintaining current export volumes demanded major improvement in the notoriously low energy efficiency of the economy. Gas prices in particular had to be increased to reach international levels. Households and jobs could no longer be subsidized by artificially low energy prices. Modernization and diversification were badly needed. That was the message of the first "Russia 2020" economic program that was passed in late 2008. The 2008 global crisis, however, postponed most attempts to implement the program, whose target of making Russia an innovation-based society by 2020 was utopian at best.

The problems were real enough, and another attempt was needed. In January 2011, then prime minister Vladimir Putin gave the Russian economic expert community, under the joint chairmanship of the rectors of two leading Moscow economics universities, the task of "writing the economic program of the post-May 2012 government." The document produced by more than one thousand experts was published in March 2012.[24] At 864 pages it is not a policy program but rather a wide-ranging survey of policy tasks, many of them complex and demanding. According to underlying program assumptions, the growth model of the 2000s is no longer relevant, as many of the drivers of growth then were transient and the world economy can no longer be expected to be as benign an environment for Russia as it was then. Russia's social policy framework also needs to be reformed. Additional finance is needed, especially for health, education, and the infrastructure, but what is needed even more is private initiative and public-private partnerships. The Putin regime believes in state-led development, but also in harmony between public and private initiatives.

Space does not allow a detailed discussion of the huge, far-reaching, and uneven document. Nonetheless, the document is remarkable, and several underlying themes emerge. The most important theme is that as Russia can no longer rely on utilizing capacities inherited from the Soviet Union, future growth must be based on investment. Vladimir Putin has accepted the goal of increasing investment in GDP from the pre-crisis peak of some 20 percent to 25, and then 28 percent.[25] In this respect the approach is closer to reality than in the original Russia 2020 program that was adopted in 2008. The goal is feasible, but it raises fundamental issues. Where can needed financial resources be raised? How can the business environment be improved to facilitate long-term investment? And where should investment be made? Currently, Russia has a competitive advantage in the resource economy, agriculture, and—potentially at least—in mathematics-based services.

In monetary policy, the new "Russia 2020" program aims to continue inflation targeting (keeping inflation low), and a floating currency. It proposes that the share of public expenditure in GDP is stable, with modest budget deficits and some debt finance. Pension reform is badly needed, but also difficult to plan and implement. It is, however, possible that Russia will engage in a new wave of reform, but many of the relatively easy tasks have already been tackled. Current and future challenges are complex and difficult, and Russia is unlikely to match its growth performance of the 2000s.

SUGGESTED READINGS

Alexeev, Michael, and Shlomo Weber, eds. *Handbook of the Russian Economy.* Oxford and New York: Oxford University Press, 2012.

Åslund, Anders. *Russia's Capitalist Revolution*. Washington, DC: Peterson Institute for International Economics, 2007.

Sutela, Pekka. *The Political Economy of Putin's Russia*. London and New York: Routledge, 2012.

Treisman, Daniel. *The Return: Russia's Journey from Gorbachev to Medvedev*. New York: Free Press, 2011.

NOTES

1. Pekka Sutela, *The Political Economy of Putin's Russia* (London and New York: Routledge, 2012).

2. David Owen and David O. Robinson, eds., *Russia Rebounds* (Washington, DC: International Monetary Fund, 2003).

3. BOFIT Russia Statistics, www.suomenpankki.fi/bofit_en/seuranta/venajatila stot/Pages/default.aspx (accessed June 11, 2012).

4. Clifford G. Gaddy and Barry W. Ickes, "Resource Rents and the Russian Economy," *Eurasian Geography and Economics* 45, no. 4 (2005): 559–83; Clifford G. Gaddy and Barry W. Ickes, "Russia after the Global Economic Crisis," *Eurasian Geography and Economics* 50, no. 3 (2010): 281–311.

5. Michael Alexeev and Robert Conrad, "The Russian Oil Tax Regime: A Comparative Perspective," *Eurasian Geography and Economics* 49, no. 2 (2009): 93–114.

6. BOFIT Russia Statistics, www.suomenpankki.fi/bofit_en/seuranta/venajatila stot/Pages/default.aspx (accessed June 11, 2012).

7. International Monetary Fund, *World Economic Outlook* (Washington, DC: International Monetary Fund, 2012), Table A12, www.imf.org/external/pubs/ft/ weo/2012/01/pdf/text.pdf (accessed June 11, 2012).

8. Daniel Berkowitz and Daniel N. DeJong, "Growth in Post-Soviet Russia: A Tale of Two Transitions," *Journal of Economic Behavior & Organization* 79, nos. 1–2 (2011): 133–43.

9. *Russian Economic Barometer*, ecsoc.ru/en/reb/ (accessed June 11, 2012).

10. Seija Lainela and Alexey Ponomarenko, "Russian Financial Markets and Monetary Policy Instruments," *BOFIT Online* no. 3 (2012).

11. Lainela and Ponomarenko, "Russian Financial Markets."

12. Lainela and Ponomarenko, "Russian Financial Markets," 26.

13. Employment share obviously grows when a wider definition of the energy sector is used, including refining, trading, and manufacturing branches that are dependent on providing energy producers with pipes, machinery, and so forth. The figure grows further if jobs dependent on low energy costs are added, but doing that makes distinguishing the energy and the non-energy parts of the economy impossible.

14. Sutela, *The Political Economy of Putin's Russia*, 94–95.

15. Denvil Duncand and Klara Sabirianova Peter, "Does Labour Supply Respond to a Flat Tax? Evidence from Russian Tax Reform," *Economics of Transition* 18, no. 2 (2010): 333–63.

16. Migara A. De Silva, Galina Kurlyanskaya, Elena Andreeva, and Natalia Golovanova: *Intergovernmental Reforms in the Russian Federation: One Step Forward, Two Steps Back?* (Washington, DC: The World Bank, 2009).

17. Ekaterina Zhuravskaya, "Federalism in Russia," in *Russia after the Global Economic Crisis*, eds. Anders Åslund, Sergey Guriev, and Andrew W. Kuchins (Washington, DC: Peterson Institute for International Economics, 2010), 59–78.

18. De Silva, Kurlyanskaya, Andreeva, and Golovanova, *Intergovernmental Reforms in the Russian Federation*.

19. International Monetary Fund, *Russian Federation: Selected Issues Paper*, IMF Country Report no. 11/295 (Washington, DC: International Monetary Fund, 2011), 48–89.

20. Jaromir Benes, Marcelle Chauvwer, Ondra Kamenik and others, "The Future of Oil: Geology versus Technology," *IMF Working Paper* WP/12/109, May 2012.

21. *BOFIT Weekly* 16 (April 17, 2009).

22. International Monetary Fund, *Fiscal Monitor: Navigating the Fiscal Challenges Ahead* (Washington, DC: International Monetary Fund, 2010).

23. Yevsei Gurvich, "Vse schitaiut sebya obdelennymi," *Ogonyok*, June 6, 2011.

24. *Strategiia-2020: novaia model rosta – novaia sotsialnaia politika*, www.2020strategy.ru (accessed March 21, 2012).

25. "Predsedatel' Pravitel'stva Rossiiskoi Federatsii V.V. Putin prinial uchastie v s'ezde obshcherossiiskoi obchestvennoi organizatsii 'Delovaia Rossiia,'" premier.gov.ru/events/news/17451 (accessed December 28, 2011).

9

Crime, Organized Crime, and Corruption

Louise Shelley

Almost two decades after the collapse of the Soviet Union, organized crime and corruption remain intractable problems for the Russian state. Violent crimes rates are high, especially for homicide. Organized crime is no longer as visibly violent and gang wars are no longer fought for the control of the aluminum industry, as was the case in the 1990s. However, the extent of the crime problem has not diminished, and its form has merely transformed over time. With the enormous growth of Russia's drug markets, its crime groups are now more deeply involved in the narcotics trade than in the past. Moreover, the pervasive problem of corporate raiding, by which valuable businesses are taken over by force and legal manipulation, reflects the fact that organized crime activity remains focused on acquiring valuable property.[1]

The Russian state, because of an absence of political will and pervasive high-level corruption within its ranks, has been ineffective in dealing with these problems. Compounding the problem is the political-criminal nexus and the fact that politicians who assume political office have legal immunity from investigation and prosecution.[2] The police reform launched under President Dmitry Medvedev failed. The specialized police units to combat organized crime were abolished in September 2008 without any alternative enforcement strategy.[3] Moreover, the problem of corruption has become a highly political issue that has driven tens if not hundreds of thousands of Russian protesters to the streets. The anticorruption blogs of Aleksei Navalny make him a popular political figure within Russian society.[4]

President Putin has returned to power in a society whose citizens are fed up with pervasive corruption.

Russia's crime problems are not just national; they are international. Russian criminals were among the first to take full advantage of globalization.[5] Many criminals who initially set up operations overseas were the so-called *vory-v zakone* (thieves-in-law), or the traditional elite of the Soviet-era criminal world who lived according to rigidly established rules.[6] In addition, many smaller groups of criminals from the former USSR are operating within Western Europe, involved in serious organized crime, tax evasion, and money laundering.[7] The groups often combine Russian criminals with their compatriots from other post-Soviet states. Whereas their activities were once focused primarily on the acquisition of key sectors of the Russian economy, more recently they have become greater participants in the international drug trade, complementing their international role in the trade of women, arms, and endangered species and timber.[8] Moreover, the technical capacity of the criminals has pushed them to the forefront of computer crime with major involvement in the production of child pornography marketed through the Internet, "pfishing," and even wholesale coordinated attacks on the Internet and websites of foreign countries such as Estonia and Georgia.[9]

In Russia, there is a unique integration of the licit and illicit economies. Key sectors of the economy are controlled by oligarchs with criminal pasts or close ties to organized crime. But the parallels that many commentators have tried to draw between the oligarchs and the robber barons have been proven invalid. Robber barons used corruption and coercion to eliminate competition and to intimidate laborers. In Russia, the order was reversed. Criminality was crucial to the acquisition of key sectors of the energy sector, aluminum, and natural resources. Then violence was used to eliminate competitors.

Russia's licit and illicit economies operate on a natural resource model, which is not surprising, as illicit business is shaped by the same cultural and historical factors that shape the legitimate economy. The illicit economy mirrors the patterns of the legitimate one. Historically, Russia was never a society of traders. Before the 1917 revolution, Russian trade was dominated by non-Russians, Armenians, Greeks, Germans, and others who lived in distinct districts of Moscow. Russians did not trade. Instead they sold natural resources such as fur, timber, and the vast natural mineral wealth of their vast empire. With the reintroduction of capitalism in 1992, old patterns of business quickly reemerged. Oil sales represent one-third of the national economy, bringing into question the economic future of Russia when this precious resource is dissipated or when prices might drop. The trafficking of women operates on the natural resource model. Russia criminals sell off the women like a raw commodity, selling them to other crime groups who will exploit the women in the destination countries, maximizing their profits.[10] The Russian state shows little will to protect its citizens even though it is facing a severe demographic crisis, and the export and sale of its women of childbearing age threatens the very survival of the Russian nation. The natural resource model of both licit and illicit trade is extremely harmful to the long-term health of the Russian economy and the Russian state.

This chapter is based on a wide variety of sources, including analyses that have been carried out in Russia by researchers affiliated with TraCCC (Terrorism, Transnational Crime and Corruption Center) centers in Russia. Over the past decade centers have existed in all the major regions of Russia. At first, the centers concentrated on the largest cities in Russia—Moscow, St. Petersburg, and Ekaterinburg. But more recently, research has been conducted in smaller cities throughout Russia such as in Saratov on the Volga, Chelyabinsk near the Kazakh border, Stavropol in the conflict-ridden North Caucasus, and in Vladivostok, a crime center in the Far East.[11] Research has also been carried out in Siberia and many other regions that face serious and distinctive crime problems, thereby facilitating analysis of regional differences in crime. Insight has been obtained from the sponsored research of these centers that has resulted in the publication of dozens of books and hundreds of articles since the mid-1990s. The multidisciplinary research has focused on particular aspects of crime, such as human trafficking, money laundering, the role of crime groups in the process of privatization, overall crime trends, and many other topics.

Interviews have been conducted with large numbers of law enforcement in Russia and in other parts of the world concerned with post-Soviet organized crime. Legal documents of criminal cases in Russia and abroad have been studied to understand the mechanisms of organized crime activity. Civil litigation in the West among key industrial figures with criminal pasts have also been examined to shed light on the acquisition of businesses through criminal tactics.[12]

In addition, the chapter draws upon the Russian press and national and regional data to understand the evolution and geography of crime in Russia. The chapter also uses Western scholarship on crime and policing in Russia, which has increased in recent years.[13] Analysis of crime data reveals striking regional differences from west to east, in part a legacy of the Soviet era where labor camps were concentrated in Siberia and new industrialized cities gave rise to particularly high rates of criminality.[14]

OVERALL TRENDS IN CRIME

The growth of crime and the absence of an effective law enforcement response have affected the quality of daily life, the longevity of the population, and the economy. Beccaria, the Enlightenment thinker, wrote that the certainty of punishment is more important than its severity. In Russia, at the present time, there is no certainty of punishment although there is severity for those who are caught and either cannot pay the bribes to get out of the criminal justice system or who are subjects of particular political concern to the government, such as the former oil magnate Mikhail Khodorkovsky.[15]

The following trends characterize Russian crime and organized crime:

- High rates of homicide.
- High rates of youth crime and child exploitation.
- Very high rates of drug abuse and a rapidly escalating problem of international drug trade.
- Large-scale human smuggling and trafficking from, into, and through Russia.
- Corporate raiding resulting in insecure property rights and undermining entrepreneurship.
- Organized crime involvement in all sectors of the economy.

These trends are discussed in more detail below.

Homicide

In the immediate post-Soviet period, Russia had very high rates of homicide, the result both of high rates of interpersonal violence and the contract killings associated with organized crime. Increased violence was also explained by the availability of weapons, which had been tightly controlled during the Soviet period.[16] The availability of arms, facilitated by the small-weapons trade of Russian organized crime and former military personnel, made many ordinary acts of crime more violent than in the past.[17] The decline in Russian medical care meant that many individuals who were merely assault victims in the past now became homicide victims. Even though contract killings have declined, intrapersonal violence remains very high, partly explained by enduring problems of alcohol abuse. A scholar of Russian violence has written, "Post-communist Russia's homicide mortality rate has been one of the highest in the world, exceeding that of European countries by a factor of 20–25, and for most of the post-communist period has also been significantly higher than that of other ex-Soviet states."[18] Homicide rates differ enormously by region, as low as 7 per 100,000 persons in Kabardino-Balkaria (North Caucasus) to 118 per 100,000 persons in the Republic of Tuva (Siberia).[19]

Youth Crime and Child Exploitation

Youth crime and child exploitation are enduring problems in Russia, explained by the high rates of abandoned children, street children, and the number of institutionalized children whose parents have left them or whose parents have been declared incompetent to raise their children.[20] Parents have been determined unfit parents because of alcoholism, drug use, domestic violence, and child sexual exploitation. The number of homeless or abandoned children is estimated to be at the same level as after World War II. There are 700,000 orphans and 2 million illiterate youths.[21] Children exposed to high levels of violence in their youth often replicate these patterns in adolescence and adulthood. Moreover, the absence of programs to help deinstitutionalized youth after eighteen return to their communities has made many of the females susceptible to sex traffickers.

Commercial sexual exploitation of children is recognized as an increasing problem, and the State Duma has not yet passed adequate legislation to combat all aspects of this phenomenon.[22] Much of the child pornography marketed on the Internet is produced in Russia and sold internationally. Russia now assumes second place in the production of marketed pornography, contributing 23 percent of international production.[23]

There are now fifty transit homes throughout Russia, but these are intended only to provide temporary shelter for children who are found abandoned or begging on the streets. Many children are not able to enter these homes because they are forced to beg or prostitute themselves by organized crime. Sometimes collusion between the criminals and the police prevents children from being brought to the transit homes. The huge influx of migrants from the former successor states has contributed to the large number of abandoned and homeless children who are not Russian and may have a poor knowledge of Russian, making them even more vulnerable to exploitation.[24]

Drug Abuse

Drug addiction has skyrocketed in Russia. This increase has occurred in the number of users, the geographical reach of the problem, and the variety of drugs used. As the market has grown, there appears to be also a presence of large and more powerful organized crime groups involved, although no monopolization of markets has yet emerged. According to the head of the Federal Service for the Control of Narcotics, the last decade has seen a fifteenfold rise in the number of drug-related crimes and a tenfold increase in the number of drug users.[25] A new designer drug called *krokodil* or crocodile, related to morphine, has spread rapidly in Russia.[26]

According to the Ministry of Internal Affairs, there are now 4 million youth who use drugs, starting as young as age eleven. The rate of drug abuse is 2.5 times higher among youth than among adults. Mortality connected to drug abuse is now 42 times higher for youth than in the 1980s, while the comparable figure for adults is 12 times higher.[27]

Russian official statistics reveal an alarming trend in the quantity and the distribution of the drug trade. For example, in 1985, the Ministry of Internal Affairs had identified only four regions in Russia with over 10,000 serious abusers of drugs. By the beginning of the twenty-first century, that figure had climbed to over thirty regions. Today there is hardly a city in Russia in which there are not drug addicts.[28] Drug abuse is not evenly distributed.[29] Whereas 310 addicts were registered per 100,000 people in Russia as a whole in January 2004, the figure in the Russian Far East was 542 per 100,000.[30] With approximately 500,000 registered users, and millions of unregistered users, representing 2 to 4 percent of the Russian population, narcotics now assume a notable share of the $15 billion of the Russian shadow economy.[31] Several years ago Mark Galeotti estimated an even more severe problem than do these estimates, suggesting over 6 million drug users, of which 2 million are addicts.[32] In a very short period Russia has developed one of the world's most serious problems of drug abuse.

The drug problem in Russia does not consist of only one commodity. *Krokodil* is just the latest of a variety of synthetic and natural drugs that plague Russia. According to the 2012 U.S. State Department Report on Drugs, Russia is a market for opium, hashish, marijuana, synthetics, and other dangerous illegal substances.[33] According to the United Nations in 2011, Russia was the world's largest market for heroin produced in Afghanistan, and 1.7 million users consumed 70,000 kilos of heroin.[34] Opiates in particular are highly problematic. The Russian domestic opiate market has been valued at $12 billion, or roughly one-fifth of the world market, explained by Russia's proximity to Central Asia and drug production in Afghanistan. Synthetic drugs enter Russia from Western Europe (coming through Ukraine, Belarus, and the Baltic States) and Asia. Cocaine enters from Latin America.[35]

The drug business appears to be employing an ever-larger number of Russian citizens annually. Not only are crime groups more actively engaged in the drug trade, but many impoverished Russian citizens serve as drug couriers. Russian governmental sources estimate that the number of organized criminal groups involved in the drug trade have increased by 85 percent since 1993.[36] By 2004, 950 criminal groups were estimated to be involved in the drug trade.[37] Other explanations for the growth lie in the political-criminal nexus and the links that Russian organized crime has formed with crime groups in many other parts of the world. In the early 1990s, 30 percent of the drugs in Russia came from abroad, whereas the comparable figure at the beginning of the twenty-first century is more than double that. In several regions of Russia, for example, Moscow, St. Petersburg, and Khabarovsk, 80 percent of the confiscated drugs are of foreign production. The range of countries supplying drugs to Russia includes not only Central Asia and China but also more remote countries such as Peru, Colombia, and the Netherlands.[38]

Russia is also increasingly a transit country for drugs from Afghanistan, Pakistan, and Iran into European markets.[39] In the past decade, the so-called northern route of heroin smuggling has linked Afghanistan via Central Asia to Russia and Europe. Approximately 25 percent of Afghanistan's drug production exits along the northern route. This route has become an ever more important part of the drug route out of Afghanistan and has assumed an ever larger share of Afghan's drug exports. Perhaps first intended as a transshipment country, Russia's main importance in the global heroin industry is now as a consumer. Many of the consumers are young, and some are former military personnel formerly deployed on the borders in Central Asia and in the Chechen conflict.

The actors in this illicit economy range from Russian military personnel, law enforcement, and ordinary criminals to Soviet ethnic crime groups and illegal immigrants from Asian countries. Corrupt relationships that exist among the drug traffickers and local and regional officials allow these crime groups to operate throughout Russia, even in the capital. Furthermore, crime groups from many other countries are active in Russia. These include crime groups from not only the neighboring states of the former USSR but also Eastern Europe, Japan, China, South and possibly North Korea, Vietnam, Nigeria, and Latin America.[40]

The Russian situation also recalls the Colombian situation, where drug trafficking is used to finance nonstate violent actors, including separatist and terrorist movements.[41] Dagestan, a region adjoining Chechnya, is now a major entry point for drugs into Russia.[42] Although the links between insurgencies and the drug trade is not as strong in Russia as in Colombia, there is an important link in both drug markets between drugs and violent conflict. Organized crime including drug trafficking has been a factor prolonging the war in Chechnya, providing income and the motivation to continue warfare on both sides of the conflict.

Human Smuggling and Trafficking

Human trafficking persists on a large scale. Trafficking is not just of Russian women exported for sexual exploitation abroad; there is also a large importation of trafficked women from poorer Soviet successor states. Moreover, there is a significant illegal migrant population. Many of the workers find themselves in situations of severe labor exploitation. There is also an increasing problem of the exploitation of the children of illegal migrants who have no legal status and cannot attend school.

Even as the Russian economy has grown and the middle class has expanded, the problem of sex trafficking of Russian women persists on a large scale because of the poverty, vulnerability, and the hopelessness of many adolescents and women. Many youth live in poorly supported children's homes. Others are living in the streets, having been abandoned by their parents or having run away from drunken and violent parents. Even teenagers from intact families can be victims of trafficking. In 2007, a pit was found outside Nizhnii Tagil, in the Urals. Young girls were lured by a group of criminals who invited young women for ice cream and then tried to compel them into prostitution. Many of the girls resisted and were murdered. Forty missing women were found in the pit, including the daughter of one of the traffickers. Many of the murdered young women had previously been reported to the police as missing by their families, but there had been no follow-up. When the facts became known, a public outcry followed.[43]

This is just a small element of trafficking victimization in contemporary Russia. With its increasing affluence, labor shortages, and a male population not ready to do hard physical labor, a rapid influx of illegal immigrants into Russia occurred, primarily from impoverished countries in Central Asia such as Tajikistan and Kyrgyzstan. Even though there has been less demand for labor since the economic slowdown in 2008, there has been less employment and a decline in wages of workers and of remittances.[44] Russia estimates that there are now 5 to 10 million illegal migrants in Russia. This figure is in addition to the legal migrants, a new category of workers recently introduced in Russia that now gives temporary work permits for stays up to three months. Despite this new category of legal migrants, 80 percent of all migrants are employed in the informal or "shadow" economy, receiving a fraction of the wages paid to Russian workers. Survey research reveals that one-quarter of those surveyed knew migrants who had been enslaved: their passports were taken away, their wages withheld, and they were kept in confinement by those who controlled them. The number of those subject to labor trafficking is now estimated to exceed the number of victims of sex trafficking.[45] Despite this massive exploitation, aiding these people is not a priority for either Russian citizens or the state. There is very little concern for individual rights, a legacy of the Soviet period and even prerevolutionary traditions. Sixty percent of the population is not ready to help migrants.

Corporate Raiding

Corporate raiding combines the use of illegal acts and the misuse of criminal law to deprive business owners of valuable property. It exists on a broad scale in Russia. The problem of corporate raiding is not merely a problem of insecure property rights, but also involves significant threats to the life and welfare of individuals whose property is sought by highly protected and connected individuals. "Reiderstvo" (raiding) is often initiated at the behest of powerful government people and is often executed by law enforcement officials. Therefore, its victims are not just threatened by private citizens but are persecuted with the full force of the state. As the long-serving U.S. Department of Justice prosecutor assigned to the U.S. embassy in Moscow, Tom Firestone, explained:

> "Reiderstvo" differs greatly from the U.S. hostile takeover practice in that it relies on criminal methods such as fraud, blackmail, obstruction of justice, and actual and threatened physical violence. At the same time, though, "reiderstvo" is not just simple thuggery. In contrast to more primitive criminals, Russian "reideri" rely on court orders, resolutions of shareholders and boards of directors, lawsuits. In short, it is a new more sophisticated form of organized crime.[46]

The problem of corporate raiding remains pervasive in Russia. In 2009, the highly reputable director of the Audit Chamber of Russia, Sergei Stepashin, reported that there were 40,000 cases of raiding annually in different sectors of the economy throughout Russia. Of these, only fifty-five were investigated, according to President Medvedev.[47] Some Western sources estimate the number of raiding cases is as high as 70,000 annually.[48] This reveals the almost total impunity of the raiders. There is even less protection for victims of corporate raiding in the Caucasus. This impunity points to high-level complicity in corporate raiding.

Organized Crime

Post-Soviet organized crime is distinct from organized crime in many regions of the world because it initially focused on the legitimate economy and only more recently assumed a larger role in the drug trade and other aspects of the illicit economy.[49] Organized crime was able to grow so rapidly in the first decade of the post-Soviet period because of pervasive corruption among government officials, the incapacity of the demoralized law enforcement, and the perception by the criminals that they could act with almost total impunity.[50] During the Soviet period, party sanctions placed some curbs on government misconduct; but with the collapse of the Communist Party, and in the absence of the rule of law, there were no limits on the conduct of government officials. The crime groups could function effectively because they corrupted or co-opted government officials and were rarely arrested and incarcerated.[51] Corruption, bribery, and abuse of power escalated rapidly, but there was a sharp diminution of prosecutions for these offenses.[52]

The law enforcement system was decimated by poor morale and dangerous work conditions, as well as the dismissal and departure of many long-
term personnel. For these reasons it was ill-equipped to deal with the
increasing number of serious crimes. Moreover, law enforcement's inexpe-
rience with investigating and prosecuting crimes in a market economy gave
organized crime groups the opportunity to expand their financial reach
enormously. A whole business of private protection evolved, often staffed
and run by organized crime, and crime groups extracted payments from
those in need of protection rather than actually providing a service. They
have been named "violent entrepreneurs" by the Russian researcher Vadim
Volkov.[53]

The diversity of post-Soviet organized crime is one of its hallmarks.
Crime groups are multiethnic and often involve cooperation among groups
that are antagonistic outside the criminal world.[54] Foreign groups not only
operate on Russian territory but also provide partnerships with Russian
crime groups to carry out their activities. For example, Japanese Yakuza
work with Russian organized crime in the Far East to illegally secure needed
timber in exchange for used Japanese cars for the Russian market.

Organized crime groups are not involved exclusively in one area of criminal activity. Crime groups may specialize in drug trafficking, arms trafficking, or auto theft, but most crime groups are multifaceted, spanning many
aspects of the legitimate and illegitimate sectors of the economy simultaneously. In any one region of the country, most forms of illicit activity will be
present. There are regional differences as well; for example, organized crime
involvement with environmental crime will be greater in Siberia and the
Far East than in the more densely populated regions of western Russia.

Russian organized crime's involvement in the banking sector undermined the integrity of the banking system and facilitated massive money
laundering out of Russia. Russian money laundering, as distinct from capital flight, was so significant in the 1990s that it drained Russia of much of
its investment capital.[55] Only after the Russian financial collapse in 1998,
and after Russia was cited early in the following decade by the Financial
Action Task Force for noncompliance with international money laundering
standards, were substantial improvements made in the banking sector.[56]
But there are still problems with organized crime having influence over
some banks and capital flight associated with it.[57] This problem has not
ended, and with Putin's reassumption of the presidency, the pace of capital
flight has exacerbated, with tens of billions leaving Russia in the first
months of 2012.[58]

THE GEOGRAPHY OF CRIME

The vastness of Russia's enormous territory results in significant variations
in crime by region. Compounding these geographical differences is the fact

that many regions of Russia, such as the North Caucasus, Tatarstan, and parts of the Volga region, have strong ethnic influences that also shape the characteristics of crime. Furthermore, there are certain regions characterized by particularly high rates of crime, such as the major cities of Moscow, St. Petersburg, and Ekaterinburg, as well as the regions of Siberia and the Russian Far East. Crime rates escalate as one moves from the western part of the country to the east. This phenomenon is a legacy of Soviet-era policies of strict population controls, a massive institutionalized penal population that often settled in Siberia after release close to their former labor colonies, and the development of new cities east of the Urals without necessary infrastructure and social support systems.

Siberia and Urals

During the Soviet era, new cities were established, particularly in Siberia, which were populated primarily by young men, and there was no planning to attract women to the same communities. With the existing internal passport and registration system that restricted mobility, women could not move to these communities without employment. Therefore, these new cities quickly became areas with high rates of alcohol consumption, violent crime, and other forms of criminality.

At the end of the Soviet period, these communities that were the basis of Soviet industrial production went into significant decline. The rich natural resources of the Urals and Siberia, however, provided large revenues for the corrupt bureaucrats and crime groups that appropriated this state property as their own. Furthermore, the Urals region was a major center of the Soviet Union's military-industrial complex. With the decline of Soviet military production, many of these factories ceased to function, leaving many citizens without incomes. The economic crisis that hit this region helps explain the large number of children-at-risk. Although economic prosperity has come to many cities in the area in the 2000s, serious problems endure. The Nizhnii Tagil case of teenage girls who resisted prostitution and were found dead in a pit is illustrative of the problem of poverty. High levels of drug addiction characterize Siberia, especially the area around Irkutsk.[59]

There is an enormous diversity of organized crime groups operating in Siberia. The Trans-Siberian railroad that traverses Russia is a key area for crime groups to operate. Moreover, the railroad's proximity to China contributes to the active presence of crime groups, facilitated by serious problems of corruption along the border. In addition to such powerful local crime groups as the Bratsk criminal society, there are groups from Central Asia and the Caucasus, including Ingush and Chechen organizations.[60]

The Russian Far East

The Russian Far East has seen a significant decline in population since the collapse of the Soviet Union. The absence of economic development in the region and its isolation from more populous eastern regions of Russia have provided an enormous incentive for citizens to leave. The region had extremely high crime rates in the 1970s, and the region continues to be characterized by very high rates of crime and violent crime. Exacerbating the criminality of the region has been the criminalization of the region. Epitomizing this problem was the former mayor of Vladivostok, Vladimir Nikolayev, an organized criminal with the "klichka" or criminal name of Winnie the Pooh, who was elected in 2004.[61] His ouster in 2007 was made all the more difficult because he held the second position in United Russia Party for the Russian Far East. Sergei Darkin, the criminalized governor of the Russian Far East, was forced out in 2012.[62] His removal is not the result of an increase in integrity in Russia, but rather due to the fact that his criminality was undermining Russia's credibility in the advance of APEC meetings. Funds allocated for development of the region in advance of the meeting were being siphoned off by a criminalized and corrupt regional elite.

Organized crime groups from the Russian Far East work with South Korean, Japanese, Chinese, and Vietnamese crime groups. Much of the criminality is connected with the ports and the massive shipping that flows through this region. Many of the shipping and fishing companies are dominated by organized crime.[63] The impoverished military in the region has contributed to massive unauthorized arms sales to foreign governments and organized crime groups. A sale of Russian helicopters to North Koreans was averted in the late 1990s only when members of the police, who were not part of the scheme, stumbled on the helicopters just prior to delivery.[64]

Much of the crime is connected with the exploitation of natural resources. Fish and timber represent 93 percent of the exports from the Russian Far East. Overfished waters, according to crime data from the organized crime authorities in the Russian Far East, wind up in Japanese and Korean markets.[65] Since the fall of the Soviet Union, there has been a fourfold decline of forested land.[66] Half the hardwood in the Russian Far East is illegally harvested either by corrupt officials or by gangs in the communities. Japanese and Chinese crime groups are actively involved in the illegal purchase of timber. In an investigation documented in the *New Yorker*, the illegally harvested timber was used in Chinese factories to make furniture for Wal-Mart.[67]

Crime in Major Urban Centers

Moscow, as Russia's largest city and economic powerhouse, is home of the largest and most important crime groups such as Soltnsevo and Izmailovo. These groups have penetrated into the most lucrative sectors of the economy such as banks, real estate, and raw materials. These groups are part of a very diverse picture of criminality in the city. Ethnic crime groups have been deeply involved in the consumer markets for food and consumer goods. Restaurants, clubs, and casinos have been centers of criminal activity and investment. But in this rich investment environment, it is often hard to differentiate where the criminality ends and the corruption of government officials begins.

Moscow has become one of the most expensive cities in the world. The absence of competition, the large sums extracted by organized crime as their share of profits, and the domination of real estate by organized crime groups in cooperation with corrupt officials help explain the extremely high cost of business and of daily life. The wife of former Moscow mayor Luzhkov was a billionaire, much of the fortune made from real estate before her husband's ouster.[68] Corruption in the real estate sector also exists in St. Petersburg.

The criminalization of real estate continues, even though its form has evolved over time. In the past, many citizens simply lost their apartments and disappeared without trace. No protection was available from the government to protect tenants who were threatened by high-level organized crime. High-level officials in Moscow and St. Petersburg demanded significant bribes for information about the availability of property for rent and purchase. Construction companies that built much of the new construction often have organized crime figures as major shareholders or financiers. Corporate raiding of valuable urban real estate remains a serious problem.

Moscow is still a major center of money laundering, despite enhanced controls. The close relationship between the banks and powerful individuals, the cash-reliant economy, and the lack of regulation of financial markets still make it relatively easy to move illicit funds from the very large shadow economy.[69]

CONCLUSION

Crime rates were suppressed in the Soviet years, a consequence of its high levels of social control, high rates of incarceration, and controls over places of residence. With the liberalization of the Gorbachev era, fundamental changes occurred in Soviet crime patterns. Crime rates rose rapidly, and organized crime became a formidable actor in the new economy. The 1990s were traumatic. Many Russians lost their lives' savings in bank failures. Unemployment rose dramatically, particularly among women. The social safety net collapsed. In the absence of effective state enforcement, organized crime filled the vacuum and became a visible force in society, not only through its displays of violence and its role in private protection but also through the key role it played in privatization and politics in the transitional period.

The Putin-Medvedev years brought greater stability, but Russia has not been able to eliminate the high rates of violent crime, endemic corruption, or pervasive organized crime. High levels of money laundering and export of capital have continued to deprive Russia of the capital it needs for investment, although the record profits obtained during the boom years of oil revenues masked the impact.

Crime problems have evolved over the years and remain an important element of the structure of the Russian economy, society, and political system. The number of homicides associated with organized crime has declined, but homicide rates remain among the highest in the world. Conflicts over property are no longer decided by shootings but often instead by expensive litigation in the West, particularly London, where many of Russia's richest citizens have placed their assets.[70]

Property rights are still not secure. Property acquired by force, deception, and coercion in the early days of the post-Soviet period is now often redistributed by corporate raiding. Russia is an exporter of trafficked women, an importer of large numbers of migrants, and a transit and destination country for trafficking victims. Although Russia has provided temporary work permits for many foreign workers, there are still large numbers of illegal migrants from poor Soviet successor states who come to Russia to earn money. Significant numbers become victims of labor and sexual trafficking.

Despite the centrality of the crime and corruption problem, there has been no concerted state action commensurate with the size of the problem. Without an effective law enforcement apparatus, an empowered civil society, or a free media, it is very difficult to curb the rise of organized crime or the pervasive corruption. The criminal trajectories set in motion in the early post-Soviet period have continued. Organized criminals have so much power because they assumed critical investment positions in key sectors of the economy in the transitional period. Massive collusion with and corruption of politicians have ensured this continued ownership. In fact, many criminals have sought governmental positions to acquire immunity from prosecution.

Crime in Russia is a major political and economic influence on society. The heavy involvement of criminals and corrupt politicians in the legitimate economy are key explanations for the absence of transparency in Russian financial markets. This contributed to the especially precipitous decline of the Russian markets relative to other international exchanges in fall 2008. Furthermore, the existence of widespread monopolies as a result of organized crime and oligarch dominance of the economy has led to high prices. Pervasive criminal activity is an enormous impediment to entrepreneurship and the emergence of small and medium-sized businesses that are crucial to long-term economic development and a middle class that could be the backbone of a more democratic society.

Corruption remains endemic and a major factor in citizen discontent. The long-term destabilizing influence of this corruption should not be underestimated. It has contributed to human brain drain, capital flight, and a disillusionment of many citizens with government not just in Moscow, but in many more remote regions as well.[71]

SUGGESTED READINGS

Karklins, Rasma. *The System Made Me Do It: Corruption in Post-Communist Societies.* Armonk, N.Y.: M. E. Sharpe, 2005.

Kegö, Walter, and Alexandru Molcean. *Russian Speaking: Organized Crime Groups in the EU.* Stockholm: Institute for Security and Development Policy, 2011.

Orttung, Robert, and Anthony Latta, eds. *Russia's Battle with Crime, Corruption and Terrorism.* New York and London: Routledge, 2008.

Stoecker, Sally, and Louise Shelley, eds. *Human Traffic and Transnational Crime: Eurasian and American Perspectives.* Latham, Md.: Rowman and Littlefield, 2005.

Varese, Frederico. *Mafias on the Move: How Organized Crime Conquers New Territories.* Princeton: Princeton University Press, 2011.

———. *The Russian Mafia: Private Protection in a New Market Economy.* Oxford: Oxford University Press, 2005.

Volkov, Vadim. *Violent Entrepreneurs: The Use of Force in the Making of Russian Capitalism.* Ithaca: Cornell University Press, 2002.

NOTES

1. Thomas Firestone, "Criminal Corporate Raiding in Russia," *The International Lawyer* 42, no. 4 (2008): 1207–29.

2. Roy Godson, ed., *Menace to Society: Political-Criminal Collaboration around the World* (New Brunswick, N.J.: Transaction, 2003); Leslie Holmes, "The Corruption-Organised Crime Nexus in Central and Eastern Europe," in *Terrorism, Organised Crime and Corruption: Networks and Linkage,* ed. Leslie Homes (Cheltenham, U.K.: Edward Elgar, 2007), 84–108.

3. Mark Galeotti, "Medvedev's First Police Reform: MVD Loses Specialised Organised Crime Department," inmoscowsshadows.wordpress.com/2008/09/11/medvedevsfirst-police-reform-mvd-loses-specialised-organised-crime-department/ (accessed May 29, 2012).

4. See Navalny's blog on corruption, rospil.info/ (accessed June 1, 2012).

5. They have globalized and moved to different locales to increase their business opportunities in different markets. See Frederico Varese, *Mafias on the Move: How Organized Crime Conquers New Territories* (Princeton: Princeton University Press, 2011).

6. These organized crime groups are not the product of post-Soviet society, they also flourished under the Soviet regime. Frederico Varese, *The Russian Mafia—Private Protection in a New Market Economy* (Oxford: Oxford University Press, 2001); Yakov Gilinskiy and Yakov Kostjukovsky, "From Thievish Cartel to Criminal Corporation," in *Organised Crime in Europe*, eds. Cyril Fijnaut and Letizia Paoli (Dordrecht: Springer, 2004), 181–202.

7. Europol, *Organised Crime Threat Assessment 2011*, May 4, 2011, www.europo l.europa.eu/content/press/europol-organised-crime-threat-assessment-2011-429 (accessed June 1, 2012); Walter Kegö and Alexandru Molcean, *Russian Speaking Organized Crime Groups in the EU* (Stockholm Paper Series, Stockholm: Institute for Security and Development Policy, 2011), 26.

8. For trade of women see Louise Shelley, *Human Trafficking: A Global Perspective* (Cambridge and New York: Cambridge University Press, 2010), 174–200; G. M. Zherebkin, *Otvetstvennost' za nezakonnuiu rubku lesnykh nasazhdenii. Analuz nelegal'-nykh rubok na rossiiskom Dal'nem Vostoke i metodika ikh rassledovaniia* (Vladivostok: Apel'sin, 2011); Nicholas Schmidle, "Disarming Victor Bout: The Rise and Fall of the World's Most Notorious Weapons Trafficker," *The New Yorker*, March 5, 2012, 54–65.

9. "Marching Off to Cyberwar: The Internet: Attacks Launched over the Internet on Estonia and Georgia Highlight the Difficulty of Defining and Dealing with 'Cyberwar,'" December 4, 2008 www.economist.com/node/12673385 (accessed June 1, 2012).

10. Shelley, *Human Trafficking*, 113–21.

11. The publications of these centers can be accessed through policy-traccc .gmu.edu, under the section on study centers in Eurasia. The website of the Center in Vladivostok, www.crime.vl.ru, has about 400,000 readers annually, making it one of the most read academic websites in Russia. Together the three websites have approximately a million readers annually.

12. Steven Swinford and Jon Ungoed-Thomas, Peter Mandelson, "Oligarch Oleg Deripaska Linked to Mafia Boss," *Sunday Times*, October 26, 2008, www.timeson line.co.uk/tol/news/politics/article5014782.ece (accessed October 30, 2008). Simon Goodley, "Oleg Deripaska Accuses Rival Bringing £1.6bn Suit of Running Protection Racket," February 13, 2012, www.guardian.co.uk/world/2012/feb/13/ olegderipaska-rival-crime-claims (accessed June 1, 2012).

13. Gilles Favarel-Garrigues, *Policing Economic Crime in Russia: From Soviet Planned Economy to Privatization*, translated by Roger Leverdier (New York: Columbia University Press, 2011); Brian Taylor, *State Building in Putin's Russia: Policing and Coercion after Communism* (Cambridge and New York: Cambridge University Press, 2011); Vadim Volkov, *Violent Entrepreneurs: The Use of Force in the Making of Russian Capitalism* (Ithaca: Cornell University Press, 2002).

14. Louise Shelley and Yuri Andrienko, "Crime, Violence and Political Conflict in Russia," in *Understanding Civil War: Evidence and Analysis*, ed. Nicholas Sambanis (Washington, DC: World Bank, 2005), 87–117; Elina Alexandra Treyger, *Soviet Roots of Post-Soviet Order*, Doctoral Dissertation, Harvard University, Cambridge, Mass., June 2011; A. Lysova, N. G. Shchitov, and W. A. Pridemore, *Homicide in Russia, Ukraine and Belarus*, in M. Liem and W. A. Pridemore, eds. *Sourcebook of European Homicide Research* (New York and Dordrecht: Springer, 2011), 451–69.

15. Serge Schmemann, "The Case Against and For Khodorkovsky," *International Herald Tribune*, October 19, 2008, www.nytimes.com/2008/10/20/opinion/20mon 4.html (accessed June 1, 2012); Alena Ledeneva, "Telephone Justice in Russia," *Post-Soviet Affairs* 24, no. 4 (2008): 324–50; Kathryn Hendley, "Telephone Law and the 'Rule of Law': The Russian Case," *Hague Journal on the Rule of Law* 1, no. 2 (2009): 241–64.

16. Louise I. Shelley, "Interpersonal Violence in the Soviet Union," *Violence, Aggression and Terrorism* 1, no. 2 (1987): 41–67.

17. N. F. Kuznetsova and G. M. Minkovskii, *Kriminologiia: Uchebnik* (Mosow: Vek, 1998), 553.

18. Treyger, *Soviet Roots of Post-Soviet Order*, 8, see also W. A. Pridemore, "Social Structure and Homicide in Post-Soviet Russia," *Social Science Research* 34, no. 4 (2005): 732–56.

19. Treyger, *Soviet Roots of Post-Soviet Order*, 18.

20. Clementine K. Fujimura, Sally W. Stoecker, and Tatyana Sudakova, *Russia's Abandoned Children: An Intimate Understanding* (Westport, Conn.: Praeger, 2005).

21. "V Rossii—'tretiia volna' bezprizornosti, beznadzornosti, negramotnosti, i prestupnost' podrostov (statistika)," June 1, 2005, www.newsru.com/russia/01 jun2005/generation.html (accessed May 29, 2012).

22. See the mission of Stellit, http://eng.ngostellit.ru/# (accessed June 1, 2012).

23. Innocentjustice.org/know-more/ (accessed June 1, 2012).

24. Discussion by Marina Ryabko, director of the "Priyut-Tranzit" government-funded shelter for children and teens in St. Petersburg. The event was entitled "Child Trafficking and Exploitation in Russia: Scale and Scope," held on September 24, 2008, George Mason University, Arlington, Va.

25. V. Cherkesov, "Otvechaet na voprosi glavnovo redaktora almankha 'organizovannaia prestupnost, terrorism, i korruptsiia,' Professor V.V. Luneev," *Organizovannaia Prestupnost, Terrorizm, i Korruptsiia*, no. 4 (2003): 8.

26. Simon Schuster, "The Curse of the Crocodile: Russia's Deadly Designer Drug," June 21, 2011, www.time.com/time/world/article/0,8599,2078355,00.html (accessed May 30, 2012).

27. "V Rossii, 'tretiia volna' bezprizornosti," June 1, 2005.

28. B. Tselinsky, "Sovremennaia Narkosituatsiia v Rossii: Tendentsii i Perspektivii," *Organizovannaia Prestupnost, Terrorizm, i Korruptsiia*, no. 4 (2003): 21.

29. A. G. Museibov, "Regional'nye praktiki po preduprezhdeniiu nezakonnogo oborota narkotikov," *Sotsiologicheskie issledovaniia*, no. 7 (2003): 125–30.

30. Based on the analysis of Vladivostok branch of the Transnational Crime and Corruption Center, www.crime.vl.ru/index.php?p=1202&more=1&c=1&tb=1& pb=1 (accessed October 29, 2008).

31. United States Department of State Bureau for International Narcotics and Law Enforcement Affairs, *International Narcotics Control Strategy Report*, vol. 1, *Drug and Chemical Control*, March 2007, 467–70, www.state.gov/documents/organiza tion/81446.pdf (accessed October 30, 2008).

32. Mark Galeotti, "Russia's Drug Crisis," *Jane's Intelligence Review* 18, no. 10 (2003): 52–53.

33. www.state.gov/j/inl/rls/nrcrpt/2012/vol1/184101.htm#Russia (accessed May 29, 2012).

34. *UNODC World Drug Report*, 2011, www.unodc.org/wdr (accessed June 1, 2012).

35. Aaron Beitman, "Perspectives on Illicit Drugs in Russia," December 5, 2011, traccc.gmu.edu/category/traccc-posts/page/2/ (accessed June 3, 2012).

36. "Narkobiznes—ugroza natsional'noi bezopasnosti," Press Release, Federal Narcotics Control Service, July 15, 2003.

37. Vladimir Vorsobin, "Putin prizval bortsov s narkotikami rabotat' 'na polnuiu katushku'," *Komsomol'skaia Pravda*, March 31, 2004.

38. Tselinsky, "Sovremennaia Narkosituatsiia v Rossii," 6.

39. Tselinsky, "Sovremennaia Narkosituatsiia v Rossii," 23. Kairat Osmonaliev, "Developing Counter-Narcotics Policy in Central Asia, Washington and Uppsala: Silk Road Paper," Central Asia-Caucasus Institute and Silk Road Studies Program, 2005; "Drug Dealers, Drug Lords, and Drug Warriors-cum-Traffickers: Drug Crime and the Narcotic Market in Tajikistan," traccc.gmu.edu/category/traccc-posts/page/2/ (accessed June 3, 2012); Letizia Paoli, Victoria A. Greenfield, and Peter Reuter, The World Heroin Market: Can Supply be Cut? (Oxford and New York: Oxford University Press, 2009).

40. Sergei Golunov, "Narkotorgovlia cherez Rossiisko-Kazakhstanskuiu granitsu: Vyzov i problemy protivodeistviia," traccc.gmu.edu/topics/drug-trafficking/traccc publications-on-drug-trafficking/ (accessed May 30, 2012); Aaron Beitman, "Perspectives on Illicit Drugs in Russia," December 5, 2011.

41. Tamara Makarenko, "Terrorism and Transnational Organised Crime: The Emerging Nexus," *Transnational Violence and Seams of Lawlessness in the Asia-Pacific: Linkages to Global Terrorism* (Hawaii: Asia Pacific Center for Strategic Studies, 2004). Kimberley Thachuk, "Transnational Threats: Falling Through the Cracks?" *Low Intensity Conflict & Law Enforcement* 10, no. 1 (2001); Sabrina Adamoli, et. al., *Organized Crime around the World* (Helsinki: HEUNI, 1998); Barbara Harris-White, *Globalization and Insecurity: Political, Economic and Physical Challenges* (Hampshire and New York: Palgrave-Macmillan, 2002); Ian Griffith, "From Cold War Geopolitics to Post-Cold War Geonarcotics," *International Journal* 49, no. 1 (1993–1994): 1–36; R. Matthew and G. Shambaugh, "Sex, Drugs, and Heavy Metal: Transnational Threats and National Vulnerabilities," *Security Dialogue* 29, no. 2 (1998): 163–75.

42. Louise I. Shelley and Svante E. Cornell, "The Drug Trade in Russia," in *Russian Business Power: The Role of Russian Business in Foreign and Security Relations*, eds. Andreas Wegner, Jeronim Perovic, and Robert W. Orttung (London and New York: Routledge, 2006), 200.

43. "Na Urale nashli tainoe zahoronenie seks-rabyn," *Komsomolskaia Pravda*, February 2, 2007, kp.ru/daily/23848.4/62919/ (accessed June 1, 2012); Valentina Blinova, "Proshchanie," *Ogonek* 7 (February 12–18, 2007): 18–20.

44. Sudharshan Canagarajah and Matin Kholmatov, "ECA Knowledge Brief: Migration and Remittances in CIS Countries During the Global Economic Crisis," web.worldbank.org/WBSITE/EXTERNAL/COUNTRIES/ECAEXT/0,contentMDK:2 2445169~pag ePK:146736~piPK:146830~theSitePK:258599~isCURL:Y,00.html (accessed June 1, 2012).

45. Elena Tyuryukanova, "THB, Irregular Migration and Criminal Gains," Paper presented at OSCE-UNODC-CYPRUS Regional Meeting on Human Trafficking and Money Laundering, September 18–19, 2008, Larnaca, Cyprus.

46. Firestone, "Criminal Corporate Raiding in Russia," 1207.

47. Maria Antonova, "Kremlin Tightens Screws on Corporate Raiders," May 14, 2010, www.themoscowtimes.com/business/article/kremlin-tightens-screws-on-cor porate-raiders/405960.html (accessed May 1, 2011).

48. Luke Harding, "Raiders of the Russian Billions," *The Guardian*, June 24, 2008, www.guardian.co.uk/world/2008/jun/24/russia.internationalcrime (accessed May 1, 2011).

49. Svetlana Glinkina, "Privatizatsiia and Kriminalizatsiia-How Organized Crime is Hijacking Privatization," *Demokratizatsiya* 2, no. 3 (1994): 385–91.

50. Louise Shelley, "Organized Crime Groups: 'Uncivil Society,'" in *Russian Civil Society: A Critical Assessment*, eds. Alfred B. Evans Jr., Laura A. Henry, and Lisa McIntosh Sundstrom (Armonk, N.Y.: M. E. Sharpe, 2006), 95–109.

51. G. F. Khohkriakov, "Organizovannia prestupnost' v Rossii: 60-e gody-pervaia polovina 90-x godov," *Obshchestvennye nauki i sovremmenost'*, no. 6 (2000): 62–74.

52. See Louise Shelley, "Crime and Corruption," in *Developments in Russian Politics*, eds. Stephen White, Alex Pravda, and Zvi Gitelman (Houndsmills: Palgrave, 2001), 239–53; Alena Ledeneva, *How Russia Really Works: The Informal Practices That Shaped Post-Soviet Politics and Business* (Ithaca and London: Cornell University Press, 2006); Leslie Holmes, "Crime, Organised Crime and Corruption in Post-Communist Europe and the CIS," *Communist and Post-Communist Studies* 42, no. 2 (2009): 265–87.

53. Volkov, *Violent Entrepreneurs*; Vadim Volkov, "Silovoe predprinimatel'stvo v sovremennoi Rossii," *Sotsiologiecheskie issledovaniia*, no. 1 (1999): 55–65.

54. Varese, *The Russian Mafia*; Alexander Kupatadze, *Organised Crime, Political Transitions and State Formation in Post-Soviet Eurasia* (Houndsmill and New York: Palgrave Macmillan, 2012).

55. Center for Strategic and International Studies, *Russian Organized Crime and Corruption, Putin's Challenge* (Washington, DC: CSIS, 2000), 32–39.

56. Christopher Kenneth, "FATF Not Satisfied with Russia's Anti-Money Laundering Efforts," April 11, 2002, *The Russia Journal*, www.russiajournal.com/node/6112, (accessed June 1, 2012); see continuing problems with Russian money laundering, Bureau of International Narcotics and Law Enforcement Affairs, *2012 International Narcotics Control Strategy Report (INCSR)*, vol. 2, March 7, 2012, www.state.gov/j/ inl/rls/nrcrpt/2012/vol2/184117.htm#Russia (accessed May 30, 2012).

57. N. A. Lopashenko, *Begstvo kapitalov, peredel sobstvennosti i ekonomicheskaia amnistiia* (Moscow: Iuridicheskie programmy, 2005).

58. Ira Iosebashvili, "Capital Flees Russia, Damping Official Hopes Over Putin's Win," April 4, 2012, online.wsj.com/article/SB10001424052702303299604577 323401787710184.html (accessed June 1, 2012).

59. The problem first identified by Anna Repetskaya a decade ago still endures. See Anna Repetskaya, "Irkutsk Organized Crime Press Review," *OC Watch* 5 (October 1, 1999): 16.

60. Mark Galeotti suggests that Chechen organized crime may be seen as a franchise, as there is more Chechen organized crime than Chechens. See "'Brotherhoods' and 'Associates': Chechen Networks of Crime and Resistance," in *Networks, Terrorism and Global Insurgency* ed. Robert J. Bunker (London and New York:

Routledge, 2005), 175; Aaron Beitman, "Organized Crime in Western Siberia," part 3, discusses Repetskaya's research on the crime groups present in Western Siberia, April 26, 2012, traccc.gmu.edu/2012/04/26/organized-crime-in-western-siberia part -3/ (accessed May 30, 2012).

61. "Vladivostok Mayor Stripped of Power among Corruption Investigation," Associated Press, March 1, 2007, www.nytimes.com/2007/03/01/world/europe/ 01iht-russia.4763829.html?_r = 1.

62. "Russian Far East Governor Steps Down," February 28, 2012, RIA-Novosti, en.rian.ru/society/20120228/171590672.html (accessed May 30, 2012).

63. See website of Vladivostok Center, www.crime.vl.ru.

64. V. A. Nomokonov, ed., *Organizovannia prestupnost': tendentsii, perspektivy bor'by* (Vladivostok: Dalnevostochnogo universiteta, 1998).

65. P. V. Korovnikov, "Problemy dekriminalizatsii sfery prirodopol'zovaniia Primorskogo kraiia i nekotorye puti ikh resheniia," in *Rossiia i ATR Problemy bezopasnosti, migratsii i prestupnosti* (Vladivostok: Dal'nevostochnogo universiteta, 2007), 88–89.

66. Dal'nii Vostok: Khronika organizovannoi prestupnosti (Obzor pressy 1997-August 2003) www.crime.vl.ru/index.php?p = 1385&more = 1&page = 4 (accessed November 1, 2008).

67. Raffi Khatchadourian, "The Stolen Forests Inside the Covert War on Illegal Logging," *New Yorker*, October 6, 2008, www.newyorker.com/reporting/2008/10/ 06/081006fa_fact_khatchadourian (accessed November 1, 2008).

68. Vadim Nikitin "Feminism as Cronyism for Russia's Power Women," March 1, 2009, foreignpolicyblogs.com/2009/03/01/feminism-as-cronyism-for-russias power-women / (accessed June 1, 2012).

69. Bureau of International Narcotics and Law Enforcement Affairs, *2012 International Narcotics Control Strategy Report (INCSR)*.

70. "Court Battle between Roman Abramovich and Boris Berezovsky Ends," January 19, 2012, www.guardian.co.uk/world/2012/jan/19/court-battle-abramovich berezovsky-ends. (accessed June 1, 2012).

71. See for example, "Astrakhan Focus of Anti-Putin Protests," April 14, 2012, www.euronews.com/2012/04/14/astrakhan-focus-of-anti-putin-protests/ (accessed June 4, 2012).

10

Agriculture

Stephen K. Wegren

Since 2000, two stages of agrarian policy have been pursued by the Russian government. The first stage was the development of an institutional and legislative base to stabilize the agricultural sector and pave the way for growth. The second stage, from 2005–2006 onward, witnessed the introduction of governmental financial assistance to increase domestic production, make Russian agriculture internationally competitive, and reduce dependence on foreign imports. This chapter begins with a review of Russia's agricultural situation and achievements under former president Dmitry Medvedev. The chapter then considers priorities and challenges that face Putin in his second tour as president (his third term, hereafter referred to as Putin 3.0). Medvedev's agrarian policy did not depart significantly from Putin's, and it is unlikely that Putin 3.0 will depart from policy directions defined during the Medvedev presidency. By 2018, when Putin's third term expires, Russia is likely to have had eighteen years of consistency in agrarian policy. Russia's agriculture has a twofold global importance. First, its production rebound influences world supply and affects global commodity prices. A Russia that is a supplier in a hungry world is better than a Russia that subtracts from global surplus. Second, a competitive agricultural sector is an integral part of the profile of a global power. Inasmuch as Putin hopes to return Russia to international influence, a strong agricultural sector furthers his goals.

AGRICULTURE FROM PUTIN TO MEDVEDEV

Compared to the agricultural situation that Putin confronted when he became president in 2000, Dmitry Medvedev inherited a favorable agricultural situation when he became president in 2008. During the 1990s, food production had fallen precipitously. Large farms (state and collective farms and their legal successors) suffered the biggest decrease in food production. Based on an index of physical volume of output (1990 = 100), in Boris Yeltsin's last year in office agricultural production by large agricultural enterprises declined to 36 percent of its 1990 level. Moreover, during the 1990s the structure of output changed so that by the end of the decade, households and not large farms were the predominant producer as measured in ruble value.

Food production on large farms declined due to input prices that rose faster than wholesale food prices, the shifting of responsibility for rural social services and rural infrastructure to farm budgets, a general shortage of credit to cover seasonal operating and production costs, and a decline in domestic demand for food as a result of rapidly escalating retail food prices. In other words, large farms felt a multidimensional financial squeeze. By the latter Yeltsin era, the combination of extraordinarily bad harvests and devaluation of the ruble in 1998 led to regionally imposed price controls on food products in the fall of 1998 and winter 1998–1999. To prevent starvation, some regions received Western food aid well into 2000. Nor did it appear that Russia's agriculture could rebound quickly, because rural infrastructure crumbled at an accelerated rate during the 1990s as government capital investments dried up. Each year large numbers of capital stock became unusable as farm equipment fell into disrepair or was removed from use. Thus, in many ways, when Putin assumed the presidency, the agricultural situation was bordering on catastrophic.

Once elected in 2000, Putin made agricultural recovery a priority and introduced many steps to help large farms recover.[1] With Putin as president it became clear that a primary goal was to pursue and protect "state interests." In agriculture, this orientation led in turn to (1) priority attention to the recovery of large farming enterprises in terms of both their financial strength and their food production; (2) import protection policies for several food commodities; and (3) government intervention in the domestic grain market for the purpose of "stabilizing" wholesale prices for grain producers, regional supplies, and retail prices for consumers. Since large farms produce the overwhelming majority of grain products, they benefited the most from governmental market intervention. The government's goals were initially laid out in a document called "Basic Directions of Agrofood Policy to 2010," which former minister of agriculture Aleksei Gordeev presented in July 2000.[2] The "Basic Directions" reflected a broad-based strategy of governmental support for agriculture. Gordeev indicated that the highest priority for agricultural policy would be increasing domestic food production and lowering reliance on food imports, and improving the nation's food security. During the next few years, this first stage of the government's agrarian strategy created an institutional and policy foundation that would facilitate economic growth, in contrast to Yeltsin's agrarian policies that had been destructive.

The agricultural situation inherited by Medvedev was different from what Putin had been bequeathed. In 2008 food production was trending upward in both volume and ruble value, farm profits were rising, consumer food consumption was increasing, and Russia was emerging as a major grain exporter. In 2008, Russia attained a post-Soviet record grain harvest, and gross farm profitability (pre-tax) rose to a high of R117.4 billion in 2008.[3] In 2009 the ruble value of Russia's agricultural production reached its apex for the post-Soviet period. The situation changed, however, when the global financial crisis hit, followed by a devastating drought and heat wave in 2010, which cost Russia one-third of its harvest and forced it to ban grain exports during the 2010–2011 agricultural year. In 2009 farm profitability dropped, and the volume of production declined compared to 2008.[4] In 2010 the drought led directly to significant production declines for many agricultural commodities, although government financial emergency assistance was able to mitigate much of the damage to animal husbandry. Overall, even though Medvedev faced a difficult situation in agriculture during two of his four years in power, the agricultural situation was again trending positively as he left office. Production trends for several basic commodities are indicated in table 10.1.

The impact of the weather in 2010 is clear in the production numbers displayed in the table. The 2010 heat wave and drought caused major damage to Russia's agriculture—destroying more than 13.3 million hectares of grain crops, and more than 30 percent of the cultivated area in 43 affected regions. Former minister of agriculture Elena Skrynnik estimated that R41 billion of damage was caused to Russia's agricultural sector.[5] After the grain harvest fell to 61 million tons in 2010, production rebounded to nearly 94 million tons in 2011 and Russia resumed grain exports. Russia also received record harvests of sunflower and sugar beets in 2011. The production of beef and poultry also hit post-Soviet highs. Overall, the value of food output in 2011 was R3.4 trillion, up substantially from R2.6 trillion in 2010 (in current rubles).

In my opinion, Medvedev's agrarian policies are best understood as a continuation of the course begun by former (and current) president Putin.[6] The basis for agrarian policy since 2006 is the law "On the Development of Agriculture," which was adopted in December 2006 after many years of debate. As a result, Medvedev's agricultural policies extended preexisting policy and did not define any fundamentally new directions. Under Medvedev, three main achievements occurred in Russia's agriculture: (1) continuation and expansion of government financial support programs to agriculture, despite the financial downturn; (2) priority development of the

Table 10.1. Annual Agricultural Production 1998–2010 (All Categories of Producers)

	1998–1999[a]	2000–2001[a]	2002–2003[a]	2004–2005[a]	2006–2007[a]	2008	2009	2010	2011
Grains (mil. tons)[b]	51.2	75.3	76.9	78.1	80.1	108.2	97.1	61	93.9
Sugar beets (mil. tons)	13.0	14.3	17.5	21.6	29.9	29.0	24.9	22.3	46.3
Sunflower seeds (mil. tons)	3.6	3.3	4.3	5.6	6.2	7.4	6.5	5.3	9.6
Potatoes (mil. tons)	31.2	34.5	34.7	36.6	37.7	28.8	31.1	21.1	32.6
Vegetables (mil. tons)	11.4	12.7	14.0	14.8	15.5	13.0	13.4	12.1	14.7
Meat and poultry (mil. tons, carcass weight)	4.5	4.4	4.8	4.9	5.2	6.3	6.7	7.1	10.9
Milk (mil. tons)	32.4	32.4	33.4	32.0	31.6	32.4	32.6	31.9	31.7
Eggs (billion)	32.8	34.4	36.3	35.7	37.8	38.1	39.4	40.6	41.0

Sources: *Rossiiskii statisticheskiy ezhegodnik* (Moscow: Goskomstat, 1999), 363–71; *Agropromyshlennyi kompleks Rossii* (Moscow: Goskomstat, 2001), 61–81; *Rossiia v tsifrakh* (Moscow: Goskomstat, 2004), 209–11; *Rossiia v tsifrakh* (Moscow: Rosstat, 2011), 277, 280; *Sotsial'no-ekonomicheskoe polozhenie Rossii* (Moscow: Rosstat, 2012), 2, 5, and author's calculations.

[a] Two-year averages.
[b] Grain totals after cleaning.

private farming sector; and (3) entry into the WTO, with special attention paid to effects on agriculture. Each is discussed in turn.

Government Financial Assistance Programs

During Medvedev's presidency both he and Putin spoke publicly numerous times about the need to support and improve the sector. Both men also visited farms and food processing plants in different regions, thereby signaling their support for agricultural development. As prime minister, Putin took a personal interest in agrarian affairs by attending various agricultural conferences and congresses of AKKOR, the Rossiyskoe agrarnoe dvizhenie (Russian Agrarian Movement, RAD), and other agricultural associations and organizations. When Vladimir Putin was reelected president in March 2012, government support for agriculture continued to be a national priority.

Medvedev's policies were an outflow from initiatives that were begun under Putin. In the later years of Putin's second term, a program called "Development of the Agroindustrial Complex" was introduced, with planned expenditures of more than R30 billion during 2006–2007, of which R14.2 billion would come from the federal budget primarily in the form of loans with subsidized interest rates (the term of the loans could range from two to eight years).[7] This program represented the first serious attempt in the post-Soviet period to infuse substantial financial support into the agricultural sector. The program ended up spending more than originally anticipated, as by the end of 2007 just under R48 billion had been directed to agriculture.[8]

As president, Medvedev wanted to improve agricultural performance and competitiveness. He not only supported government financial assistance to agriculture but also oversaw the renewal and expansion of the original program with a slightly different title, "The Development of Agriculture during 2008–2012."[9] According to the original indices in the program, state expenditures for agriculture were expected to increase from R76.3 billion in 2008 to R130 billion in 2012. Overall, R551.3 billion was to be financed from the federal budget and R1.5 trillion from the consolidated budget (regional and federal budgets) during the program's five years. In mid-2009 President Medvedev pledged to fund the program in full despite the financial crisis and economic downturn in Russia.[10] Due to the 2010 drought and other factors, however, the federal government ended up allocating supplemental monies in an attempt to consolidate the gains that had been achieved.[11] In 2011, a record R163 billion from the federal budget was spent on agriculture in support of the program, thereby surpassing planned expenditures.[12] Medvedev remained committed to supporting agriculture to the end of his administration. In October 2011 he met with agricultural workers and stated that the government's approach to agriculture in the 1990s, an approach that saw the sector as a "black hole," was "an absolutely mistaken ideology." Instead, the agricultural sector needs constant attention, even in developed nations, in order to keep the sector productive and competitive. Medvedev said that the Russian government will "always" provide support for the sector, stating, "Have no doubt, this policy will continue. It is my position . . . and the position of everyone who manages agriculture."[13]

The expansion of support for agriculture was not just monetary. Under Medvedev, branch programs were adopted and funded in the following areas: animal husbandry (cattle and milk cows), rural housing, private farming and small forms of farming, the development of family milk farms, land reclamation, rural community development, modernization of food processing, the fishing industry, development of the pig industry, and development of the poultry industry. Some of these branch programs are planned to extend to 2020. Starting in January 2012 he also funded a crop insurance program to protect producers from catastrophic losses, backed by R5 billion in federal funding for 2011.[14] According to this insurance program the federal government will pay 50 percent of the insurance premiums. Starting in 2009 a system of rural credit and consumer cooperatives was funded by the federal government to provide private farmers and private plot operators with small-scale loans and services. On January 1, 2011, more than 4,500 cooperatives were operating throughout the country, including 1,216 credit co-ops, 762 processing co-ops, and 2,525 service co-ops.[15] Thus, during his term Medvedev not only maintained government support to agriculture, but actually expanded its scope.

The Private Agricultural Sector

A second arena where Medvedev extended previous policy concerns the development of private farming. Although the large farm sector was Putin's first priority in 2000, during Putin's first two terms a series of steps was taken to aid private farmers. For example, in 2003 an updated federal law on private farming was passed that established the legal status of private farmers, an important step for farmers who wanted to obtain credit. In 2004 a program was introduced that allowed private farmers to lease agricultural machinery at state-subsidized rates, significant because few farmers had the financial means to purchase machinery outright. This law was an important step in helping private farms address the problem of chronic undermechanization. In 2004, a law on land mortgaging allowed private farmers to mortgage their privately owned land in order to raise capital for investment. By 2007, thirty-five of Russia's eighty-six regions had implemented pilot projects that provided financial credit based on land mortgaging.[16] In early 2007, the government announced it would subsidize private farmers who raised pedigree livestock. Finally, private farmers were eligible to receive direct production subsidies, subsidies for the transport of grain on state railroads, and subsidies for fuel and mineral fertilizer.

As government support for private farming increased, the sector began to show significant improvement in food production. By 2008 when Medvedev took office, private farms produced 21 percent of the nation's grain, 10 percent of its sugar beets, and about 30 percent of its sunflowers.[17] Under Medvedev a number of additional initiatives were begun. The first initiative came in June 2009 when a special financial program was adopted by the Ministry of Agriculture entitled "The Development of Peasant Farms and Other Small Scale Forms of Farming in the Agro-industrial Complex during 2009–2011."[18] The program spelled out goals and tasks for the program, monetary allocations to address existing problems, and expected results. This document represented the first attempt to systematically address problems in the sector.

A few months later, in August 2009, a project called "The Development of Family Milk Farms on the Basis of Private Farms during 2009–2011" was adopted, with the goal to create 300 such farms. In the program's first year eight regions signed an agreement with the Ministry of Agriculture to create fifty pilot farms, and in reality fifty-two farms were created in those eight regions. The farms, grouped in eight-to-ten farm clusters, fulfill the production cycle from the production of milk to processing to delivery of finished milk products.[19] In 2011 the Ministry of Agriculture decided to extend the program to 2020 and in 2012 allocated R1.5 billion to this program.[20]

Also in 2009, a program was announced by the Ministry of Agriculture called "The Development of Family Livestock Farms on the Basis of Private Farms." The purpose of this program is to provide financial support for family private farms, which average just a few head of livestock per farm. The goal is to expand livestock holdings to 20 to 100 cattle per farm, from 50 to 300 sheep and goats, and 1,000 or more chickens.[21] Speaking before the State Duma in February 2012, former minister Skrynnik reported that 470 family livestock farms had been created under this program during 2009–2011, and from 2012 to the end it was planned to add 150 additional family farms annually. In February 2012 Skrynnik indicated that seventy-six regions had indicated a willingness to participate and develop regional programs. She also stated that this program receives R3 billion annually from federal and regional budgets.[22]

Other initiatives were also started. Starting in 2012, another branch project called "Support for Beginning Farmers during 2012–2014" was introduced. This program intends to facilitate the conversion of subsidiary agricultural operations into private farms, in other words, turning registered private plots into viable private farms.[23] At the beginning of 2012 Skrynnik stated that seventy-one regions had expressed an interest in setting up regional programs.[24] In 2012, R2 billion was allocated to this program in order to create 1,700 new private farms and 5,000 new jobs.[25] According to this program, beginning farmers could receive up to R1.5 million from federal funds to obtain animals and equipment. In addition, a one-time supplement of R250,000 was available for housing construction/repair, or to build animal sheds, bringing federal assistance up to R1.75 million per new farmer.[26] Overall, almost R10 billion will be spent in support of this program during 2012–2014, with R4.9 billion coming from the federal government.[27] In Kurgan *oblast*, near the city of Kurgan, the agricultural academy has established a special office called "business incubator" that is staffed by a qualified graduate student. The student offers free consultation to persons wishing to apply to the Beginning Farmer or the Family Livestock Farm program. If the farmer-to-be chooses to proceed following the consultation, assistance to develop a business plan is provided on a sliding fee basis, depending on the complexity of the plan. The business plan is then submitted to a regional committee comprised of ministry officials and agricultural experts, who decide whether to fund the application.[28]

Furthermore, starting in 2012 a program called "Young Farmer" was introduced that hopes to attract young people to start private farms. The federal government encourages regional governments to create similar local programs and offers various financial incentives to do so. The federal government also offers subsidies to private farmers for the purchase of agricultural equipment, pedigree livestock, and seed.

Despite these programs, private farmers continue to face problems. One of the problems is converting land shares or rental land to private property, a process that is complicated, lengthy, and not entirely transparent.[29] Added to those problems is the cost. Any land that is to be sold, purchased, or converted to private property has to be cadastred, which is quite expensive. In Moscow *oblast*, for example, which has among the highest land prices in the nation, the cost to convert one hectare of agricultural land to private property can run R5,000 to 10,000. Thus, in order to convert 150 hectares a farmer would face costs of R1.5 million, a sum that relatively few farmers can afford. The importance of converting land to private ownership is that it gives private farmers more control over the land they use and ability to make wise economic decisions. In addition, privately owned land can be mortgaged in order to raise capital for investment. In December 2010 Medvedev signed a revised federal law on agricultural land turnover that came into effect in July 2011.[30] The intent of the revised law is to help private farmers convert land that they may lease or own as land shares to private ownership. The program will allow up to 800,000 hectares of land to be converted to ownership. The main types of land that are eligible in this program include agricultural land that has been leased for at least three years, and state and municipal land that is to be used for the creation or expansion of private farming.[31] At the end of October 2011 the federal government issued instructions that specified how the new law would be implemented. According to the published rules, the federal government is to pick up 40 percent of the cost of conversion, and regional governments would cover the remaining 60 percent.[32] The problem, however, was that budgetary allocations for the remainder of 2011 were only R120 million, an average of only R3.7 million *per region* from federal and regional funds, sufficient to cover the expenses of one private farmer in Moscow *oblast*. For 2012 the federal government allocated R1.4 billion to cover the costs of property conversion, but as one Russian scholar has noted, that sum is sufficient to help only one in ten farmers.[33]

Another major problem faced by private farmers is access to credit to fund their farm operations or to invest in production capacity. Officials in AKKOR (the organization that represents private farming interests) often complain that private farmers receive a small percentage of available credit; official government reports indicate that in 2009 the total borrowing level of the private agricultural sector was R93.3 billion, of which private farmers accounted for R26.8 billion (29 percent). In 2010, private farmers accounted for 23 percent of total private sector borrowing (R23.7 billion out of total credit of R104 billion).[34] The state-owned Rossel'khozbank (Russian Agricultural Bank) is the primary lender to private agricultural producers. To simplify the process for obtaining a loan, in February 2011 AKKOR signed an agreement with Rossel'khozbank to reduce the number of documents that farmer-applicants need to provide. Further, for farmers with a positive credit history, the bank could make a decision within thirty calendar days, an important consideration for farmers with seasonal costs.[35] Thus, a broad-based effort to support private farming existed under Medvedev and is likely to continue under Putin 3.0, although challenges remain.

Entry into the WTO

Russia's accession into the WTO took almost eighteen years, the longest of any major country. Russia's negotiation process was concluded in November 2011, and in December 2011 a WTO ministerial conference accepted Russia as a member, awaiting only Russia's ratification. Russia ratified the agreement in June 2012. Within Russia, opinions about accession were far from consensual. Former president Medvedev tried to assuage concerns when he promised that Russian agriculture will become one of the leaders in the world economy in coming years and "no WTO will stop that."[36] Despite government assistance programs and the influx of financial resources into agriculture since 2006, concerns were expressed in the run-up to accession. Critics in Russia argued that protection of domestic producers would be hurt by a reduction in import tariffs and by better access for foreign competitors in the Russian market; that financial support from the government for Russian agriculture would be limited; that Russia will be less able to regulate its foreign economic trade activities; and that as Russia integrates into the world market, Russian consumers would be hurt by domestic food prices becoming more closely tied to global commodity prices.[37] Even rural liberals expressed concerns. The former president of AKKOR, Vladimir Bashmachnikov, was troubled by the prospect that price supports and subsidization of interest rates for loans would not be permitted under WTO rules. The president of the regional branch of AKKOR in Rostov *oblast* worried that budget limitations would mean that small forms of farming receive even less government support, and that Russia's private farms would not be able to compete with highly subsidized farms in the EU. A private farmer from Voronezh *oblast* was apprehensive that "if we open our borders for WTO, we will be supplied with Australian kangaroos and Dutch butter."[38]

So why should Russia's entry into the WTO be considered an achievement? First, WTO membership gives Russia status that it did not have before, essentially allowing it equal status with other major nations and providing a psychological lift. Second, accession is expected to increase economic growth in the medium and long term, lower import prices, increase competition, and spur foreign investment. Further, accession helps to enforce the rule of law and provide investors access to the WTO's dispute resolution process. Third, although there is no consensus on the effects WTO membership will have on agriculture, former minister Skrynnik went on record as saying that Russia joined on advantageous terms, "some of the best of any country that joined this organization."[39]

Putin has promised that support for agriculture will continue after membership. In July 2011 Putin stated that "we will strictly defend the interests of domestic consumers and producers. We will not adopt any decision that would place our producers in a disadvantageous position or would undermine their competitiveness."[40] In January 2012 Putin indicated that "we are thinking about what we need to do in order to support domestic producers. I have no doubt that we will find these instruments. Within the parameters of the WTO exist instruments to support the domestic market."[41] And in February 2012 at a forum of agricultural interests Putin publicly guaranteed that "we will continue to support the agricultural branch."[42] In 2012, the Russian government will spend the equivalent of $5.6 billion for agriculture, and Skrynnik noted that under the WTO agreement Russia would be able to increase government expenditures in agriculture to $9 billion in the short term.[43] In other words, policy statements suggest that agriculture will not be a "loser" as a result of WTO membership.

Moreover, there are benefits to membership. For example, Russia will be able to use the dispute process to reduce the chance of trade conflicts and give Russia alternatives other than to take unilateral steps that aggravate relations with other nations. Russia will benefit from access to foreign markets without facing punitive tariffs. Finally, membership will create stimuli for Russian agriculture to become efficient and to use government support more effectively, both of which will make the agricultural sector more attractive to foreign and domestic investors who bring much-needed capital for modernization. In the long run, therefore, the competition that WTO ushers in may make Russia's agricultural sector more competitive and profitable, with benefits to farms and their employees, food processors, as well as other agribusiness. As First Deputy Prime Minister Igor Shuvalov argued, "Everybody will make gains, there will be no losers."[44]

PRIORITIES IN AGRICULTURE

For the past ten years the main goals of agrarian policy have been to increase domestic production and make Russian products globally competitive, increase national food security, and increase food exports. These core objectives are unlikely to change under Putin 3.0. The food security doctrine, which guides the formulation of agrarian policy, is discussed first. I then turn to domestic production and the 2013–2020 program of agricultural development. Last, I examine prospects for increasing food exports.

Improve National Food Security

In January 2010 former minister Skrynnik identified Russia's food security as a central problem in overall national security.[45] After many months of discussion over a draft released by the Ministry of Agriculture, at the end of January 2010 former president Medvedev signed a doctrine of food security.[46] Article 1 of the food security doctrine states that food security is part of the National Security Strategy to 2020. Article 4 states that the doctrine serves as the basis for development of the agroindustrial complex. The doctrine calls for "food independence of the Russian Federation" based upon quantitative and qualitative measures. Article 8 establishes quantitative indicators for food supply that domestic production should fulfill. For example, to achieve food security Russia aims to produce 95 percent of the grain it consumes, 95 percent of its potatoes, 85 percent of its meat and meat products, 80 percent of its fish products, and 90 percent of its milk and milk products.[47]

The food security doctrine is important for several reasons. First, it is unlikely that the targets for domestic production can or will be met completely, especially since Russia's WTO membership is likely to lead to more food imports, not less. In that respect the doctrine represents a worldview, a perspective that sees food policy and food trade as national security issues rather than ways in which the diet of Russian citizens may be enriched. According to this worldview, it is dangerous to depend upon foreign nations for food, a view that does not lend itself well to global integration. Harking back to the Soviet era, autarky is seen to provide greater national security, however unattainable true food independence may be in reality.

Thus, I see this doctrine as more of a political statement than a plan that can be fulfilled.

Second, despite the fact that complete fulfillment is unlikely, we should not be quick to dismiss the doctrine as mere political rhetoric. Public statements by Medvedev, Putin, Viktor Zubkov, and Skrynnik (among others) repeatedly referred to the food security doctrine as a guide for policy. For example, during the 2010 drought the government's reactions and measures were intended to protect livestock herds so as to avoid increasing meat imports, and both Zubkov, who was First Deputy Prime Minister in charge of Agriculture under Medvedev, and Skrynnik were explicit that food security was driving their actions.[48] It *might* be the case that the food security doctrine is used as rationalization and justification. But at the same time, political leaders just as easily could have avoided reference to the doctrine without political consequence, so the fact that agrarian leaders often make reference to doctrine probably is meaningful at some level. Thus, my sense is that this doctrine is taken seriously as a paradigm for food policy and agrarian strategy. The government's development plan for 2013–2020, which is discussed next, refers to the program as a mechanism to fulfill the goals of the food security doctrine.

Increase Domestic Production and Competitiveness

In October 2011 the Ministry of Agriculture completed a draft program for agricultural development during 2013–2020 and circulated that document for commentary. At the time this chapter was written only a draft of the new program had been published.[49] The program envisions retaining government support for projects begun in the 2008–2012 program and adding several new projects. The 2013–2020 program contains six subprograms and three special federal programs.[50] According to the draft program the average rate of growth is forecast to be no less than 2.4 to 2.5 percent annually, with growth rates for meat and meat products increasing at a somewhat higher rate. Overall, food production should grow by almost 43 percent by 2020 compared to 2010. The production of processed food should expand by 4.3 to 5.0 percent annually, and 60 percent by 2020.[51] In addition, the program intends to increase investment into agriculture by nearly 9 percent annually, modernize food processing enterprises, expand irrigated and drained land by more than 10 million hectares, increase labor productivity by 70 percent by 2020 compared to 2009, increase profitability of farm enterprises by 20 percent, and raise the standard of rural life and create stable communities by bringing agricultural incomes up to 95 percent of the average level in the nation.[52]

To meet these goals the draft program envisions expenditures of R2.37 trillion from the federal budget, with another R2.3 trillion from regional budgets and R2.2 trillion from commercial sources. At the end of November 2011 representatives from the Ministry of Agriculture and Ministry of Finance met to discuss the proposed budgetary outlays. The Ministry of Finance disagreed with increasing federal expenditures to fund the program, calling the proposal "unfounded," and it also did not feel it possible to fund new goals that were not contained in the 2008–2012 program.[53] Thus, the process of budgetary negotiation was begun, and at this writing the outcome was not known, but it is likely that spending will be scaled back.

Expansion of Food Exports

Off the radar screen of most Western analysts, Russia became a food exporter during Putin's second term (2004–2008) and this continued when Medvedev was president. Cereals are Russia's main cash crop. During 2007–2009 Russia averaged between 17 and 20 million tons of cereal exports. An export ban was imposed as a result of the 2010 heat wave, but during the 2011–2012 agricultural year Russian exports rebounded. Because of a good harvest, nearly 94 million tons, by January 2012 Russia had already exported nearly 19 million tons. In February 2012 former vice premier Zubkov stated that Russia could export 27 million tons by the end of the agricultural year.[54] Although Skrynnik had previously indicated that the government would consider imposing export tariffs on volumes exceeding 24 million tons in order to maintain grain reserves and ensure enough feed for livestock, Zubkov said that reserves were adequate to meet domestic needs and he did not see any basis for introducing any kind of restrictions on exports.[55] Going forward, the expansion of grain exports is "one of the strategic directions for the development of agriculture" according to Deputy Minister of Agriculture Aleksandr Solov'ev.[56] Although meat is a high-value product, Russia does not have significant export earnings from this commodity, although Zubkov indicated in early 2012 that Russia intends to export up to 400,000 tons of poultry meat by 2015.[57]

Since 2005, the value of food exports has increased, but food exports only account for about 2 percent of Russia's export revenue. Expressed in U.S. dollars, food exports rose from $1.6 billion in 2000 to $5.5 billion in 2006 and to a high of $9.9 billion in 2009, before declining to $9.3 billion in 2010 as a result of the prohibition of grain exports from mid-August 2010 to July 1, 2011, in response to drought and harvest losses.[58] In 2009, prior to the devastating drought in 2010, the export of cereals accounted for nearly 35 percent of total food export earnings.

Two main trading blocs are the Commonwealth of Independent States (CIS), comprised of former Soviet republics, and the Far Abroad (which includes the EU). The problem for Russia is that it has a chronic trade deficit in food trade with both trading blocs. By far the largest trade deficit is with the Far Abroad, equal to –$24.8 billion in 2008, –$19 billion in 2009, and –$24 billion in 2010.

Eschewing traditional markets for Russian grain such as Northern Africa and Middle Eastern nations, the region that Russian policy makers have eyed for expansion of grain exports is East and Southeast Asia. In May 2009 Zubkov called the development of export policy a "strategic task for Russia" and specified Pacific Rim countries as a future market for the export of cereals.[59] At the June 2009 World Grain Forum held in St. Petersburg, former president Medvedev stated that Russia intends to expand grain exports to new geographical regions, including Southeast Asia.[60] The development of export markets in Asia comports with the priorities that Putin articulated in a speech to the State Duma in April 2012. In that speech he outlined four main priorities for his third term, one of which was the economic development of Russia's far eastern region.[61]

At present, however, Russia has a very small presence in grain trade in the Far East. At the beginning of the 2011–2012 agricultural year, no East Asian country ranked in the top forty of recipient nations of Russian grain.[62] Moreover, transportation costs for Siberian grain to export terminals in the Far East are significantly higher than grain deliveries from southern Russia to Black Sea terminals. In this respect trade may be limited by cost. Nonetheless, expected population increases by midcentury and with them rising demand make Southeast Asia an attractive market. That said, Russia's hope for expansion will face competition from the United States and Australia, whose market access to Southeast Asia is better than to nations in Central Asia or around the Black Sea.[63] Toward this end, grain terminals and ports for the export of grain are being expanded and updated.[64]

CHALLENGES: PAST, PRESENT, AND FUTURE

The discussion of the rebound in Russian agriculture since 2000 is not meant to suggest that agricultural problems have been solved. The recovery in Russian agriculture since 2000 has been impressive, but more needs to be done. Below I discuss some of the challenges that need to be addressed in Russian agriculture during Putin 3.0. I focus on long-term structural challenges.

An enduring challenge is the fact that Russia does not feed itself. Despite an increase in food production since 2000, Russia has yet to reach the average production levels of the late Soviet period for many commodities, a fact that speaks to the magnitude of the decline during the 1990s, the bottom from which the recovery began. Among G8 nations, only Japan and Russia are net food importers. Indeed, during 2007–2010 the value of Russia's food imports was $129.2 billion, whereas the value of its food exports was only $37.2 billion, so imports exceeded the value of exports by about 3.5 times.[65] Moreover, despite government financial assistance, during 2008–2010 Russia spent about seven times as much on food imports as was allocated for financial support to domestic producers. The relationship between expenditures on food imports and export earnings, and between expenditures on food imports and domestic support, is unlikely to shift significantly anytime soon, despite the food security doctrine.

Why doesn't Russia just produce more if consumer demand is growing? There is no single cause to the food problem but rather a confluence of factors that contribute to the inability of Russia's domestic producers to meet demand. One reason concerns financial considerations. Increases in the cost of fuels, feed, and fertilizers have created price disparities between inputs and farm gate prices whereby input prices have risen faster than wholesale prices received by food producers, especially for livestock products. To cover higher costs, farms borrow, and therefore even though production has increased, so too has farm debt. Despite increased production and profitability on large farms, their aggregate debt increased significantly during 2000–2010. Moreover, Russia's farms have been exposed to worldwide commodity price increases, and rapidly rising feed and transportation costs offset to a certain degree the infusion of state financial assistance to the animal husbandry sector. Thus, many large farms are not in a position to expand production because of insufficient credit, as well as because of labor or machinery deficiencies, poor management, climatic factors, and other reasons. About 25 percent of Russia's large farms continue to be unprofitable, and that number would be considerably higher absent government subsidies and assistance programs. Consequently, domestic production cannot satisfy increased demand that has resulted from higher real incomes. With WTO membership, Russian expenditures on food imports are likely to increase.

A second contributing factor is that Russia is a country where a high percentage of the labor force still is employed in agriculture, about 13 percent, compared to developed nations such as the United States, Germany, and Great Britain, where 2 to 4 percent of the workforce is employed in agricultural production. Although on a comparative basis a large number of people work in Russian agriculture, one factor that hinders the expansion of food production is human capital; specifically, there is a shortage of skilled workers. In mid-2008, former minister Gordeev indicated that there was a deficit of 70,000 agricultural specialists.[66] According to data from the Ministry of Agriculture, in 2006 large farms employed less than 42 percent of the number of agricultural specialists as in 1990, 19 percent the number of workers in animal husbandry, and 25 percent the number of tractorists and machinists as in 1990.[67] As a result, less-skilled labor is used, which decreases efficiency. Moreover, because average incomes for agricultural workers are about one-half of the national average, large farms often lose skilled labor to other professions or other branches of the economy.

Aggravating the problem of rural labor, it is estimated that 70 percent of young rural families "are in need of serious improvement in housing conditions."[68] The government has adopted a program for rural social development that runs through 2013, and new housing is being constructed and efforts made to attract and/or retain young people in the countryside. But the number of families that receive new housing is low compared to need, and affordability is often problematic, particularly for young families. Therefore, the outflow continues—in 2010 more than 635,000 people migrated out of the countryside; almost one-half of them were aged fourteen to twenty-nine.[69] Despite government efforts, substandard rural housing is often the norm, as only 53 percent of rural housing is equipped with gas; in other words, 47 percent of rural housing uses wood for cooking and heat.[70] The government also has adopted a program for rural regional development for 2014–2017 and to 2020, with the goal to create sustainable rural communities. Even so, fewer educational and cultural opportunities make it difficult to retain skilled rural labor. For example, compared with 1991, by 2011 the countryside had 13,500 fewer schools and nearly 21,000 fewer recreational clubs.[71] The need to improve the quality of human capital is especially great if Russia hopes to compete with advanced farming sectors among many EU nations and in the United States, where government support of agricultural education and science is greater.

The development of sustainable rural communities to retain labor and rural youth is complicated by the decline in the size of the rural population. Between the 1989 and 2002 censuses almost 10,800 villages disappeared, an average of 825 a year. By 2002, more than 34,000 Russian villages had fewer than ten persons.[72] In 2005, former minister Gordeev noted that 72 regions in Russia were experiencing rural depopulation, and 13,000 villages had no permanent residents (three-quarters of which are located in the central and northwest federal districts).[73] Official figures show that over 3,000 villages in Russia became deserted in 2010 alone.[74] The Ministry of Agriculture released data that show a decline in the number of persons employed at agricultural enterprises from 4.5 million in 2000 to 1.6 million in 2010.[75] The prognosis is for continued decline. As a whole, the rural population is predicted to decline by 2.2 million between 2010 and 2021.[76] Clearly, therefore, it is difficult to sustain rural communities in an environment of depopulation.

The maintenance of sustainable rural communities is complicated by widespread rural poverty. One Russian sociologist notes that 27 percent of the population was rural, but rural areas contained 42 percent of Russia's poor in 2010.[77] Two well-known Russian experts estimate that 77 percent of rural children aged sixteen or less live in households in which the average monetary income is below the subsistence minimum, 67 percent of workers in agriculture and forestry have monetary incomes below the poverty line, and 54 percent of rural management personnel have monetary incomes below the poverty line.[78] The unemployment rate for rural dwellers aged fifteen to twenty-four is almost 3.5 times higher than among urban youth of the same age.[79] Poverty and high unemployment create incentives for rural youth to migrate to urban centers, thus undercutting the long-term future of rural communities.

Rural poverty is exacerbated by limited alternative employment opportunities, particularly in remote or small villages. Overall, only 58 percent of working-age adults living in rural areas are employed.[80] Moreover, there is a poverty trap whereby poorer households are disadvantaged, thereby making the alleviation of poverty more difficult. For example, poorer households tend not to engage with the market in order to earn extra money, despite the fact that there is a statistical association between market engagement and level of household income: households that engage more have higher income. Poor households tend to consume more of the food they produce and sell less, and they have virtually no income from entrepreneurial activity. Why? Households in poverty are disadvantaged in their demographic structure, they have smaller land holdings, and they are more risk averse.

A final problem that restricts food production is antiquated agricultural machinery and technology. Theoretically, the contraction in rural labor can be offset by modern agricultural equipment and machinery, but it is estimated that much of Russia's technological base is two to three generations behind the developed world, a reflection of years of neglect and lack of investment. Putin argued that 70 to 80 percent of tractors and combines are "shabby" and in need of replacement.[81] Moreover, the number of tractors, grain combines, and feed combines is declining. The number of tractors, for example, fell from 531,000 in 2006 to 305,800 in September 2011. Going forward, the number of tractors, grain combines, and feed combines is forecast to decline about 10 to 15 percent a year, so that in 2020 there will be 49 percent of the tractors, 64 percent of the grain combines, and 71 percent of the feed combines as in 2012.[82] These trends mean that machinery cannot offset the loss of labor, and present and future food production levels may be affected. The need to modernize the stock of agricultural machinery, both quantitatively and qualitatively, led to the adoption of a subprogram within the larger program of development that runs 2013–2020, and in 2012 the government allocated R3.5 billion to acquire new machinery. Thus, as the discussion above suggests, the problem of sufficient food production is multifaceted and requires resolution of long-standing socioeconomic and demographic problems.

CONCLUSION

The contours of Russia's agricultural model are identifiable. The goal of Putin 1.0 was to revitalize agriculture by bringing the state back. Since 2000 the state has been much more interventionist, seen, for example, in the numerous assistance programs discussed above.[83] These developments did not occur accidentally, but rather were the result of deliberate policies. While Russia's agricultural economy is not regulated as it was during the Soviet period (nor is there any chance of Russia reverting to a planned economy), the agricultural sector is more regulated than the original neo-liberal model of the early 1990s had envisioned. The Russian model for agriculture, therefore, is state-led growth. The government has assumed the leading role in achieving these goals, and in general one could argue that the state continues to fulfill roles that are filled by nonstate actors in developed capitalist systems (for instance being the main provider of investment credit).

In 1992, it was an open question what Russia's agricultural system would look like ten years later: who would be the predominant producers, how would the system operate, and what would be the role of the state. Today, those questions are much less open. The trajectory of reform has been defined, and today the agricultural sector and its policies are not dissimilar from 2004. It is very likely that in 2015, or even in 2020, the structure of Russia's agricultural system and the nature of its policies will look very much like today. That is not to deny that individual policies may be modified or even changed, but the essential features may be reasonably predicted going forward. The state will remain interventionist for the foreseeable future.

In terms of agricultural policy, the contours are clearly discernible. The core goals are to increase domestic food production, work toward national food security, and increase food exports. Clearly, a strong agricultural sector is perceived to be an important component of global power. Inasmuch as Putin has ambitions to return Russia to international influence, agriculture is not to be the weak link. From 2004 onward, Putin's policy approach to agriculture was broad based and strategic in nature. In terms of priorities and policy direction, Putin 3.0 is very likely to look a lot like Putin 2.0.

At the same time, Putin and his government face challenges ahead that are not easy to resolve. Resolution of the food problem is multifaceted and requires resolution of long-standing socioeconomic and demographic problems. An integrated program must address many problems simultaneously, including but not limited to infrastructure, educational, recreational, and cultural opportunities, rural housing, low incomes and high poverty, and the quality and quantity of human capital. As Russian leaders have indicated, the long-term health of agriculture and its competitiveness depend on rural areas offering employment opportunity that pays adequate wages. But rural development is easier said than done, especially when considering the size of rural Russia. Contemporary Russia is attempting to undo a legacy of unmet goals—we should remember that the Soviet leadership under Brezhnev in the 1960s also wanted to raise rural standards of living and bring living conditions closer to those found in urban areas. Four decades later, those goals remain unfulfilled. Going forward, therefore, despite notable improvements in aspects of Russian agriculture, the challenges that confront Putin 3.0 are formidable, and success is not assured.

SUGGESTED READINGS

Lerman, Zvi, ed. *Russia's Agriculture in Transition*. Lanham, Md.: Lexington Books, 2008.

Pallot, Judith, and Tat'yana Nefedova. *Russia's Unknown Agriculture: Household Production in Post-Socialist Rural Russia*. Oxford: Oxford University Press, 2007.

Wegren, Stephen K. "Russian Agriculture in 2009: Continuity or Change?" *Eurasian Geography and Economics* 50, no. 4 (2009): 464–79.

———. *Land Reform in Russia: Institutional Design and Behavioral Responses*. New Haven, Conn.: Yale University Press, 2009.

———. "Russia's Food Policies and Foreign Policy." *Demokratizatsiya: The Journal of Post-Soviet Democratization* 18, no. 3 (2010): 189–207.

———. "Food Security and Russia's 2010 Drought." *Eurasian Geography and Economics* 52, no. 1 (2011): 140–56.

———. "The Impact of WTO Accession on Russia's Agriculture." *Post-Soviet Affairs* 28, no. 3 (2012).

NOTES

1. Stephen K. Wegren, "Agriculture in the Late Putin Period and Beyond," in Stephen K. Wegren and Dale R. Herspring, eds., *After Putin's Russia: Past Imperfect, Future Uncertain*, 4th ed. (Lanham, Md.: Rowman and Littlefield, 2010), 201–8.

2. See Stephen K. Wegren, "Russian Agrarian Policy under Putin," *Post-Soviet Geography and Economics* 43, no. 1 (2002): 27–28. Gordeev was minister of agriculture from August 1999 into early 2009. On March 12, 2009, President Medvedev signed a decree replacing him with Elena Skrynnik. In May 2012 Skrynnik was replaced by Nikolai Fedorov, a lawyer by training, and former president of the Republic of Chuvashia.

3. National'nyy doklad, "*O khode i resul'tatakh realizatsii v 2010 gody gosudarstvennoi programmy razvitiia sel'skogo khoziaistva i regulirovaniia rynkov sel'skokhoziaistvennoi produktsii, syr'ia i prodovolstviia na 2008–2012*," 2011, 63, www.mcx.ru (last accessed June 3, 2011).

4. An agricultural year runs July 1 to June 30. Gross farm profitability declined to R83.6 billion in 2009, and to R82.2 billion in 2010 because of harvest losses due to the drought.

5. Stephen K. Wegren, "Food Security and Russia's 2010 Drought," *Eurasian Geography and Economics* 52, no. 1 (2011): 148.

6. For an early analysis see Stephen K. Wegren, "Russian Agriculture in 2009: Continuity or Change?" *Eurasian Geography and Economics* 50, no. 4 (2009): 464–79.

7. Expenditures included R7.45 billion in 2006 and R7.18 billion in 2007 for the development of animal husbandry; and R6.6 billion in 2006 and R9.37 billion in 2007 for the stimulation of small farming enterprises and various types of cooperatives. During 2006–2007, there was a link at the Russian Ministry of Agriculture's website called "The National Project," from which these data were taken. In 2012, there are two links, one called "State Program for 2008–12" and another called "State Program for 2013–20." See www.mcx.ru.

8. A. Slepnev, "Razvitie sel'skogo khoziaistva na blizhayshuiu perspektivu," *APK: ekonomika, upravlenie*, no. 6 (June 2008): 2.

9. *Sel'skaia zhizn'*, March 20, 2007, 1. The goals of the five-year plan are discussed by Medvedev in *Krest'ianskie vedomosti*, no. 9 (March 2007): 10. The program was renewed in July 2007, with a January 2008 start date. The goals of the 2008–2012 program are (1) improve regional rural development; (2) increase rural employment and standards of living; (3) increase competitiveness of Russian food products; (4) achieve financial stability in the sector and begin a process of modernization in agriculture; (5) accelerate the development of priority sub-branches within agriculture; and (6) protect and reclaim land and other natural resources that are used in agricultural production.

10. *Sel'skaia zhizn'*, June 25–July 1, 2009, 1.

11. Yelena Vassilieva, "Agriculture Development Program Annual Report is Prepared," GAIN Report no. RS 1120, April 25, 2011.

12. *Sel'skaia zhizn'*, October 4, 2011, 1.

13. *Sel'skaia zhizn'*, October 25, 2011, 2.

14. *Sel'skaia zhizn'*, July 12, 2011, 1; and *Rossiiskaia zemlia*, no. 10 (May 2011): 2.

15. *Pokazateli proizvodstvo sel'skokhoziaistvennoi produktsii i udel'nyi ves malykh form khoziaistvovaniia za 2009-2010*, 2011, www.akkor.ru (accessed February 21, 2012).

16. Cited in V. N. Khlystun, "Zemel'no-ipotechnoe kreditovanie: Sostoianie i perspektivy," *Ekonomika sel'skokhoziaistvennykh i pererabatyvaiushchikh predpriiatii*, no. 4 (April 2008): 12.

17. *Rossiia v tsifrakh* (Moscow: Rosstat, 2010), 246.

18. "Razvitie krest'ianskikh (fermerskikh) khoziaistv i drugikh malykh form khoziaistvaniia v APK na 2009-2011," June 9, 2009, prikaz no. 218, Ministry of Agriculture, Moscow, 2009, www.mcx.ru (accessed July 10, 2009, no longer available on the ministry website in 2012).

19. *Sel'skaia zhizn'*, October 29–November 4, 2009, 1; *Rossiiskaia zemlia*, no. 4 (February 2010): 4.

20. "Vystuplenie na vstreche s rabochei gruppoi Rossiiskogo soiuza sel'skoi molodezhi po razvitiiu molodezhnogo predprinimatel'stva, 14.11.2011, Moskva," November 14, 2011, www.mcx.ru (accessed November 25, 2011).

21. *Krest'ianskiie vedomosti,* nos. 47-48 (December 2011): 4.

22. "Vystuplenie na 'Pravitel'stvennom chase' v Gosudarstvennoi Dume, 08.02.2012, Moskva," February 2, 2012, www.mcx.ru (accessed February 21, 2012).

23. This conversion will not apply to all or even more private plot operations. Of the 16 million or so registered private plots, only about 31,000 (less than 1 percent) are commercially oriented, that is, food sales comprise the bulk of household income. See V. Uzun and V. Saraikin, "Ekonomicheskaia klassifikatsiia lichnykh podsobnykh khoziaistv," *APK: ekonomika, upravlenie,* no. 1 (January 2012): 41–8. Some private plots are registered as such in order to escape income taxes, but otherwise are not distinguishable from private farms in their operations. It is to those two groups that the program is directed.

24. "Nachinaiushchego fermera podderzhat," *Rossiiskii fermer,* no. 1 (January 2012): 11.

25. "Vystuplenie na 'Pravitel'stvennom chase' v Gosudarstvennoi Dume, 08.02.2012, Moskva."

26. *Sel'skaia zhizn',* November 29, 2011, 1.

27. *Krest'ianskie vedomosti,* nos. 5–6 (February 2012): 3.

28. Interview, Evgeny Strelkov, Kurgan State Agricultural Academy, Kurgan, May 15, 2012.

29. Natalya Shagaida, "Agricultural Land Market in Russia: Living with Constraints," *Comparative Economic Studies* 47, no. 1 (2005): 127–40.

30. The text of the revised law is found in *APK: ekonomika, upravlenie,* no. 2 (February 2011): 68–81.

31. *Agro Zhizn',* no. 6 (April 2012): 3.

32. The text of the government instruction (*pravila*) is found in *Rossiiskii fermer,* no. 12 (December 2011): 6–7.

33. Vasilii Uzun, "Komu bublik, a komu dyrka ot bublika," *Rossiiskii fermer,* no. 2 (February 2012): 20.

34. *National'nyy doklad "O khode i resul'tatakh realizatsii v 2010 gody gosudarstvennoi programmy razvitiia sel'skogo,* 76–77.

35. *Rossiiskaia zemlia,* nos. 1-2 (January 2011): 3.

36. "Putin Says Protective Measures for Agricultural Equipment Producers Possible," December 21, 2011, www.wto.ru/en/news.asp?msg_id=28746 (accessed December 28, 2011).

37. This list of concerns is drawn from V. V. Miloserdov, "A Nuzhna li Rossii VTO?" *Ekonomika sel'skokhoziaistvennykh i pererabatyvaiushchikh predpriiatii,* no. 12, (December 2008): 5; *Krest'ianskie vedomosti,* nos. 45–46 (December 2010): 8; *Sel'skaia zhizn',* March 1, 2011, 3.

38. *Sel'skaia zhizn',* October 19, 2010, 1.

39. *Sel'skaia zhizn',* February 28, 2012, 1.

40. V. V. Putin, "APK—Lokomotiv razvitiia strany," *Rossiiskii fermer,* no. 8 (August 2011): 5.

41. *Sel'skaia zhizn',* January 31, 2012, 1.

42. *Krest'ianskie vedomosti,* nos. 5–6 (February 2012): 2.

43. *Sel'skaia zhizn',* December 27, 2011, 1.

44. "Government to Support Industries That May Suffer from WTO Membership," December 19, 2011, www.wto.ru/en/news.asp?msg_id=28736 (accessed December 28, 2011).

45. E. Skrynnik, "Prodovol'stvennaia bezopasnost'—vazhnaia sostavliaiushchaia sistemy natsional'no bezopasnosti Rossii," *APK: ekonomika, upravlenie*, no. 1 (January 2010): 3.

46. "Doktrina prodovol'stvennnoi bezopasnosti Rossiiskoi Federatsii," 2010. www.mcx.ru (last accessed March 17, 2010). At the time this chapter was written (April–May 2012), the link still existed at the ministry's website.

47. See Stephen K. Wegren, "Russia's Food Policies and Foreign Policy," *Demokratizatsiya: The Journal of Post-Soviet Democratization* 18, no. 3 (2010): 189–207.

48. Wegren, "Food Security and Russia's 2010 Drought," 140–56.

49. "Proekt Gosudarstvennaia programma razvitiia sel'skogo khoziaistva i regulirovaniia rynkov sel'skokhoziaistvennoi produktsii, syr'ia i prodovol'stviia na 2013–2020 godu," October 7, 2011, www.mcx.ru (accessed October 8, 2011). The draft was updated in March 2012, but the discussion herein is based upon the version released in October 2011. A cursory examination suggested only minor changes.

50. *Sel'skaia zhizn'*, November 29, 2011, 1.

51. *Sel'skaia zhizn'*, November 29, 2011, 1.

52. For commentary and early analysis, see I. Ushachev, "O proekte Gosudarstvennoi programmy razvitiia sel'skogo khoziaistva i regulirovaniia rynkov sel'skokhoziaistvennoi produktsii, syr'ia i prodovol'stviia na 2013–2020 godu," *APK: ekonomika, upravlenie*, no. 1 (January 2012): 3–13.

53. *Krest'ianskie vedomosti*, nos. 45–46 (December 2011): 2.

54. *Sel'skaia zhizn'*, February 7, 2012, 1.

55. *Sel'skaia zhizn'*, October 18, 2011, 1; *Sel'skaia zhizn'*, February 7, 2012, 1.

56. *Krest'ianskie vedomosti*, nos. 45–46 (December 2011): 3.

57. *Krest'ianskie vedomosti*, nos. 3–4 (January 2012): 2.

58. *Torgovlia v Rossii* (Moscow: Rosstat, 2009), 277; *Rossiiskiy statisticheskiy ezhegodnik* (Moscow: Rosstat, 2011), 712.

59. *Sel'skaia zhizn'*, May 26, 2009, 1.

60. *Sel'skaia zhizn'*, June 18-24, 2009, 3.

61. Maria Zhebit, "Vladimir Putin Outlined Priorities of His Future Presidency," *Izvestiia*, April 12, 2012, *Johnson's Russia List*, no. 68 (April 12, 2012).

62. *Krest'ianskie vedomosti*, nos. 29–30 (August 2011): 2.

63. *Krest'ianskie vedomosti*, nos. 47–48 (December 2011): 9.

64. Stephen K. Wegren, "The Impact of WTO Accession on Russian Agriculture," *Post-Soviet Affairs* 28 (2012): 3.

65. *National'nyy doklad "O khode i resul'tatakh realizatsii v 2010 gody gosudarstvennoi programmy razvitiia sel'skogo khoziaistva,"* 14.

66. *Sel'skaia zhizn'*, June 5–11, 2008, 3.

67. I. Ushachev, "Nauchnoe obespechenie programmy razvitiia sel'skogo khoziaistva na 2008–2012 gg.," *Ekonomist*, no. 4 (April 2008): 21.

68. I. Buzdalov, "Obespechit' prioritet sel'skogo razvitiia," *APK: ekonomika, upravlenie*, no. 7 (July 2011): 17.

69. Aleksandr Rybakov, "Palki v Kolesa," *Rossiiskii fermer*, no. 1 (January 2012): 10.

70. Rybakov, "Palki v Kolesa," 10.

71. Rybakov, "Palki v Kolesa," 10.

72. Genrikh Sil'vestrov, "Sokhranit' krest'ianskii liud," *Rossiiskii fermer*, no. 10 (October 2011): 26.

73. A. V. Gordeev, "Aktual'nye problemy razvitiia sel'skogo khoziaistiva Rossi-iskoi Federatsii," *Ekonomika sel'skokhoziaistvennykh i pererabatyvaiushchikh predpriiatii*, no. 8 (August 2005): 4.

74. "Exodus Leaves Russia's Villages to Ghosts," August 30, 2011, www.russiatoday.com, *Johnson's Russia List*, no. 156 (August 31, 2011).

75. L. V. Bondarenko, "Zaniatost' na sele i resursnoe obespechenie organizatsii malogo biznesa sel'skimi bezrabotnymi," *Ekonomika sel'skokhoziaistvennykh i pererabatyvaiushchikh predpriiatii*, no. 12 (December 2011): 59.

76. Rybakov, "Palki v Kolesa," 17.

77. L. Bondarenko, "Bednost' i sotsial'no-psikhologicheskii klimat v Rossiiskoi derevne," *APK: ekonomika, upravlenie*, no. 11 (November 2011): 49.

78. I. Ushchachev and L. Bondarenko, "Kontseptsiia snizheniia sel'skoi bednosti," *APK: ekonomika, upravlenie*, no. 1 (January 2007): 5.

79. T. V. Blinova and S. G. Bylina, "Prognoznoe modelirovanie chislennosti zaniatykh v sel'skom khoziaistve RF," *Ekonomika sel'skokhoziaistvennykh i pererabatyvaiushchikh predpriiatii*, no. 5 (May 2011): 63.

80. Rybakov, "Palki v Kolesa," 10.

81. Putin, "APK—Lokomotiv razvitiia strany," 4.

82. *Krest'ianskie vedomosti*, nos. 45–46 (December 2011): 6.

83. Other interventions include commodity intervention (the state buying grain in good years to support prices and selling grain from reserves in bad years to restrain inflation), wholesale price controls, export levies and import embargoes on food commodities, and a credit program that has made the state-owned agricultural bank the lender of first resort to agricultural producers of all types.

III

FOREIGN POLICY AND THE MILITARY

11

Foreign Policy

Andrei P. Tsygankov

In autumn 2009 Russia's foreign policy began to depart from the assertive course that had culminated in the war with Georgia in August 2008. An assertive foreign policy had addressed many of the key tasks the Kremlin had since 2005. Since that time, the country revived its status as great power and defended its international prestige using available economic, military, and diplomatic means. Russia exploited its energy clout to expand its relations abroad. It cemented its military presence in the strategic area of the Southern Caucasus by defeating Georgia and recognizing South Ossetia and Abkhazia's independence. Having established itself as a major power, Russia was now turning to domestic modernization and inviting the outside world to contribute to it. Under the presidency of Dmitry Medvedev, the country gradually adopted a more nuanced approach to the outside world—one that was dictated by need to modernize the domestic economy.

The new approach to foreign policy did not mean that Russia was returning to its pro-Western course of the early 1990s or attempting to build special ties with the United States in the manner that followed 9/11. Not only did Russia become stronger, but the international context in which Russia had to defend its interests changed dramatically. The world was no longer West-centered. The global financial crisis revealed the United States' and Europe's economic vulnerability; the Russia-Georgia war undermined the West's monopoly for the use of force in world politics. In the meantime, China and India kept growing during the crisis by consolidating new regional centers of power and establishing politico-economic interdependence outside the West.[1] Under these new conditions, Russia has worked to broaden its existing ties with countries across the world, from Europe and the United States to Asia and Afghanistan. The Kremlin has also mobilized its soft power to reverse the color revolutions in Kyrgyzstan and Ukraine and strengthen Russia's influence in the former Soviet region. Finally, Russia remained critical of the U.S. proposal to develop the Missile Defense System (MDS) jointly with Europeans but separately from Russia.

This chapter documents the new policy shift away from the Kremlin's assertive foreign policy, explaining it by Russia's revealed economic vulnerabilities and new international opportunities. In addition, the chapter analyzes the challenges ahead as Putin returns to the presidency. Contrary to some common views that attribute Russia's foreign policy to the nation's traditionally imperialist and anti-Western political culture, the primary drivers in the Kremlin's foreign policy have remained contemporary and domestic. They include new opportunities for economic growth and stability, as well as the need to address increasing security threats. Because Russia was seriously affected by the global financial crisis, it remains keenly interested in developing economic and technological ties with the Western nations. At the same time, the Kremlin's priorities have begun to shift. Initially the country's leadership was hoping to develop a grand strategy by engaging Western nations, in particular the United States, into projects of common significance, such as counterterrorism and energy security. However, as Russia grew stronger and the West began to decline relative to the rising powers in Asia and Latin America, the Kremlin made important adjustments to its policy.

CHANGED CONDITIONS AND
RUSSIA'S WORLDVIEW

International Conditions

Three factors—the global financial crisis, new relations with the United States, and revolutions in the Middle East—served as global conditions that have shaped Russia's current foreign policy perspective. During 2008, Russia's economy was hit by the global financial crisis. The crisis ended an era of unprecedented growth that lasted nine years (1999–2008), during which the economy not only caught up with 1990 levels but continued to grow at an annual pace of about 7 percent. The global economic crisis, however, revealed the tenuous nature of Russia's recovery and the remaining weaknesses of its power base. During the crisis, Russia, which is heavily dependent on energy exports, experienced a decline in GDP by about 9 percent in 2009, while China and India continued to grow, albeit at a slower pace. Russia had to spend a considerable portion of its financial reserves to bail out domestic enterprises, including noncompetitive ones, and to scale back its activist foreign policy in Central Asia and the Caucasus.[2] During the crisis Russia met some of its economic and security challenges, but the downturn also perpetuated an insufficiently diversified economic structure and failed to address some serious gaps in its social infrastructure.

Another important factor that affected Russia's foreign policy was the U.S. decision to improve relations with the country. Despite Russia's war with Georgia in August 2008, President Barack Obama quickly moved to "reset" relations with Russia and establish strong ties with Russia's president Dmitry Medvedev in early 2009. The "reset" diplomacy alleviated the Kremlin's fear of NATO expansion and the region's destabilization in response to Washington's strategy of global regime change.

For several reasons, Russia had previously condemned the liberalizing and democratizing instincts coming from the United States as directed against the Kremlin's power and security. The so-called color revolutions in Georgia, Ukraine, and Kyrgyzstan during 2003–2005 failed to bring greater stability and prosperity, but greatly politicized the international environment in the region. Georgia and Ukraine expressed their desire to join NATO, which added to Russia's sense of strategic insecurity. In the aftermath of the NATO summit in April 2008, President Putin stated, "We view the appearance of a powerful military bloc on our borders . . . as a direct threat to the security of our country. The claim that this process is not directed against Russia will not suffice. National security is not based on promises."[3] Russia also felt vulnerable to the radicalization of Islam in response to the U.S. methods of fighting a war on terror. Although some of Russia's problems with Islamic terrorism could be attributed to its own errors, such as attempts by some of its authorities to close local mosques, other aspects were related to U.S. policies that tended to isolate moderate Muslims, which in a global world translated into a greater support for Islamic radicals inside Russia.

Finally, Russia was affected by transformations in the Middle East from regime changes in Egypt, Tunisia, and Libya to rising instability in Syria. From Russia's perspective, the Middle Eastern changes had the potential to destabilize the region and contribute to growing terrorist violence including inside Russia. Russia's domestic ties with 20 million to 25 million Muslims were far from balanced, constantly testing the relationships between ethnic Russians and residents from the Islamic republics of the Northern Caucasus.

Russia's Worldview

It took Russia's leadership some time to adjust its foreign policy perspective to the new global conditions. Until the fall of 2009, the country's officials refused to fully acknowledge the debilitating effects of the global financial crisis and continued to issue generally optimistic assessments. For example, the new National Security Strategy to the year 2020 provided a long list of potential threats to the country's security, but stated in its preamble confidence in the country's ability "to reliably prevent internal and external threats to national security and to dynamically develop the Russian Federation and to turn it into a leading power in terms of technological progress, people's quality of life and influence on global processes."[4]

As time passed, Russia began to draw fundamental lessons from the crisis. In September 2009, Medvedev published the article "Forward, Russia!" with a highly critical assessment of the country's domestic conditions. By pointing to "a primitive economy based on raw materials and endemic corruption," a "semi-Soviet social sphere, fragile democracy, harmful demographic trends, and unstable Caucasus," the former president posed a rhetorical question: "If Russia cannot relieve itself from these burdens, can it really find its own path for the future?"[5] His proposed solutions included the modernization of the economic and the political system, technological changes, and strengthening the judiciary to fight corruption. In his address to the Federation Council in November 2009, Medvedev further insisted that the effectiveness of foreign policy must be "judged by a simple criterion: Does it improve living standards in our country?"[6] Finally, in his meeting with Russia's ambassadors in July 2010, he further highlighted the need to establish "modernization alliances" with the United States and other Western nations.[7] Official documents too began to reflect the new vision. The Foreign Ministry document prepared for the president in February 2010 sought to strengthen Russia's economic position. By reflecting the realities of the global financial crisis, the document builds on Medvedev's notion of "modernization alliances" and provides detailed recommendations for attracting Western investments and creating favorable conditions for Russia's technological modernization.[8]

The new vision responded to the new realities without undermining the established foreign policy consensus in Russia. Such consensus assumes that the currently "unipolar" structure of the international system diminishes Russia's global influence and that its leadership must work to revive the country's status and remain tough in defending its national interests.[9] In addition, both Putin and Medvedev advocated essentially economic means for achieving Russia's international objectives. Both sought to position their country for successful competition in the world economy, including by capitalizing on Russia's rich energy reserves. Both were pragmatically focused on exploiting opportunities outside the West and building flexible coalitions with members of BRIC (Brazil, Russia, India, China), Shanghai Cooperation Organization (SCO), and other non-Western countries to promote Russia's global interests. Finally, both were concerned that political changes in the Middle East and elsewhere may further complicate the already painful global economic recovery.

The Domestic Reception

Medvedev's foreign policy vision was met with a mixed reaction at home. The initially skeptical members of the business community became increasingly supportive of the president's priorities, which included new incentives for investments from the private sector.[10] Critical of what they viewed as an excessively centralized and energy-oriented model of development, members of the business class supported Medvedev's emphasis on modernization as essential for the country's integration with the world economy and Western institutions. In particular, the Institute of Contemporary Development (INSOR), led by the head of Russia's Union of Industrialists and Entrepreneurs Igor Yurgens, published a number of reports and statements supportive of Medvedev's domestic and foreign policy agenda. One such report described Russia's future aspirations in the twenty-first century, presenting the country as bound to the European Union by shared values, security interests, visions of world order, and a system of treaties on strategic partnerships in military, energy, political, and cultural areas.[11] Foreign policy analysts with ties to the West also supported Medvedev and encouraged him to go further in developing Russia's pro-Western orientation. For example, director of the Moscow Carnegie Center Dmitry Trenin argued that "Russia is not a distinct civilization or a world unto itself," and therefore "Russia's non-inclusion into the European security architecture is a problem, while China's absence from the U.S.-led system of security arrangements in Asia is not."[12]

More critical was the reaction from those groups within the political class who read Medvedev's policies as excessively pro-Western and detrimental to the nation's sovereignty. Those with strong ties to the defense and security establishment demonstrated that their foreign policy priorities differed from those with commercial and political relations to the West. By highlighting Russia's obligations to preserve global strategic balance and influence in Europe, Eurasia, and other regions, these groups defended a more muscular and assertive foreign policy, and not the one "judged by a simple criterion: Does it improve living standards in our country?" These groups' modernization priorities also differed from those of Medvedev, placing emphasis on the development of the energy and military sectors, as opposed to diversification highlighted by Medvedev. Importantly, Putin too was often sympathetic to the groups' ideas.[13] The Middle Eastern changes deepened fears that similar developments could take place inside Russia and destabilize the existing political structure. Moreover, as the 2012 presidential election approached, foreign investors were divided, with some showing signs of nervousness about political stability and leaving the country's markets.[14] Outside the Kremlin, the divide widened between successful professionals in large cities and those dependent on additional state assistance for survival during the economic crisis.

In September 2011, Putin responded to the growing divide by making public his decision to run for presidency. Quite possibly, the decision reflected Putin's skepticism regarding his protégé's vision and ability to act on his perspectives on the country's future. On March 4, 2012, after running an aggressive and populist campaign, Putin was elected in the first round with the impressive 64 percent of the vote. The Medvedev project therefore remained half completed. The system was again stabilized on Putin's terms. However, the cities-based middle class, which was critical of Putin's system, grew restless and increasingly ready for political protest. The elections to Duma on December 4, 2011, amply demonstrated the public fatigue with the system, which worked to promote the ruling party, United Russia (UR), at the expense of other parties and movements. Even the official count recognized that UR gained 49 percent of the vote by losing 15 percent of what it obtained in 2007. In addition, the vote was widely contested across the country, especially in large cities. The new power structure assumed the need to incorporate Medvedev's supporters, to which Putin responded by nominating Medvedev for prime minister.

RELATIONS WITH THE WEST

"Reset" with the United States

Russia's ties with the United States began to improve soon after Washington's proclaimed desire to "reset" relations with Moscow and President Obama's trip to Russia in July 2009. The two sides cooperated in several areas. They signed and ultimately ratified the new START by replacing the old treaty of 1991. Signed in Prague on April 8, 2010, the new agreement further limited the number of strategic nuclear missiles to the level of 1,500, renewed a verification mechanism, and banned the deployment of strategic weapons outside the national territories. Russia also cooperated with the Western nations on Iran. The United States had earlier supported Russia's proposal to reprocess spent nuclear fuel outside Iran as a way for the country to continue with its nuclear program for peaceful purposes. However, Tehran refused to go along with the Russian proposal, and Moscow opted to support the United Nations' resolution on Iran. In addition, U.S.-Russia relations notably improved in the area of stabilizing Afghanistan. Russia agreed to U.S. military overflights and overland transportation of nonmilitary cargoes. The two countries jointly raided several opium laboratories in Afghanistan, destroying more than 2,000 pounds of heroin.[15] In March 2012, the Kremlin went as far as approving NATO use of an airport in Ulyanovsk as a transit point for moving soldiers and cargo to and from Afghanistan.[16] Finally, Russia renewed a strong interest in developing economic relations with the United States. Medvedev stressed the importance of investments to the information technology sector. Russia also completed negotiations over its membership in the World Trade Organization—the end of the road that began in 1993. In addition, Russia's state oil company Rosneft concluded an agreement with ExxonMobil to explore and develop Russia's Arctic Basin.[17] The deal's success depends on Moscow's commitment and approval by the U.S. Congress.

The progress in relations with the United States did not overshadow a number of unresolved issues between the two countries. The Kremlin remained critical of the U.S. proposal to develop the missile defense system (MDS) jointly with the Europeans. Russia was worried about being isolated from Western security developments and viewed as potentially threatening the expansion of American military infrastructure closer to Russia's borders, which had been taking place within and outside NATO. Even after Obama's election, the United States remained rhetorically supportive of the former Soviet states' bid for NATO membership.[18] Russia maintained its right to protect its interests in Georgia and elsewhere in the former Soviet region, whereas the United States continued to demand that the Kremlin withdraw its military from North Ossetia, Abkhazia, and Moldova. The two sides also competed, rather than cooperated, on energy transportation issues. As Russia worked to increase the exports of Central Asian energy via Russia's pipelines, the United States tried to persuade potential investors and former Soviet nations to build alternative transportation routes, such as the Trans-Caspian route under the Caspian Sea. Outside Europe and Eurasia, Russia remained concerned about U.S. foreign policy interventions, which became evident from Moscow's decision to abstain in the United Nations Security Council (UNSC) resolution that authorized airstrikes against Libya.[19] The list of unresolved issues between the two countries also included Russia's arms sales to non-Western countries, the Soviet era Jackson-Vanik amendment that blocked development of bilateral economic ties, and human rights. In particular, against objections from the Russian government, the U.S. Congress considered the bill that would impose visa bans and asset freezes on human rights violators in Russia. The bill was named after Russian lawyer Sergei Magnitsky, who was defending a foreign firm but was arrested and died while in detention.[20]

Relations with Europe

The "reset" in U.S.-Russia ties assisted the development of Russian ties with European countries. Speaking in Berlin in June 2008, President Dmitry Medvedev articulated a broad perspective on Europe "from Vancouver to Vladivostok," and proposed a new all-European treaty to establish a new security architecture by moving beyond NATO expansion and the conflict over Kosovo.[21] He cited the need to strengthen international law and urged to move beyond Atlanticism by developing an equal partnership between the European Union, the United States, and Russia. Medvedev further suggested that, if the West and Russia were able to sign the Helsinki Act of the Conference on Security and Cooperation in Europe in 1975, then they would be in an even better position to negotiate a new security treaty after the end of the Cold War.

Moscow's intervention in Georgia's conflict with South Ossetia in August 2008 created new tensions in Russia-West relations, yet Medvedev saw the conflict as an opportunity to strengthen his case. According to him, the fact that neither NATO nor the Organization for Security and Cooperation in Europe (OSCE) were able to prevent military confrontation in Georgia indicated the need for an improved security framework in Europe. The two organizations, Medvedev argued, were important yet insufficient for filling the existing security vacuum. Comparing the significance of the Caucasus conflict to Russia to that of September 11, 2001, to the United States, Medvedev insisted that "[w]e simply have to create a new security system, otherwise there will be no guarantees that someone like Saakashvili could not . . . try something similar to what happened in August."[22] In November 2009, Russia published its proposal for a new security treaty by pledging to legally restrict its unilateral use of force in exchange for European nations and the United States doing the same. The Kremlin presented the draft as the document that would "finally do away with the legacy of the Cold War."[23]

In the economic arena, Russia remained focused on greater integration with the EU's economy, and the two sides concluded a number of important agreements to this effect. Russia's largest natural gas company, Gazprom, built a direct pipeline to Germany underneath the Baltic Sea. It also negotiated an agreement with Southern European nations to build a new oil pipeline to Bulgaria and Greece by bypassing the crowded Bosphorus. Russia also managed to achieve greater integration with European economies by exchanging some companies' shares. In addition, it began to negotiate deals with European companies over joint development of the Arctic. Furthermore, Russia made progress in political relations with EU nations by seeking to develop a common understanding on solving the Middle Eastern conflict and Iran's nuclear program. Many Europeans shared the Kremlin's commitment to multilateralism and negotiations, rather than sanctions and force. Finally, Russia worked on improving bilateral relations with Eastern European states, such as Poland and Latvia.

Nonetheless, the development of relations with European countries faced important obstacles. The idea of a new security pact did not receive the foreign support that Russia wanted. Although some Western nations welcomed Russia's efforts to reach out to Europe, they offered only general support and remained wary of Medvedev's initiative. Germany and France responded by proposing to establish the EU-Russia Political and Security Committee as an institution to consult on strategic issues on the continent.[24] They agreed with the need to address the vacuum of European security, but did not find Russia's proposal satisfactory. NATO secretary-general Anders Fogh Rasmussen said he saw no need for the new legally binding security treaty "because we do have a framework already."[25] The United States was equally dismissive. U.S. Secretary of State Hillary Clinton found that a new European treaty was unnecessary—the position that Medvedev described as reflecting "a certain envy" among "our American partners."[26] Washington expressed full confidence in the NATO-centered security system in Europe and proposed that any revisions should be discussed in the OSCE context.[27] Finally, the Eastern European nations were concerned that Russia's initiative was about recognizing Russia's sphere of interests and giving Moscow a veto over NATO's international operations. They shared the perspective of Georgia and viewed Russia as the most important threat to their security.[28] At the end of 2010 Medvedev expressed disappointment with the lack of international support and acknowledged that two and half years of discussions did not lead to any breakthrough. Citing the power of stereotypes, he said his initiative may have appeared ahead of its time and would have to wait before being considered in the future.[29]

Progress was also slow regarding Western plans for an MDS in Europe and handling of the Middle Eastern crisis. Moscow threatened to develop new intercontinental ballistic missiles that could spark a new arms race. The Kremlin maintained that NATO's missile defense plans could undermine Russia's security as soon as 2020, when the system's fourth phase would be deployed. Russia also took issue with the West pursuing regime change in Libya and going after Muammar Gadhafi personally. Although Moscow had originally not vetoed the UNSC resolution of the use of force against him, it later criticized the implementation of the resolution and then vetoed a much weaker resolution on Syria. Divergent perceptions of interest by Russia and the West continued to be a problem. Russia, through its initiatives— from merging the two missile defense systems to negotiating a new pan-European security treaty—demonstrated a desire to have strong cooperative relationships, whereas Western nations wanted more favors from Moscow, allowing transit routes to Afghanistan, pressuring Iran into nuclear compliance, and negotiating a political exit for Middle Eastern leaders.

Economically, Russia and the EU continued to disagree over what defines economic security. The EU perceived Russia's energy disputes with former Soviet republics as a threat to its own interests. The EU insisted that Russia ratify the Energy Charter. The charter had been signed by Boris Yeltsin during the 1990s, and stipulated the access of third parties to Russia's energy

pipelines. The EU also saw the issue in terms of market diversification principles and wanted to have a room for changing energy partners should such
an opportunity present itself. However, Russia was an energy producer, not
a consumer, and it wanted to sign long-term contracts with Europeans,
resisting access to its pipelines. Given the significance of high energy prices
for its economic development, Russia wanted to avoid repetition of 1986,
when a sharp decline in prices undermined the Soviet economy. In addition, Russia was wary of European efforts to negotiate separate energy
agreements with Azerbaijan, Turkey, and the countries of Central Asia. Russia also had limited success in gaining greater access to the EU retail markets
and distribution networks, as well as shares in prominent European companies.

CHINA AND THE MIDDLE EAST

Russia improved its standing in the non-Western world by participating in
international coalitions, such as the SCO and BRIC, and by fostering bilateral ties. Relations with China, Russia's largest neighbor, obtained a strategic dimension in the areas of commerce and regional security. Furthermore,
the two nations demonstrated an increased convergence in global priorities
and solutions to existing issues in world politics.

Imperatives of Modernization and Security in Asia

Although Russia saw itself as a country of European identity, it sought to
take advantage of its strategic proximity to Asia for the purpose of modernizing its economy. China and the Asia-Pacific region were important
because of the potential of becoming a gateway for Russia's entrance to the
global economy. With one-half of the world's population and accounting
for one-fifth of global trade, the Asia-Pacific region was viewed by many as a
success story of modernization and globalization. Rich in natural resources,
Russia was poised to satisfy the region's growing demand for energy while
modernizing its own domestic economy along the way. Russia moved from
primitive accumulation of capital to the stage of generating a stable flow of
investments in the economy, and it was turning its forward-looking vision
and growing resources into a more active foreign policy. In addition, the
region faced some long-standing security challenges, such as the nuclear
ambitions of North Korea and China's relations with Taiwan.

Russia's first interest was to increase its role in solving vital security issues
in East Asia. For years, Russia's officials argued for the development of a
multilateral security framework in the region and beyond. The Kremlin

insisted that security problems could only be solved through the systematic coordination of state efforts, and not through use of force by ad hoc coalitions. For instance, it developed the Shanghai Cooperation Organization with China and four Central Asian states for addressing threats from terrorism and the security vacuum in the area. In East Asia, Moscow advocated multilateral solutions to the nuclear crisis with North Korea, and contributed to creating the six-party format for dealing with the crisis. It is critical for Russia that changes in the region, such as reunification of the two Koreas, be orderly and not destabilizing in nature.[30] Russian analysts considered a unified Korea a potential strategic partner, provided that the shape of unification was not overly determined by the United States. For these reasons, Russia insisted on preserving even-handed relations with both Koreas.

Russia's most important priority remained economic modernization, and that required determination to win markets in arms and energy. China and India remained Russia's largest buyers, purchasing more than 90 percent of Russia's annual arms exports. Russia viewed itself as connected with Asia in an economically open region, in which Russia, due to its richness of natural resources, occupies an important role and reaps considerable economic, as well as political, benefits. Although Russia's main energy market remained in Europe, accounting for about 50 percent of foreign trade, Russia continued to aggressively promote itself as an energy pipeline hub connecting Asia, Europe, and North America. Russia's sales of weapons and energy to China decreased, yet the two nations' economic and political interests are compatible and there is hardly an alternative to their growing cooperation in the future. In September 2010, Russia completed an oil pipeline connecting to northeastern China, and two gas pipelines are planned.[31]

Of course, none of this meant that Russia faces no constraints on advancing its influence in the region. One such constraint has to do with progressive power differentials. As Russia continues to supply China with energy and weapons and China continues to grow at a considerably higher rate than its northern neighbor, the risk of Moscow becoming a junior partner in a Beijing-led coalition increases. However, a way out of this "relative gains" dilemma is not to reduce bilateral interactions, but rather to continue strengthening multilateral security institutions and be versatile in developing economic relations in the region. For example, in an effort to promote trilateral cooperation with South Korea and North Korea, Moscow hosted a trip by North Korea's leader Kim Jong Il. As Kim and President Medvedev met at a Siberian military base, they agreed to create a bilateral commission to investigate possibility of constructing a trans-Korean pipeline. Russia pledged an annual supply of 10 billion cubic meters of gas for the projected pipeline, two-thirds of which would go through North

Korea.[32] Moscow also hoped that participation in the APEC summits, such as the one scheduled for June 2012, had the potential of helping Russia's regional integration and development in the Far East.

Relations with the Middle East

In the Middle East, Russia has worked to develop relations across the region, sustain its influence on Iran, and has considerably expanded ties with Turkey, Israel, and Afghanistan. Although Moscow failed to persuade Tehran to send its spent nuclear fuel to Russia, the Kremlin continued a dialogue with Iranian leaders. Russia sought to restrain Western leaders from military intervention or imposing additional sanctions on Iran, while welcoming negotiations. In February 2012, Putin warned that the consequences of a military strike on Iran "will be truly catastrophic."[33] In Afghanistan, Russia attempted to introduce its own policy by appointing a presidential special representative for the country, fostering ties with its official leadership, and establishing separate lines of communication to the Taliban leadership.[34] Despite Russia's traditionally strong ties with Syria, Palestine, and other Arab states, the Kremlin also managed to deepen its relations with Israel. For example, the two sides signed a $100 million deal for Israel to provide Russia with unmanned aerial vehicles, thereby enabling the Russian security forces to tighten surveillance over Georgia.[35] In addition, Turkey has emerged as especially important to Russia, with the two converging on perceptions of world order, developing ambitious energy plans, and cooperating on improving security in the Black Sea area. In May 2010, the two countries signed an agreement to carry Russian oil from the Black Sea to the Mediterranean. The two nations were also connected by important gas projects such as a pipeline from Russia to Greece, Italy, and Israel, and from Russia to Southern Europe—both through Turkey or the Turkish sector of the Black Sea waters.[36]

Finally, the pragmatic, nonideological orientation of Russia's leadership assisted it in making adjustments to the postrevolutionary realities in the Middle East. For example, the Kremlin sought to distance itself from Libya's Muammar Gadhafi by not vetoing the United Nations Security Council resolution on the use of force against him.[37] At the same time, Russia was worried about revolutions in the Middle East, and Russian officials continued to voice concern about the possible radicalization of Middle Eastern states. Acting jointly with China, Russia vetoed the U.S.- and European-sponsored UNSC resolutions regarding Syria. Fearful that such resolutions would lead to a military intervention and regime change in Syria, as happened in Libya, the Kremlin instead pushed for negotiations between Bashar al-Assad and the military opposition. The BRIC summit held in April 2012 in India then further supported negotiations in Syria. As of May 2012, the

Kremlin moved closer to accepting the possible removal of Assad, but not at the cost of dismantling the Syrian regime or losing Russia's influence over it.[38]

Russia's Middle East activism had roots in both global and domestic developments. Globally, the Kremlin was seeking to increase political influence and commercial gains. Domestically, Russia remained concerned about the potential reverberations of the Middle Eastern destabilization. An explosive environment emerged from growing influence of radical Islamist ideologies, rising immigration from Muslim ex-Soviet republics, and insufficient state policy on the Northern Caucasus's economic and political integration. During 2010–2011, Russia was confronted with growing terrorist violence. Previously contained in Chechnya, terrorism spread throughout other parts of the region—Dagestan, Ingushetia, Kabardino-Balkaria, and North Ossetia. Since the October 2002 seizure of a Moscow movie theater, Chechen jihadists have worked to stage violent actions in Russia's capital. On March 29, 2010, two female suicide bombers trained by the Caucasus-centered Doku Umarov detonated their explosives inside a Moscow metro train, killing forty people and injuring many more. Another major attack came in March 2011, when a bomb detonated in the largest Moscow airport, Domodedovo, killing thirty-six and injuring 180 people. The Kremlin responded by outlining a new antiterrorism strategy for the region,[39] but the violence was far from curtailed.

THE FORMER SOVIET REGION

"Privileged Interests" and Russia's Regional Aspirations

In the former Soviet region, Russia insisted on its own sphere of influence. The regional component of Russia's policy was supposed to reinforce the global one, moving Russia on the path of becoming an independent center of power and influence in the world. Russia's foreign policy consensus assumed the importance of domination in the region by remaining "pragmatic" and avoiding the use of brute force in achieving its objectives. Although the Kremlin was unapologetic about using force against Georgia and recognizing the independence of South Ossetia and Abkhazia in August 2008, both Putin and Medvedev viewed regional dominance in terms of soft power, rather than direct control over its neighbors' domestic and international priorities. They assumed that Russia has sufficient economic, diplomatic, institutional, and cultural capacity to regionally negotiate the preferred international postures of the former Soviet states.

Medvedev's concept of "privileged interests" served to reinforce this thinking after the 2008 war with Georgia. Russia sought to downplay the use of force in the Caucasus and obtain international recognition of its regional vision. Immediately following the Georgian war, the president set out five principles in conducting foreign relations: the primacy of international law; multipolarity as a basis of global stability; nonconfrontational relations and active development of ties with Europe, the United States, and other nations; protection of Russia's citizens and business needs; and special ties with close neighbors.[40] It is the fifth principle that former president Medvedev articulated using the term "privileged interests." Following Russia's earlier expressed position, Medvedev sought to clarify that his country did not want an area of geopolitically exclusive influence.[41] Rather, Medvedev was referring to a common historical experience, and spoke of "countries with which we have been living side by side for decades, centuries, now, and with which we share the same roots . . . countries where Russian is spoken, and that have a similar economic system and share much in terms of culture."[42]

Following the idea of strengthening Russia's ties with its neighbors, in fall 2011 Putin proposed to build a new Eurasian Union among the CIS states.[43] Similar to Medvedev, Putin emphasized an open nature of the proposed union and laid out economic incentives from joining it, including increase in trade, common modernization projects, and improved standards of living.

Aiming at Low-Cost Political Stabilization

Russia sought to strengthen its influence in the former Soviet region by relying on diplomatic, economic, and cultural tools. By capitalizing on high oil prices, it strengthened its presence in neighboring economies and contributed to reversing the color revolutions in Ukraine and Kyrgyzstan, which the Kremlin viewed as dangerous for Russia and destabilizing for the larger region. In both countries, anti-Kremlin governments were replaced with those in favor of stronger ties with Russia. Following a change in government, Russia negotiated new terms for its political influence. In April 2010 Ukraine and Russia agreed to extend the lease on Russia's Black Sea fleet for twenty-five more years in exchange for a reduction in natural gas prices by 30 percent.[44] In 2011, Russia invited Ukraine to join a Customs Union, promising another major discount for gas prices.[45] While the Black Sea deal probably closes NATO's door for Ukraine, the gas agreement and potential membership in the Customs Union keeps Ukraine in Russia's area of economic influence. The Customs Union was originally conceived in 2010 and includes Russia, Belarus, and Kazakhstan—it became operative in January 2012. Ukrainian leaders declined the Customs Union offer, but indicated willingness to accommodate Russia in strengthening its presence in the Ukrainian economy.

In Kyrgyzstan, following the 2010 "Tulip" revolution that the Kremlin had helped to foment,[46] Russia sought to bring to power a pro-Russian coalition and establish a political system with a strong central authority.[47] In early November 2010, the pro-Russian candidate Almazbek Atambayev was elected new president in the first round of elections. Even in Georgia, the Kremlin was now finding a way to influence events without relying on force—by developing ties with Georgian opposition to President Mikhail Saakashvili.[48]

The Kremlin also wanted to consolidate its military presence in the region. In Kyrgyzstan, Russia sought to create a new antiterrorism center under the auspices of the Collective Security Treaty Organization (CSTO) in the southern part of the country.[49] In Tajikistan, Moscow negotiated redeployment of 6,000 troops to patrol the border with Afghanistan in exchange for a promise to rearm the Tajik army. Finally, the Russia-controlled CSTO, which also includes Armenia, Belarus, Uzbekistan, Tajikistan, Kazakhstan, and Kyrgyzstan, amended its mission by pledging to defend its members from internal "unconstitutional disturbances." In an apparent response to Arab-like uprisings, the CSTO also conducted ambitious military exercise by imitating defeat of an attempted coup in Tajikistan.

The preservation of Russia's influence in the region would have not come without the country's attempts to act globally and win at least some support for its policies from established powers in the West and rising non-Western powers. For example, the Kremlin would not have been as successful in its offensive against U.S. "unilateralism" were it not for France's and Germany's tacit support that had resulted from the three's opposition to the U.S. invasion of Iraq. Were the two Western European states to support NATO membership for Ukraine and Georgia, it would have taken longer for the Orange and Rose revolutions to run out of steam (in Ukraine and Georgia, respectively). In addition, Russia probably could not have been as successful in its war against Georgia were China to take a strong critical stance toward it. Although Beijing refused to endorse Russia's recognition of Abkhazia and South Ossetia's independence, the Chinese informally supported Russia during the crisis in the Caucasus, and the issue has not complicated the two nations' relations.[50]

However, Russia's increased influence has not translated into stability in the region. The reversal of the color revolutions in Ukraine and Georgia has yet to bring more order to Eurasia. Evidence of instability has included the tense atmosphere in the Caucasus following the war with Georgia, renewed terrorist attacks, the persistent failure of Western forces to stabilize Afghanistan, the inability of Central Asian rulers to reign in local clans and drug lords, and the weakness of legitimately elected bodies of power in Moldova and Ukraine. Kyrgyzstan may serve as an example of instability in the

region. When the second violent round of power struggle occurred in Kyrgyzstan in June 2010, the new interim government in Bishkek failed to gain
control over the country, and the southern part—a stronghold of the
ousted president Kurmanbek Bakiev—became de facto independent.[51] Yet
the crisis elicited little serious response from key powers or international
organizations in the region. Despite the relative recovery of the economy,
Russia could ill afford efforts to single-handedly stabilize and pacify the
region. At best, the Kremlin could defend its core interests in regional settings and address its economic interests.

Maximizing Economic Opportunities

Having reversed the color revolutions in Eurasia, Russia sought to gain
economically. Not in the position to become the regional center, Russia
instead emphasized "pragmatic" bilateral ties and issue-specific multilateral
contacts. Energy remained its main card. In addition to gaining control over
the most valuable assets abroad and increasing Russian shares in foreign
companies, the Kremlin's general economic objective remained strengthening its energy position in world markets by coordinating its activities with
other energy producers, building pipelines in all geographic directions, raising energy prices for its oil- and gas-dependent neighbors, and moving to
control transportation networks in the former USSR.

In Ukraine, Russia was primarily interested in gaining control over energy
infrastructure. In order to overcome the dependence on Ukrainian transit
in transporting natural gas to European markets, the Kremlin developed a
dual-track approach. It worked with Turkey and Southern European states
in order to obtain their permission to build the southern pipeline that
would deliver Russian energy to Europe via the Black Sea by circumventing
Ukraine. On the other hand, Moscow continued to pressure Kyiv to agree
to joint ownership of Naftogas, Ukraine's state-controlled gas company.[52]
The Kremlin wanted to avoid additional energy disputes with Ukraine similar to those in 2005 and 2006 by purchasing controlling stakes in Naftogas.
As articulated by Konstantin Kosachyev, chairman of the International
Affairs Committee of the State Duma, the idea was for Ukraine and Russia
to "become a single transit space between Europe and China, between
European and Asian markets."[53]

In Central Asia and the Caucasus, Russia sought to obtain valuable assets
and renegotiate price arrangements with oil- and gas-rich states, such as
Azerbaijan, Turkmenistan, and Kazakhstan, leaving them with less incentive to sell to Europe and China. With attractive prices and an energy transportation system in place, the Caspian states would be less likely to
construct new pipelines that are favored by non-Russian nations. In the
energy-poor Kyrgyzstan, the Kremlin worked to gain controlling stakes in

valuable companies, such as the enterprise that has supplied the U.S. military base with energy and the Dustan torpedo plant on the shore of the country's mountain lake.[54]

CONCLUSION

Although it is too early to offer a definitive assessment of Russia's evolving international course, this survey suggests a generally successful record. Following the difficult months after its military assertiveness in Georgia, Russia has revived its relations with the Western nations. Not only has Russia preserved the existing level of ties with France, Germany, and other Western European nations, but Moscow has worked to strengthen these ties. European leaders have reciprocated by proposing to establish the EU-Russia Political and Security Committee as an institution to consult on strategic issues on the continent. The U.S. attempts to "reset" relations with Moscow have further assisted the continuous development of Russian ties with Europe. With respect to Asia and the Middle East, Russia has continued to develop economic and political ties across the two regions by prioritizing relations with China and Turkey. In the former Soviet world, the Kremlin has found new partners in the postrevolutionary governments of Ukraine and Kyrgyzstan. By capitalizing on "pragmatic" economy-driven ties and high oil prices, Russia has also made some advancement in reviving the old Kremlin's initiative, the Customs Union.

The new course, which combines elements of cooperation and assertiveness, is yet to be fully consolidated, and it remains to be seen whether the course will gather sufficient political support at home. Having met the challenge of power transition in 2012, the country needs to concentrate on solving its formidable demographic and institutional problems including reforming the military, education, and health-care systems. Externally, Russia's new course depends on favorable developments in the global political and economic system. For Russia's pragmatic modernization course to continue, U.S.-Russia relations need to be predictable, reciprocal, and develop in the direction of strengthening mutual trust. Lack of progress with issues such as MDS in Europe, or of coordination of policies toward Afghanistan, the Middle East, and former Soviet states may encourage the Kremlin to strengthen the rhetoric of assertiveness in relations with the West. Development of the global economy is another critical factor. A global recovery and stable energy prices may facilitate Russia's engagement with the world, whereas major disturbances, such as a recession or a sharp decline in oil prices, are bound to undermine the process.

SUGGESTED READINGS

Official Statements

Medvedev, Dmitry. "Speech at Meeting with Russian Ambassadors and Permanent Representatives in International Organizations." eng.kremlin.ru, July 12, 2010.
Putin, Vladimir. "Russia and the Changing World." *Moskovskie novosti*, February 26, 2012, available in English at: en.rian.ru/world/20120227/171547818.html?id.

Books

Legvold, Robert, ed. *Russian Foreign Policy in the 21st Century and the Shadow of the Past*. New York: Columbia University Press, 2007.
Mankoff, Jeffrey. *Russian Foreign Policy: The Return of Great Power Politics*. 2nd ed. Lanham, Md.: Rowman & Littlefield, 2011.
Tsygankov, Andrei P. *Russia's Foreign Policy: Change and Continuity in National Identity*. 3rd ed. Lanham, Md.: Rowman & Littlefield, 2013.

NOTES

1. Some observers pointed to importance of these trends before the crisis. See Naazneen Barma, Ely Ratner, and Steven Weber, "The World Without West," *National Interest* 90, no. 4 (2007).

2. Jeffrey Mankoff, "Internal and External Impact of Russia's Economic Crisis," *Proliferation Papers*, no. 48 (March 2010).

3. Vladimir Putin, "Press Statement and Answers to Journalists' Questions Following a Meeting of the Russia-NATO Council," Bucharest, April 4, 2008, www.kremlin.ru.

4. *Interfax-AVN*, May 13, 2009. The full Russian text of the strategy is published on the website of the Russian Security Council, www.scrf.gov.ru.

5. Dmitry Medvedev, "Forward, Russia!" www.kremlin.ru, September 10, 2009.

6. Dmitry Medvedev, "Address to Federation Council of the Russian Federation," November 12, 2009, www.kremlin.ru.

7. Dmitry Medvedev, "Speech at Meeting with Russian Ambassadors and Permanent Representatives in International Organisations," July 12, 2010, www.kremlin.ru.

8. *Programma effektivnogo ispol'zovaniia vneshnepoliticheskikh faktorov v tseliakh dolgosrochnogo razvitiia Rossiiskoi Federatsiii*, February 10, 2010, www.runewsweek.ru/country/34184.

9. For a more detailed description of Russia's global strategy, see Andrei P. Tsygankov, "Preserving Influence in a Changing World: Russia's Grand Strategy," *Problems of Post-Communism* 58, no. 1 (2011).

10. See, for example, Medvedev's speech in Magnitogorsk that stressed the need to improve the business climate. Dmitry Medvedev, "Meeting of the Commission

for Modernization and Technological Development of Russia's Economy," March 30, 2011, eng.kremlin.ru/news/1981.

11. *Rossiia XXI veka* (Moscow: Institut sovremennogo razvitiia, 2010), 44–45.

12. Dmitry Trenin, "Blowing Both Hot and Cold," *Moscow Times*, March 24, 2009.

13. Vladimir Putin, "Speech at Meeting with Deputies of State Duma," April 20, 2011, premier.gov.ru/events/news/14898/.

14. Tai Adelaja, "Competitive Constraints. A New Report Says Russia Is Losing the Global Battle for the Hearts and Minds of Investors," *Russia Profile*, September 8, 2011, russiaprofile.org/business/44937.html.

15. Michael Schwartz, "Russia Joins Drug Raid in Afghanistan, Marking Advance in Relations with U.S.," *New York Times*, October 29, 2011.

16. "NATO Base in Russia 'Pragmatic Decision'—Analysts," *RIA-Novosti*, March 21, 2012.

17. Roland Nash, "Rosneft and Exxon—A Big Deal," *Business New Europe*, September 7, 2011, www.bne.eu.

18. Arshad Mohammed, "Hilary Clinton Tells Ukraine Door to NATO Open," *Reuters*, July 2, 2010, www.reuters.com/article/2010/07/03/us-usa-clinton-ukraine-idUSTRE66051S20100703.

19. Putin criticized the resolution as "defective and flawed" and resembling "medieval calls for crusades." Medvedev rebuked Putin's criticism. Alexei Anishchuk, "Russia's Medvedev raps Putin's Libya 'crusade' jibe," *Reuters*, March 21, 2011, us.mobile.reuters.com/article/topNews/idUSTRE72K5AJ20110321.

20. For a discussion, see Cory Welt, "Russia, Trade, and Human Rights: Thinking through U.S. Policies," *American Progress*, April 30, 2012, www.americanprogress.org/issues/2012/04/us_russia_magnitsky.html.

21. Dmitry Medvedev, "Speech in Berlin," *Izvestiia*, June 6, 2008.

22. Dmitry Medvedev, "Meeting with the Participants in the International Club Valdai, Moscow," September 12, 2008, www.kremlin.ru; Dmitry Medvedev, "Interview of the President with the Spanish Media," March 1, 2009, www.kremlin.ru.

23. Conor Humphries, "Russia Drafts 'Post-Cold War' East-West Security Pact," *Reuters*, November 29, 2009, uk.reuters.com/article/2009/11/29/uk-russia-treaty idUKTRE5AS1OZ2 0091129.

24. Judy Dempsey, "Russia Wants to Formalize Relation with E.U.," *New York Times*, October 18, 2010.

25. Robert Bridge, "Moscow Looking for European 'Re-think' at Munich Security Conference," *Russia Today*, October 21, 2010, www.russiatoday.com.

26. "Europe Will Need European Security Treaty Sooner or Later—Medvedev," *RIA Novosti*, December 1, 2010, english.ruvr.ru/2010/12/01/36016876.html.

27. For a more detailed analysis of the U.S. position from a conservative perspective, see Sally McNamara, "Russia's Proposed New European Security Treaty: A Non-Starter for the U.S. and Europe," *Heritage Foundation Backgrounder* no. 2463, September 16, 2010.

28. For documentation that Baltics and Poland wanted NATO to develop secret contingency plans in response to the war in the Caucasus, see Ivo Daalder, "Action Request: Baltic Contingency Planning," October 18, 2009, wikileaks.ch/cable/2009/10/09USNATO464.html.

29. "Europe Will Need European Security Treaty Sooner or Later."

30. Russia conducted several military exercises in the Far East to rehearse actions for accepting up to 100,000 North Korean refugees in case of a North Korean destabilization.

31. Gillian Wong, "Russia Wants to Supply All of China's Gas Needs," *AP*, September 27, 2010, www.guardian.co.uk/world/feedarticle/9284274.

32. Khristina Narizhnaya, "Kim Endorses Trans-Korean Pipeline," *Moscow Times*, August 25, 2011.

33. Vladimir Putin, "Russia and the Changing World," *Moskovskie novosti*, February 26, 2012.

34. M. K. Bhadrakumar, "Mullah Omar Gets a Russian Visitor," *Asia Times*, March 23, 2011.

35. M. K. Bhadrakumar, "Israel Joins Russian Ballet School," *Asia Times*, September 11, 2011.

36. Anna Smolchenko, "Medvedev Hails 'Strategic' Turkey Ties," *AFP*, May 12, 2010, georgiandaily.com/index.php?option = com_content&task = view&id = 185 81&Item id = 66.

37. The Kremlin also recalled Russia's Libya Ambassador for criticizing Moscow's decision. "Former Russian Ambassador to Libya Chamov on Dismissal, Situation There, UN Vote," *Zavtra*, March 30, 2011, www.zavtra.ru.

38. Simon Tisdall, "Syria: Why Russia Changed Tack," *The Guardian*, May 28, 2012.

39. "Medvedev Outlines Anti-terrorism Strategy for North Caucasus," *RIA Novosti*, April 1, 2010, en.rian.ru/russia/20100401/158395373.html.

40. Paul Reynolds, "New Russian World Order: The Five Principles," *BBC News*, September 2, 2008, news.bbc.co.uk/2/hi/europe/7591610.stm.

41. For example, see Putin's insistence that Russia seeks not the post-Soviet states' territory or natural resources, but the human dignity and the quality of life of its citizens, whom it regards as its own cultural compatriots. Vladimir Putin, "Address to Federation Council of the Russia's Federation," March 25, 2005, www .kremlin.ru.

42. Dmitry Medvedev, "Meeting with Members of the Council on Foreign Relations, Washington, DC," November 15, 2008, www.kremlin.ru.

43. Vladimir Putin, "The New Integration Project for Eurasia," *Izvestia*, October 3, 2011.

44. Lyubov Pronina, "Russia Gas Deal Shuts NATO Door for Ukraine, Opens Asset Access," *Bloomberg*, April 23, 2010, mobile.bloomberg.com/news/2010-04-23/ russian-gas-deal-may-close-nato-door-for-ukraine-open-access-to-assets?category = & BB_NAVI_DISABLE = PULSE.

45. Sergei Sidorenko, "V Rade buri," *Kommersant*, April 7, 2011, http://kommer sant.ru/doc/1616500.

46. Philip P. Pan, "Russia Helped Fuel Unrest in Kyrgyzstan," *Washington Post*, April 12, 2010. One element of Russia's pressures concerned export duties for gasoline and diesel fuel. By shifting from selling fuel duty-free to raising duties for dependent neighbors, the Kremlin could achieve impressive results. In the second half of 2010, Russia also tried the approach in Tajikistan by seeking its permission

to install a military base there. Russia supplies 93 percent of the country's petro-leum products. "Russia Ends Fuel Duties for Kyrgyz, Raises Them for Tajiks," March 25, 2011, *CentralAsiaOnline.com*.

47. Steve Gutterman, "Russia, U.S. at Odds on Kyrgyzstan's Future," *Reuters*, October 6, 2010, www.reuters.com/article/2010/10/06/us-kyrgyzstan-russia-usa-idUS TRE6952ZU20101006.

48. Yuri Simonyan, "Nino Burdzhanadze obiavili 'predatelem Guziyi'," *Nezavisi-maia gazeta*, April 3, 2010.

49. Bruce Pannier, "Russia's Star On Rise Again in Kyrgyzstan," *RFE/RL*, April 8, 2011.

50. As Elizabeth Wishnik wrote, "Prior to the recognition, Chinese media coverage largely echoed Russian positions, and, even afterwards, Chinese experts sympathized with Russian opposition to NATO's expansion." Elizabeth Wishnik, *Russia, China, and the United States in Central Asia* (Carlisle, PA: Strategic Studies Institute, U.S. Army War College, 2009), 41.

51. Andrew Higgins, "In Central Asia, a New Headache for U.S. Policy," *Washington Post*, September 1, 2010.

52. Tatyana Ivzhenko, "Ukrayina i Rossiia mogut izmenit' gazovo-flotski dogo-vor," *Nezavisimaia gazeta*, March 15, 2011.

53. "Moscow to Counteract 'Anti-Russian' Form of Ukraine's Integration with EU," *Interfax*, March 4, 2011, www.kyivpost.com/news/russia/detail/99007/.

54. Aleksandr Gabuyev, "Rossiisko-kirgizskie otnosheniia smazali i zapravili," *Kommersant*, March 22, 2011.

12

Relations with Central Asia

Gregory Gleason

Vladimir Putin's return to the presidency in May 2012 represents a new stage in the rapidly changing relationships between Central Asia and Russia.[1] Central Asia is important for Russia. As one Russian foreign affairs analyst recently expressed it, "If Russia loses its preeminent positions in Central Asia, it would lose control of the southern sector of its traditional sphere of influence. This, in turn, would create entirely new conditions in which immense challenges and risks emanating from Central Asia could threaten the stable and steady development of Russia itself."[2] Similarly, Russia is important for Central Asian states. The tsarist colonial period and the seventy-three years of Soviet practice have left a deep imprint on Central Asian societies. With the breakup of the USSR in December 1991, the five Central Asian countries—Kazakhstan, Kyrgyzstan, Tajikistan, Turkmenistan, and Uzbekistan—became independent. Even after their independence, Russia remains a major commercial partner for all the Central Asian states.

In addition to the close economic relationships between Russia and the Central Asian states, there is an important political dimension to the relationship. But the political relationship is much more complicated. The rising influence of Russia in international affairs, often referred to in the Russian language as *usilie* or "resurgence," is highly visible in Central Asia. What might be called Russia's "political-gravitational field" is palpable throughout the Central Asian states, where many of the media, financial, and technological influences originate primarily from Russia. Much of the competition pits Russian-based firms against the commercial prowess of firms from other countries of the world, including China, India, Europe, Turkey, the United States, and others. There is clearly competition over

Central Asia's resources, markets, and future prospects. But despite the competition, Central Asian states are not merely balancing "East against West" as was often rightly or wrongly perceived as the key foreign policy choices in the past two decades since independence.[3] Today there are many competing sectors of influence: the energy sector, chiefly gas and oil but also electric power; the minerals sector; the agricultural sector; and, at least in Kazakhstan, the emerging banking sector. Today there are many vectors of influence—the Slavic relationship to the north is paralleled by a strong Turkic-language and cultural relationship to the west and a Persian cultural relationship to the south. China represents a new and rapidly accelerating commercial influence on Central Asia.[4] Moreover, the Central Asian states have conflictual relations with one another in ways that magnify the influences of foreign countries. These conflicts do not seem to be diminishing but rather to be growing in intensity and importance.

In this context, the role of Russia is not simply one of dominance or competition; it is more complex than that. It is based on a subtle but important—and quite possibly impractical—distinction between leading and dominating. Russian leaders are attempting to exert a leading but not dominating role within the former Soviet space. In theory it is possible to recognize a distinction that in practice does not exist; in practice leading is often synonymous with dominating. Russian political leaders and doctrines of political guidance expressly state that Russia has no intention of occupying a position of dominance in the space of the countries of the former Soviet Union. Yet for Russia to fully relinquish the dominating role of the past while assuming a new leadership role as first among equals is invariably fraught with misunderstanding and conflict.

Russia's influence is on the rise and is quite visible. A more confident and more assertive Russia is exerting greater political and economic influence over Central Asia than it has for the past two decades of independence since the disintegration of the USSR. On the other hand, even though Russian leadership is more confident than it has been in the past, it is also more internally conflicted, more challenged by its own constraints, and more apt to pursue policies that create greater problems for future economic and political development in Russia in particular and in the Eurasian regional sphere in general. The more assertive is Moscow's pursuit of reestablishing political primacy throughout Eurasia, the more Russia motivates its neighbors to seek refuge in striving to gain greater distance. The more Moscow seeks to "integrate" its neighbors into a single economic and political space, the more Moscow's agenda is preempted or shifted according to the agendas of its neighbors.

It is difficult for Russia to exert its influence in Central Asia without creating the impression that it is seeking to intervene in order to preempt the influence of other states. But today's situation is not truly comparable to competition over power and territory such as that of the "Great Game" of past centuries where great powers' objectives and actions were fairly transparent. The rules of the nineteenth-century great games were fairly well understood. Today the situation is different. The Soviet past has left mixed populations throughout the region, leaving a truly multinational legacy within the context of increasingly salient national sentiments.[5] Power in the globalized world is not simply the control over territory as it was in the past; it is the competition for sustained influence.[6] Today's competition, as one Russian analyst accurately characterized it, is in the form of a "Great Game with unknown rules."[7] It is difficult to excel in a game in which the rules are shifting or elusive.

This chapter surveys the relationship between Russia and its southern neighbors, Kazakhstan and the other Central Asian countries. Beginning with the assumption of authority by newly elected president Vladimir Putin in May 2012 and looking backward, this chapter describes Russian political objectives in terms of the foreign policy stature of each of the countries of the region. Many of the factors that play an important role are essentially the same as those in the past. The influence of the Soviet Union lingers on in the form of habits in thought, practice, and cultural traditions. New problems have emerged or are barely perceptible on the horizon. These problems present challenges and opportunities for both Russia and Central Asian countries. Among the issues are the rapidly rising influence of China; the continuing instability in Afghanistan and Pakistan; the threat of insurgency and insurrection, particularly in the densely populated and underemployed Fergana Valley; the pressures created by volatility in energy markets; and the marked differences among the Central Asian states themselves over such issues as the water-and-energy nexus, migration, and commercial interactions.

RUSSIA'S NEW LEADERSHIP AND NEW STRATEGIES

Russia's May 2008 presidential election brought Dmitry Medvedev to power as president. Shortly thereafter, in July 2008, a new "Russian Foreign Policy Concept," the main strategic guidance document of the Russian government in foreign affairs, was adopted. While the strategy was announced as an expression of the new Medvedev government foreign policy, in fact the document was very much a product of the Putin presidency. It immediately served as a statement of the programmatic objectives of Medvedev as president and the guiding doctrine for implementation by Putin as prime minister. The 2008 Russian Foreign Policy Concept was followed in May 2009 by the issuance of a more comprehensive doctrinal statement, the

Russian National Security Strategy. In February 2010 the security aspects of the foreign policy were stated in a more detailed fashion in a new Russian Military Doctrine.[8]

Russia's presidential election of 2012 reversed the roles of Putin and Medvedev, but essentially represented political continuity. To be sure, Putin's return to the post of the president was conducted with a well-calculated and determined surge in activity. But Putin's early postelection efforts merely represented a renewed effort to bring to closure many of the foreign policy initiatives of the previous decade. Soon after reassuming the presidency, Vladimir Putin announced that the Russian government would issue a new Russian State Strategy before the end of 2012.[9] All indications are that this new strategy document will retain the priorities and mechanisms of the past decade.

The Russian Foreign Policy Concept refers to international and technological trends and developments and shifts in the "multipolar" international system. The document emphasizes Russia's newly ensconced position as a leading partner in the international community, seeking to pursue national interests in the context of international law and the framework of an increasingly integrated and globalized international community. The document emphasizes the challenges posed by what it calls "outmoded international institutions and patterns of thinking tied to solutions for problems of the past rather than challenges of the future." The document asserts that Russia pursues an open, predictable, and pragmatic foreign policy determined by its national interests. In terms of national priorities, the document asserts that the "balanced and multivector character of Russia's foreign policy is its distinguishing feature." The document continues that the development of bilateral and multilateral cooperation with the nations of the Commonwealth of Independent States (CIS, former Soviet republics), constitutes a priority in Russia's foreign policy. "Russia forges friendly relations with all the CIS member states on the basis of equality, mutual benefit, respect and regard for the interests of each other. Strategic partnerships and alliances are developed with states that demonstrate their readiness to engage in them."[10]

Russian strategy is built upon a few fairly simple premises. First, Russia seeks to restore the country's role as a major world power. Second, Russia seeks to promote new or revised international organizations that provide Russia with a role more significant than that of the UN Security Council. Third, Russia seeks to assign a special importance to the countries of the former USSR and to pursue its interests through regional international organizations. The emphasis on regional multilateral organizations begins with the CIS, the organization that was formed during the disintegration of the USSR. At its inception the CIS was established as a "consensus organization," meaning that it works on the basis of consensus and affords every member a veto power. The past two decades have illustrated that the CIS has not always worked in directions desired by Moscow. Accordingly, Russia has put greater emphasis on alternative organizations that emerged out of willing coalitions. In security respects, that has been the Collective Security Treaty Organization (CSTO). In economic respects, it has been the Eurasian Economic Community (EvrAzEs). And in counterterrorism respects, it has been the Shanghai Cooperation Organization (SCO). These organizations have become Russia's preferred venues for asserting influence throughout the region, particularly after Georgia's Rose Revolution, Ukraine's Orange Revolution, and Kyrgyzstan's Tulip Revolution awakened anxiety over impending systemic transformation.[11]

The broader foreign policy initiatives pursued by both Medvedev and Putin are aimed at what is called an "architectural" reorganization designed simultaneously to address a host of Russia's problems, some of which are East-West oriented and some of which involve Central Asia in the East-West dimension, in particular with respect to the energy trade. Some of the issues are global in nature. Former president Dmitry Medvedev introduced the "Berlin Initiative" in a speech to more than 1,000 German businessmen in June 2008, calling for a wholesale reassessment of the European security architecture, and essentially proposing to retire NATO in favor of restructuring international financial institutions. In November 2009, Medvedev began circulating among foreign chancelleries and media outlets a draft document calling for establishing a new international security organization structured around a European security treaty.

Nongovernmental organizations and civic organizations are not an influential part of the Russian political tradition. The influence of civic society in Western countries has come to be seen in Russia as an important corollary to official government action. As revenue from government-controlled exports began to flow into Russia, the government began sponsoring foundations of their own design and under their own direction. One of the most significant organizations is *Nashi* (Ours), which grew to be a very effective youth organization, plying a mixture of nostalgic reminiscences of the past with strident nationalism. Efforts to bring under greater measure of management virtually all efforts devoted to international affairs included the universities and the establishment of new organizations such as the Valdai Club. Once Putin reassumed the presidency, he announced the establishment of a Presidential Council on International Affairs in June 2012, which brings nongovernmental groups and entities such as cultural organizations into the ambit of an official governmental institution.[12]

The use of NGOs abroad to influence international politics is also important. Russian government-sponsored NGOs began assuming active roles in the Russian borderland regions. One illustration is Aleksandr Knyazev's foundation, the Social Foundation of Aleksandr Knyazev.[13] The Knyazev

Foundation since its establishment in 2002 has been financing numerous research projects, conferences, publications, interviews, and movies on Central Asian regional political and economic affairs. The theme of Knyazev's foundation is simple: whatever is good for the United States is bad for Russia; whatever is bad for the United States is good for Russia.

RELATIONS WITH CENTRAL ASIA

The past decade has witnessed many changes in Central Asian countries that have a profound influence on Russia's foreign policy. Kazakhstan is a country marked by continuity and success. Kazakhstan's pragmatic yet principled president, Nursultan Nazarbayev, in office since April 1990, was reelected in April 2011 to another five-year term. Kazakhstan's relations with Russia have remained positive in nature. Nazarbayev recently noted that Kazakhstan and Russia are members of a strategic union, close neighbors and partners, saying, "I think that the relations between Russia and Kazakhstan are illustrative for all the entire post-Soviet territory, as an example of how close relations can be."[14] Nazarbayev's observations are particularly important because he was essentially the author of the modern idea of "Eurasian integrationism." Nazarbayev is also credited with being the first proponent of modern-day "multivectoralism" in foreign policy. Nazarbayev has spurred on Russia's diplomatic drive to re-create many of the commercial and political relationships of the former USSR in the form of customs and trade agreements under the general rubric of "integration." In early 2012 Nazarbayev pilloried the OSCE for unproductive emphasis on elections and human rights and an inability to address issues of economic security and military cooperation.[15] He called for the establishment of a new entity, the Organization on Interaction and Confidence-Building Measures in Asia, the OICA, to replace the OSCE.[16]

If Kazakhstan's close association with Russia is based on the country's successes and achievements, its neighbor Kyrgyzstan's close association with Russia is based on the country's tribulations and shortcomings. Kyrgyzstan's initial pro-Western inclinations have fallen victim to economic woes and internecine conflicts. Kyrgyzstan's president since 1990, Askar Akayev, lost power in a so-called Tulip Revolution in March 2005. A former Kyrgyz official, Kurmanbek Bakiev, took control as acting president and then was elected but lost power in April 2010 in a popular revolt. The diplomat Roza Otunbayeva served as president on an interim basis until Almazbek Atambayev took office in December 2011. Atambayev regards close cooperation with Russia as a first principle of Kyrgyzstan's foreign policy and actively seeks closer economic and political ties with Russia. But problems remain. In meeting with Dmitry Medvedev in February 2012,

President Atambayev pleaded for Russia's help in rescheduling the nearly $493 million of sovereign debt to Russia. Medvedev's response to Atambayev's request for debt rescheduling was illustrative, suggesting that Russia adopt the role of regional patron for Kyrgyzstan. Medvedev said, "It is important for Russia to coordinate with its close partners the efforts to bring the situation to a more stable state than it is today, and all the more important to prevent what might happen as a result of negative developments."[17]

Tajikistan, Turkmenistan, and Uzbekistan remain a greater distance from Russian foreign policy objectives. Tajik president Emomali Rahmon gained office in 1992, in large measure as a result of Russian military support in the country's unfolding civil war. He was first elected in 1994 and in 2006 won a third term of office along with a change in legislation changing the term to seven years and allowing him to run two terms. Tajikistan is a strategic partner with Russia and maintains important close economic and cultural ties, but trends and interests are pushing Tajikistan in other directions. Tajikistan's high priorities are to the east with China, to the west with Afghanistan and Iran, and to the south with India and Pakistan. Even the connections with Russia are interpreted in this connection. In a May 2012 meeting with Vladimir Putin, Rahmon noted that "along with you we have very good results from our regional integration process in the context of the South-Asian four-partner relationship—Russia, Tajikistan, Afghanistan, Pakistan."[18]

Turkmenistan's relationship with Russia is designed to be simple, but in reality it is complicated. Turkmenistan officially maintains a foreign policy of "positive neutrality." In reality it is a foreign policy of isolation and avoidance that is based almost entirely on the country's rich endowment of hydrocarbon (basically methane) resources. The "positive neutrality" foreign policy was the brainchild of Saparmurat Niyazov, the Communist Party leader who appointed himself president and ruled for twenty-one years until his death in December 2006. Gurbanguly Berdimuhamedov, previously Niyazov's physician, took over and was elected president in February 2007 and then again in February 2012. Berdimuhamedov's foreign policy statements typically consist of one principle—to improve conditions for the Turkmen people.[19]

Uzbekistan's relationship with Russia is yet more complex. Uzbek president Islam Karimov took office in 1990 and was popularly elected in 1991, again in 1995, again in 2000, and again in 2007 with modifications in electoral law along the way. From Russia's point of view, the most important regional organizations in Eurasia are the Collective Security Treaty Organization and the Eurasian Economic Community. Uzbekistan is a member of the Collective Security Treaty Organization but not very active, and in November 2008 it suspended participation in the Eurasian Economic

Community. Uzbekistan has defined its foreign policy in terms of its national interests, not in terms of allegiance or fealty.[20]

CENTRAL ASIA'S ENERGY
AND MINERAL RESOURCES

One of the most important factors in Central Asia's relationship has been the energy trade. This was important in the early years of independence and has grown steadily more important, and can be expected to continue along this trend into the foreseeable future. Kazakhstan, a major oil producer, has entered into the natural gas business and has become the world's largest producer of uranium ore for nuclear power generation. Kazakhstan expects to double its crude oil production in the next decade, an accomplishment, if successful, that will propel Kazakhstan into the list of one of the world's top five oil exporters.

Russia's ability to use energy resources to fuel a dynamic foreign policy is apparent. Russia is clearly an energy power, although some analysts object to the accuracy of the notion of an "energy superpower."[21] Whatever the terminology, Russia's energy leverage is great, and its relationship to energy in general is unique. A survey of features regarding reserves, production, and export illustrates this. Russia holds the first place in gas reserves, second place in coal reserves, and is within the top ten in oil reserves. In 2011 Russia was first in oil production, surpassing the world's major oil producer, Saudi Arabia. Russia was second in oil export and fifth in oil consumption. In natural gas production Russia was in first position, first position in gas export, and second in gas consumption. Russia was fifth in coal production, third in coal export, and fifth in coal consumption. Russia is in first place as a supplier of industrial uranium enrichment services with 40 to 45 percent of global capacity and with a very competitive enrichment industry (according to various estimates). There are other countries with concentrations of production, exporting, and consumption, but there is no other country that ranks at the very top of world lists in all categories. There is no other country whose foreign policy instruments are so fixed to the success of energy industries. The close linkage between Russia's energy industry and foreign policy means that Russian policy makers must always bear in mind global energy demand and scientific-technical developments. Demand is rising. "The era of cheap energy," as Vladimir Putin observed at a meeting of natural gas producers in December 2008, "is coming to an end." But this does not necessarily mean that the path to greater success is simply to increase production. Neil King Jr. has expressed the role of energy in present circumstances starkly: "The current world order has been built on cheap and abundant oil more than any other commodity but the role of oil and gas in the future can be expected to be very different."[22]

To see the importance of energy and minerals for Russian foreign policy, it is necessary to look backward a few years. In the early 1990s Russia's foreign trade was minimal. The Russian financial crisis of 1998 and default on sovereign debt forced a painful adjustment, driving down the exchange rate and making Russian exports much more competitive. The result has been distinctly beneficial for Russian exports to countries outside the former Soviet trading zone. As a result, every year since 1999 Russia has been running a substantial balance of payments surplus. The influx of foreign payments primarily for energy fuels and minerals are reflected in the mounting international reserves—the so-called gold reserves of the Russian Central Bank. As the Russian economy began to recover in export sales as a result of the currency depreciation following the 1998 financial default, foreign currency began to flow back into Russia. The cash-strapped Russian government of the 1990s turned in the first decade of this century toward strategies for spending more, not less, in domestic markets.

The Putin government's first objective was government spending in ways that restored government political control. This entailed government investment in private industry through a strategy of mixed control of key industries in energy and minerals, either through establishing "state corporations," buying out controlling interests in the private corporation, or through manipulating the private companies for political means. The idea of "national champions" refers to a state-owned enterprise or an enterprise in which the state has controlling interests either officially or unofficially. The Russian government took pivotal positions in key sectors, energy, minerals, manufacturing, R&D, transportation infrastructure, and media.

As a spin-off of "national champions," the idea of "development corporations" arose to link government-sponsored industrial and banking conglomerates with the goal of addressing chronically underdeveloped or politically unstable regions such as the South Caucasus. In the past two years numerous development corporations have been established throughout Russia (*Mezhgosudarstvennaia korporatsiia razvitiia*, or MKR). The MKR idea has been further adapted to extend to areas outside of the Russian Federation, purportedly based on the American concept of the Millennium Challenge Corporation (MCC).[23] The MKR concept involves a coordinated sector or region-specific development program led by the Foreign Development Bank (*Vneshekonombank*). Some Russian foreign policy activists have long urged a Russian government-sponsored "Central Asian Development Project" to help spur Central Asian development and at the same time bring Central Asian countries into line with Russian development objectives, thus heading off emerging threats. Russia's "drug czar," Viktor Ivanov, the head of the Russian Federal Drug Control Service, has urged the creation of a

"Russian Corporation for Cooperation in Central Asia" to serve as an instrument for counternarcotics purposes and at the same time to spur Central Asian economic development.[24]

The energy import dependency of the European countries and the growing demand for energy resources driven by rapid economic expansion in China, India, and other Asian countries caught the Central Asian countries in a new political dynamic. Newly accessible oil and gas discoveries in Azerbaijan, Kazakhstan, Turkmenistan, and Uzbekistan began coming on line, linking suppliers with distant consumers through a complicated web of pipelines traversing great distances or third-party countries.[25]

Russia's resurgent influence over energy resources as an instrument of foreign policy has stimulated fears among Europeans over dependence on Russian energy resources. In Russia, the increasingly close coordination between diplomatic goals and the commercial goals of energy producers and distributors drew toward making the two agendas virtually indistinguishable. In response, European Union (EU) negotiators began drawing attention to the importance of a negotiated foundation for assurances of energy security for European nations. By energy security, the negotiators principally had in mind assured energy deliveries at agreed-upon prices without the threat of disruption to gain political advantage.

While recent improvements in energy efficiency in power generation, transfer, and utilization have been considerable, energy supplies will continue to be scarce. This is significant for the relationship between Russia and the Central Asian energy exporters because there will be increasing competition for available energy resources in ways that may portend an increasingly important role for energy security in national policies. Changes in national policies have spurred technological development in unexpected directions. The invention of technology making the extraction of unconventional natural gas—such as shale gas and coal bed methane—commercially viable caught energy markets and national policy makers by surprise. Just a few years ago shale gas was regarded as a scientific novelty that would never result in a commercially viable product. Now shale gas is viewed as the most dynamic area of energy development in several countries. Just a few years ago energy planners spoke of the emergence of a "nuclear renaissance," which was expected to restore nuclear power to a position where it could be expected to compete with oil and coal as a main source of electricity generation. The tragedy at the Fukushima Daichi nuclear power plant in March 2011 dramatically reversed the expectation of nuclear power replacing oil and gas. Nuclear power may continue to play an important role as a base load provider in conjunction with oil, gas, and coal. But whatever its technical and commercial merits, nuclear power may continue to encounter strong public apprehension and anxiety.

AFGHANISTAN

More than three decades of armed conflict in Afghanistan have taken a heavy toll on the country's capability to interact with the outside world. At the turn of the twenty-first century Afghanistan was one of the least globally integrated countries in the world. Road, rail, and air linkages were backward, small in number, and limited to connections with only a few countries. In October 2001, the first international coalition forces entered Afghanistan to dislodge al Qaeda from political influence in Afghanistan and to bring an end to terrorist military preparations in Afghanistan. The December 2001 Bonn conference held under UN auspices sketched the basic outlines of a new national government of Afghanistan. International Security Assistance Force (ISAF) forces assumed the responsibility to establish security conditions for Afghanistan's reconstruction as international organizations, multilateral donors, and private business began the process of reconstruction. During this time the great bulk of the movement of freight for both military and economic purposes was conducted through Afghanistan's southern transportation routes passing through Pakistan.

The international community and America in particular has an enormous investment in the success of stabilization and normalization in Afghanistan. America acted to eliminate the threat of terrorists against America and its allies following of a wave of premeditated sneak attacks against the United States in September 2001, which claimed the lives of 2,996 innocent Americans and citizens of other countries. The Afghanistan government did not play a direct role in the September 11, 2001, attacks; however, it allowed the existence of havens for political extremists, harbored them after they carried out terrorist attacks, and did nothing to prevent terrorists from carrying out these and other acts in the future.

America, invoking its right to self-defense, acted to prevent these attacks in the future by dispatching expeditionary military forces to Afghanistan in order to eliminate this danger. In addition, America sought to help establish a government that could prevent attacks from occurring in the future. In December 2001 the UN Security Council resolved to establish the ISAF to address the lawless situation in Afghanistan (United Nations Security Council Resolution 1386 of December 20, 2001). On August 11, 2003, NATO took command of military operations in Afghanistan in response to a request from the Afghan government and the UN Security Council. In July 2011, President Obama designed a strategic program toward Afghanistan to stabilize during a bridge period in preparation for the transfer of military and law enforcement capacity to the Afghanistan government beginning with withdrawal of American combat troops.[26]

The NATO Lisbon summit in November 2010 resulted in a broadly based and coordinated commitment to the expansion of transport and communication relations. President Obama specifically referred to withdrawal, transition, and long-term cooperative commitment in Afghanistan, saying, "We have full agreement on our new Strategic Concept, tomorrow our NATO allies, ISAF partners and the Afghan government will work to align our approach on Afghanistan, particularly in two areas: our transition to full Afghan lead between 2011 and 2014, and the long-term partnership that we're building in Afghanistan."[27] The OSCE Astana Summit in December 2010 reflected a similar commitment. The final communiqué noted, "We underscore the need to contribute effectively, based on the capacity and national interest of each participating State, to collective international efforts to promote a stable, independent, prosperous and democratic Afghanistan."[28] The NATO Summit of May 2012 specified the campaign plan for the reduction of the use of force in Afghanistan and the transition to local authorities.

The importance of bringing an end to the protracted conflict in Afghanistan has shifted attention to the network of transit routes for civilian and military transport passing through Afghanistan's northern neighbors and for cooperation among Afghanistan's neighboring states. As ISAF troops draw down in Afghanistan, more responsibility will be in the hands of countries that were incapable or unwilling to address the challenges of insurgency in Afghanistan in the 1990s. The governor of Moscow *oblast*, Boris Gromov, and ambassador Dmitry Rogozin—neither of whom can be regarded as biased apologists of American foreign policy—have claimed, "We insist that NATO troops stay in the country [Afghanistan] until the necessary conditions are provided to establish stable local authorities capable of independently deterring radical forces and controlling the country."[29]

But Afghanistan's southern transport routes, limited in number and vulnerable to disruption by insurgents in such key narrow bottlenecks as the Khyber Pass, are inadequate to the demands of Afghanistan's reconstruction. From the earliest days of U.S. presence in Afghanistan there was an effort to sponsor and facilitate greater regional cooperation in Afghanistan's stabilization and reconstruction efforts. In 2005 the U.S. State Department reorganized its bureaus, establishing a Central Asia and South Asia department with the goal of linking the U.S. diplomatic and humanitarian assistance programs in such a way as to promote better relations between Afghanistan and its northern Central Asian neighbors. In 2008 the U.S. Department of Defense undertook an effort to shift transport routes to the northern part of Afghanistan, creating new corridors for transport through the countries of Central Asia and Eurasia. The international coalition has shifted a large proportion of its freight movement from the southern routes to the northern routes. The "northern distribution network" promised to reduce the vulnerabilities of reliance on southern routes. At the same time, the northern routes offered a number of other very important advantages.

Regional cooperation in South Asia faces real challenges. Some observers have argued that cross-cutting regional and ethnic differences are so salient that the best solution is through promoting a de facto internal partition to reduce competition.[30] Others have argued that the best solution is to promote broad extraregional cooperation. Central Asia has historically been a connecting rather than separating region, connecting East and West, for centuries maintaining transit corridors of the "silk road." The reopening of the age-old transit routes across Afghanistan, as S. Frederick Starr put it, would be "the single greatest achievement of U.S. foreign policy in the new millennium."[31] Other observers urge caution with respect to the challenges to cooperation. Ali Jalali, former minister of internal affairs in Afghanistan, pointed out the scope of the challenge, noting, "Despite the presence of international military forces in Afghanistan and the stated commitment of the United States, United Kingdom, and NATO to uphold the independence, territorial integrity, and sovereignty of Afghanistan, the country is still vulnerable to those neighbors' influence, and that has the potential to either spoil or promote Afghanistan's development.[32] Afghanistan's regional challenges lead some observers to approach future prospects with a pessimistic realism. Ashley Tellis argues that "the regional approach to Afghanistan—understood as an effort to incorporate all of Kabul's major neighbors into a cooperative enterprise led by the United States, and aimed at stabilizing Afghanistan through successful counterterrorism, reconstruction, and state-building—is unlikely to succeed, first and foremost, because the key regional stakeholders have diverging objectives within Afghanistan."[33] This leads some to raise caution that progress toward regional cooperation and stabilization could become more challenged by the recognition of the impeding withdrawal of combat forces. As David Abshire and Ryan Browne note, "Afghanistan's neighbors have begun jockeying for influence in a bid to gain the upper hand in the region's future balance of power. This struggle for regional hegemony greatly undermines . . . South and Central Asia's long-term stability."[34]

The speed and scale of the drawdown of ISAF combat forces has direct implications for Afghanistan's northern-neighboring and partner countries. The withdrawal of ISAF combat forces poses specific questions regarding Afghanistan's eastern neighbors. India, the largest contributor other than the United States to Afghanistan development assistance, maintains a disputed territory on Afghanistan's eastern border. Pakistan views India's role in Afghanistan reconstruction as a form of strategic encirclement. Pakistan regards its deep cultural connections with Afghanistan as justifying its continued influence in post-transition Afghanistan as an expression of a policy of "strategic depth." Iran, on Afghanistan's western border, considers influencing the direction of Afghanistan's stabilization as an important way to avoid returning to the period of deterioration of relations Iran experienced with Afghanistan in the 1990s. Relations with Afghanistan's neighbors to the east, west, and south are dynamic. The ability of Central Asian states to cooperate with Russia and the international community will be a test of Russian foreign policy in the region.

LOOKING FORWARD: RESURGENCE OR RESTORATION?

Surveying the economic and political terrain of Central Asia in terms of Russia's political influence in the region, it is impossible for analysts of foreign affairs to avoid a very simple question: is the rising tide of Russian influence a resurgence or does it constitute a restoration of Russian power in the region?

Both historical and future-looking considerations are relevant to the answer. Reflecting on the past, it is apparent that Russian influence expanded to the south in the latter part of the nineteenth century in a preemptive expansion for territorial control. In a struggle with the expanding Victorian Empire, Russia eventually played a role in defining the contours of modern-day Asia and the Middle East, through defining the outlines of West China, Afghanistan, and Iran. These international borders remain today. The idea of territorial expansion was romanticized in the geopolitical doctrines of the nineteenth century and the political geography of Sir Halford Mackinder, who is credited with proclaiming that the "hand that controls the heartland of Asia controls the world."[35] Russian influence in Central Asia receded in the period of World War I, but Bolshevik leaders in St. Petersburg and Moscow were unwilling to relinquish any measure of control over the territories of the Russian Empire. Soviet power brought great misfortune to Central Asia but also brought many benefits. Now the question is what benefits can Russian influence bring in the future.

Mackinder's idea of the "heartland of Asia" swells Russian postcolonial spirits today, particularly those of the Eurasianist faction of national expansionists in Russia. The Russian Eurasianists argue for a modern, broader version of Uvarov's concepts of *samoderzhavie*, *Pravoslavie*, and *Narodnost*—the nationalist troika of autocracy, Russian Orthodoxy, and populism. These ideas give sustenance to those who argue for the primacy of the Russian state but have no corresponding concepts in the culturally distinct countries of Central Asia.

Interpreting the dynamics of Russian foreign policy in Central Asia should not start with gauging the influence of Russian Eurasianism, but rather in calculating the impact of the "lessons" of the Soviet Union. As the first decade of postcommunist experience proceeded, Russia's capacity to exert decisive influence over the regions of Central Eurasia receded. Independent-minded states such as Uzbekistan challenged Russia's claim to a dominant voice in the security and economic arrangements throughout the entire Eurasian region. Russia's own internal political disputes, shrinking government revenues, the Russian financial markets crisis in 1998, weak world market commodity prices, and the rising European and U.S. influence throughout the Eurasian region hampered Russia's ability to maintain Moscow's former sphere of influence in Central Asia. Russia lost the capacity to influence the development of infrastructure, as international organizations and large multilateral lending institutions moved into the region, establishing new mechanisms and new priorities for economic development. Russian foreign-policy makers found their hands tied and their choices crimped. For these reasons, Russian grand policy toward Central Asia and the Caucasus gradually devolved into a situation in which Russia was conducting numerous parallel but not always complementary bilateral foreign policies.

That situation changed dramatically as Putin came to power in 2000. Russia's changed financial capabilities, buoyed by surging oil prices, rekindled Moscow's vision of increased influence throughout Eurasia. Russian leaders adopted a sophisticated program for gaining control over Eurasian infrastructure through cooperative projects, through targeted investment and debt equity swaps, as well as through other mechanisms. The rise of Russian influence in Central Asia was supported by many policy makers. In Ashgabat, Astana, Bishkek, Dushanbe, and Tashkent many welcomed a restoration at least in part of the influence of Moscow. The decade of the 1990s had changed the Russian approach. In the Putin period the Russians returned not as overlords but as partners. Decisions could be made not on ideological maxims but on national interests.

Central Asian national interests in some cases are consonant with Russian policy objectives, but not in all. For this reason, Russia's rising influence has been resisted in some respects, driving Central Asian leaders to seek other, counterbalancing influences or partners. Some leaders feared that the return of an expansive Russia to the Central Asian region portends aspirations of a return of larger Russian imperial ambitions. Some feared that the new Russian "liberal imperialism" so enthusiastically endorsed by Russia oligarchs was merely a strategy for great Russian chauvinism in another guise.[36] Some saw in the outline of Russia's return to Central Asia a stealth strategy to displace European or American initiatives in the form of a "Great Game" of contest over Central Asian sovereignty. Some saw Russia's rising influence as only the first stage of a vast strategy to unfold a new form of political influence over infrastructure in rail, shipping, air routes, electricity grids, oil and gas pipelines, and finance with geopolitical objectives first and commercial objectives taking only a second position. Some saw Russia's moves to harness the hydroelectric potential of Kyrgyzstan and Tajikistan as the first steps in a strategy for gaining control of power resources throughout the entire region. And some feared that Russia's historical indifference to civil rights and freedoms were likely to motivate Russian leaders' willingness to overlook human rights violations in the Central Asian countries in favor of Russia's narrow national interest.

Does Russia's renewed influence constitute resurgence or restoration? In fact, the statement of the question in this form itself distorts the situation in a way that does an injustice. As the supporters and critics of Russia's foreign policy initiatives in Central Asia illustrate, there is no return in this modern world to the Great Game competitions of the past and the dividing of the world between powerful states willing to pursue coercion to achieve their goals. Nothing of the past can be restored without distortions in this contemporary world. The greater the benefit that Russian policy can bring to the Central Asian states, the more successfully the states will be able to pursue their own national interests.

SUGGESTED READINGS

Collins, Kathleen. *Clan Politics and Regime Transition in Central Asia*. Cambridge: Cambridge University Press, 2006.

Cummings, Sally N. *Understanding Central Asia: Politics and Contested Transformations*. London and New York: Routledge, 2012.

Jones Luong, Pauline. *Institutional Changes and Political Continuity in Post-Soviet Central Asia: Power, Perceptions, and Pacts*. Cambridge: Cambridge University Press, 2002.

Khalid, Adeeb. *Islam after Communism: Religion and Politics in Central Asia*. Berkeley: University of California Press, 2007.

Laumulin, Chokan, and Murat Laumulin. *The Kazakhs*. London: Brill Publishers, 2009.

Marat, Erica. *The Tulip Revolution: Kyrgyzstan One Year After, March 15, 2005–March 24, 2006*. Washington, DC: Jamestown Foundation, 2006.

McGlinchey, Eric. *Chaos, Violence, Dynasty: Politics and Islam in Central Asia*. Pittsburgh: University of Pittsburgh Press, 2011.

Olcott, Martha Brill. *Central Asia's Second Chance*. Washington, DC: Carnegie Endowment for International Peace, 2005.

Promfred, Richard. *The Central Asian Economies Since Independence*. Princeton, N.J.: Princeton University Press, 2006.

Schatz, Edward. *Modern Clan Politics: The Power of "Blood" in Kazakhstan and Beyond*. Seattle: University of Washington Press, 2004.

NOTES

1. The author wrote this chapter while on leave from the University of New Mexico, when serving at the George C. Marshall European Center for Security Studies. The views presented in this chapter do not necessarily represent the views of the U.S. Department of Defense or the George C. Marshall Center.

2. Alexei Vlasov, "Russia, China, and the U.S. in Central Asia," Valdai Discussion Club, May 15, 2012, valdaiclub.com/asia/42740.html.

3. The East-versus-West competition is an important aspect of Bertil Nygren's arguments in his comprehensive study of Russia's interaction with the post-Soviet "near abroad." See Bertil Nygren, *The Rebuilding of Greater Russia: Putin's Foreign Policy Towards the CIS Countries* (London: Routledge, 2007).

4. Marlene Laruelle and Sebastian Peyrouse, *China As a Neighbor: Central Asian Perspectives and Strategies* (Stockholm: Institute for Security, Development and Policy, 2009), www.isdp.eu/images/stories/isdp-main-pdf/2009_laurelle-peyrouse_book_china-as-a-neighbor.pdf.

5. Igor Zevelev, "Russia's Policy toward Compatriots in the Former Soviet Union," *Russia in Global Affairs* 6, no. 1 (2008): 49–63, eng.globalaffairs.ru/number/n_10351.

6. Dmitri Trenin, "Russia's Spheres of Interest, not Influence," *The Washington Quarterly* 32, no. 4 (2009): 3–29.

7. Andrei Kazantsev, *Bol'shaia igra s neizvestnymi pravilami* (Moscow: New Eurasia Foundation, 2008), www/fundeh/org|files|publications|132|kazancev_a_a_bolshaya_igra_s_neizvestnymi_pravilam/pdf.

8. "Voennaia doktrina Rossiiskoi Federatsii," February 5, 2010, news.kremlin.ru/ref_notes/461.

9. "Sovet dlia natsii," *Rossiskaia gazeta*, May 13, 2012, www.rg.ru/2012/06/09/nacpolitika-site.html.

10. Text of the Russian Foreign Policy Concept is available in English and Russian on the Russian government website: archive.kremlin.ru/eng/text/docs/2008/07/204750.shtml.

11. As one senior U.S. State Department policy official expressed it, "The 'Revolution of Roses'" . . . had huge reverberations in the former Soviet Union. It has caused governments throughout the region to take stock of their internal political situation." A. Elizabeth Jones, assistant secretary for European and Eurasian Affairs, testimony before the Senate Foreign Relations Committee, Oversight of Foreign Assistance Programs. Washington, DC, March 2, 2004, www.state.gov/p/eur/rls/rm/30059.htm.

12. "V Rossii sozdan prezidentskii Sovet po mezhnatsional'nym otnosheniiam," *Rossiskaia gazeta*, June 7, 2012, www.rg.ru/printable/2012/06/07/sovet-anons.html.

13. Knyazev founded the organization in Kyrgyzstan but has moved activities to Kazakhstan after repeated threats upon his life, presumably from Kyrgyz nationalists (www.knyazev.org).

14. "Meeting with Kazakhstan President Nursultan Nazarbayev," May 15, 2012, news.kremlin.ru/transcripts/15351/print. Also see Andrei Vasileev, "Nursultan Nazarbayev: V nashei druzhbe net nikakikh sekretov," *Rossiskaia gazeta*, November 2, 2010, www.rg.ru/2010/11/02/nazarbaev.html.

15. See "Remarks by President Nursultan Nazarbayev at a Meeting with Heads of the Diplomatic Missions Accredited in Kazakhstan," Astana, Kazakhstan, March 2, 2012, portal.mfa.kz/portal/page/portal/mfa/en/content/news/nws2012/2012-03 02.

16. In 2011 Kazakhstan had the chairmanship-in-office of OSCE, a rotating position occupied by a county with the country's foreign minister as chairperson-in-office. Kazakhstan was the first former Soviet state to occupy the position. Kazakhstan's contribution as OSCE chairman was widely regarded as highly successful.

17. "Vstrecha s prezidentom Kirgizskoi Respubliki Almazbekom Atambayevym," February 24, 2012, news.kremlin.ru/transcripts/14587.

18. "Vstrecha s Emomali Rahmon," May 15, 2012, news.kremlin.ru/transcripts/ 15349/print.

19. See for instance, Berdimukhamedov's presidential campaign address on the Turkmen government website. "Programnoe zayavlenie kandidata na post Prezidenta," www.turkmenistan.gov.tm/?id=533.

20. Gregory Gleason, "Uzbekistan Charts a New 'Uzbek Path,'" *Security Insights*, George C. Marshall European Center for Security Studies, November 2008, www .marshallcenter.org/mcpublicweb/en/component/content/article/44-cat-pubs-secur ity-insights-/616-art-pubs-sec-insights-3.html?directory=20.

21. Peter Rutland, "Russia as an Energy Superpower," *New Political Economy* 13, no. 2 (2008), prutland.web.wesleyan.edu/Documents/Energy%20superpower.pdf.

22. Neil King Jr., "Peak Oil: A Survey of Energy Concerns," *Occasional Paper*, Center for New American Security (September 2008), 6, www.cnas.org/node/182.

23. The frequent references to the U.S. MCC are simply offered as a plausible justification of the MKR. In fact the Russian undertaking shares little in conception or practice with the MCC. In fact the MKR model of a state-owned, state-guided conglomerate is not American; it is Chinese.

24. See "FSKN predlagaet borot'sia s narkotrafikom s pomoshchiu milliardnykh investitsii," *Kommersant*, no. 41, March 7, 2012, kommersant.ru/doc/1888886. Ivanov's proposals resemble the project called the "New Middle East" proposed by the political activist Yury Krupnov. The project calls for Russian leadership in driving economic development in Central Asia in order to prevent threats from arising out of anarchy and extremism. Krupnov's proposals are available in Russian on the "Party of Development" website, www.drazvitiia.ru/index.php?modul=project& action=prev&id=76.

25. Russia and China had sometimes conflicting, sometimes complementary stakes in consuming, transporting, processing, and marketing Caspian Basic energy resources.

26. Barack Obama, "Remarks by the President in Address to the Nation on the Way Forward in Afghanistan and Pakistan," Eisenhower Hall Theatre, United States Military Academy at West Point, West Point, New York, December 1, 2009, www .whitehouse.gov/the-press-office/remarks-president-address-nation-way-forward afghanistan-and-pakistan.

27. Barack Obama, "Remarks by the President on the NATO Summit and the New START Treaty," Lisbon, November 20, 2010, www.whitehouse.gov/the-press office/2010/11/19/remarks-president-nato-summit-and-new-start-treaty.

28. "Astana Commemorative Declaration: Toward A Security Community," December 2, 2010, www.osce.org/mc/73962.

29. Boris Gromov and Dmitry Rogozin, "Russian Advice on Afghanistan," *The New York Times*, January 12, 2010. Gromov was the former highest ranking Soviet military officer in Afghanistan in February 1989 and Rogozin is presently the Russian ambassador to NATO.

30. Robert D. Blackwill, "Plan B in Afghanistan: Why a De Facto Partition Is the Least Bad Option," *Foreign Affairs* 90, no. 1 (2011): 42–50. Also see Paul D. Miller, "Finish the Job: How the War in Afghanistan Can be Won," *Foreign Affairs* 90, no. 1 (2011): 51–64.

31. S. Frederick Starr, "Afghanistan Beyond the Fog of Nation Building: Giving Economic Strategy a Chance," *Silk Road Paper*, Caucasus and Central Asia Institute (January 2011), 13, http://www.silkroadstudies.org/new/docs/silkroadpapers/1101 Afghanistan-Starr.pdf.

32. Ali A. Jalali, "The Future of Afghanistan," *Parameters* 36, no. 1 (2006): 4–19, at 17.

33. Ashley J. Tellis, "Implementing a Regional Approach to Afghanistan: Multiple Alternatives, Modest Possibilities," in *Is a Regional Strategy Viable in Afghanistan* (Washington, DC: Carnegie Foundation, 2010), 123. www.carnegieendowment .org/publications/index.cfm?fa = view&id = 40760

34. David M. Abshire and Ryan Browne, "The Missing Endgame for Afghanistan: A Sustainable Post-Bin Laden Strategy," *The Washington Quarterly* 34, no. 4 (2011): 59–72, at 61.

35. Halford J. Mackinder, "The Geographical Pivot of History," *The Geographical Journal* 23 (1904): 421–37.

36. Anatoly Chubais, "We Are Proposing a Few Changes," *Izvestiia*, October 8, 2004.

13

Relations with the European Union

Jeffrey Mankoff

Russia's relationship with the European Union (EU) is deeply paradoxical. The EU is simultaneously Russia's most important economic partner and a multilateral, sovereignty-questioning, value-based organization that fits uncomfortably with Moscow's state-centric view of international relations. Though Russia is deeply tied by history and culture to Europe, and all three of its post-Soviet presidents (Boris Yeltsin, Vladimir Putin, and Dmitry Medvedev) have described Russia as part of Europe, the organizing principles of Russian politics and foreign policy are far removed from those at the heart of the EU. The tension between Russia's European history and identity on the one hand, and its reluctance to embrace the EU's normative foundations on the other, is at the heart of the foreign policy challenges facing both Moscow and Brussels in their mutual interactions.

This intra-European divide has played out in debates over EU outreach to the states in Russia and Europe's shared "neighborhood"—the post-Soviet countries of the Caucasus (Armenia, Azerbaijan, Georgia) and, especially, Eastern Europe (Belarus, Moldova, Ukraine). For Poland and the other East European EU members, promoting political and economic reform in Belarus, Moldova, and Ukraine is critical to stabilizing the EU's eastern borders and extending the benefits of integration to neighboring countries.[1] Moreover, by encouraging non-EU members in the east to tackle corruption, strengthen civil society, and promote democratic development, Warsaw and its partners hope to move these states gradually out of Russia's orbit. Russia, however, continues to regard its onetime dependencies as an area where it has special interests, and resents what it views as meddling in such a strategically sensitive area.

Needless to say, relations between Russia and the EU have been profoundly shaped in recent years by the deep economic and institutional crisis affecting all of Europe, including Russia itself. Within the EU, the crisis
precipitated a fundamental debate about the nature of European integration, while forcing governments and EU institutions to focus relentlessly on
limiting the consequences of the worst economic downturn since the
1930s. Under these circumstances, Brussels has had to pursue a more
restrained set of ambitions with regard to both Russia and its neighbors
than had been the case before 2008. While the crisis hit Russia too, Russia's
economy returned to growth much faster than those of its European neighbors. Russia's recovery, coupled with the continued dynamism of developing economies in Asia, helped strengthen a perception, already widespread
in Russia, that the global center of gravity is shifting away from Europe,
even though Russia's economy remains closely tied to Europe and would
be negatively affected by a renewed European crisis.[2]

The crisis and the perception of Europe's growing irrelevance damaged
Europe's soft power, including its attraction as a model for Russia's future
development and its ability to use economic leverage to influence Russian
behavior. Yet the resulting focus on economic issues has underlined the
interdependence between Russia and the EU, creating incentives on both
sides for cooperation in pursuit of a return to growth. It has also sidelined
some of the more contentious areas in EU-Russian relations, such as the
emergence of an independent EU defense identity and disputes over gas
pipelines. Within the EU, the crisis also reinforced the disparity between
Europe's core and periphery, enhancing further the influence of the EU's
bigger and more developed states—above all, Germany, which continues
to enjoy a kind of privileged partnership with Russia. In this way, the crisis
has helped ameliorate tension between Russia and the EU, as the attention
of both has increasingly focused elsewhere. Given the depths to which relations plunged in 2007–2008, that may be not only a positive development
but also an indication that the relationship remains in flux, as both Russia
and the EU confront fundamental questions about their identities and roles
in the world. The purpose of this chapter is to survey relations between Russia and the EU, focusing on the duality in the relationship over regional
identity and economic relations.

RUSSIA'S PLACE IN EUROPE

The EU's very existence challenges some of the fundamental assumptions
underpinning official Russia's view of the world—namely, that states reign
supreme and that cold calculations of national interest trump the abstract
values driving European integration. The EU's emphasis on liberal values

has often put it at odds with Russia, whose foreign policy has always been driven much more explicitly by the pursuit of narrowly defined interests and the personal profit of its elites.[3] The EU has pursued varying degrees of integration toward both Russia and its neighbors to promote democratic transition in Russia itself, even as many EU member states maintain a more *realpolitik* approach to Moscow.

For much of the early post-Soviet period, engagement between Russia and the EU was limited. Boris Yeltsin's administration paid more attention to cultivating a special relationship with the United States, even as Europe focused much of its effort on getting its own house in order after the formal establishment of the EU in 1993. Brussels's recognition that expansion into the old Eastern Bloc would make Russia a close neighbor laid the foundation for the first attempt at formally defining the relationship between Russia and the EU. The result was the 1994 Partnership and Cooperation Agreement (PCA), which granted Russia most-favored nation status with the EU and created an institutional framework for interactions between Russian officials and their European counterparts.[4] The highly structured dialogue that resulted ensured regular interactions, keeping channels of communication open even during moments of tension and creating a habit of consultation that over time helped to stabilize the relationship.

Even though the PCA was signed in June 1994, it was not ratified until 1997. The delay was largely due to European unease over the war in Chechnya, where Russian troops were acting with great brutality. The basic aim of the PCA was to use the prospect of improved access to European markets as an inducement for the post-Soviet countries to assimilate European values relating to human rights, democracy, and respect for international law— principles that Russia appeared to be blatantly violating in Chechnya.[5] Similar agreements were signed with a range of post-Soviet countries on the assumption that with the proper mix of incentives, the EU could bring about their gradual adoption of European values. Even if Russia was never seriously considered for potential EU membership, Brussels pursued the PCA and similar steps to promote convergence around EU standards out of a belief that Russia would eventually follow the path toward political and economic liberalization being trod by Poland and other postcommunist states of Eastern Europe.[6]

In practice, Russia's postcommunist transition did not follow the smooth path many Europeans foresaw during the institution-building boom of the early 1990s. Partially in consequence, the PCA and related EU initiatives have tended to take a back seat to calculations of political and economic interest in day-to-day interactions, which has favored the EU's member states over the more value-driven EU apparatus in Brussels.[7] The institutionalization of ties through agreements such as the PCA have nevertheless provided a forum for continuing engagement at multiple levels, even if the resolution of specific problems continues to depend on decisions by national political leaders.

The spat over Chechnya also provided one of the first indications that, even in its post-Soviet guise, Russia did not share many of the fundamental values driving the process of European integration. This values gap would be a recurring theme, one that was in many ways more problematic in the context of EU-Russian relations than in Moscow's relationship with the United States, which like Russia remains jealous of its sovereignty and more comfortable with the use of large-scale military force. Since the EU is as much a moral community as a geopolitical entity, Russia's rejection of the liberal principles underlying European integration remains a barrier to further integration.

Yet the establishment of a superstructure for EU-Russian relations under the auspices of the PCA, coupled with the EU's relative weakness as an international security actor in the 1990s, allowed Moscow to see the EU as a generally benign force, in contrast to the hostility with which it continued to view NATO. While each round of NATO expansion provoked a crisis in relations, Moscow was comparatively sanguine about EU expansion, which in any event lagged several years behind NATO expansion. Russian officials went out of their way to emphasize that Moscow did not object to new states joining the EU. Indeed, as eight former communist states in Eastern European states prepared to join the EU in March 2004, Russian foreign minister Sergei Lavrov noted that the only difficulties expansion would pose for Russia had to do with the extension of EU regulations to new members and the potential impact on trade with Russia.[8]

In practice, the EU's new members helped push Brussels into taking a more assertive stance toward Russia, for instance on renewal of the expiring PCA (which Poland and the Baltics vetoed until Moscow lifted politically motivated boycotts) and on relations with Georgia, steps that exacerbated intra-EU tensions between old and new members. And if Russia did not initially raise much objection to "widening" of the EU, it was generally more concerned by the parallel process of "deepening," particularly insofar as it entailed the development of the EU into an autonomous security player. Attempts to create an integrated European Defense and Security Policy (EDSP) and Common Foreign Policy (CFP) forced Moscow to confront the possible emergence of a united, powerful Europe with close links to Washington on its borders.[9]

With Russia's turn back toward authoritarianism following Vladimir Putin's ascension to the presidency in 2000, the gap between Russian and EU political practice continued to widen. European officials and multilateral institutions frequently condemned Russia's seeming retreat from democratic liberalism and its still spotty record on human rights. The Council of Europe has been especially outspoken on these issues, criticizing Moscow for the continued detention of former Yukos oil company chairman Mikhail Khodorkovsky, the killing of Russian journalists such as Anna Politkovskaia, and ongoing human rights abuses in the North Caucasus.[10] In 2011–2012, the European Commission, the Council of Europe, and several national governments condemned Russia's failure to hold free and fair elections for the Duma and the presidency, along with the Kremlin's occasionally heavy-handed response to the protests that broke out after the results were announced.[11] Yet both Medvedev and Putin have been firm in emphasizing Russia's sovereign right to organize its internal affairs as it sees fit—rejecting the implication that European values enjoy universal applicability.[12] This gap between the EU's promotion of what it views as universal rights and Russia's invocation of sovereignty as an absolute principle remain among the most significant barriers to integration as a model for structuring relations between Russia and the EU.

THE RUSSO-EUROPEAN ECONOMIC PARTNERSHIP

A deep chasm in values and institutions overlays increasingly extensive economic ties between Russia and Europe. Despite diverging views of politics and foreign policy, Russia and the EU are bound together in a number of ways, notably through an interdependent economic relationship. Taken as a whole, the EU is by far Russia's most important economic partner, both as a source of investment capital and as a trade partner. The EU as a whole is Russia's largest trading partner, accounting for 47 percent of Russian foreign trade turnover in 2010.[13] Individual EU countries, including Germany and the Netherlands, are themselves among Russia's leading trade partners and sources of foreign investment as well. Russia is the third largest trading partner for the EU as a whole—and an increasingly important market for European manufacturers given the EU's own economic malaise.[14] These economic ties provide ballast in relations with countries such as Germany and Italy, which is lacking particularly in Russian-U.S. relations. The EU is also an important market for other Russian commodities, including metals, timber, as well as petrochemicals and textiles.[15] Europe is also a major source of the technology and expertise necessary to modernize Russia's economy. For this reason, former president Medvedev targeted the EU and several of its member states as partners in "modernization alliances" designed to leverage increased Russian political cooperation to gain access to technology Russia lacks.[16] A broader objective was to deepen mutual economic dependence between Russia and the EU, creating a community of interests within both the political elite and the business community.[17] With the return of Vladimir Putin to the Kremlin, Moscow may have dropped the rhetoric of modernization alliances, but the centrality of European investment and technology for the future of the Russian economy remains unchanged.

The EU's large, diversified economy relies heavily—but unevenly—on Russian energy. Energy and mineral fuels are Russia's major export to Europe (comprising almost 80 percent of total exports to the EU). Postcommunist states in Central and Eastern Europe in particular rely on Russia as a supplier of oil and gas. This dependence has been the source of repeated problems, as deliveries from Russia have been curtailed on multiple occasions as a result of tensions between Russia and transit states Ukraine and Belarus, or, during the winter of 2011–2012, because of inadequate supplies. Yet Moscow has fiercely resisted Europe's attempts to diversify its supplies through the construction of new oil and gas pipelines that bypass Russia, while Brussels has been at best ambivalent about Russian attempts to build its own offshore pipelines that bypass Ukraine and Belarus (Nord Stream and South Stream).

Russia's proposed pipeline projects have exacerbated tensions within the EU, especially between countries, such as Germany and Italy, that would directly benefit from the new pipelines, and those, such as Poland and the Baltic states, that fear being further marginalized. Indeed, tensions between the large Western European states that have long since ceased viewing Russia as a direct threat to their security, and many of the EU's newer Eastern members with a more recent history of Russian invasion and occupation, have frequently impeded Brussels's ability to present a united front in its dealings with Moscow. Germany, Italy, and France in particular have long sought to promote mutually beneficial economic cooperation with Russia, downplaying the idea that Russia continues to represent a real threat to European security, to the frequent consternation of their postcommunist neighbors in Eastern Europe.

In the long run, though, the discovery of new energy supplies and Russia's own cautious steps to modernize its economy all hold the long-term potential to lessen the importance of energy as a source of EU-Russian discord. The economic crisis accelerated this process by reducing European gas demand, which, coupled with the discovery of significant shale gas resources in both Europe and North America and the EU's own efforts at market liberalization (strongly opposed by Moscow), have weakened Russian market power. The development of unconventional energy, including shale gas from fields in Central Europe, and facilities for importing liquefied natural gas (LNG), of which the United States may become a major exporter, all hold the potential of further undermining Gazprom's hold on the European market and fundamentally altering the current interdependent economic relationship in Europe's favor.

For all the attention given to tensions in the energy relationship, Russia continues seeking greater access to European markets through the creation of a free-trade zone and visa-free travel. European wariness about these initiatives is partially the result of concern about the practical consequences, but also of concern about Russia's intentions and ability to contribute to the broader European project of integration based on shared values. Meanwhile, Russia's accession to the World Trade Organization (WTO) was long delayed by disputes over issues such as market access for European goods, levels of food imports and sanitary standards, and protection of intellectual property rights. Even after the EU agreed to a protocol establishing conditions for Russia's WTO accession, trade disputes continued to rankle. While Russia moved slowly to implement its commitments, the EU struggled to present a common front to Moscow in the face of its own members' diverging priorities.[18]

EU outreach to the post-Soviet countries became more difficult in a Union increasingly focused on resolving its own internal problems, above all ensuring the survival of the euro.[19] While Europe's diminished foreign policy ambitions may have indirectly improved relations with Russia, Moscow too has reason to fear a protracted crisis in Europe. Given the importance of Europe as a market for Russian exports, a sustained reduction in demand, particularly for energy, would have serious consequences for the Russian economy. The impact on Russia would be exacerbated by a renewed European banking crisis, much less a collapse of the euro. A study by Sberbank (Russia's largest state-owned bank) estimated that a full-scale Greek default and exit from the euro in 2012 would shift Russian GDP growth from positive 3.8 percent to negative 2.1 percent in 2013, drive up inflation to almost 7 percent, and decimate Russia's own banking sector, which is heavily exposed to the EU.[20]

SPECIAL RELATIONSHIPS

The more introspective Europe growing out of the 2008–2009 economic crisis also halted (at least for a time) the EU's long-standing push to take on a larger international security role, creating an opportunity for Russia to reinvigorate its bilateral partnerships with key allies Italy, France, and Germany, joined by Poland, whose rapprochement with Russia has been among the most striking and most significant developments of recent years. Given its own state-centric worldview and the fact that the EU itself has been in continuous flux since its creation in 1993, Russia has frequently preferred dealing directly with individual European states to working through Brussels. While critics have portrayed this approach as a form of divide-and-rule, it has allowed particular European states to establish themselves as mediators between Russia and the EU writ large, and to enjoy the fruits of close bilateral relations with Moscow. With the EU's expansion to the East, Moscow's special relationships with Paris, Rome, and—especially—Berlin have become a source of intra-EU tension, as many newer (and usually smaller) members fear their interests being sacrificed by the big Western European powers. Ironically though, Germany's status as a trusted interlocutor in Moscow has at times made it a more effective voice for the interests of its Eastern neighbors than is Brussels.

The special relationship between Russia and the Federal Republic has a long history, dating back to the *Ostpolitik* strategy of Chancellor Willy Brandt in the 1970s. When the Cold War ended, German officials and companies were well placed to take advantage of the opportunities emerging in the new Russia. Former German chancellor Helmut Kohl took the lead in seeking Russia's integration with European structures, even while downplaying Germany's relations with its postcommunist neighbors in Eastern Europe. Even after German unification and the decision to anchor the united Germany in NATO, Moscow did not see Berlin as a potential political-military threat in the same way it viewed nuclear-armed Britain and France. Germany's pacifist constitution and forceful rejection of nuclear weapons made it unlikely to emerge as a geopolitical rival, no matter how strong its economy became in the aftermath of unification.[21]

As the EU began preparing to admit several new members from the old Eastern Bloc, Germany (and France) took the lead in seeking a special relationship with Russia to mitigate the consequences of expansion. The goal was to enlist Russia as a partner in efforts to stabilize Europe's still unsettled Eastern reaches.[22] This trilateral French-German-Russian relationship remains an important driver of European policy, even as Moscow's relations with Poland and other Eastern European states have improved in recent years.

Alongside a host of bilateral meetings with European heads of state, Russia's president continues to meet his French and German counterparts at an annual trilateral gathering that sets much of the agenda for Russia's broader security relationship with Europe. During the June 2010 trilateral summit in the German city of Meseberg, the three leaders agreed to a German proposal to focus on the long-festering conflict between the government of Moldova and its separatist region of Transnistria. German chancellor Angela Merkel sought to use Transnistria as a test case for giving Russia a more substantive role in European security, long one of Moscow's key demands.[23] Following an agreement to resume the formal "5 + 2" talks on Transnistria, Merkel and French president Nicolas Sarkozy agreed to explore Russian proposals for enhanced security cooperation at the 2011 trilateral meeting in Deauville, France—including Russia's potential participation in the EU's own political and security decision-making process.[24]

Given the baleful consequences of Russo-German collaboration in the twentieth century, from the Treaty of Rapallo to the Molotov-Ribbentrop pact, Russia's neighbors at times still voice suspicion about the development of closer relations between Berlin and Moscow. The controversy surrounding the recently completed Nord Stream gas pipeline between Russia and Germany, which bypasses Poland and other current transit states (and whose shareholder consortium is headed by former German chancellor Gerhard Schröder), is perhaps the most salient example, but is symptomatic of a broader concern shared in particular by many of the EU's newer Eastern members, who have frequently voiced their displeasure over Germany's modern-day *Ostpolitik*.[25] Of course, many German officials and journalists have also criticized Berlin's special relationship with Moscow, which seemingly runs counter to modern Germany's strongly antiauthoritarian political culture. With Putin's return to the Kremlin in 2012, even Merkel was reported questioning the value of partnership with a regime that openly scorned Western values and whose legitimacy appeared rapidly waning in the face of mounting protests.[26]

While Germany has been Russia's most important partner within the EU, other West European states have also forged strong bilateral relationships with Moscow that have at times been the source of tension with their more Russophobic neighbors in Eastern Europe, and with the European Commission in Brussels. Like Germany, Italy, under Silvio Berlusconi, sought to position itself as something of a mediator between Russia and Europe, while in the process developing mutually beneficial economic ties. This partnership received a boost from the peculiar personal relationship that developed between Putin and Berlusconi, but it also reflects the mutual interests of Russian and Italian business in developing closer cooperation, and appears set to endure despite Berlusconi's October 2011 resignation. Just as Germany is the European linchpin for the Nord Stream pipeline, Italy plays a similar role vis-à-vis South Stream, which is planned to run across the Black Sea and the Balkans to Central Europe via Italy (Italian energy company Eni is a major investor, alongside Gazprom). Italy was also the European country most supportive of Russia during the war with Georgia. Rome opposed Brussels's decision to suspend the EU-Russia PCA over the war, and Berlusconi even declared in October 2008 that he favored Russia's joining the EU.[27] Italy and Russia have also signed a series of agreements on defense cooperation, including contracts for Russia to purchase Italian armored vehicles, along with an agreement to conduct joint military and naval exercises in 2011.[28]

France's relationship with Russia has been more nuanced than the personality-driven partnership between Rome and Moscow, but Paris too has often pursued an independent policy toward Russia that frustrated many of its European allies. Former president Jacques Chirac's government shared Russian concerns about the consequences of the U.S.-dominated world order and joined with Germany and Russia in 2003 to spearhead opposition to the U.S. invasion of Iraq.[29] After replacing Chirac in 2006, Sarkozy maintained Paris's close ties with Moscow. Sarkozy touted France's own modernization partnership with Russia, which included participation by French companies in the controversial Nord Stream and South Stream pipeline projects, and a partnership between Renault and troubled Russian automaker AvtoVAZ.[30]

Sarkozy's France also approved the sale of two French Mistral-class amphibious assault ships to the Russian navy (with two more to be constructed at Russian shipyards), over vociferous protests at home, elsewhere in Europe, and in the United States—protests that intensified following an offhand comment by the chief of the Russian naval staff that Moscow's 2008 war with Georgia would have been over in forty minutes if Russia had had the Mistrals in its arsenal at that point.[31] Of course, some European countries eager to sign their own arms deal with Moscow, such as Spain and the Netherlands, welcomed the deal for the precedent it set.[32] Sarkozy meanwhile dismissed the concerns of Georgia and others, arguing that "if we expect Russia to behave like a partner . . . we should treat it like a partner."[33]

If Germany (and France and Italy to a lesser degree) has served as Russia's bridge to the EU, Poland and the Baltic states have been the most wary of European attempts to engage and integrate Russia. A long history of Soviet (and in many cases, tsarist) occupation inclined the newly sovereign states of Eastern Europe to seek rapid integration with Euro-Atlantic structures following the 1989 revolutions to guard from any renewed danger from the East. Many of them continued to regard Russia as a continued threat to their independence, and urged the EU and NATO to play a more active role in defending them from this perceived threat. They were instrumental in the development of new policy instruments to engage postcommunist states that remained outside the EU and NATO, including the Yugoslav successor states in the Western Balkans and Russia's European post-Soviet neighbors (Belarus, Ukraine, and Moldova). They also frequently pushed Brussels into taking a harder line with Moscow, for instance, over the 2008 war between Russia and Georgia.

While the newer EU members have been frequent critics of the special relationships with Moscow pursued by Paris, Rome, and Berlin, these special partnerships have not been all bad for the Eastern Europeans. Germany's demand that Russia drop its politically motivated boycott of Polish meat imports (in place from 2005–2007) as a condition of pursuing a replacement for the expiring PCA convinced Moscow that its attempts to split Warsaw from its EU allies had failed and contributed to the Kremlin's decision to pursue a wide-ranging reconciliation with Poland. This rapprochement took on additional momentum in the aftermath of the April 2010 plane crash near Smolensk that killed Polish president Lech Kaczyński and several other members of the Polish political-military elite, but it started earlier when Moscow realized that even the Germans would prioritize intra-EU solidarity over their bilateral partnership with Russia. Similarly, it was Germany's ability to act as a go-between that laid the foundation for the establishment of a new trilateral Polish-German-Russian security forum (paralleling the French-German-Russian summits).[34] In the case of the Baltic states, NATO's decision to put in place a contingency plan for defending them from a potential Russian invasion helped give substance to the Alliance's commitment to their defense, and signaled to Moscow that its aggressive tactics, such as holding military exercises near the Lithuanian border and threatening to target missiles, were counterproductive.[35]

RUSSIA, THE EU, AND THE SHARED NEIGHBORHOOD

The ability of the EU to confer prosperity and security on its members has made integration an appealing prospect for nonmembers, including Russia's post-Soviet neighbors. While Brussels argues that it is in Russia's interest to have secure and prosperous neighbors, Moscow is ambivalent, fearing that Brussels's gravitational pull represents a threat to Russian influence in countries like Ukraine and Belarus, even if Russia does not see the EU as such a threat.[36] The ten eastern EU members (the original eight would be joined by Bulgaria and Romania in 2007) have in particular pushed Brussels to pay more attention to the still unstable area between the EU's new eastern borders and Russia. Since Moscow considers the post-Soviet region to be of primary importance for its own security interests, the EU has struggled to match Russia's degree of engagement in countries such as Belarus and Ukraine.[37] To Poland and other Eastern European EU members, this lack of attention to the "neighborhood" has both weakened Brussels's hand in dealing with Moscow and undermined European security by allowing corruption and misgovernance to flourish just beyond EU borders.

Of course, the EU has never been indifferent to developments on its borders. It has often struggled, however, to engage the region in a coherent way, given the competing interests of member states and a lack of clarity regarding ultimate goals. For much of the post–Maastricht Treaty era, Brussels crafted agreements with neighboring states on a bilateral basis, relying on PCA. These accords were designed as an *à la carte* menu of steps to promote cooperation between the EU and former Eastern Bloc states. For some, the PCAs were portrayed as a stepping-stone to full EU membership, whereas for others, they were more limited agreements designed to address specific problems but lacking the force of law.

The European Neighborhood Policy (ENP), which Brussels elaborated in 2003, was the first attempt at developing a unified strategy for the countries East (and South) of the EU. Designed to standardize the existing patchwork of PCAs, the ENP highlighted Russia's anomalous position relative to the institutional Europe of the EU. While the association agreements signed under the auspices of the ENP would be tailored to the interests of each partner state, they were all governed by the principle of encouraging convergence on the basis of the EU's *acquis communautaire* (i.e., the basic statutes defining the obligations of EU membership).[38] Brussels extended the offer of ENP membership to Moscow as well. The Russians categorically refused, however, believing that Russia's large size and special role in Europe would not allow it to accept a partnership that would put it on par with its smaller neighbors. Moreover, the ENP was explicitly designed to bring partner states' legislation—and values—into harmony with the EU. Since Russia was not an aspiring EU member, it rejected the argument that it should adjust its legislation in line with the *acquis*, particularly given that Moscow had no role in writing them. Instead of being rolled into the ENP, Russia instead agreed with the EU on the creation of the so-called Four Common Spaces, covering economics, freedom/security/justice, external security, and education/culture. The Common Spaces laid the foundation for convergence of Russian and EU practices in the four covered fields, but without the implication that Russia was being forced to adopt EU standards as the price of cooperation.[39]

Meanwhile, Brussels was coming to the conclusion that the ENP was insufficient as a mechanism for integrating its Eastern neighbors into a Europe that was increasingly viewed as coterminous with a zone of peace and prosperity. During France's 2008 European Council presidency, Paris had pushed for the adoption of a targeted strategy for engaging the countries of the Mediterranean and North Africa, many of which were former French colonies. As several of these states were already ENP members, the establishment of what would become the EU's so-called Mediterranean Union seemed to imply that Brussels would henceforth be prioritizing the Southern vector of its foreign policy over the Eastern (the EU already had a parallel Northern Dimension covering relations with Norway, Iceland, and—on the basis of the Common Spaces—Russia). Germany, Poland, and other non-Mediterranean states objected to the French proposal for a special Mediterranean club, especially since Sarkozy's original plan envisioned that only states along the Mediterranean coast would be included, an arrangement that seemed to violate the principle of EU solidarity.

Largely to balance this perceived tilt toward the South, Poland and others proposed a similar program for engaging the EU's Eastern neighbors. The result was the Eastern Partnership (EaP), a Polish-Swedish initiative unveiled in May 2008 focusing on the six post-Soviet states around Russia's borders: Belarus, Ukraine, Moldova, Azerbaijan, Armenia, and Georgia. The EaP sought to channel EU funds into these six countries to promote economic and institutional development, improve border management, and enhance EU energy security. Among the proposed steps on energy security was the formation of the so-called Southern Corridor to bring gas from the Caspian region to Europe through new pipelines bypassing Russia (the largest of which, Nabucco, was designed to run from Turkey through Southeastern Europe to Austria), thereby reducing Gazprom's hold over European economies.[40]

Russia, though, condemned the EaP as an attempt by the EU to carve out a new sphere of influence and weaken Russian access to European energy markets.[41] This skepticism was not entirely off the mark. The Russo-Georgian war had increasingly led EU members to overlook their concerns about the poor state of political freedom and human rights in several of the EaP states out of a growing belief that Moscow had rejected the post-1991 territorial status quo, and that consequently Moscow and the West were again engaged in a contest for influence across the whole post-Soviet region.[42]

European leaders nevertheless argued that Moscow was overreacting, and that the EaP would actually benefit Russia by stabilizing conditions along its own borders—an argument that overlooked Russia's primary interest in the region as a zone of political influence and a strategic glacis against the West. The EaP (or any successful EU attempt to bring about political change in Russia's post-Soviet neighbors) would moreover break the link between corrupt elites in Russia and other post-Soviet states, undermining the very notion of the "post-Soviet space" as a coherent geographical and political expression. Before long, though, the EaP became a victim of the EU's own internal difficulties and the outbreak of civil unrest in many of the Mediterranean Union countries, which increasingly monopolized EU attention and resources.[43] With Brussels pulling back its rhetorical and financial commitments to the EaP, by 2011 Russian officials even started hinting at Moscow's interest in participating in some EaP projects, a sure sign that Moscow no longer took the EaP seriously.[44]

Yet Belarus, Moldova, and Ukraine in particular remain a significant source of tension between Brussels and Moscow. Despite the EaP's waning ambitions, Brussels continues to view the promotion of political and economic reform in the eastern neighborhood as a foreign policy priority. Russia still remains wary of what it sees as attempts to reorient these states away from Moscow, which Russian leaders fear will undermine Russia's geopolitical influence and undermine its quest for strategic depth along its borders.

Ukraine, by far the largest and most consequential of the eastern neighborhood states, has been a source of particular tension. Sharply divided between a Ukrainian-speaking West, much of which was under Austro-Hungarian or Polish rule until World War II, and a Russian-speaking East and South that was long part of the Russian Empire, Ukraine continues to live up to its name (the word *Ukraina* means "borderland"). Within the Ukrainian elite, relations with Russia and the EU continue to serve as a proxy in power struggles between competing regional factions. Ukraine's internal divisions have made it difficult for Kyiv to simultaneously pursue close relations with both Moscow and Brussels. In the aftermath of the 2004 Orange Revolution, Ukraine's new leaders sought a rapid path to Euro-Atlantic integration, in part to secure their hold on power against a Russian-backed opposition. Yet even since the election of the easterner Viktor Yanukovych in 2010, Kyiv continues to view deeper economic integration with the EU as the key to the country's future development and prosperity, as well as a hedge against overweening Russian influence.

Following Ukraine's 2008 accession to the WTO, Brussels proposed signing a new Association Agreement to replace the 1993 EU-Ukraine PCA. An important component of the new agreement would be the establishment of a deep and comprehensive free trade area (DCFTA) that would cover a whole range of trade-related issues, both at and beyond the border.[45] The proposed DCFTA was the most far-reaching trade agreement pursued in the post-Soviet region, aiming not just at eliminating tariffs, but at harmonizing Ukraine's domestic regulations with EU standards in areas such as intellectual property protection, customs regulations, and government procurement.[46]

Given Russian sensitivities about the Euro-Atlantic ambitions of Ukraine's leadership, Moscow reacted with alarm to the prospect of such far-reaching economic integration, even when President Viktor Yushchenko was replaced by the more pro-Russian Viktor Yanukovych in February 2010. Russia feared that the proposed trade agreement would not only reorient Ukraine's economy increasingly toward Europe and away from Russia, but would facilitate Ukraine's break from the post-Soviet institutional setup that facilitated Russia's continued influence. Moscow instead pressured Kyiv into joining the Customs Union it was in the process of establishing with Belarus and Kazakhstan—and which nearly derailed Russia's own WTO accession in 2009.

Despite Russian pressure, Yanukovych continued calling for completion of the Association Agreement talks with the EU and establishment of the DCFTA, which he argued would strengthen Ukraine's economy and lay the foundation for eventual membership in the EU itself.[47] Though negotiations between Kyiv and Brussels were completed in October 2011, the new Association Agreement was soon put on hold following the conviction and jailing of former prime minister Yulia Tymoshenko after what the Europeans argued was a politically motivated trial. The Yanukovych government nevertheless maintained its rhetorical commitment to deeper integration with the EU, even as it moved further away from EU standards for governance, democracy, and human rights.[48]

In March 2009, the EU signed an agreement to modernize the Ukrainian gas transportation infrastructure, to reduce the waste and corruption that left Kyiv vulnerable to Russian pressure over payment arrears and had contributed to the 2006 and 2009 gas crises in Europe. Apart from commercial considerations, Brussels feared that the Ukrainians would transfer control of the country's pipeline network to Moscow to settle the outstanding debts that had precipitated the gas crises in the first place (following years of pressure, Moscow reached just such a deal with Belarus in November 2011).[49] Brussels worried that Russian control of the Ukrainian pipelines, coupled with the construction of Nord Stream and South Stream, would strengthen Gazprom's monopoly over gas supplies, along with Moscow's political influence in both Kyiv and Brussels itself. Russia argued that any attempt to bring in foreign assistance to modernize the pipeline network would threaten the interests of Gazprom and make further disruptions more likely. Kyiv meanwhile suggested a tripartite consortium that would keep the network in Ukrainian hands while tamping down pressure from Russia.[50]

The drama over Ukraine's pipeline network and Association Agreement highlight some of the dilemmas facing European policy makers over their outreach to the countries between the EU and Russia. While the EU does not want this region to turn into a geopolitical and legal gray zone, its attempts to use the tools of integration to stabilize the region and draw it closer to Europe continue meeting resistance from Moscow, which sees its influence in the region as the foundation for Russia's existence as a major global power and recognizes the importance of trade and investment for Russia's own economy. At the same time, states like Ukraine suffer from many of the same political and institutional shortcomings as Russia itself. The EU consequently faces a chicken-and-egg dilemma: integration is designed as a tool to promote reform, but (as with Russia itself), the EU is wary of pursuing even limited integration with countries that have not fully embraced European values and practices. The result is that Ukraine and its neighbors remain on the periphery, subject to the competing ambitions of Brussels and Moscow, with no clear vision of a future in Europe.

CONCLUSION

Notwithstanding the cultural, historical, and economic ties between Russia and the EU, relations between Moscow and Brussels have been subject to frequent swings. In early 2007—more than a year before the war between Russia and Georgia created an unprecedented crisis in EU-Russian relations (including suspension of the PCA)—a leading European official warned that relations with Russia "contain a level of misunderstanding or even mistrust we have not seen since the end of the Cold War."[51] Yet, not long after the smoke had cleared in the South Caucasus, Moscow and Brussels were signing a "partnership for modernization," while Germany, France, and even Poland were pressing the EU to resume close cooperation with Russia, including security cooperation.

This instability testifies to the paradoxical nature of EU-Russian relations. Despite continued, and often quite heated, disagreements over Russia's domestic development (including adherence to European standards for democracy and human rights), Russia and the EU continue to need each other. Russian leaders may talk about Asia's growing importance, including the need to "catch the Chinese wind in the sails of [Russia's] economy," as Putin expressed it in a February 2012 preelection essay, but Europe will remain Moscow's indispensable economic partner for the foreseeable future.[52] Similarly, Europe's quest for energy diversification is beginning to bear fruit, but given existing infrastructure and future uncertainty, Europe for now has little choice but to continue buying large quantities of Russian gas. Nor can Europe's major security challenges be solved without Russia playing a constructive role. These include the protracted conflicts in Moldova and the South Caucasus, the status of conventional forces in Europe, and the ongoing dispute over European missile defense. For Russia, mounting uncertainty along its Southern and Eastern borders provide a powerful argument for keeping tensions in Europe to a minimum.

Russia and the EU may be uncomfortable partners, but their partnership is permanent and inescapable for both sides. Unfortunately the EU's preferred strategy of using the EU's own body of law and regulation as a tool for drawing neighboring countries into its orbit seems to have hit a wall with Russia. Russia is too big, too *sui generis*, and too ambivalent about what the EU stands for to become truly "European" as defined by the EU itself. Moscow's ambivalent position with respect to Europe reflects in some ways a centuries-old dilemma of Russian identity. Russia is in Europe, but not of it. The EU's challenge lies in learning to reconcile values and interests in its dealings with Russia—a task for which the strategy of integration it has pursued for much of the past two decades appears inadequate.

SUGGESTED READINGS

Gomart, Thomas. "Europe in Russian Foreign Policy: Important but No Longer Pivotal." IFRI, *Russie.Nei.Visisions* no. 50, www.ifri.org/downloads/ifrigomartrussi aeuengavril2010.pdf.

European Union External Relations Directorate-General. "Russia: Country Strategy Paper, 2007–2013." eeas.europa.eu/Russia/docs/2007-2013_en.pdf

Kulhánek, Jakub. "EU and Russia in Search of a New Modus Operandi: Time is Running Out." www.amo.cz/publications/eu-and-russia-in-search-of-a-new-modus operandi-time-is-running-out.html?lang=en.

Moshes, Arkady. "Russia's European Policy under Medvedev: How Sustainable Is a New Compromise?" *International Affairs* 88, no. 1 (2012): 17–30.

Stehenmüller, Constanze. "Germany's Russia Question." *Foreign Affairs* 88, no. 2 (2009): 89–100.

NOTES

1. For an overview of EU efforts to address these cross-border challenges, see European Commission, "Country Cooperation: Moldova," and "Country Cooperation: Ukraine," ec.europa.eu/europeaid/where/neighbourhood/country-coopera tion.

2. Thomas Gomart, "Europe in Russian Foreign Policy: Important but No Longer Pivotal," *Russie.Nei.Visisions* no. 50, www.ifri.org/downloads/ifrigomartrus siaeuengavril2010.pdf.

3. Jeffrey Mankoff, *Russian Foreign Policy: The Return of Great Power Politics*, 2nd ed. (Lanham, Md.: Rowman & Littlefield, 2011), 1–21, 77–79. Also see Philip Hanson and Elizabeth Teague, "Big Business and the State in Russia," *Europe-Asia Studies* 57, no. 5 (2005): 657–80.

4. "Russia-EU Agreement on Partnership and Cooperation," December 1, 1997, eurlex.europa.eu/LexUriServ/LexUriServ.do?uri-CELEX:21997A1128(01):EN:HTML.

5. "Partnership and Cooperation Agreements (PCAs): Russia, Eastern Europe, the Southern Caucasus, and Central Asia," europa.eu/legislation_summaries/ external_relations/relations_with_third_countries/eastern_europe_and_central_ asia/r17002_en.htm.

6. See Fyodor Lukyanov, "Russia-EU: The Partnership That Went Astray," *Europe-Asia Studies* 60, no. 6 (2008): 1109.

7. Angela Stent, "Berlin's Russia Challenge," *The National Interest* 46, no. 88 (2007): 46–47.

8. Sergei Lavrov, "Stenogramma vystupleniia i otvetov na voprosy rossiiskikh i zarubezhnykh SMI Ministra inostrannykh del Rossii S.V. Lavrova na press-konferentsii v Press-tsentre MID Rossii Moskva," March 17, 2004, www.ln.mid.ru/bdomp/brp_4 .nsf/2fee282eb6df40e643256999005e6e8c/ae18e363299c3077c3256e5b002d6297! OpenDocument.

9. Dov Lynch, "Russia's Strategic Partnership with Europe," *The Washington Quarterly* 27, no. 2 (2004): 100.

10. Council of Europe, "PACE Rapporteur on Media Freedom Expresses His Deep Frustration at the Lack of Progress in Investigating the Murder of Anna Politkovskaia in Russia," Press Release, February 2, 2009, wcd.coe.int/ViewDoc.jsp?id= 1410219&Site=COE; Council of Europe, "Chechnya: PACE Committee Demands Full Elucidation of the Recent Spate of Murders," Press Release, January 27, 2009, wcd.coe.int/ViewDoc.jsp?id=1398813&Site=DC (accessed June 4, 2012).

11. European Union, "Statement by Catherine Ashton, High Representative of the European Union, on the Presidential Elections in Russia on 4 March 2012," www.consilium.europa.eu/uedocs/cms_Data/docs/pressdata/EN/foraff/128733.pdf.

12. See Thomas Gomart, "EU-Russia Relations: Toward a Way Out of Depression," *CSIS/IFRI Report*, July 2008, 3, www.ifri.org/files/Russie/Gomart_EU_Russia.pdf (accessed June 4, 2012).

13. European Commission, "Bilateral Relations Statistics (Russia)," trade.ec.eur opa.eu/doclib/docs/2006/september/tradoc_113440.pdf.

14. Ben Aris, "Retail Wave Hits Russia," *Financial Times*, April 3, 2012, blogs.ft .com/beyond-brics/2012/04/03/retail-wave-hits-russia (accessed June 4, 2012).

15. European Commission, "Trade Statistics: Russia, 2011," ec.europa.eu/trade/ creating-opportunities/bilateral-relations/cou ntries/russia/.

16. Sergei Lavrov, "Vystuplenie i otvety Ministra inostrannykh del Rossii S.V. Lavrova na voprsy SMI v khode sovmestnoi press-konferentsii po itogam peregovorov s Vysokom predstavitelem ES po inostrannym delam i politike bezopasnosti, zamestitelem Prededatelya Yevropeiskoi kommissii K. Ashton," November 17, 2011, www.mid.ru/bdomp/ns-dos.nsf/162979df2beb9880432569e70041fd1e/c 32577ca00173dbb4425794b0069bd0f!OpenDocument (accessed June 4, 2012).

17. Russian Ministry of Foreign Affairs, "Programma effektivnogo ispol'zovaniia na sistemnoi osnove vneshnepoliticheskikh faktorov v tseliakh dolgosrochnogo razvitiia Rossiiskoi Federatsii," May 11, 2010, www.runewsweek.ru/country/341 84.doc. Also see Angela Stent and Eugene Rumer, "Russia and the West," *Survival* 51, no. 2 (2009): 95.

18. For competing interpretations of the EU's difficulties, see H. Haukkala, "The Role of Solidarity and Coherence in the EU's Russia Policy," *Studia Diplomtica* 52, no. 2 (2006): 35–50; and Tuomas Forsberg and Antti Seppo, "Power without Influence? The EU and Trade Disputes with Russia," *Europe-Asia Studies* 61, no. 10 (2009): 1805–23.

19. Arkady Moshes, "Russia's European Policy Under Medvedev: How Sustainable Is a New Compromise?" *International Affairs* 88, no. 1 (2012): 19–20.

20. "Ot redaktsii: Pora gotovit'sia k krizisu," *Vedomosti*, May 30, 2012, www.vedo mosti.ru/opinion/news/1797180/pora_gotovitsia_k_krizisu (accessed June 5, 2012).

21. See Alexander Rahr, "Germany and Russia: A Special Relationship," *The Washington Quarterly* 30, no. 2 (2007): 137.

22. Thomas Gomart, "France's Russia Policy: Balancing Interests and Values," *The Washington Quarterly* 30, no. 2 (2007): 147.

23. See Vladimir Socor, "Meseberg Process: Germany Testing EU-Russia Security Cooperation Potential," *Jamestown Eurasia Daily Monitor* 7, no. 191 (October 22,

2010), www.jamestown.org/single/?no_cache = 1&tx_ttnews[tt_news] = 37065. (accessed June 4, 2012).

24. Katrin Bennhold, "At Deauville, Europe Embraces Russia," *New York Times*, October 18, 2011, http://www.nytimes.com/2010/10/19/world/europe/19iht-sum mit.html (accessed June 4, 2012).

25. Constanze Stehenmüller, "Germany's Russia Question," *Foreign Affairs* 88, no. 2 (2009): 89–100.

26. Ralf Neukirch and Matthias Schepp, "German-Russian Relations Enter a New Ice Age," *Der Spiegel*, May 30, 2012, www.spiegel.de/international/germany/german and-russian-relations -are-at-an-im passe-a-835862.html (accessed June 4, 2012).

27. "Berlusconi Says He Wants Russia to Join the EU," Agence France Presse, October 15, 2008, afp.google.com/article/ALeqM5g2INfqbAE6C9LjlXFkwDrF1l8zbw (accessed June 4, 2012).

28. Jorge Benitez, "Italy and Russia Deepen Defense Relationship during Berlusconi Visit," December 3, 2010, www.acus.org/natosource/italy-and-russia-deepen defense-relationship-during-berlusconi-visit.

29. Gomart, "France's Russia Policy," 147–51.

30. Liubov Pronina, "AvtoVAZ to Start Producing Renault-Based Lada Cars," *Bloomberg*, January 31, 2012, www.bloomberg.com/news/2012-01-27/avtovaz-to start-producing-rena ult-based-lad a-cars-next-month.html; John Bowker, "Western Carmakers Lift Russian Capacity," *Reuters*, March 20, 2012, www.reuters.com/article/2012/03/20/russia-cars-idUSL6E8EK0JX20120 320 (accessed June 4, 2012).

31. Vladimir Socor, "Mistral Warship Offer Symbolizes New Franco-Russian Strategic Partnership," *Jamestown Eurasia Daily Monitor* 6, no. 221 (December 2, 2009), www.jamestown.org/programs/edm/single/?cHash = 6fd9ade8b0&tx_ttnews[tt_news] = 35790 (accessed June 4, 2012).

32. Eka Janashia, "Mistral Deal Raises Georgian Security Concerns," *Central Asia-Caucasus Analyst*, February 2, 2011, http://www.cacianalyst.org/?q = node/5489 (accessed June 4, 2012).

33. Quoted in "France Committed to Naval Cooperation with Russia—Sarkozy," *RIA-Novosti*, June 8, 2010, en.rian.ru/world/20100608/159348291.html (accessed June 4, 2012).

34. Alexander Rahr, "The Russia-Germany-Poland Trialogue Continues," April 3, 2012, valdaiclub.com/europe/40740.html.

35. Moshes, "Russia's European Policy under Medvedev," 24.

36. F. Stephen Larrabee, "Russia, Ukraine, and Central Europe: The Return of Geopolitics," *Journal of International Affairs* 63, no. 2 (2010): 33–52; Filippos Proedrou, "Ukraine's Foreign Policy: Accounting for Ukraine's Indeterminate Stance between Russia and the West," *Southeast European and Black Sea Studies* 10, no. 4 (2010): 443–56.

37. Paul Flenley, "Russia and the EU: The Clash of New Neighbourhoods?" *Journal of Contemporary European Studies* 16, no. 2 (2008): 191–93.

38. European Commission, "The Policy: What Is the European Neighborhood Policy?" October 30, 2010, http://ec.europa.eu/world/enp/policy_en.htm (accessed June 5, 2012).

39. See Thomas Gomart, "Predstavlenie pri polupustovom zale," *Nezavisimaia Gazeta*, May 11, 2005, www.ng.ru/politics/2005-05-11/2_kartblansh.html (accessed June 4, 2012).

40. "Eastern Partnership," Europa Press Release, March 12, 2008, europa.eu/ rapid/pressReleasesAction.do?reference=MEMO/08/762. Russia's proposed South Steam pipeline is generally viewed as an attempt to preempt the construction of Nabucco.

41. Valentina Pop, "EU Expanding Its 'Sphere of Influence' Russia Says," *EU Observer*, March 21, 2009, euobserver.com/9/27827.

42. Ahto Lobjakas, "EU's Eastern Partnership Strains to Juggle Interests, Values," *Radio Free Europe/Radio Liberty*, April 29, 2009, www.rferl.org/content/EU_Eas tern_Partnership_Summit_Strains_To_Juggle_Interests_And_Values/1618551.html (accessed June 4, 2012).

43. Peter Rutland and Kateryna Shynkaruk, "There Goes the Eastern Neighbor-hood," *Moscow Times*, June 3, 2011, www.themoscowtimes.com/opinion/article/ there-goes-the-eastern-nei ghborhood/438 125.html (accessed June 4, 2012).

44. "Russian Attitude to EU Eastern Partnership Program Changing—Diplomat," Interfax, July 15, 2011, www.interfax.co.uk/ukraine-general-news-bulletins-in english/russ ian-attitude-to-eu-eastern-partnership-program-changing-diplomat/ (accessed June 4, 2012); Fyodor Lukyanov, "The Secure Eastern Partnership," *Russia in Global Affairs*, October 7, 2011, eng.globalaffairs.ru/redcol/The-secure-Eastern-Partnership-15345 (accessed June 4, 2012).

45. European Commission, General Directorate for Trade, "Ukraine," ec.euro pa.eu/trade/creating-opportunities/bilateral-relations/cou ntries/ukrain e/.

46. Karel de Gucht, "EU-Ukraine Trade Negotiations: A Pathway to Prosperity," Address to INTA Committee Workshop, October 21, 2011, trade.ec.europa.eu/ doclib/docs/2011/october/tradoc_148296.pdf.

47. Viktor Yanukovych, "Ukraine's Future Is with the European Union," *Wall Street Journal*, August 25, 2011, online.wsj.com/article/SB10001424053111903 46130457652467220915 8138.html (accessed June 4, 2012).

48. On Ukraine's attempts to balance between the EU and Russia, see Proedrou, "Ukraine's Foreign Policy"; Steven Pifer, "Understanding Ukraine's Foreign Policy," *Den'* (Kyiv), April 13, 2010, www.brookings.edu/opinions/2010/0413_ukraine_ pifer.aspx/ (accessed June 4, 2012).

49. Andrew E. Kramer, "Gas Deal with Belarus Gives Control of Pipeline to Rus-sia," *New York Times*, November 25, 2011, www.nytimes.com/2011/11/26/world/ europe/in-deal-with-belarus-russia-gets-control-of-yamal-europe-pipeline.html (accessed June 5, 2012).

50. "Putin Warns EU over Ukraine Pipeline Deal," EurActiv, March 24, 2009, www.euractiv.com/energy/putin-warns-eu-ukraine-pipeline-deal/arti cle-180577. Robert M. Cutler, "Ukraine Seeks Pipeline Threesome," *Asia Times*, April 9, 2010, www.atimes.com/atimes/Central_Asia/LD09Ag01.html (accessed June 4, 2012).

51. "EU-Russia Relations 'at Low Ebb,'" BBC Online, April 20, 2007, news.bbc .co.uk/2/hi/europe/6574615.stm.

52. Vladimir Putin, "Rossiia i meniaiushchiisia mir," *Moskovskie Novosti*, Febru-ary 27, 2012, mn.ru/politics/20120227/312306749.html (accessed June 4, 2012).

14

Is Military Reform Over?

Dale R. Herspring

Our armed forces remained in the 1970s–1980s level until recently.

—Dmitry Medvedev (August 8, 2011)

The Russian political leadership claims that the military reform process is over.[1] This chapter presents an analysis that disagrees with that assessment. Similar to the rest of Russia, the military faces two serious problems. First, it is struggling to find a way to rearm and reequip and modernize itself after the starvation diet it was placed on during Boris Yeltsin's presidency. His policies led to a quantitative drop in the number of modern weapons, and it also resulted in a technological gap that put it far behind the West.

The second problem facing the military is organizational. The Russian military has contracted since the end of the USSR. Unfortunately, during most of that time its shrinkage was not the result of a well-thought-out plan. Instead, actions—even to the current day—seem to be taken on the spur of the moment with little thought given to their long-term implications. Indeed, there have been occasions when one policy was contradicted by another policy. While the Kremlin entitled this policy the New Look, Russian officers and others have found it difficult to understand what it means in practice.

Needless to say, Russian military officers at all levels have not only been confused by the arbitrary and contradictory directions that military reform has taken, but many officers who have devoted their lives to the Russian military are increasingly discouraged by reform. In many cases they feel embittered at the way their advice has been ignored, and they feel as if they have been treated like peasants under the tsarist regime. Before looking at

297

the many structural problems, however, the next section focuses on the background of Russian executive actions in areas such as structural change and modern military technology.

WEAPONS AND TECHNOLOGY

The conflict over weapons has led to a difficult period in Russian civil-military relations. It has resulted in an open conflict between civilian and military elites over a variety of issues. This is not to suggest that the Russian Federation is facing a crisis in civil-military relations. It is not. Vladimir Putin is in charge and senior military officers and civilians know it.

The problem facing Russian civilians and military officers in the design and procurement of weapons is complex. First, it is important to understand that historically the Russians have not had the kind of capitalistic structure common in the United States, where several companies compete to obtain a contract to build ships, planes, or tanks. The lowest bidder, provided the U.S. government (USG) has confidence in its ability to deliver the product, wins the contract to build the item in question. Officers have been trained to deal with these civilian corporations.

The Russian tradition has been much different. All weapons development and procurement take place within government bureaucracies. There have been two or three firms competing to build planes or ships, but in the past competition has not revolved around cost, instead focusing on a weapon's performance. Competition existed but took place under the umbrella of the Soviet government. During the post-Soviet era most of these firms were privatized and with a new emphasis on consumer goods, many fell into disuse. The new world left the military more than a bit confused about how to manage development and procurement.

With the exception of the war in Chechnya, under Russian president Boris Yeltsin acquiescence to Western interests meant that there was little chance of a major war, so he saw no need to pour money into the military industrial complex. In addition, Yeltsin's primary concern was to keep the military from becoming too strong; he did not want it to pose a political threat to him. That is why he changed the relationship between the chief of the General Staff and the minister of defense (MoD). Traditionally in Russia, the chief of the General Staff worked for the defense minister. However, Yeltsin changed that relationship and made both men subordinate to the president. The result was a healthy dose of chaos in the upper ranks of the military as the defense minister issued orders, but could not ensure that the chief of the General Staff would carry them out.[2] This served Yeltsin's purpose perfectly—keep both men fighting each other so neither could represent an internal political challenge.

From the standpoint of weapons and technology, Yeltsin largely ignored the military. He was not willing to spend money on a military he did not think necessary. Not surprisingly, morale among military officers plummeted, as one Russian author observed:

> The actual situation is as follows: the troops are manned by 45 to 50 percent; troops' material provision has been cut by nearly 60 percent, as a result of which approximately 70 percent of games and maneuvers had to be scraped; combat flying practice has been reduced sharply; from 100–120 hours to 30–35 hours a year; and only one to two divisions are deemed fully combat-ready in each military district, and one to two ships in each fleet.[3]

In 1995 it was reported that only 20 percent of the entire fleet of tanks was usable, and that "the supply of combat aircraft had fallen twenty times."[4] In fact, by 1995 the number of aircraft declined 90 percent in comparison with 1991.[5] The situation was so bad that pilots often spent most of their time sweeping runways. Indeed, many were reassigned to other branches because there was nothing for them to do.

Weapons modernization and procurement was also a major problem under Yeltsin. For example, in 1991 the Air Force purchased 585 aircraft, but in 1995 it bought only two![6] The same year the Army received only twelve new battle tanks. It should have received 300 just to keep its armor at its current level.[7] To get an idea how bad the situation was, consider that in most developed countries "between 60 and 80 percent of all weapons are new; in Russia the figure is 30 percent."[8] In fact, the situation would get worse.

When Vladimir Putin became president, he was determined to reverse Yeltsin's policy of neglect, and Putin began to pay attention to the military and its needs. He started by reversing Yeltsin's starvation budget. The generals argued for 3.5 percent of GNP in accordance with a 1998 presidential decree. Putin was not prepared to put that much money in the military, but he did increase its budget. However, given the depth of the problems facing the military, the money allocated to it was not enough for it to catch up with the rest of the world. As one Russian analyst indicated, "There has been no mass production of new technology such as the KA-32 helicopter, T-90 tank, close-battle radar-location stations, and closed communications radio stations for the Russian Army."[9] General Yury Baluyevsky, then chief of the General Staff's Operations Department, underlined the seriousness of the problem in 2001 when he noted that arms procurement accounted for only 6 percent of total defense expenditures, compared to a "minimum of 20 percent in NATO countries. The greater share of Russia's defense budget goes to wages, food, uniforms, and so on."[10] Russia was five to twelve years behind the United States in the production of weapons.[11]

In an effort to deal with the situation, in January 2002 the Putin administration adopted a State Program for Armaments for the period up to 2010, which increased spending on arms and research. One key official stated that the procurement plan topped the preceding year's expenditures by nearly 40 percent.[12] In 2004, some new weapons began to appear, albeit in extremely small numbers. For example, in July the Army announced that it had obtained fourteen T-90S tanks, and it hoped to get another 20 to 30 in 2005.[13] However, the next year, defense minister Sergei Ivanov announced that the Army would get only eighteen.[14] Meanwhile, the Air Force announced that during 2005 it would purchase one Tu-160 strategic bomber and repair a second one. It planned "to modernize seven Su-27 fighters, purchase four Topol-M strategic missiles, two Iskander tactical missile systems . . . one warship and one diesel submarine."[15] Despite Putin's efforts to treat the military more evenhandedly, the situation only worsened.

STRUCTURAL MODIFICATIONS

In the post-Soviet period it soon became clear that Russia's military needed structural reform. One could not maintain the same kind of structure for a military that was soon reduced to two million, and would eventually number less than one million troops. Unfortunately, Yeltsin was of little help. There were two critical problems facing any effort to reform the armed forces. The first was money. It costs a lot to modify structure, especially moving from a conscript military to a professional military, which most of the generals wanted. Not only is there the problem of paying for those who leave the service, there is also the need to provide a whole new infrastructure for the new professional force: apartments, schools, hospitals, playgrounds. Further, pay would have to be raised significantly so that the military could attract the "best and the brightest."

The second requirement was for leadership. If there were a military that was ultraconservative and resistant to change, it was the Russian Army.[16] Nevertheless, the military would find good leaders, such as General Igor Rodionov, whom Yeltsin picked to be defense minister. Rodionov was a dynamic officer, one respected throughout the armed forces. He saw the need for change and was determined to create a new and different kind of military. To do that he needed support from the top—to help convince the many officers who were still living in the past of the need to change—a factor that was ignored despite the problems exposed by the conflict in Afghanistan and the first Chechen war. Russia needed to develop forces capable of conducting substate conflict. Unfortunately, Yeltsin refused to give Rodionov his backing. Combining this with the structural arrangement mentioned above (having the chief of the General Staff work for Yeltsin rather than Rodionov) ensured that nothing was accomplished.

When Putin took over, it soon became clear to him that chaos existed in the military. Defense Minister Igor Sergeyev was a gentlemanly missile officer whose focus was primarily on the nuclear balance between the United States and Russia. The chief of the General Staff, Anatoly Kvashnin, was a very different type of individual, a rough and tough Ground Forces officer who had fought in Chechnya and who believed that the majority of the country's military budget should be spent on conventional forces.

The tug-of-war between Kvashnin and Sergeyev continued under Putin. Kvashnin wanted to reduce strategic forces while Sergeyev wanted to build up nuclear forces. After Putin attended a meeting on August 11, 2000, where he listened to the two officers battle over funds, he decided that something had to be done. As he put it at the meeting, "When pilots do not fly and sailors do not go to sea, can it be said that everything is right and proper in the structure of the Armed Forces today?"[17] Kvashnin won the first round, as the Strategic Rocket Forces were downgraded. On March 28, 2001, Sergeyev stepped down. He was replaced by Putin's close confidant from his days in the KGB, Sergei Ivanov.

Unfortunately, Sergeyev's departure did little to improve the relationship between the defense minister and the chief of the General Staff. Kvashnin continued to defy Ivanov just as he had Sergeyev. By the end of 2003, it was clear that something had to be done. On June 14, the Duma changed Article 13 of the Law on Defense to read, "Oversight for the Armed Forces of the Russian Federation is carried out by the Defense Minister via the Defense Ministry."[18] Putin then fired Kvashnin after seven years on the job. In addition, Putin increased the military's budget. He promised that defense spending would be increased 20 to 25 percent a year, "remaining at 2.5 percent to 2.7 percent of GDP."[19] Although Putin had not provided the generals and admirals with everything they wanted (i.e., 3.5 percent of GDP), they now had the stability and predictability that is so critical in managing a military budget.

In 2007, the bottom fell out of Putin's plan to revamp the military. Ivanov commissioned an audit of the military budget, as something did not seem right. The audit discovered that corruption was even more extensive than he had anticipated. Then on April 3, 2008, the Audit Chamber announced that more than R164.1 million had been stolen from the ministry through fraud and outright theft. The report said, "The Ministry of Defense accounts for 70 percent of the budgetary resources used for purposes other than those officially designated."[20] Ivanov took this information to Putin, and they both decided that something had to be done.

ENTER SERDIUKOV

Putin felt it was time for a major shock to the military. He elevated Ivanov to the position of first deputy prime minister on February 15, 2007. In his place as defense minister he brought in Anatoly Serdiukov, a former furniture salesman and at that time head of the Tax Service. Serdiukov brought twenty civilian auditors with him. The job he faced was enormous: military morale was at rock bottom,[21] corruption was out of control,[22] and there was even anger among "officers, generals and the Russian public at large vis-a-vis the state the military finds itself in."[23] The bottom line is that the military needed help—both financial and leadership—if it were to carry out the tasks assigned to it. If that were not enough, the military was facing a radical reorganization process. Indeed, it was literally being turned upside down. Everything was subject to change, and what may come as a surprise, under Serdiukov, even the country's senior military officers knew little about the changes being introduced. Their civilian defense minister often just announced the changes, leaving it up to the uniformed military to adapt.

Modernizing the Military

Putin came to realize that if he hoped to attract better-qualified officers and NCOs (noncommissioned officers) he would have to begin by raising salaries and provide the military with the money it needed to modernize its forces. As prime minister, that is exactly what he did in 2012. Taking money from social programs, Putin announced that the government had decided to allocate R20 trillion to modernizing the military and an additional R3 trillion to modernizing the defense-industrial complex. This means that for the period 2012–2020, 2.8 percent of the country's gross domestic product will be devoted to the military.[24] New programs and/or weapons systems will be introduced in all branches of military service. In short, the Kremlin decided to follow Henry Kissinger's advice that no foreign policy is worth much unless it is backed up by a strong military.[25]

Dmitry Rogozin, who previously served as Russia's representative to NATO and is currently a deputy vice premier (which makes him senior to the chief of the General Staff), has been given the task of revitalizing the country's defense-industrial establishment. The latter has equipment from the 1960s and 1970s and has a workforce whose average age is in the sixties. Modernizing this force is not an easy task, especially at a time when the uniformed military has decided that Russian-produced weapons are of inferior quality and instead attempts to fill its needs with the purchase of weapons abroad.

Realistically before military reform can go any further, the Makarov Rogozin (Nikolai Makarov is chief of the General Staff) dispute will have to be resolved, which is real and involves more than personalities. The heart of the dispute goes to the question of who will make Russia's weapons for the next eight years. Will Putin give the money to domestic industries, or will part of it be spent on weapons from abroad as Russia is doing currently? The most obvious example is the three French Mistral landing craft being built. The weapons systems will be Russian but the platform will be French. The problem facing the Russian military is enormous. As noted by a Russian admiral, "Russia is building too few ships and the U.S. Navy has the advantage of ten times more."[26] However, the problem is not just one of numbers. Quality is a very serious issue as the following quote indicates.

> The reasons the Russian Navy is in such a state are not new either. They are well known. They include neglect and underfunding for the program to build new combat ships, the technological backwardness and dearth of production facilities, catastrophic loses of highly qualified engineering and technical personnel and a poor work ethic.[27]

This is not just a problem for the Navy; it impacts all branches of military service. In the Air Force, for example, "In the USA the development of the F-35 fifth-generation is being completed, which could potentially become the main adversary for Russian aircraft in future conflicts." Unfortunately, in the Russian Air Force, the authors note, "Time seems to have frozen at the level of the mid-1980s both for fighter and other types of aircraft."[28] Makarov made similar comments about Ground Forces equipment. "Take the T-90 tank, about which much has been said, much has been written, and Israel's Merkava. Compare its weapons system to our tank's, not to mention the T-72 tank and all the rest. Nor does our tank (T-90) provide any anti-mine protection. Take our artillery. Foreign armies everywhere have precision-guided munitions, and their range is longer. That is to say, this advance puts our Armed Forces at a disadvantage."[29] Faced with this technological disadvantage, Makarov argued that the Mistral is only the tip of the iceberg. As he commented in 2011, "The Russian Army will continue acquiring foreign weapons which will be manufactured under license on Russian territory."[30]

In fact, Moscow has been importing a variety of weapons; for instance, Moscow has purchased Austrian sniper rifles,[31] Italian armored vehicles,[32] Israeli UAVs (unarmed aerial vehicle),[33] French Panhard armored vehicles,[34] Italian light helicopters,[35] and French underwater breathing equipment,[36] to name only a few. Indeed, the strongest slap in the Russian defense complex's face came from the commander of Ground Forces, Colonel-General Aleksandr Postnikov, who stated,

The newest T-90 tank, which is a modification of the Soviet T-72, . . . is unjusti-
fiably expensive—118 million rubles. In the opinion of the commander in
chief, it would be better for this money to buy three German "Leopard" tanks,
meeting all the necessary requirements, than for it to be spent on the old
domestic one.[37]

Russian generals understand the problem. However, they also know that
they need modern weapons if they are to field a military able to fight and
win wars.

The War in Georgia

The 2008 war in Georgia demonstrated to everyone, but especially to
Moscow's conservative military, that Russia's armed forces were inept and
that it was time for some major changes. When the war began, the General
Staff was in the process of moving from its building to the old Warsaw Pact
headquarters. As a result, "many officers learned the news that Georgia had
begun a military operation against South Ossetia from morning news publications."[38] As a result, the military operation was a disaster from the
beginning. And it did not improve as time went on. A former airborne chief
of intelligence reflected the views of most of his colleagues when he commented,

> Our army is still being trained based upon regulations which were written in
> the 1980s! The regulations, manuals, combat training programmes, and the
> volumes of standards have become obsolete. An old friend recently sent me
> the volume of standards that is in force, which we wrote already in 1984, 25
> years ago. This volume is a reflection of the operational and combat training
> of the troops and their operating tactics. If the Airborne Troops have remained
> at that prehistoric level, then we can confidently say that the General Staff and
> the rest of the troops continue to train for a past war.[39]

In essence, this five-day war was a watershed for Russia and its military; it
represented the last war of the twentieth century, fought exclusively with
dated tactics, equipment, weapons, and structures more suited to waging
large-scale conventional warfare than being deployed in a local, noncontact
conflict.[40] Even the country's conservative generals realized that major
changes were required.

SERDIUKOV'S CHANGES

While many people in and outside of Russia have criticized the changes
that have taken place under Serdiukov—and there is good reason for that

criticism—the reality is that some of the changes introduced under Serdiu-kov's New Look policy have been long overdue and are a move in the right direction. First, let us consider some of those positive changes.

Reduction in Size

The heart of Serdiukov's New Look policy was his decision to cut the Russian military from around two million to one million men (if that is the correct number; some suggest it is currently no more than 800,000).[41] As noted above, the war in Georgia demonstrated that the mass armies of World War II were useless (even if some Russian generals had and still have a hard time understanding that).[42] To face the problems of the post-Georgia world, the General Staff decided that Russia needed a smaller military. Ideally, they believed it should be one staffed by soldiers, sailors, airmen, and marines who *want* to be part of it—that means a minimum of conscripts. In many ways, this bears a strong similarity to militaries in the West. For example, the original decision to reduce the officer corps to 150,000 was justified by the military because it would ensure an officer-enlisted ratio would be 1:15, similar to that in Western militaries rather than the 2:1 common at the time.[43]

Introducing Chaplains

For many years, Russian military officers resisted the idea of chaplains; not surprising for an army that emerged from atheistic communism. However, there were also practical reasons for their hesitation. First was the issue of authority, as commanders were justifiably worried about having a new voice in the chain of command. Second, there was concern over the emergence of Muslim Imans who might create a security problem.[44] Both problems have been resolved (at least in theory). Based on the most recent information, there are now nineteen chaplains serving in the military with the number shortly to triple to sixty.[45] It is not clear if any of the chaplains are Muslim, Jewish, or Buddhist; to date they all appear to be Russian Orthodox. Moscow clearly understands the morale problem and has also increased the number of Army psychologists in military units to 3,000.[46] But the military soon recognized that unit psychologists alone would not solve the problem. There are many instances where they cannot resolve important issues, such as marital problems with the spouse and children, not to mention drugs, dealing with the loss of a loved one, morale, and spiritual matters.

Educational Reform

Moscow has also introduced a major reform of its military educational institutions. On the one hand, this change was driven by the reduction in the size of the military. From the early 1990s to 2009, the military was reduced by a factor of four. There were 166 military higher educational institutions graduating around 60,000 officers a year in the early 1990s. By 2009 the number of schools was down to sixty-four, and they turn out 15,000 to 17,000 officers a year.[47] One of the results of the abundance of schools and graduates at the precommissioning level was that it filled the military with many more officers than needed. For example, the deputy head of the Defense Ministry's Main Personnel Department commented, "Of some 15,000 graduates, only 4,000 to 5,000 best graduates will receive guaranteed placement" in military ranks as officers."[48] As a consequence, the military took the unprecedented step of closing the military academies for two years because there were too many officers, and producing more would only make the matter worse. As a consequence, many students after four years of undergraduate education at an academy were not commissioned, but were given the option of being released into civilian life, or placed in service as a noncommissioned officer until an officer position became available.

Changing Logistics

Several years ago, the Kremlin decided that instead of relying on military personnel to provide logistical support for the armed forces, it would outsource this task as in the West.[49] This means employing civilian commercial corporations to carry out jobs such as food preparation and procurement, assistance with barracks maintenance, and providing basic security such as that found on most bases. With the reduction of conscript service to one year the military could no longer expect them to take on preparing food (e.g., peeling potatoes), standing guard duty, or cleaning the base. According to Russian military sources, as a result, "the norms of the provisions of the servicemen are determined by orders of the Defense Ministry, but the soldiers are fed by outside organizations, which conclude contracts with Voyentorg (a civilian food services organization) who organize the entire process, including the food delivery, preparation of the meal, and its distribution to the servicemen. Goodbye to poor meals!"[50]

Military Police

There was a long and lively debate over the decision whether to create military police.[51] The major problem was command authority. While everyone agreed in principle that they were needed to deal with issues such as *dedovshchina* (the process whereby junior recruits are harassed by more senior ones), no commander wanted to lose control over his unit to an outside force, even if it was military. The problem now appears to have been solved.

Pay

Probably the most important recent action taken by the Kremlin was the decision to substantially increase pay.[52] It was controversial and led to the resignation of the finance minister, Aleksei Kudrin, who preferred to stay within strict budget parameters. Kudrin was not happy that money would be taken from social programs to pay for the increase.[53] Kudrin also opposed increased spending in other policy areas that would increase the budget deficit.

Restructuring

Moscow's decision to create four large military districts based on a joint command is also a step forward. It helps overcome service parochialism and does an excellent job of creating an efficient military force. It helps ensure that the officer in charge has the right service background to make sound decisions based on the situation at hand, not on service loyalty. The key question is what or which service will work best given the mission to be carried out.

Physical Fitness

In the past, outsiders often had the impression that the number of stars on a general's shoulder was related to his girth. The bigger around the middle, the higher the rank. A commander should set an example for his troops. A senior officer should set an example for his troops. Assuming the Russians are serious about physical fitness, it will mark a major step forward.

NEEDED CHANGES

Let us turn now to areas where major changes still need to be taken.

Personnel

An army is only as good as its officers, NCOs, and enlisted personnel. The key is to have a fully manned unit led by highly trained officers and NCOs. But as everyone wearing the uniform of the Russian Federation knows, attracting (to steal a term used by the U.S. military) "the best and the brightest" is not easy. As it is now, the Russian military is undermanned, but more about that below.

Stability in the Upper Ranks

There was a day when the senior ranks of the Russian military remained fairly stable. One learned their names and could follow their careers along a regular path. Now, however, the situation has changed. Officers no sooner take a senior position than they are transferred—often to the retirement list. These frequent changes not only make it difficult for outside observers to keep track of who is who, it also undermines efforts to build cohesion and leadership, two factors that are key to the performance of any military force.

The Draft

Among NATO members, only Turkey still has the draft. For its part, it is clear that many senior officers in the Russian military would like to continue to rely on it. There are problems, however. Not only is it extremely unpopular, there are not sufficient numbers of young fit Russians to continue it. The reduction to one year of service was sensible, but it is not a solution to the country's problems. According to Russian statistics, "The military needs to recruit about 300,000 men during each draft to keep the number of personnel at the required level of 1 million." However, it was only possible to recruit 135,000 in the fall draft of 2011.[54] In the meantime, the new training program that tries to train conscripts in six months so they will have some time to put their training into practice, is commendable. But the realities of demographics mean the military is not going to be able draft 300,000 soldiers twice a year to fill its ranks in the future, given the birth rates in the year-groups of 1992, 1993, or 1994. (It could draft those with criminal records as was the case in the past.) The staffing problem is made even worse by the number of young men who avoid the draft. For many, the idea of serving in the Russian military appears to be the equivalent of a death sentence. In public opinion polls conducted in 2011, comments were negative. "They do not believe the army, where those who drive soldiers to suicide are shielded while attempts are made to prosecute officers who fight for the truth."[55] Or, as another source put it, "The current form of the army should not exist! The army maims and kills its soldiers."[56] The desertion rate appears manageable, but given the demographic situation there is little chance that the military will reach the one million level that the generals claim to be their goal.

The General Staff is fully aware of the numbers problem. In response, the Kremlin came up with a new approach. The General Staff is putting renewed emphasis on the *kontraktniki*, those who have voluntarily signed a contract to become a professional. However, as everyone in uniform knows, the *kontraktniki* program has had a checkered past. At present, the general consensus (including among senior generals) is that the program is not working. Instead of the best and brightest, the armed forces are attracting individuals who are unemployable or have personal problems.

The military has stated that it needs 450,000 *kontraktniki*. The question is how to find that many volunteers in a country that has no history of a volunteer army. Furthermore, public opinion polling indicates that at this time not only is morale low among those in the military, the military's reputation among civilians has fallen precipitously since the days of the Soviet Army. More changes are needed. The military infrastructure must be radically changed. Housing, kindergartens, schools, medical service, and leisure time activities will all need to be improved, at least if the Russian experience is anything like what happened when the United States changed to a professional military.

The NCO

Another critical problem with which the Russians must deal is the NCO. NCOs are the heart of Western militaries. They run the units or sections. They take care of minor disciplinary problems, and they are the ones who have daily contact with enlisted soldiers and who, in the field, sleep, eat, and train/exercise together with them. Platoons are commanded by and accompanied by a junior officer, but the life of the unit depends heavily on senior NCOs. In practice, they also train these junior officers, who are normally on their first assignment. The problem for the Russian military is that it cannot make up its mind what to do with NCOs. Are they technical experts (as in the Navy) or regular line/combat soldiers? A school was set up at Ryazan to train them—one taking two years. Such a step is all well and good, but how does a private move to become a master sergeant (*Starschina*)?

The heart of the NCO problem is the delegation of authority. Unfortunately, the Russians find the delegation of authority to be extraordinarily threatening. Delegating authority to an NCO does not mean giving him or her permission to use violence against his own soldiers. An American Marine Corps drill instructor will get within millimeters of a recruit's nose, and will yell in his face, but never touch him. There are other things one can do to get his attention—like one hundred push-ups, running at night, and extra duty.

A Plan

One of the biggest problems facing the Russian military is the lack of a carefully thought-out plan. Actions, including important structural modifications, appear to be done in an ad hoc fashion, decided upon on the spur of the moment. Chaplains are created. Why? How do they fit into the over-all reform plan? Apparently, someone in Moscow decided that chaplains could help solve morale problems. Or consider officers. At first, there was a need for 150,000 officers. But then, just when the personnel offices in Moscow were getting used to dealing with these restrictions, including retiring around 200,000 officers, 70,000 more were added. One can only imagine the chaos and confusion that must have been created in every section of the military from housing, to pay, to personnel, training, and so on, deciding what to do with these officers. It certainly conveys the impression that no one seems to know who is in charge or what the military will look like in five or ten years. Someone from the Defense Ministry needs to sit down in the General Staff and put all of these pieces together. This is one of the major causes of low morale among many officers. They have no idea what to expect. What about their families, their children, their wives? Will they have housing? Will there be schools and medical facilities? Then, of course, the question of their future looms over them. Will they have a future in the years ahead?

General Staff Academy

The same sort of chaos exists at the General Staff Academy. First, it was stated that the General Staff Academy would have thirteen to fifteen students for two years at the 0–7 level (brigadier general or navy rear admiral), with the second year heavily involved in civilian subjects. Then, in 2011, it was announced that the term was reduced to ten months. That meant that the students now have to cover the two-year program in ten months. It means that courses are being dropped (probably from the second year), and that what is taught is being simplified.

Housing

Housing is another problem facing the military. Horror stories abound of families quartered in horrendous housing—for example, two former colonels and their families living in what used to be a chicken coop in Siberia! Fortunately, Putin appears to have taken this issue on with a vengeance and has promised to resolve it. If he does, and housing is at a decent qualitative level and located near a big city, I suspect that more than one officer will be more than ready to say, "God bless him!"

Corruption

Everything is dependent on the fight against corruption. Western sources call Russia one of the most corrupt countries in the world, and Russian sources openly admit that there are more problems with corruption in the military than any other segment of society. Former defense minister Ivanov told Putin that 40 percent of the military budget was being siphoned off!

Corruption impacts everything. Some Russians claim it is so built into the system over the years, that despite President Medvedev's efforts to attack it, nothing seriously will happen in our lifetime. One cynical Russian commented to this writer, "Well, they will plan for ten frigates, but by the time corruption is over, there will only be enough money for seven, and they will call it a success."[57] It was equally shocking to read that the chief of medicine in the Russian military was arrested for corruption, at a time when Russian military medicine needs all the help it can get. About the only thing worse would be to hear that the chief of chaplains was arrested for corruption. The military should be one of the easier bureaucracies in which to attack corruption, but it looks like it will take many years and major structural changes to get control of it.

Minister of Defense Anatoly Serdiukov is to be commended for his restructuring of the procurement system. His setting up of a civilian coterie to deal with the actual purchase of weapons and thereby remove serving officers from direct involvement in the procurement process was a positive step. However, it did not solve the problem. Now, civilians tell the military officers what to order and how much it will cost (the kickback it built into the overall cost). Then the civilians order it, the military officer gets a kickback, and everyone is happy. Unfortunately, however, the problem remains.

Data

Another problem that haunts the Russian military (and anyone who seeks to understand it) is the lack of reliable data. If it hopes to be taken seriously by the outside world, it is critical that the Defense Ministry develop better statistical and accounting procedures. This does not refer to classified information. However, there is no reason for the ministry to not know exactly how many service personnel are serving at any given time or what is being spent on particular items. Without good data, there's no way of setting valid benchmarks for military reform.

Crime

Crime continues to be a problem according to Sergei Fridinsky, the chief military prosecutor. Recently, he reported that crime among enlisted men is up 15 percent. The Russian approach in dealing with crime or problems like *dedovshchina* (which continues to be a serious issue) is to blame the commanding officer (CO). Effective NCOs would help minimize the problem.

Technology

Technological backwardness remains a serious problem. The Russian military is becoming increasingly decrepit and outdated. Only around 10 to 15 percent of its weapons are now modern.[58] In many ways, the problems of the 1990s still exist (e.g., three ships were finally produced based on 1980s technology!). According to one article by a Russian observer, if Russia did everything possible to raise the technological level of its military by 2025, it would catch up with the West.[59] The only problem was that the West would be far beyond that technological point by then. Purchasing new equipment from the West not only provides the Russian military with modern equipment, it also acts as a very strong incentive for the indigenous Russian defense-industrial complex to modernize, and it encourages political authorities to support such an effort.

The Military and Defense Industries

The latest problem facing the Ministry of Defense has been the effort to reach agreement between the MoD and the military-industrial complex over the cost of various weapons systems. On the one hand, we have the most senior uniformed military officer—the chief of the General Staff (Nikolai Makarov) and on the other a civilian—the vice premier in charge of the military-industrial complex (Dmitry Rogozin). In contrast to many who held his position, Makarov is not afraid to stand up to Rogozin, especially when it comes to procuring weapons and equipment from the West. This is an issue that Putin will have to settle himself. What is unusual, however, is the willingness of the country's top general to publicly stand up to the country's top civilian when dealing with such matters. After all, a ship can only go in one direction at a time.

CONCLUSION

Modernizing the Russian military is and will continue to be both a lengthy and frustrating process. It reminds one of Lenin's dictum of "two steps forward, and one step backward." Not everything that the Kremlin attempts will work. As noted above, the Serdiukov regime has taken some positive actions. For example, the structure has been modified to create a more efficient organization; many of the mundane, nonmilitary tasks have been outsourced; the size of the Army has been reduced; chaplains have been introduced; the educational system is being revamped; military police have been introduced, which may help reduce the omnipresent harassment of soldiers; pay has been increased; and physical fitness programs have been introduced. Those are all positive steps.

However, there is much left to be done. For example, the lack of stability in the upper ranks, the failure of the draft, the unwillingness to give NCOs authority, the lack of a plan, the chaos at the General Staff Academy, the insufficient housing and other types of "creature comforts," corruption, the continued existence of crime, and in particular, the lag in technology. Until these latter issues are dealt with in a serious fashion, the Russian Army will remain far behind its Western neighbors.

SUGGESTED READINGS

Bartles, Charles. "Defense Reforms of Russian Defense Minister Anatoly Serdiukov." *The Journal of Slavic Military Studies* 24, no. 1 (2011).

Blank, Stephen. "Lurching toward Militarization: Russian Defense Spending in the Coming Decade." *Eurasia Daily Monitor* 6, no. 3 (January 5, 2011).

Blank, Stephen, ed. *Russian Nuclear Weapons, Past, Present, and Future.* Carlisle, Pa.: U.S. Army War College, 2011.

de Hass, Marcel. *Russia's Foreign Security Policy in the 21st Century; Putin, Medvedev and Beyond.* Routledge: London, 2010.

Finch, Ray. "One Face of the Modern Russian Army: General Vladimir Shamanov." *Journal of Slavic Military Studies* 24, no. 3 (2011).

Gresh, Jason. "The Realities of Russian Military Conscription." *Journal of Slavic Military Studies* 24, no. 2 (2011).

Herspring, Dale. *Military Culture and Civil-Military Relations, the German, Canadian, Russian and American Cases.* Baltimore: Johns Hopkins University Press, 2013.

———. "Creating Shared Responsibility Through Respect for Military Culture: The Russian and American Cases." *Public Administration Review* 71, no. 4 (2011).

———. "Is Military Reform in Russia for 'Real?' Yes, but. . . .". In *The Russian Military Today and Tomorrow: Essays in Memory of Marcy Fitzgerald,* ed. Stephen Blank and Ricard Weitz. Carlisle, Pa.: Strategic Studies Institute, 2010.

Herspring, Dale, and Roger McDermott. "Serdiukov Promotes Systematic Russian Military Reform." *Orbis* 54, no. 2 (2010).

———. "Chaplains, Political Officers, and the Russian Armed Forces." *Problems of Post-Communism* 56, no. 4 (2010).

McDermott, Roger. *The Reform of Russia's Conventional Armed Forces.* Washington: The Jamestown Foundation, 2011.

Tsypkin, Mikhail. "What's New in Russia's New Military Doctrine?" *Radio Free Europe/Radio Liberty,* February 27, 2010.

NOTES

1. "Russia's Military Development Remains Priority for State Policy," *Rossiia* 24, March 20, 2012.

2. This is discussed in Dale Herspring, *The Kremlin and the High Command: Presidential Impact on the Russian Military from Gorbachev to Putin* (Lawrence: University of Kansas Press, 2006).

3. Charles Dick, "The Russian Army—Present Plight and Future Prospects," *Jane's Intelligence Review Yearbook, 1994–1995* (London: Janes, 1995), 43.

4. "The Defense Minister Has It in for Everyone," *Novaia ezhednevaia gazeta,* December 9, 1994.

5. "Russia's Red Army Has Lost Its Rear," *Christian Science Monitor,* June 2, 1997.

6. "Russia: Damage and Casualty Effect of Advanced Weapons," *Technika i vooruzhennie,* February 2, 1998.

7. Anatol Lieven, *Chechnya: Tombstone of Russian Power* (New Haven, Conn: Yale University Press, 1998), 278.

8. "Conversations without Middlemen," Moscow TV, September 14, 1995.

9. Vladimir Mukhin, "Reshuffle Brings Putin People to the Top," *Russian Journal,* May 4, 2001.

10. Mukhin, "Reshuffle Brings."

11. "Duma Defense Committee Head Says Military Reform Not Yet Under Way," *RFE/RL Daily Report,* March 22, 2002.

12. "State Oks $2.5 Billion Arms Budget," *Moscow Times,* January 18, 2002.

13. "Russian Army to Acquire 14 T-90S Tanks in 2004," *RIA-Novosti,* November 30, 2004.

14. "Defense Minister Says Russian Army to Get First T-90 Tanks in 2005," *RIA Novosti,* November 30, 2004.

15. "Russia without an Army," *Vedomosti,* November 18, 2004.

16. In Russia, "army" refers to all the services.

17. "Development Strategy of the Armed Forces Defined," *Military New Bulletin,* no. 8 (August 2000).

18. *Federalnyi zakov 'Ob oborone,'* April 24, 1996; in www.mil.ru/articles/articles .3863.shtml.

19. "Ivanov's Budget," *Rossiiskie vesti,* September 8, 2005.

20. "Defense Ministry Will Shed Excess Equipment," *RFE/RL Newsline,* April 3, 2008.

21. "Permanent Military Reform," *Nezavisimaia gazeta,* March 16, 2011.

22. "What the Market Will Bear," *Russia Profile.org,* January 12, 2012.

23. "Complete Zero: Serdyukov's 'Reforms' in Facts and Figures," *Pravda,* March 18, 2010.

24. "Russia's Military Development Remains Priority for State Policy—Medvedev," *Rossiia 24,* March 20, 2012.

25. This writer heard Kissinger make such a comment when the latter was secretary of state, and this writer was a foreign service officer.

26. "Admiral Komoyedov Answered Questions from Readers of RIA Novyy Region." *Novyi Region,* July 23, 2010.

27. "There's Nothing Disgraceful about Building Ships Overseas," *Nezavisimoe voennoe obozrenie,* August 20, 2009.

28. "Russian Air Force Has Fallen Behind Other Leading Military Powers," *Interfax,* January 18, 2011.

29. "Russia's Top General Complains about Russia's Inferior Capabilities," *Interfax*, November 19, 2011.

30. Defense Ministry will Continue Buying Foreign Weapons, Technologies," *Interfax*, December 7, 2011.

31. "Russian Courts Exchange Dragunov Rifles for Austrian Sniper Weapon," *rewsru.com*, December 25, 2011.

32. "Russia to Get First 57 Italian Armored Vehicles in 2012," *RIA Novosti*, March 14, 2012.

33. "Will Our Army Fight with Imported Weapons," *Komsomolskaia pravda*, May 23, 2009.

34. "Russia to Purchase 500 French VBL Armored Vehicles," *Lenta.ru*. November 11, 2011.

35. "Defense Ministry Announces Tender for Eurocopters—No One Russian Light Helicopter Meets the Air Force Requirements Specified in the Competition Documentation," *Izvestiia*, February 23, 2012.

36. "New French Rebreathers for Russian Navy Divers," *RIA Novosti*, April 2, 2012.

37. "The General Staff: Russia Has Delayed Army Reform for 20 Years. It Is Necessary to Take an Example from NATO," newsru.com, March 30, 2011.

38. "Sword of the Empire," *Zavtra*, October 5, 2008.

39. "Confusion Reigns in the Russian Troops" www.utro.ru, May 19, 2009.

40. "The Price of Victory: Military Experts on the Mistakes of the Campaign in South Ossetia," *Trud*, August 18, 2008; Viktor Baranets, "Army Sent to Fight in Old Suit of Armor," *Komsomolskaia pravda*, August 26, 2008; "Interview with Anatoly Nogovitsyn,"*Toddidksys gazeta*, September 9, 2009.

41. See "Doubling the Contract, the Russian Army Will Become 70% Professional within Five Years," *Rossiiskaia gazeta*, July 8, 2011; "A Still Unresolved Problem. Who Will Reliably Protect the Country from Military Attack: Conscript or Contract Soldier," *Voenno-Promyshlennyi Kuryer*, November 11, 2010; "Russian Army's Dead Souls," *Nezavisimaia gazeta*, October 2, 2009.

42. "Supreme Commander in Chief's Five Tasks. New People Are Needed to Fill Them," *Nezavismaia gazeta*, March 30, 2011; "Russia Has Fallen Twenty Years Behind NATO," *Komsomolskaia pravda*, March 29, 2011.

43. "Generals Reduction: They Will Reduce the Armed Forces and Change Their Look," *Rossiiskaia gazeta*, October 15, 2008.

44. Based on conversations with retired Russian and Soviet military officers.

45. "Number of Chaplains in Russian Armed Forces to Triple," *RIA Novosti*, November 17, 2011.

46. "Politics: Military Psychologist Corps Will Be Doubled Due to Soldiers' Inadequacy: Without Help, Every Fourth Draftee in the Army Can Be a Suicide," *Izvestiia*, October 4, 2011.

47. "Where Is the Guarantee that Reform Will be Carried to Completion," *Nezavisimoi voennoi obozrenie*, February 9, 2009.

48. "Military Education Reform to Be Completed by 2012," *Interfax*, August 31, 2010.

49. See, for example, "Rear Services on the Road to Reform," *Krasnaia zvezda*, November 26, 2008; "Russian Army's Rear Services Face Personnel Cuts, Switch to

Civilian Suppliers," *Rossiiskaia gazeta*, November 24, 2008; "Rear Services: A Time of Change. Notes from the Assembly of Leadership Personnel of the Armed Forces Rear Services," *Krasnaia zvezda*, December 16, 2008; "Russian General Details Changes to Military Logistics as Part of Reform," *Interfax*, May 15, 2009; "In From the Rear: The New Battalions Will Be Able to Fight Autonomously for a Whole Week," *Rossiiskaia gazeta*, November 21, 2009; Dmitry Bulgakov, "The RF Armed Forces Logistics Support System at the Contemporary Stage and the Prospects for its Development," *Ekho Moskvy*, June 22, 2011; "Russian Troops Relieved of House- keeping Duties, Spend More Time in Training," *Interfax*, June 29, 2011; "Russian Army Continues to Transfer Everyday Services for Servicemen to Civilian Organiza- tions—Deputy Prime Minister," *Interfax*, August 22, 2011; "Who Is Feeding the Rus- sian Soldier Now? Outsourcing and Catering," *Argumenty i Fakty*, October 17, 2011.

50. "Back to the Meal," *Komsomolskaia Pravda*, February 21, 2012.

51. "Russian Minister Details Plans for Military Police with Defense Ministry," *Interfax*, February 3, 2006; "Military Police Seeks a Home, Ivanov, Lukin, Krashen- innikov and Zavarzin Propose Various Options for a New Security Structure," *Rossi- iskaia gazata*, February 8, 2006; "State Duma Unprepared to Draft Military Police Bill Yet—Legislator," *ITAR-TASS*, February 13, 2006; "Russian Armed Forces Decide Against Establishment of Military Police," *Interfax*, May 18, 2006; "The Comman- dants Will Become Police Officers: Military Police Will be Appearing in the Field Right Now. But They Will for the Time Being Be Manned by Old Regulars," *Vedo- mosti*, December 4, 2009; "Russian Defense Ministry Shelving Plans to Set Up Mili- tary Police," *RIA Novosti*, February 10, 2010; "Defense Ministry Drafting Documents on Military Police Introduction," *Interfax*, February 10, 2010; "Realities: Generals Back to School. Police on the Post, Military Reform Revealed Many Weak Points," *Nezavisimaia voennoe obozrenie*, October 31, 2010; "The Russian Army Will Continue to Have No Police," *Komsomolskaia pravda*, January 15, 2011, "Russian Defense Min- istry Ready to Install Police to Trouble Hazing," *RIA Novosti*, July 7, 2011; "Military Police to Appear in Russia by 2012," *RIA Novosti*, July 7, 2011; "The Ministry of Defense Needs Its Own Police: The Ministry of Defense Does not Plan to Drop the Military Police," Gazeta.ru, July 9, 2011; "Russia to Introduce Policing in the Mili- tary," *RIA Novosti*, November 22, 2011.

52. "Vladimir Putin: Compensation for All Military Personnel Will Be Increased Twofold," *Rossiiskaia gazeta*, July 28, 2011; "Russia's Putin Announces Army Pay and Pensions Rise, Pledges Help with Housing," *RIA Novosti*, Sept 21, 2011; "Police and Military Salaries to Double," *The Moscow Times*, September 22, 2011; "Russian Mili- tary, Police Pensions to Rise by at least 50%," *Interfax*, November 3, 2011.

53. "Kudrin's Dismissal Good for Russia's Defense Capability," *Interfax*, Septem- ber 27, 2011; Defense Spending Threatens Social Programs, Kudrin Says," *The Mos- cow Times*, October 11, 2011; "Military-Budget Monster: In the Next Three Years the Social Programs of Servicemen and Retirees Will Thus Not Be Resolved," *Nezavisi- maia gazeta*, October 27, 2011.

54. Russia Faces Shortage of Military Draftees," *RIA Novosti*, January 18, 2012.

55. "Society: Our Authors: Fewer and Fewer People Want to Put Their Complete Trust in Putin—The Country's Population Is Ceasing to Trust Either the Premier and President or Their Entourages," *Svobodnaia Pressa*, August 16, 2011.

56. "Society: Our Authors." *Svobodnaia Pressa.*

57. Private communication to the author.

58. "Most Russian Army's Weapons Obsolete," *Interfax,* July 19, 2010; "Failed Course of Soviet Weapons Modernization: Robbing Peter to Pay Paul Is a Symbol of Russian Defense Department's Technical Policy," *Nezavisimoi voennoi obozrenie,* September 11, 2010; So Where Are the Missiles?" *Rossiiskaia gazeta,* May 19, 2011.

59. "Retrograde Arms: Latest Innovations of Russian Defense Establishment Were Developed 20 Years Ago," *Nasha Versiia,* August 25, 2011.

Index

Note: Page numbers in *italics* indicate figures and tables.

About the Contributors

Alfred B. Evans Jr. is professor emeritus of political science at California State University, Fresno. He is the author of *Soviet Marxism-Leninism: The Decline of an Ideology* (1993) and an editor or coeditor of three books, including *Change and Continuity in Russian Civil Society: A Critical Assessment* (2006). He has published many book chapters and articles in scholarly journals. His current research focuses on civil society in Russia, with particular emphasis on organizations that engage in public protests.

Gregory Gleason is professor of political science at the University of New Mexico, where he has taught international relations since joining the university in 1988. Gleason is the author of *Federalism and Nationalism* (1991), *Central Asian States* (1997), and *Markets and Politics in Central Asia* (2003), as well as many scholarly articles. He has served as a consultant to Lawrence Livermore National Laboratory, Sandia National Laboratories, the Asian Development Bank, and the U.S. Agency for International Development. His research has been sponsored by the National Science Foundation, the National Academy of Sciences, as well as other public and private foundations. While on leave from the University of New Mexico, Gleason served at the George C. Marshall European Center for Security Studies, where he authored the contribution for this book.

Timothy Heleniak is director of the American Geographical Society. He has researched and written extensively on demographic trends, migration, and regional development in Russia and the other countries of the former Soviet Union. He previously worked at the U.S. Census Bureau, the World Bank, and UNICEF, and is currently researching migration and regional development in Russia's Arctic and northern regions with support from a National Science Foundation grant. He is the editor of the journal *Polar Geography*.

Kathryn Hendley is William Voss-Bascom Professor of Law and Political Science at the University of Wisconsin, Madison. Her research focuses on legal and economic reform in the former Soviet Union and on how law is actually experienced and used in Russia. Her research has been supported by grants from the National Science Foundation, the Social Science Research Council, the National Council for Eurasian and East European Research, and the International Research and Exchanges Board. She has been a visiting fellow at the Woodrow Wilson Center, the Kellogg Institute for International Affairs at Notre Dame University, the Russian Economic School (Moscow), and the Program in Law and Public Affairs at Princeton University. She has published widely in journals such as *Post-Soviet Affairs, Law and Social Inquiry,* and the *American Journal of Comparative Law.*

Dale R. Herspring, University Distinguished Professor of Political Science at Kansas State University, is a member of the Council on Foreign Relations. He is the author of twelve books and more than eighty articles dealing with Russian/Soviet, U.S., German, and Polish national security affairs. His most recent books include *The Kremlin and the High Command: Presidential Impact on the Russian Military from Gorbachev to Putin* (2006); *Rumsfeld's Wars: The Arrogance of Power* (2008); and a forthcoming book entitled *Military Culture and Civil-Military Relations: The American, Canadian, German and Russian Cases.*

Maria Lipman is editor of *Pro et Contra,* a policy journal published by Carnegie Moscow Center. She has also been a deputy editor of two Russian newsweekly magazines and was a cofounder and deputy editor of *Itogi,* the first newsweekly magazine in Russia. *Itogi,* published in cooperation with *Newsweek,* was part of Russia's first privately owned media group Media-Most, destroyed by the Russian government in 2001. Lipman cofounded the newsweekly *Ezhenedel'ny Zhurnal.* Since 2001, Lipman has written an op-ed column on Russian politics, media, and society for the *Washington Post.* She also has contributed to several Russian and U.S. publications and has been featured as an expert on a range of international broadcast media. She holds an M.A. from Moscow State University.

Jeffrey Mankoff is a Visiting Fellow in the Russia and Eurasia Program at the Center for Strategic and International Studies. In 2010–2011, he was an International Affairs Fellow at the Department of State and was previously adjunct fellow for Russian studies at the Council on Foreign Relations and associate director of International Security Studies at Yale University. He has held fellowships at Harvard, Yale, and Moscow State universities and is the author of *Russian Foreign Policy: The Return of Great Power Politics* (2011). He has a Ph.D. in diplomatic history from Yale.

Nikolai Petrov is scholar-in-residence at the Carnegie Moscow Center, where he directs the Society and Regions project. He also heads the Center for Political-Geographic Research. Petrov is a columnist for the *Moscow Times*, a member of the Program on New Approaches to Research and Security in Eurasia (PONARS Eurasia), and a member of the scientific board of the *Journal of Power Institutions in Post-Soviet Societies*. During 1990–1995, he served as an advisor to the Russian parliament, government, and presidential administration. He is the author or editor of numerous publications dealing with analysis of Russia's political regime, post-Soviet transformation, socioeconomic and political development of Russia's regions, democratization, federalism, and elections, among other topics. His works include the three-volume *1997 Political Almanac of Russia* and the annual supplements to it. He is the coauthor of *Between Dictatorship and Democracy: Russian Post-Communist Political Reform* (2004), *The Dynamics of Russian Politics: Putin's Reform of Federal-Regional Relations* in two volumes (2004, 2005), and *Russia in 2020: Scenarios for the Future* (2011).

Thomas F. Remington is Goodrich C. White Professor of Political Science at Emory University. He is the author of numerous books and articles on Russian political institutions. His books include *The Politics of Inequality in Russia* (2011); *The Russian Parliament: Institutional Evolution in a Transitional Regime, 1989–1999* (2001); and, with Steven S. Smith, *The Politics of Institutional Choice: Formation of the Russian State Duma* (2001).

Richard Sakwa is professor of Russian and European politics at the University of Kent and an Associate Fellow of the Russia and Eurasia Programme at the Royal Institute of International Affairs, Chatham House. He has published widely on Soviet, Russian, and postcommunist affairs. Recent books include *Russian Politics and Society* (4th ed., 2008), *Putin: Russia's Choice* (2nd ed., 2008), *The Quality of Freedom: Khodorkovsky, Putin and the Yukos Affair* (2009), and *The Crisis of Russian Democracy: The Dual State, Factionalism, and the Medvedev Succession* (2011).

Louise Shelley is a university professor at the School of Public Policy at George Mason University and the founder and director of the Terrorism, Transnational Crime, and Corruption Center (TraCCC). Her latest book is *Human Trafficking: A Global Perspective* (2010), which discusses organized crime, corruption, and terrorism. She has written *Policing Soviet Society* (1996), *Lawyers in Soviet Worklife* (1984), and *Crime and Modernization* (1981), as well as numerous articles and book chapters on all aspects of transnational crime and corruption. Shelley has collaborated with Russian scholars for more than fifteen years on issues of organized crime through centers that she has helped to establish and support throughout Russia.

Darrell Slider is professor of government and international affairs at the University of South Florida. He has received numerous awards and authored more than thirty-five articles, primarily concerning regional and local politics in Russia and other countries of the former Soviet Union.

Pekka Sutela is affiliated with Aalto University School of Economics (Helsinki), Sciences Po (Paris), and the Carnegie Endowment for International Peace (Washington, DC). He is also in 2012 the president of the Association of Comparative Economic Studies (ACES). Until 2011 he worked with the Bank of Finland, including as head of BOFIT, the Bank of Finland Institute for Economies in Transition. His most recent book is *The Political Economy of Putin's Russia* (2012).

Andrei P. Tsygankov is professor of political science and international relations at San Francisco State University. A native Russian, he is the author of many books and articles on Russia's international relations. His latest book is *Russia and the West from Alexander to Putin: Honor in International Relations* (2012).

Stephen K. Wegren is professor of political science at Southern Methodist University. He is the author or coauthor of several books on the political economy of postcommunist nations. He has published numerous articles and book chapters in a wide range of journals and books. His research has been supported by the Social Science Research Council, the National Council for Eurasian and East European Research, the Ford Foundation, and the International Research and Exchanges Board. His recent books include *Land Reform in Russia: Institutional Design and Behavioral Responses* (2009) and *Rural Inequality in Divided Russia* (2013).